AFRICA

AFRICA

VOLUME 2

AFRICAN CULTURES AND SOCIETIES BEFORE 1885

Edited by

Toyin Falola

Carolina Academic Press
Durham, North Carolina

Cover: Fang mask from Gabon
© museé de l' Homme, photo D. Ponsard.

Library of Congress Cataloging-in-Publication Data

Africa / edited by Toyin Falola.
    p.   cm.
Includes bibliographical references and index.
ISBN 0-89089-768-9 (v. 1) — ISBN 0-89089-769-7 (v. 2)
1. Africa — History — To 1884. I. Falola, Toyin.

DT20 .A61785 2000
960 — dc21

                                                    00-035789

Carolina Academic Press, LLC
700 Kent Street
Durham, North Carolina 27701
Telephone (919) 489-7486
Fax (919) 493-5668
E-mail: cap@cap-press.com
www.cap-press.com

Printed in the United States of America
2017 Printing

For Olabisi, Dolapo, Bisola, and Oloruntoyin

Contents

Contents

Preface and Acknowledgments

This book is intended as a text for college students and for all readers interested in the precolonial cultures of Africa. It covers many subjects, with each chapter written both to educate and to stimulate further research. Culture is important as a way of understanding a people and their history. With respect to Africa, culture defines its identity and offers answers to many of its contemporary problems. Through culture, a greater understanding of the past is made possible. In this book, "culture" refers to the totality of the African experience and all the ideas that Africans have evolved over time.

No one can claim to understand Africa and its place in the modern world without a clear awareness of its cultural past. Perhaps no other continent has placed more emphasis on the use of culture than Africa. Its long and brutal history of enslavement and imperial domination, and their consequences—racism, attacks on dignity and self-worth, loss of confidence—have all combined to drive Africans during the twentieth century to bold and systematic efforts to reclaim their history and culture. In the struggle for the continent to move forward and be on an equal footing with the rest of the world, many African thinkers see culture as a weapon of liberation. The strong belief is that African cultures have to be liberated from Western and imperial domination, by analyzing their specific aspects and reasserting their values in the modern world. Africans are advised to fall on culture to liberate themselves from political and economic domination, ensure empowerment, and attain the integration of diverse groups into more coherent and stable nation-states. Thus, culture has been of both practical and academic relevance in Africa. Its knowledge must ensure its understanding and its preservation. It must provide the great source to sustain morality and combat external domination. It must be the bedrock of contemporary nationalism, providing a positive inspiration to motivate Africans to strive for ideals to attain sustainable development. This book provides insights on cultures of the past, that great knowledge that Africans seek to capture and understand in all its ramifications. Volume 1, the companion to this, provides the historical basis.

I owe a great deal of debt to all my contributors. There is a commitment on their part to understand African cultures and present them in a readable form. Topics and issues are many, and no single volume can treat them comprehensively. What this volume accomplishes is an overview of the essence of African cultures, by focusing on many leading themes. At the planning stage, I received encouragement and support from many colleagues. At the preparation stage, Joel Tishken,

Rebecca Gower, and Steven Salm assisted in managing correspondence. Steven Salm assisted in reading the entire volume for style and consistency. Saheed Adejumobi did a last-minute checking, Joel Tishken worked on the illustrations, while Dr. Ann O.Hear copy-edited the manuscript.

Toyin Falola
The University of Texas at Austin

List of Illustrations and Maps

Notes on the Authors

Saheed A. Adejumobi holds B.A. and M.A. degrees in history and is currently a doctoral candidate at the University of Texas at Austin. He has contributed to other publications on Africa. His interests include ethnicity, nationalism, and African diasporic cultural politics.

Julius Adekunle holds a Ph.D. from Dalhousie University, Canada. He has been a college teacher of history since the 1970s, and has written many essays on different aspects of precolonial Africa. He is preparing for press *A History of West Africa.*

Austin M. Ahanotu obtained his Ph.D. from the University of California at Los Angeles. He is at the moment the Chairperson of the History Department, California State University, Stanislaus. He is the author of many articles and books, and has over twenty years experience as a college teacher.

Vik Bahl, Ph.D., teaches at Green River Community College (Auburn, WA). His research and teaching interests include postcolonial literature and theory, comparative ethnic studies, transnationalism, social movements, and distance education. His current work includes a co-edited volume on the politics of creativity, the development of a critical pedagogy project over the Internet, an article investigating the relationship between the state and immigrant cultural identities in contemporary England, and participation in various publication projects relating to the Zapatista revolution in Mexico.

William C. Barnett graduated from Yale University in 1988 with a B.A. in History. He taught United States, African, Latin American, and World History at Brewster Academy in New Hampshire for three years. He earned an M.A. in History from the University of Texas and is currently a Ph.D. student at the University of Wisconsin–Madison. Barnett's speciality is environmental history, and he has written on a variety of regions.

Felix Ekechi is professor of History and co-ordinator of the African Studies Program at Kent State University, Ohio. He received his Ph.D. from the University of Wisconsin-Madison. Dr. Ekechi has published several books and articles, including *Missionary Enterprise and Rivalry in Igboland, 1857-1914* (1972); *Owerri in Transition* (1984); and *Tradition and Transformation in Eastern Nigeria* (1995). He co-edited *African Market Women and Economic Power* (1989) and his essays have appeared in various journals. Professor Ekechi is currently completing a biography of Rev. M.D. Opara of Nigeria, 1905-1965.

Toyin Falola, Ph.D., has been teaching since the 1970s in different countries. Author of many books and articles, editor of journals and a monograph series, he is a professor of history at the University of Texas at Austin. Falola has participated in the drafting of history syllabi for two countries and has contributed to numerous texts on African history.

dele jegede, after graduating with First Class Honors from Ahmadu Bello University, Zaria (Nigeria) with a major in Fine Arts, dele jegede worked for a while as the Art Editor of the *Daily Times* of Nigeria before joining the faculty of the University of Lagos. With a Ph.D. from Indiana University, Bloomington, he became the director of the Center for Cultural Studies of the University of Lagos in 1989, the same year that he was elected president of the Society of Nigerian Artists. He left Nigeria in 1993 for Indiana State University, Terre Haute, where he is currently an associate professor of Art History. Cartoonist, painter, art historian, and art critic, dele jegede has illustrated several books, held numerous solo and group shows, and published hundreds of cartoons in Nigerian newspapers. With expertise in African art, both traditional and contemporary, his research interests lie in popular and contemporary African art, an area on which he has delivered lectures and papers at national and international levels. He has been a Fulbright Scholar (Spelman, Atlanta: 1987/88), Consultant to the Studio Museum in Harlem on its 1990 contemporary art show, participant in the Rome exhibit on Sacred Art (1994), Senior Post- Doctoral Fellow of the Smithsonian Institution (National Museum of African Art: 1995), and keynote speaker in Tokyo on contemporary African art (1995). dele jegede has a strong list of scholarly publications. He recently served as the president of the Arts Council of African Studies Association (ACASA).

John Lamphear has studied and lived with pastoral societies in East Africa for over six years. His writings include *The Traditional History of the Jie of Uganda* (1976) and *The Scattering Time: Turkana Resistance to Colonial Rule* (1992), both published by Oxford University Press. He is also interested in military history, and is currently working on a military history of East Africa and on a study of mutinies by African colonial troops. Dr. Lamphear is professor of History at the University of Texas at Austin.

Appolos Nwauwa is associate professor of History at Rhode Island College in Providence. He earned his M.A. and Ph.D. from Dalhousie University, Halifax, Canada, where he was a Killam scholar from 1990 to 1993. Dr. Nwauwa has taught at the Bendel (now Edo) State University in Nigeria and at Dalhousie University in Canada. Specializing in modern African studies, he has authored many articles and commissioned entries in *The Encyclopedia of Historiography*. His most recent publication is *Imperialism, Academe and Nationalism* (1997).

Kathleen O'Connor holds a Master's degree from the University of California at Los Angeles and another from the University of Southern Californiaia. She is currently working with diviners in Bahia, Brazil, tracing the history of the *babalawo* tradition and its incorporation into candomble religious structure. She is working on her Ph.D. in Anthropology at Harvard University.

Steven J. Salm holds a B.A. in History from the University of Wisconsin–Madison and a Master's from the University of Texas at Austin where he is currently a doctoral candidate. His areas of interest include literature, music, and identity, with a particular focus on the relationships between urban youth, identity, and the development of neo-traditional forms of popular culture in late colonial Africa. He has contributed to a number of publications, including *Africa Today,* and has lived and done extensive fieldwork in Sierra Leone and Ghana.

Joel Tishken holds a Master's degree in history, and he is currently working on his Ph.D. in World History at the University of Texas at Austin. Tishken has acquired experience as a teacher at the college level. He has contributed to other publications and written reviews for *African Economic History.*

Jacqueline Woodfork has worked for many years as an administrator in the United States and Africa. After completing her M.A. degree she has embarked upon a Ph.D. program at the University of Texas at Austin. She is researching aspects of French imperialism in Africa.

Introduction

Toyin Falola

Culture As a Phenomenon

Most disciplines in the academy deal with and define cultures in various ways. All individuals use their intuition and experience to define cultures as well. Thus, there is a range of understandings of how culture is perceived, defined, and employed. Some scholars are even inclined to argue that culture is an abstract concept only used to understand a phenomenon that is difficult to observe in its totality. Among the varieties and distinctions are the following:

i.   The presentation of culture as either a historical phenomenon or a static one. In some literature, the cultures of Africa have been presented as "traditional and unchanging," whereas historians have revealed both continuity and change. The concept of a static culture assumes that the continent changed little until the intervention of colonial rule. Yet, precolonial societies demonstrated adaptation, evolution, revolution, and change.

ii.   The idea that culture can be either determinist or activist. This is an argument about culture as an agency of change. Determinists see culture as determining the activities of human beings, while activists think that people create cultures to suit their needs.

iii.   The ideological difference between a materialist perspective and an idealist one. To the materialist, what determines a cultural or social phenomenon is the interaction between human beings and their material conditions and modes of production. To the idealist, culture is determined by ideas, values, and beliefs, and any study of culture should reveal both the material and non-material dimension.

iv.   The conception of culture as holistic or sectoralist. The holistic school sees culture as the whole of existence or the life of a community. The sectoralist regards it as an aspect of life concerned with education and the cultivation of good character. When the study of culture began as an intellectual exercise, it was regarded by the European intelligentsia in the Age of Enlightenment as the process of attaining refinement, of becoming civilized.[1] Those who study Africa prefer the holistic approach. They tend to divide culture into two realms: (a) as an

---

1. See for instance, Hans-Georg Gadamer, "Culture and Words From the Point of View of Philosophy," *Universitas*, 24, 3 (1982): 179-180.

"inner process" which defines ethics, intellectual life, and aesthetics; and (b) a "general process" which deals with life in all aspects, material and others.

v.   The concept of a universal as opposed to an ethnic culture. African cultures have been presented in some circles as tribal and fragmented: it is suggested that European rule introduced more positive universalist cultures which have benefited the continent. What is described as universal is usually no more than Western culture. It is also misleading to think that "ethnic" means barbaric and primitive. There is so far no convincing argument that Africa was once a collection of primitive isolated tribes, always at war with one another until Western imperialism united and civilized them.

vi.   As a corollary to the above, there has been a vigorous debate as to whether Africa should stick to its own culture or adopt the so-called universal cultures derived from the West. This has been a great source of tension and conflict in Africa itself, with opinions divided on what to do. The majority view in this debate has been to stay with the indigenous culture. In the early years of colonial rule, an editorial in an African newspaper warned of the danger of Western cultures and concluded thus:

> The attempt to develop Africa on European lines can only end in failure. It is like rearing a bird in a cage with the result of vitiated instinct and a gradual pining away which ends in death...The African, if he wants progress, must go on his own lines, he must not suffer himself to be pushed suddenly from the twilight of a civilization which has its roots and the first impulse deep in the past of a thousand years. The glare will blind or tend to reduce him to a blinkering idiot.[2]

This line of thinking remains strong, and people with contrary opinions are described as "assimilated" and "disoriented" Africans.

vii.   The strategy of reclaiming cultures has taken various intellectual forms—nationalist, resistance-oriented and post-modernist. Nationalists want to use cultures to construct a nation-state project. They glorify indigenous cultures and refuse to discuss elements in them that might be regarded as unpleasant.[3] Resistance scholars see culture as an expression of protest against dominant and hegemonic cultures.[4] Post-modernism (with its variant, post-colonial literature) wants to turn the periphery into the center of analysis and minimize the role of the West in the expansion of any so-called universal culture.[5]

The next chapter explores many of these issues in greater details.

---

2. *The Record*, May 21, 1904.

3. See for instance, the writings of Leopold Senghor, the apostle of Negritude, a philosophy which asserted the primacy of African cultures.

4. The works of Frantz Fanon illustrate this approach.

5. See for instance Edward Said, *Orientalism* (New York: Vintage, 1978).

African Cultures

Both in the precolonial and modern periods, culture is one of the ways by which Africa is defined, by Africans and non-Africans. Africa provides sufficient data to elaborate upon all the varied meanings and approaches to the study of cultures that I have identified. In Africa and elsewhere, culture performs a set of functions. One is its adaptive function, whereby human beings interact with their environment. While they inevitably adapt to the environment, they also must shape the environment to meet their basic needs. Another is its integrative function, with culture supplying those values by which a community constructs its morality and identity. A community creates or invents those symbols, rituals, and bonds to define itself. As a community tries to reproduce itself, it also falls on culture to play a socialization function. Children are brought up in certain ways, teenagers are initiated into adulthood, and women are married only after performing certain rites. The idea of a meaningful life is defined in cultural terms, and individuals draw their motivations and goals from within this definition. Culture also performs a security-providing and protective function. It supplies the ethics and the sanctions; those who conform are rewarded and rebels are punished according to established procedures. In protecting certain privileges, culture can also define class interests. A dominant group can define ethics and rules of behavior to suit itself and then impose them on every citizen. In trying to interpret the universe and human experience, culture supplies the basis and the ideas.

Until the mid 1940s, it was fashionable in some academic quarters to deny Africans their cultures or to denigrate whatever they had. In this perspective, Africans had no history before the coming of the Europeans, they had no literature, their architecture was rudimentary, their art was tribal, that is, limited by local traditions and suffering from the absence of innovation, their philosophy and songs were unimaginative, and their artists only produced for a small audience.

This negative attitude stemmed from ignorance, prejudice, and racism. Both the trans-Atlantic slave trade and European imperialism damaged the status of Africans in world politics and contributed to their presentation to the outside world as inferior people. The preoccupation of many African writers of the post-Second World War period was to deal with the assault on African cultures. These writers believed that colonialism had enabled European cultures to dominate the African ones. To regain the lost identity, writers must now unravel indigenous cultures.

As this book demonstrates, the leading features of African cultures include the following:

i.   Many aspects of African cultures are ancient. History has clearly demonstrated the existence of such civilizations as ancient Egypt, Kush, Meroe, and Aksum, to mention but a few. In many areas, states flourished well before 1000 A.D. Many of them were able to use metals, domesticate animals, cultivate the land, build cities, engage in trade, and establish viable political institutions.

ii.   Many states emerged, varying in size and pattern of political authorities. The state comprised large ethnolinguistic groups, and many of them endured for centuries. Cities grew, and groups and states engaged in diplomacy, trade, warfare, and other relations. The states were heterogeneous, incorporating people of diverse areas and ethnicities. The states were able to build efficient bureaucracies and other administrative institutions, and women played an important role in society. There was no part of Africa where its people did not make territorial claims and recognize a sovereign authority in charge of peace and war, conflict and management, and the regulation of social and economic affairs. The area of political jurisdiction was sometimes small, not larger than a village; at other times it was big, as in the case of kingdoms. Power could be centralized, as in those areas with kings and emperors. Power could also be diffused, as in non-centralized polities where elders, priests, and lineage heads exercised authority. The state interfered minimally in the lives and activities of individuals.

iii.   To Africans, culture was a combination of their history, values, institutions, concepts, and ideas about society. History was very important, a practical device to link the past with the present and to anticipate the future. Myth and symbolism infused histories of origins, migrations, warfare, and cultures, and they also show the creative ability of Africans to think and reflect. Culture provided the source of interpretation of customs, values, and the logic of behavior. To outsiders, certain practices might appear meaningless or primitive, but not to people who experienced them on a regular basis.

iv.   The African environment contributed to shaping the culture, creating notable differences, as each area responded to its climate and other natural phenomena. Whether people ate root crops or grains or were dressed warmly or lightly can be attributed to the impact of the environment. The impact of the environment can also be seen in the emergence of states and political institutions.

v.   Africans attempted to understand and relate to their environment, in religion, music, art, and other endeavors. There was a conception of the universe as the creation of a Supreme Being. Both the visible universe (earth) and the invisible one (the land of gods) were occupied by a variety of people, objects, and spirits. The cosmology dealt with the universe and its inhabitants, creating a religion that privileged the environment.

vi.   Religion enabled other creative endeavors to fuse and have harmony and meaning. Dance, music, literature, art, and drama were all part of worship, sacrifice, and rituals. These allowed people to communicate with the spiritual sphere, to express religious intensity, and to create excellent ideas without the motive of money. Creative endeavors also satisfied the requirements of leisure, as in music and literature for entertainment.

vii.   There was a worldview, shaped by religion and other ideas. This worldview affirmed the primacy of life, emphasized the responsibility of the individual in the service of the community, and supported a belief in supernatural forces which shaped people's destinies. People were expected to worship gods, respect elders, care for members of the kinship group, and ensure lineal continuity. Africans interpreted the universe and other realities through their worldview. Beliefs in witchcraft, magic, spirits, and other forces were widespread and meant that Africans explained many things in term of supernatural forces. Fertility, lightning, thunder, and earthquakes did not occur by chance in the African worldview, but were attributed to supernatural forces.

viii.   The social building blocks included unilineal descent groups. Descent could be either patrilineal or matrilineal. The lineage was strong, and lineal continuity from one generation to another was very important. While the lineage and community promoted shared values and took care of many people, social stratification existed in many places, notably in the centralized states. Areas with complex political systems and international trade developed prestige values. In all societies, irrespective of political pattern and scale, it was the community—an agglomeration of lineages—that sustained culture. The lineage—a combination of families—shared land in common, made up an economic unit, practiced a religion, and nurtured values and mores that connected the individuals with the community at large. Marriage arrangements, notably polygyny, reflected the needs and beliefs of African societies.

ix. The transition to adulthood involved lessons in socialization, and formal and informal initiation rites. Where these were informal, lessons were offered slowly within the lineage and community about culture. Where they were formal, they involved rituals and elaborate initiation ceremonies, organized by priests and in some cases by secret societies. Formal rituals were lessons in politics, behavior, wisdom, and living a married life. The transition also involved the knowledge and performance of gender roles. Sexual identities with respect to issues of power, division of labor, and expectations were part of culture that was deliberately transmitted.

x. Material culture was highly developed in such areas as mining, manufacturing, and agroallied industries.

xi. Economic institutions were highly developed, and they showed the impact of migrations, adaptations to environment, leadership, and innovations. The basic occupations were farming and pastoralism. People worked land with minimal interference from the state. The prosperity and cohesion enjoyed by many states was owed to their sound agriculture. Culture determined how people thought and felt about work. Ethics of hard work, values relating to community property, respect for land as communal property, and the role of religion in the economy were all aspects of the economic culture.

xii. Varying access to power and economic opportunities, in addition to hereditary rights and privileges, produced distinctions among people in the various communities. There were powerful priests, chiefs, and kings, and there were ordinary people: as poor peasants, artisans, and slaves. While social classes were not clearly demarcated in many areas, there was social stratification which decided a number of opportunities, possibilities, and limitations.

xiii. Africans adapted to influences from other parts of the world. From the seventh century, Islam spread to many parts and influenced the ways of life of the people. From the fifteenth century, Europeans began to make contact with places along the coast, with major consequences for trade and eventually the spread of Christianity. The contacts demonstrated the dynamic nature of culture and the ability of Africans to adapt. In resisting and rejecting aspects of external contacts that they did not like, indigenous cultures supplied viable alternatives. Africans fell back on their cultures in order to cope with and to resist foreign domination.

Additional Reading

The chapters in this volume. Additional references can be found in the notes and bibliography in each of the chapters.

AFRICA

Chapter 1

The Study of Cultures

Vik Bahl

This chapter provides a critical history of "culture" as a category of analysis and explains the most widely applied definitions of the term, its use in a range of academic disciplines and systems of knowledge, and the implications of shifts in this usage with regard to questions of resistance and cultural difference. In particular, the chapter discusses the important distinction between the conception of culture as a static set of values and practices and one that sees culture as a dynamic process that includes local, internal negotiations of social relations, identities and larger transformations over time. Further, the chapter offers a framework and justification for the examination of precolonial African cultures as part of the ongoing project of revising the prevalent misrepresentations of Africa. Finally, it provides an account of current debates about culture within postmodernism and postcolonialism and indicates the significance of culture for the ongoing challenges of historical transformation.

Introduction

This volume offers a range of chapters that provide descriptions and analyses of various aspects of African cultures before 1885, prior to the colonial conquests that followed the "Scramble for Africa." The chapters focus on such subjects as politics and state formation, indigenous religions, cities and architecture, and art and music. Even prior to 1885, Africa, especially its coastal regions, had extensive contact with the West through various forms of trade, including slavery. The entry of European powers in the form of direct colonial rule and the integration of Africa into the global economy, however, have radically and permanently altered African societies and their forms of cultural and social organization. Part of the motivation and justification for European colonial conquest emerged from representations of Africa as the primitive and barbaric "dark continent," characterizations that had also underwritten the earlier Western slave trade. These distortions went so far as to deny altogether the possession of "culture" by African societies, relegating them instead to the denigrated realm of "nature."

Since Africa was neither a blank slate upon which Europe executed its "civilizing mission," nor was it in a state of primitive barbarism, a study of African cultures before the colonial conquest is important in order to recover, to re-examine, and to rewrite the rich and complex histories of the continent. The focus on the precolonial period is not intended as simply celebratory or nostalgic for the purpose of distinguishing "authentic" African cultures that can serve as a counter to the depredations of colonialism and the legacies of continuing Western economic domination and cultural influence. Rather, history is an indispensable resource for identifying the possibilities for and virtues of maintaining continuities and/or enacting ruptures in the ongoing processes of transformation that characterize all social contexts around the globe.

In the case of Africa today, the study of precolonial cultures serves two related needs. First, colonialism does not manifest itself in the same way everywhere as an insular system, but instead interacts with already existing social systems to ensure its rule. Colonial domination is undertaken and maintained both through brute force and through the establishment of social and political institutions that adapt and co-opt existing hierarchies and social relations and codes. A history of precolonial African cultures, then, clarifies the basis by which colonial regimes are established as the complex interaction between Western and African social systems. Second, since African cultures are today (as they have always been) heterogeneous and evolving, such a history also allows us to understand the complex mix of urban, rural, Western, "modern," "traditional," and hybrid experiences, values, identities, relations, and institutions that characterize contemporary African societies.

Definitions

There are many competing definitions of "culture" as a category of analysis. This section gives an account of some prominent usages and of the role that this category has played in the analysis of society. The academic disciplines in the social sciences and humanities have evolved several divisions for pursuing the study of societies. These can broadly be characterized as the economic, political, social, and cultural spheres of activity and development. These divisions are not, however, to be regarded as absolute, and scholars and social theorists have paid attention to the interactions between these spheres and the ways in which they are valid only in relation to each other. Indeed, much of the debate about the meaning and value of these various critical terms concerns precisely the inter-relation between them. For instance, analyses of state formation must examine the cultural organization and meaning of power and leadership within a particular context. Similarly, the history of trade and commerce reveals their importance for the spread of common cultural frameworks. Conversely, we might ask how cultural forms and values determine the elaboration of economic systems.

Within academic studies, the social and cultural aspects are perhaps the least distinguished from each other. We might distinguish them by associating the social with the givens of a particular society—for example, institutions, kinship systems, and religious forms—and by referring to the cultural aspects as the process of meaning making in relation to these structures. Note, however, that this is not a fixed demarcation, and the chapters in this volume on African cultures will often incorporate the social within the cultural.

Culture as a word and a concept is notoriously difficult to define since significant contradictions and tensions exist in both its popular and its academic uses, which have undergone shifts within individual disciplines as well. We may identify five well-established definitions that have been attached to this concept:

(i) the tending and cultivation of crops and animals;

(ii) an extension of the idea of "cultivation" in the first definition to the human mind, which gives rise to distinctly class connotations, so that only particular individuals or classes are to be considered "cultured";

(iii) from the Enlightenment, a process of secular social development, wherein European culture represented the highest achievements of human civilization, towards which all other societies would or should move;

(iv) often regarded as the anthropological definition of culture, the relativization of the concept to refer to the "distinctive ways of life, the shared values and meanings, common to different groups—nations, classes, subcultures, etc., and historical periods";

(v) with a focus more on what culture *does* than what it *is*, the fifth definition of culture refers to "the set of practices by which meanings are produced and exchanged within a group," which draws our attention to the symbolic and interpretive dimensions of social life.[1]

Aside from the first definition above, all of the others continue to play a substantial role in the thinking about culture and its importance. So paying attention to the consequences of choosing one definition over another becomes essential. The second definition leads to the elitist notion of "high" culture, where, in the Western context, literature, classical music, art, philosophy, and other forms are elevated over "popular" or "mass" culture. The third definition, which sees European civilization as universal and the necessary endpoint of all human progress, continues to find echoes in the imperative for development in the formerly colonial world, prompted by Western models and needs. The fourth definition, while important for dislodging the notion that only a single, universal culture exists, runs the risk of offering a static description of societies, without attention to internal differences or to the historic and hierarchical relations between societies. The fifth definition represents a significant innovation in examining the processes by which meaning is made and contested in any social context. It has the potential problem, however, of over-inclusiveness or loss of specificity as a critical category, since all practices, institutions, and processes are implicated in the means by which people define themselves and their relations to others, and make sense of the world. The chapters in this volume primarily make use of the fourth and fifth definitions of culture listed above.

The Analysis of Culture Across the Disciplines

The disciplines of sociology and anthropology have traditionally been concerned with the category of culture and, over time, have themselves developed new, often contradictory, paradigms for both describing and evaluating the range of social practices and relations that are considered to constitute culture. Beyond

---

1. Robert Bocock, "The Cultural Formations of Modern Society," in Stuart Hall et al., ed., *Modernity: An Introduction to Modern Societies* (Oxford: Blackwell, 1996), 152-53.

the ongoing evolution of this concept in these two disciplines, more recently we have seen a growing primacy accorded to culture as a critical category in other disciplines, such as history and literary studies, as well. Moreover, because of this conjuncture of theoretical and practical interest, a great deal of interdisciplinary scholarship has been devoted to producing "cultural histories," extending our understanding of cultural processes and interactions, both at particular historical moments and locales and, more broadly, over long periods of time. Only broad sketches of the applications of "culture" across the disciplines are provided below; further elaboration and detailed historical contextualization would illuminate more fully the consequences of developments in the various fields of knowledge.

A common distinction made between sociology and anthropology is that the former studies modern industrial societies, whereas the latter typically has examined those which are preliterate and less cosmopolitan. Founding figures in both fields, such as Emile Durkheim (1858-1917) in sociology and Claude Lévi-Strauss (b. 1908) in anthropology, are credited with formulating models for understanding the totality of social experiences as constituted by a structure of relations, events, and myths. Only through an analysis of the overall structure and the symbolic meanings of a particular society's elements can its culture be understood. According to Durkheim, members of a society share a set of "collective representations" and are bound together by common practices, allowing them to understand one another and to make sense of themselves and their relation to the world in strictly social terms. In these versions of sociology and anthropology, the elements of culture are explained according to the *function* they serve in preserving social stability.[2]

Even though this *structuralist* model recognizes the significance of cultural practices as determining meaning rather than presuming static, already existing values and ways of life, it has been subject to critique for not being able to account for large-scale historic changes. For instance, part of the concern of social thinkers has been to explain the relationship between developments in culture and other shifts, like the transition from feudalism to capitalism in Europe. Another central figure of sociology, Max Weber (1864-1920), for example, linked the rise of capitalism to the historic emergence of Protestant Christianity. In this analysis, although culture is regarded as an important engine of historic change, which goes beyond a strict focus on economic or technological changes, the effects of culture are still attributed to ideologies that operate independently of individual human initiatives.[3]

Anthropology has been a central discipline within which studies of culture have been undertaken. Corresponding to the fourth definition above, this discipline has attempted to document, classify, and analyze a wide array of non-Western cultures by identifying the meanings, values, symbols, practices, rituals, and shared beliefs that characterize a particular community. Anthropology and folklore both have somewhat vindicated non-Western and non-modern knowledges

---

2. See Emile Durkheim, *Readings from Emile Durkheim*, ed. Kenneth Thompson (New York: Tavistock Publications, 1985); and Marcel Henaff, *Claude Lévi-Strauss and the Making of Structural Anthropology*, trans. Mary Baker (Minneapolis: University of Minnesota Press, 1998).

3. See Max Weber, *From Max Weber: Essays in Sociology*, trans. and ed. H.H. Gerth and C. Wright Mills (New York: Oxford University Press, 1958).

and practices by offering detailed accounts of their internal logic and frames of reference. Like sociology, anthropology has tried to balance a focus on underlying structures with one on individual meaning and the possibilities for change and contestation. The anthropologist Clifford Geertz has suggested that individual expression is only intelligible within a general idiom, and therefore both must be regarded in relation to each other. Geertz also argues, however, that socially constructed meanings are never self-evident but must be interpreted, so the role of the anthropologist or interpreter becomes yet another factor in the analysis of social formations.[4]

Anthropological work in relation to non-Western communities was largely undertaken, historically, by European and American scholars and travelers. To what extent, then, is the validity of their studies compromised by the differences in culture and relative power between the anthropologists and the communities they studied? For instance, anthropologists often assumed that the communities they studied were virtually insulated from the larger world. This operating premise gave rise to what we know as *cultural relativism*, whereby the codes and values of individual societies are thought to be so distinct that they cannot be judged from outside their own frames of reference. This premise is also related to the notion of ethnicity, which is commonly distinguished from race. While race designates biology, ethnicity refers to the cultural identity of a particular group of people.

While cultural relativism potentially signals a modicum of respect for non-Western societies, Western culture as a standard of reference has not been displaced, and there is frequently a misreading of the level of interaction and mutual influence between different non-Western social formations and between these and the West; often unacknowledged, such traffic has typically been quite high in Africa. Anthropology has, in recent years, also been attending with greater seriousness to the question of perspective, or, "Who studies whom?" In addition to foregrounding cultural and power differences, anthropology has redirected its attention from the rural and the exotic to include the urban and the everyday; increasingly, anthropologists are also conducting work on communities that are closer to their "own" culture.

Associated with but not limited to the writings of Karl Marx (1818-1883), Marxism has also offered a powerful analytic paradigm in which society can be understood as determined by its economic base, constituted by the conditions and relations of economic production. The theoretical and practical consequence of this analysis is that any given society cannot be regarded as possessing a single culture, but must instead be seen as having several cultures corresponding to its different social classes. From this formulation, we get such descriptive and evaluative categories as "bourgeois culture," "ruling-class culture," and "working-class culture." The culture of a particular class is said to be determined by its relative economic position and also by a set of values and traditions. Within the traditional Marxist model, the basis for revolutionary social change will emerge from the contradictions between the classes and the development of a working-class consciousness that will then result in the transition to an egalitarian, classless society.[5]

---

4. See Clifford Geertz, *The Interpretation of Cultures: Selected Essays* (New York: Basic Books, 1973).

5. See Robert C. Tucker, ed., *The Marx-Engels Reader*, 2nd ed. (New York: Norton, 1978).

The traditional Marxist model, which has been very influential in various political experiments around the globe, has undergone substantial revision because of critiques from both inside and outside Marxist theory and practice. For example, thinkers from those countries that were subject to colonial rule supported the Marxist critique of Western capitalism and domination and were inspired by the promise of a new, class-free global order. They nevertheless contested the Marxist assumption that imperialism, while unfortunate and brutal, was necessary for modernization — a required set of stages, in the transition from feudalism to capitalism to communism, through which all societies had to pass. Furthermore, the traditional Marxist model regarded culture as part of the "superstructure" determined by the economic base; hence, Marxist political strategies have often concentrated exclusively on seizing control of the state and the means of production. This model leaves little room for cultural changes enacted by the people themselves to direct the course of history with their own activity. This paradigm has given way, as we shall see in greater detail below, to a model that sees culture as actually *constitutive* of rather than merely *reflective* of overall systems. Culture therefore may be regarded as a legitimate basis of transformation and struggle. There remains however an ongoing, unresolved debate about the mutual determinations of the economic base and the cultural and social superstructure.

Among the leading figures who have significantly revised the traditional Marxist model is the Italian Marxist Antonio Gramsci (1891-1937). He suggested that class domination is maintained through the establishment of *hegemony*, which includes *coercion* and force but also requires, at some level, the *consent* of the subordinate classes to accept the interests of the ruling class. This suggests that class and other forms of domination simply cannot be maintained without a particular cultural system in place to allow domination to be acceptable on a day-to-day basis. Hence, the sphere of culture becomes a viable arena within which people actively contest meanings and negotiate their positions in relation to the ruling arrangements of power.[6]

Another important development in the evolution of the category of culture is the rise of what is called *social history*. Associated with historians such as E. P. Thompson in England and the Annales school in France, social history is consciously intended as a history "from below" in opposition to traditional strategies that explained the movement of history according to the lives of leaders, diplomatic relations, or even impersonal forces such as capitalist or imperialist expansion. Central to the assumptions of social history is the premise that the common people themselves, through their activity, relations, and culture, make history and are able to alter their relations with the ruling classes. History is then seen as an indeterminate process rather than one that is the outcome of a predetermined script, playing out the inexorable forces of reason or modernization. The study of the lived experience of *everyday life* poses new challenges and requires new methodologies.[7]

---

6. See Antonio Gramsci, *Selections from the Prison Notebooks of Antonio Gramsci*, trans. and ed. Quintin Hoare and Geoffrey Nowell Smith (New York: International Publishers, 1971).

7. See E.P. Thompson, *The Making of the English Working Class* (New York: Vintage Books, 1966); Lynn Hunt, ed., *The New Cultural History* (Berkeley: University of California Press, 1989); Henri Lefebvre, *Critique of Everyday Life*, trans. John Moore (New York:

Both Gramsci and the social historians were instrumental in the rise of the critical school of thought known as cultural studies that emerged in England in the 1960s, a paradigm that has since been deployed elsewhere. Cultural Studies challenged the longstanding division between high culture and low, or popular, culture, in which the latter typically had been denigrated as either uncreative and inferior or incapable of resisting the allure of mass entertainment. By contrast, scholars associated with cultural studies sought to locate and legitimate an autonomous working class culture capable of resisting the onslaughts of industrialization and fragmentation. Largely intended as a corrective to Western national histories race and gender, over the last fifteen years, have increasingly entered cultural studies as key factors, along with class, for the analysis of Western social formations.

Cultural studies, along with the shifts in anthropology over the last twenty-five years mentioned above, holds the conviction that the process by which people make meaning in social contexts is far from obvious or straightforward. Moreover, since representations and analyses of culture are now widely recognized not to be neutral, the study of culture cannot be regarded as a science, and this challenges the claims of objectivity in the social sciences and humanities as a whole. Indeed, intellectual inquiry itself should be seen as an inextricable part of cultural processes.

Identifying the values, rituals, and social conventions of a given society in order to understand the cultural experiences of its members is no longer regarded as sufficient. Rather, cultural studies, among other disciplines, is now committed to investigating the ways in which people pursue or displace their interests in relation to various forms of power; hence, it is committed to studying the means by which domination is maintained with attention to the role of *resistance* and *struggle*.

Culture as Difference

In the preceding discussion of anthropology, the importance of the concept of "cultural relativism" was explained. However, I have argued that the differences between groups or societies do not simply denote insular identities but also the inter-relation between them. It is commonly recognized that cultural identity is only meaningful if it can be opposed to something outside of itself; therefore, any concept of the "Self" must be defined in relation to an "Other." So we can speak of the differences *between* groups, or *cultural difference*, as crucial for determining the identity of any one group, even if that identity is constantly in flux. On the other hand, *culture as difference* suggests quite another scenario.

If earlier models of culture were interested in the unity of societies, the emphasis has now shifted from community, or the assumption of social harmony, to differences *within* particular social formations.[8] Since societies develop with a

---

Verso, 1991); and Michel de Certeau, *The Practice of Everyday Life*, trans. Steven Rendall (Berkeley: University of California Press, 1984). Roland Barthes is also an important figure for his analysis of everyday objects and icons and their symbolic significance, read as texts within a cultural language; see Susan Sontag, ed., *A Barthes Reader* (New York: Hill and Wang, 1982).

8. Hunt, "Introduction," 13.

range of social and political differences within them, culture may be regarded as the process by which those differences are produced and given meaning. For example, it has been argued that race, class, and gender have no meaning in and of themselves but only come to have significance and relevance through the operations of culture as a process. While we can see culture as the means by which internal differences are mediated and resolved, we are also well advised, following Gramsci, not to consider that mediation and resolution as ever final or complete. People are positioned differently in relation to the various forms of *power* in society, a concept that should be understood broadly and not just in economic and political terms. The French philosopher Michel Foucault significantly advanced the analysis of power in his studies of its operations in and through institutions, discourses, and subjectivity.[9] Because power is dispersed across a range of social relations, sites, and events, people evolve various strategies—individual and collective, conscious and unconscious—for responding to their particular positions. Those who are relatively disempowered devise strategies of *resistance*. These are to be looked for not only in immediately visible forms of violence and rebellion, but also in more subtle instances and processes of refusal, subversion of meaning, and identity formation. In cultural studies of resistance, a central concern has been the identification and theorization of popular *agency*. How do we understand the active role that people play, both in their own subordination and in their freedom from domination? What status do we accord to everyday, tactical negotiations of power as opposed to large-scale, historic confrontations?

Investigations of *gender*, under various feminist paradigms, have been especially crucial in breaking down presumptions that culture represents a shared set of meanings and operates homogeneously for all members of a given society. This is not only because women have been typically neglected or misrepresented in analyses of history and the historical process; nor is it sufficient to contend that women are positioned differently from men in social arrangements and therefore must be seen as having a culture of their own. Rather, cultural studies of gender have concluded that gender is a constitutive system of difference that determines social life in ways more far-reaching than the simple assignment of roles to men and women. These include the production of distinctions between public and private spaces, the construction of nations as masculine or feminine, and the gendering of work and value. Again, the means by which individual gendered subjects, men and women, make sense of, negotiate, and intervene in a dominant gender cultural system is far from self-evident or predetermined. Given the centrality of gender, any understanding of the coherence and culture of a community must account for this fundamental system of difference running through it. Along with feminism, gay and lesbian studies has increasingly problematized sexuality and sexual identity and insisted upon their crucial relevance for the operations of culture.[10]

A further critical category to consider in a study of the differences within cultures is *postmodernism*. Like the term culture, postmodernism has a variety of meanings in popular and academic uses. It can simply be a term to mark our own

---

9. See Michel Foucault, *The Essential Works of Michel Foucault, 1954-1984*, ed. Paul Rabinow (New York: New Press, 1997).

10. See Henry Abelove, Michele Aina Barale, and David M. Halperin, eds., *The Lesbian and Gay Studies Reader* (New York: Routledge, 1993).

period in history, beginning with the end of the Second World War and extending to the present. It can refer to the culture and strategies of representation that accompany this period. These have often been characterized by fragmentation, the proliferation of surface effects associated with mass media technologies, and a shift in critical focus and value away from the dominant center of Europe and the United States in favor of other peripheral sites, including marginal cultures within the West.

Postmodernism also refers to a series of powerful critiques of Euro-American modernity, generated within the West itself. In spite of the celebration of modernity found in much Western writing after the Enlightenment, skepticism about its utopian claims is also found relatively early in the West. Max Weber, for instance, while documenting the increasing bureaucratization and rationalization of everyday experience, remained skeptical about the dislocations of this process, since rationality could not address the problem of how to live nor guarantee values. The idealism of Western modernity, encoded in the liberal humanist notions of equality and citizenship, has always been coupled with extreme violence, expressed, for instance, by slavery, hierarchical class and gender relations, and the ongoing expansion of Western power. The modern fantasy and promise of equality has never overcome the material realities of domination. Postmodernism extends this skepticism and rejects, as false and deluded, the promises of modernity, especially its *master narratives* of progress and freedom.[11]

With special attention to the complexities of language and meaning, postmodernism, associated with the critiques of such influential French thinkers as Michel Foucault and Jacques Derrida,[12] has persuasively unmasked *all* claims to truth and identity as contingent and provisional. This is to say that while truth claims do have real effects, they cannot claim an original foundation or permanent fixity. Hence, postmodernism argues for the primacy of representation rather than expressing faith in direct access to reality. Moreover, having rejected the truth and coherence of grand systems, such as "Western civilization," postmodernism has also called attention to those differences that were disavowed, repressed, or consigned to the margins by modernity. However, critics of postmodernism have expressed concern that the rejection of grand narratives, including Marxism, renders political activity, based on modernist notions of democracy and justice and on claims to truth and legitimate analysis, increasingly difficult. Notwithstanding this difficulty, postmodernism has convincingly shown that there are multiple and unpredictable determinations of meaning and historical development, not all of which can be reduced to the individual human subject nor to any single category such as class or nationality.

Cultural critics eager to make use of the insights of postmodernism, especially the value of highlighting rather than subsuming differences, while also attending to current political imperatives, have recently begun speaking of *hybridity* or hybrid identities. Hybridity can be described as the intersection of different cultural identities in the context of unequal relations of power. This process does not nec-

---

11. See Steven Seidman, ed., *The Postmodern Turn: New Perspectives on Social Theory* (New York: Cambridge University Press, 1994); and Douglas Kellner and Steven Best, *Postmodern Theory: Critical Interrogations* (New York: Guilford Press, 1991).

12. See Jacques Derrida, *The Derrida Reader: Writing Performances*, ed. Julian Wolfreys (Edinburgh: Edinburgh University Press, 1998).

essarily result in the victory of the more powerful cultural and political force, or in biculturalism, which might be defined as the simple, neutral mixture of elements from the cultures in question. Rather, we can relate hybridity to some versions of postmodernism that reject the notion of identity as fixed or self-sufficient in favor of a view that sees identity as itself dependent upon internal differentiation and constant negotiation. Since hybridity destabilizes both powerful and subordinate cultural identities, we can also see in the production of hybrid identities the various forms of appropriation and adaptation that characterize the colonial encounter. This acknowledgment of the ongoing historic processes of defining identity and negotiating power and the presence of multiple frames of reference, even within individual subjects, is important for going beyond the false impasse that asks Africa to choose between Western and indigenous cultures.

Challenging Western Notions of Culture

It is worth emphasizing that the writing of history is itself a cultural project of the present. That is, we can see the distinction between the "history of cultures" and "historiography as culture." Outside of the academic practice of history writing, we can see the ways in which the organization of historical knowledge has direct influence on current, local relations. Consider the importance of popular national history, museums, oral histories, and other forms of popular memory for contemporary politics. Various critiques within the field of history itself have challenged the value-neutral claims of history writing and the related faith that the past can somehow be known exactly or objectively. The intersection of the concerns of history and culture has led to the interrogation of the motives for the writing of history and to an insistence on the importance of interpretation for constructing particular versions of the past. Beyond merely describing past African cultures, then, these chapters are also self-consciously part of an intervention in and critique of the standard ways in which history and cultures have come to be regarded.

If representations of history and culture are not neutral and objective but crucially determined by the motives and location of the representers, consider that the categories of "history," "culture," "reason," and "modernity" are themselves not neutral. Each of these categories and the academic disciplines within which they appear emerge as part of the modernization of Europe, integrally linked to its colonial expansion. The need to define, classify, understand, and, most significantly, differentiate societies accompanies the rise of competing nation-states and the need for systematic knowledge of the colonial Other as a requirement for "effective" rule. Is the analysis of Western culture, then, the same kind of project as the investigation of the non-West? By and large, the critical, historical trajectory of the category of culture charted above concerns its development in the West and its systems of knowledge, even though this trajectory is determined in large part by various challenges posed by non-Western cultures.

To what extent are the critical tools of Western knowledge appropriate for an anticolonial account of African histories and cultures? The answer is not a wholesale attack on and rejection of Western categories of thought, nor a conclusion that the explanatory categories and disciplines developed in the West in conjunction with the projects of European expansion are automatically inappropriate for current investigations. Rather, what is called for is a questioning of their privileged status, wide dissemination, and universal claims. Indeed, the interaction between Western colonial powers and their subordinate populations, within both nationalist and postcolonial responses to Western domination, has been negotiated through appropriations, adaptations, and reformulations. Nevertheless, our own understanding and inquiry must proceed with a consciousness of this "history of ideas," to point to the often unacknowledged assumptions that underwrite even current representations of history and culture.

It has been argued that Western culture has been as much determined by centuries of colonial encounters as the cultures of formerly colonial countries. Recall the discussion at the opening of the previous section, "Culture as Difference," that cultural identities must construct an "Other" to mark the boundaries of the "Self." This process is not, however, innocent. The West defined itself as "civilized" in relation to the "barbarism" of its colonial Others, which allowed the colonial project to be redefined comfortably as a "civilizing mission," executed through "exploration," missionary activity, educational policy, and legal and political reforms, to say nothing of military conquest. While constructions of the Self as distinct from the Other invariably rely upon false assumptions and oppositions, they also reveal crucial features of Western culture and its development. For instance, the great popularity of adventure literature, such as H. Rider Haggard's *King Solomon's Mines* (1885) and *She* (1887), and "serious" literature, such as Joseph Conrad's *Heart of Darkness*, suggests the extent to which Africa served as a screen upon which Europe's own fantasies, desires, fears, and doubts could be projected. In our own day, the successful production of films about Western adventures in Africa, such as *Raiders of the Lost Ark* (1981), *King Solomon's Mines* (1985), and *The Ghost and the Darkness* (1996), suggests the ongoing operation of colonial cultural dynamics.[13] Prior to turning our attention to non-Western cultures and histories, then, we must expose and challenge the very powerful meanings attached to the category of culture itself, which are still in part determined by Western assumptions and needs with regard to the "Self" and "Other."

Nationalism and Postcolonialism

The studies of African cultures provided in this volume, along with work conducted about and from other non-Western societies, must contend with the history and legacies of Western domination, including critical categories of thought as well as slavery, colonialism, and the ongoing structural inequalities that continue to characterize global relations. Even though this volume concerns pre-1885 African cultures, it must still be situated within a long and diverse series of projects, extending into the present, that contest the disastrous effects of misrepresentation.

---

13. For some significant contributions to this critique, see Edward Said, *Orientalism* (New York: Vintage, 1978); Homi Bhabha, "Of Mimicry and Men: The Ambivalence of Colonial Discourse," *October* 28 (1984): 125-33; Robert Young, *Colonial Desire: Hybridity in Theory, Culture and Race* (New York: Routledge, 1995); and Anne McClintock, *Imperial Leather: Race, Gender and Sexuality in the Colonial Contest* (New York: Routledge, 1995).

Because of the distortions and violence of colonial representations, struggles for independence in Africa and elsewhere, in addition to direct forms of political engagement and confrontation, included the project of rejecting these representations. These struggles affirmed the humanity of non-Western peoples and the legitimacy of their cultures, and insisted upon identities rooted in alternative traditions. Examples of these strategies include the Négritude movement, associated with writers and artists such as Aimé Césaire and Léopold Senghor, and the elaboration of notions of nationalist culture that would support demands for independence as a historic right.[14] Theorists such as Albert Memmi, Frantz Fanon, and Amilcar Cabral further undertook the investigation of the experience of Westernized colonial subjects. They argued that this elite class must undo the internalization of Western superiority and the aspirations to which that led, in order to refuse the role of *comprador*, or colonial mediator, in favor of an allegiance to the subjugated nation and the culture still available in the everyday life of the people. This suggests that culture itself provided strategies of resistance and was regarded as a site of struggle.[15]

Nationalist writers have, to varying degrees, been aware of the dangers of nostalgia and the romanticization of tradition in projects of cultural reclamation. Nevertheless, one of the pitfalls of nationalism, both before and after formal independence, remains precisely the idealization of a precolonial past, without attention to the complexities, internal differences, and inequalities of historic African societies, nor to the ongoing evolution of cultures as they take in new influences and negotiate the current exigencies of history and power. For instance, Négritude's and pan-Africanism's assertion of the commonalities shared by Africans was not sufficient to resist the forces of neocolonialism, nor did they adequately explain the internal struggles for power within Africa. Ethnicity and post-independence nationalism, in particular the disjunctions between them, have proven to be unresolved sources of disruption and strife. Moreover, nationalism does not adequately address divisions based on class and gender. This is not to suggest that Africa is now, or was ever, only divided against itself. Chapters in this volume also trace the commonalities between groups and their histories of mutual influence and cooperation.

It is important to differentiate nationalism as a response to colonialism from the nationalisms of the post-independence period. While the latter continue to configure the West as a term of opposition, against which African reality is to be reformulated, in many cases such nationalist ideologies mask the extent to which successful post-independence regimes depend on and accommodate the West and its neocolonial practices. While the colonial encounter and the ongoing structuring of global relations should not be underestimated, current contestations and developments cannot be attributed in any single and straightforward way to colo-

---

14. See Aimé Césaire, *The Collected Poetry*, trans. Eshleman and Annette Smith (Berkeley: University of California Press, 1983) and *Discourse on Colonialism*, trans. Joan Pinkham (New York, Monthly Review, 1972); and Léopold Sedar Senghor, *Prose and Poetry*, trans. and ed. John Reed and Clive Wake (London: Heinemann Educational, 1976).

15. Important works by these anticolonial authors include Albert Memmi, *The Colonizer and the Colonized*, trans. Howard Greenfeld (New York: Orion Press, 1965); Frantz Fanon, *The Wretched of the Earth*, trans. Constance Farrington (New York: Grove Press, 1968); and Amilcar Cabral, *Unity and Struggle: Speeches and Writings*, trans. Michael Wolfers (New York: Monthly Review Press, 1979).

nialism and its legacies. The chapters in this volume, by detailing the processes that characterized precolonial Africa, are crucial in providing accounts that indicate the dynamic conditions internal to Africa that constituted those societies and that continue in complex fashion to have an impact on current realities.

If nationalist projects developed strategies for reclaiming the primacy of African cultures in opposition to Western hegemonic forms and assumptions, the postcolonial period has seen the extension and complication of these critiques. Significantly, the growing field of *postcolonialism* comprises three inter-related projects: (i) to characterize and analyze the experiences of societies after they have achieved formal independence, including an account of the effects of neocolonialism; (ii) to re-tell non-Western histories and to identify sites of political agency and meaning-making according to representational logics that exceed or escape Western colonial and neocolonial paradigms, as part of the ongoing project of decolonizing culture; and finally, (iii) as discussed in the previous section, to intervene in the histories and explanatory frameworks of Western culture and identity themselves, such as the insular story of Europe's transition from feudalism to capitalism or the development of modern Euro-American subjectivity as independent of the history of colonialism. The extent to which Western academic disciplines and postmodern critiques have developed, and are dependent upon, critiques of colonialism and the challenges posed by formerly colonial subjects has not been sufficiently noted.

These three inter-related projects make postcolonialism ambitious indeed as an intervention in contemporary theoretical and political debates since its domain and effects are not limited to a particular period or region. Some of the significant achievements of postcolonial criticism are the foregrounding of hybridity and internal differentiation in subject formation; the constitutive status of gender and sexuality in the elaboration of national narratives; and the centrality of *subaltern*, or subordinate, communities and their political agency in accounting for the unfolding of history.[16] Unlike some of the variants of nationalism discussed above, then, postcolonial critiques are more attentive to hybridity and to the range of internal differences, based on class, ethnicity, and gender, that characterize colonial and postcolonial contexts and that cannot be reduced to a strict opposition between the West and the non-West.

The focus on hybridity and the second feature of postcolonial studies listed above, namely, the ongoing production of knowledge and alternative frameworks in the interests of decolonization, has turned on the central question of modernity or modernization. Very often, the claims of modernity are uncritically and misleadingly seen in strict opposition to traditional cultures, which are seen as static and backward. This volume's project of representing and interrogating precolonial African cultures does not propose the recovery and reinstatement of lost, static traditions. Indeed, the chapters demonstrate the ongoing evolution and adaptation of African cultures to various historical developments. Some scholars have therefore rejected the tradition/modernity paradigm for one that balances continuity, through the reinvention and reinvigoration of tradition, with ruptures and development, in response to African needs as determined by African actors.

---

16. In particular the Subaltern Studies school of Indian historiography is based on this approach; see Ranajit Guha and Gayatri Chakravorty Spivak, eds., *Selected Subaltern Studies* (New York: Oxford University Press, 1988).

Many critics from the formerly colonial world have wondered about the appropriateness of the quest for modernity, especially when Western metropolitan sites are busy declaring the arrival of the postmodern moment and when the progressive and democratic claims of modernity have been revealed to be largely empty or untenable. Africa has sought appropriate models of development and modernization that can minimize internal tensions and allocate resources equitably, but we should not forget that the pursuit of development takes place in the context of the depredations of global capital, which, in part, also provide the motivation for the critiques associated with postmodernism. The violence and discord associated with the *uneven development* that formerly colonial countries have undergone further indicate the limits of uncritically accepting the desirability of modernity.

The critique of modernity should not be interpreted as a call for a return to "tradition." Africa is irrevocably enmeshed in the projects, histories, and categories of thought characteristic of the West. Beyond an oversimple choice between tradition and modernity, African history and current reality reveal the proliferation of syncretic and hybrid cultures. These still have the task in front of them of determining appropriate strategies for survival, resistance to domination, and autonomous development.

Review Questions

1. What are some of the reasons for studying precolonial African cultures in the present period?
2. In which academic disciplines has the term "culture" as a category of analysis been developed? Identify some of the important differences in the uses of the term.
3. What are the pitfalls of regarding culture as a static set of values and practices?
4. Define "civilized" and "Other." What are the dangers of such labels?
5. What was the role of cultural assumptions in the project of European colonialism? In what ways do these old assumptions about Africa continue to have currency and effects today?
6. How has the concept of culture evolved within Marxism?
7. What are the innovations of cultural studies?
8. Define and discuss the terms "agency" and "resistance."
9. Discuss the concepts "cultural differences" and "culture as difference."
10. Discuss the differences between postmodern and postcolonial conceptions of culture.
11. Why is culture important for nationalist struggles?
12. How might Western and African cultures be related to or dependent upon one another?

Additional Reading

Ashcroft, Bill, Gareth Griffiths, and Helen Tiffin, eds. *The Post-Colonial Studies Reader*. New York: Routledge, 1995.

Dirks, Nicholas B., ed. *Colonialism and Culture*. Ann Arbor: University of Michigan Press, 1992.

Fanon, Frantz. *The Wretched of the Earth*. Translated by Constance Farrington. New York: Grove Press, 1968.

Gray, Ann and Jim McGuigan, eds. *Studying Culture: An Introductory Reader*. 2nd ed. New York: Arnold, 1997.

Grinker, Roy Richard and Christopher B. Steiner, eds. *Perspectives on Africa: A Reader in Culture, History, and Representation*. Oxford: Blackwell, 1997.

Hall, Stuart et al., eds. *Modernity: An Introduction to Modern Societies*. Oxford: Blackwell, 1996.

Mongia, Padmini, ed. *Contemporary Postcolonial Theory: A Reader*. New York: Arnold, 1996.

Said, Edward. *Orientalism*. New York: Vintage, 1978.

Storey, John, ed. *Cultural Theory and Popular Culture: A Reader*. 2nd ed. Athens: University of Georgia Press, 1998.

Chapter 2

Intergroup Relations

Toyin Falola

Introduction

The purpose of this chapter is to demonstrate that, in spite of the huge size and diversity of the African continent, many African states and groups interacted with one another during their long precolonial period. This relationship was one of the reasons why many ideas of, and assumptions about, culture were common. Relationships took the form of peaceful means and also of conflicts, as imperial states tried to expand and create colonies of satellites to control. No African group or culture was insulated against change brought about by contacts with other peoples. Evidence of borrowing can be found in beliefs, dance, music, language, and politics. After 1885, with the partition and conquest, new institutions of colonial rule were set up; these separated countries and introduced new identities. Competing imperialisms destroyed a number of pre-existing linkages. Imperialism justified its "civilizing mission" by describing Africa as "tribal units," with each one so fixed in its ways that acculturation to other cultures was difficult.

Intergroup relations were based on the assumption that there were codes and rules to guide the actions and activities of groups, that one state recognized the leadership of another, and that there were avenues by which to conduct politics. No African community could be treated as an island, removed from other communities. In fact, the political and economic survival of each community depended on how well it could manage the relationships, either of friendship or of hostility, that it maintained with its neighbors. Among the major features of this relationship were trade, diplomatic relations, exchange of political and cultural ideas, and war. Peace and war are both aspects of society's relations with other societies and are linked by "an intermediate zone in which the tension caused by the interaction of two or more societies is mitigated towards one end of the scale of their relations by peaceful tendencies, while towards the other it is exacerbated by influences hostile to peace."[1] I shall analyze those factors that promoted intergroup relations in Africa and also those that indicate evidence of cultural resemblances.

---

1. Robert S. Smith, *Warfare and Diplomacy in Pre-colonial West Africa* (London: Methuen, 1976), 1.

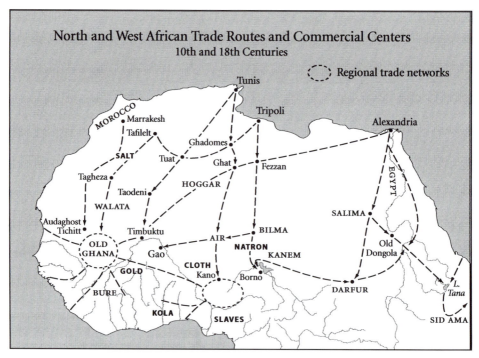

Figure 2-1. Inter-Regional Routes in West and North Africa

Migration

The history of the establishment of states, dynasties, and many other institutions reveals a great deal about migration. Traditions of origins emphasize the migration of people from their original homeland to other areas, as well as the spread of languages, crops, religions, and other ideas. Many cases of migration have been confirmed by historians in virtually all regions of Africa. Many involved massive population movements, while others related to state formation involving the mobility of armies and political leaders.

Archaeologists have equally confirmed the migrations of people in early African history. One notable case was the movement out of the Sahara region because of unfavorable conditions. Probably about the second millennium B.C., the loss of rainfall and the drying up of rivers and pastures forced people in the Sahara to relocate. Yet another major example was the spread of Bantu languages, from their original homeland in the Cross River basin to much of sub-Saharan Africa. Internal migrations were many and they contributed to the diffusion of iron technology, state formation, and urbanization, to mention but a few consequences. The spread of the knowledge of iron working was particularly significant in generating further migrations and the building of states.

Population movements were very common. To start with, the most common occupations of farming, hunting, fishing, and trading required mobility over short distances within every region. Larger-scale mobility occurred when population expanded beyond available resources, forcing people to seek opportunities elsewhere. When drought or other ecological disasters occurred, one sure way of coping was to migrate *en masse* to colonize new areas. Population movements were also brought about by warfare, conflicts, state expansion, and complicated political rivalries. Every population movement represented the expansion of cultural and ethnic frontiers. Some major examples of population movements included those by the Arabs between the ninth and the eleventh centuries to the Nile Valley, North Africa, and the Sahara; the Oromo movement to Ethiopia in the sixteenth and seventeenth centuries, and the Fulani expansion across West Africa from the eleventh to the seventeenth centuries. These and other examples of population movements reveal the ability to travel and relocate, and the spread of cultures over time.

Migration was also induced by economic factors. In some cases, it involved such occupations as nomadism and fishing which required some traveling. Nomads had to search for grazing land, occasionally moving across regional frontiers. In the case of fishermen, such as the Ewe of West Africa, they traveled on the sea, far beyond their own locality. In the process, the Ewe borrowed from the cultures of the Yoruba and Fon to their east and the Akan to the west. For instance, the Ewe attribute their divination practices to the Yoruba, in addition to a number of loan words and similar myths of origin.

Conflicts, warfare, and imperialism led to many cases of migration. Such migrations could be swift and short-distance, or they could be slow and steady, depending on the circumstances that triggered them off.

Whatever their causes, migrations enabled new areas to be colonized and expanded, ideas and beliefs to spread over wider regions, and food crops and material culture to diffuse. The spread of the knowledge of iron working and of food production transformed Africa in many ways and encouraged the emergence of states.

Cultural Agencies

There were also cultural institutions which cut across or united groups and communities. Practitioners of divination, like the *Ifa* diviners in West Africa, are known to have traveled widely. Islamic preachers and missionaries were also great travelers. In some areas, groups organized celebrations and dances that brought various peoples together. One example was the *Jengu* religious group, featuring ritual dances and sacrifices to water spirits for fecundity and good harvests. The *Jengu* was widespread among the Bantu groups in Cameroon, and was able to unite people in different areas for worship. In the forest belt of Cameroon there was another cultural organization, the *Ahon*, which brought many villages and groups together in a male dance to celebrate initiation or perform funeral rites. Initiation and secret societies could involve people among different groups, as in the case of the *Poro* secret society in Liberia, Sierra Leone, Guinea and the Ivory Coast. The *Poro* was the body which performed initiation rites and maintained law and order. By wearing the mask of identification, a *Poro* man enjoyed power beyond his own village or group.[2]

---

2. George Harley, *Notes on the Poro in Liberia* (New York: Kraus Reprint, 1968), 3.

Secret societies were organized in such a way as to unite people of different groups, backgrounds, and generations. By their very nature, they transcended village, city, and state boundaries, both in membership and operation. They involved men and women who shared similar views on many philosophical, political, and ethical matters. Membership was open to those who could keep secrets, afford the initiation fee, and defend the interests of the society. By way of signs and symbols that only the initiates could interpret, the members of these secret societies moved from one town to another, spreading messages of goodwill and receiving kind treatment from their colleagues.

The oracle system also encouraged interstate relations. The oracle was respected as an impartial judge. The priest of the oracle often performed such religious and medical duties as purging a community of witches and healing the sick. Oracles were therefore revered and priests highly respected. To take one example, among the famous oracles that united many Igbo clans and villages in Eastern Nigeria were those of Awka, Ozuzu, Umunoha, Agwu, and Arochukwu. When an oracle established a reputation for impartiality in decision making, it received clients from far and wide.

Cultural traits were diffused from one society to another in two major ways —through migration or cultural dispersion, and through borrowing. Diffusion of culture could be intraethnic, exchanging ideas between people within the same ethnic group. Examples of this abound everywhere, the diffusion being caused by forced migrations, trade relations, marital relations, or diplomacy. Material objects spread in Africa by way of population expansion.

Diffusion could also be interethnic, referring to ideas that were exchanged between two or more ethnic groups. Neighboring states influenced one another. This would explain why such ideas as divination and iron and bronze working spread rapidly and took similar forms in many areas.

More than any other aspect of culture, religion provided the strongest links among different African groups. Islam was one of the main religions that brought states and peoples together. It encouraged political centralization, which enabled kings to control vast areas with a greater degree of political cohesion than before. It also encouraged joint worship and the pilgrimage to Saudi Arabia. During the pilgrimage, people traveled across lands, and they interacted peacefully with people in different places.

With respect to indigenous religions, the stress on community, social cohesion, and respect for elders was very prominent. The mask, a sacred religious object, was found in many areas. The mask embodied a spirit, god, or ancestor and was invested with ritual meanings. Wherever the mask was used, it was associated with the promotion of social cohesion and community solidarity. If ideas of what the mask represented were common, so too were the creative talents associated with carving them.

A notable aspect of African art was the masquerade, used primarily as a form of ritual communication between the living and the dead, and secondarily as a form of entertainment with its multi-media aspects of the mask, songs, dancing, and drama. Forms and types were diverse, but the functions were similar in many places, notably as rituals for ancestors, detection of witchcraft, and initiation rites. Masquerades made political and social comments, using the anonymity offered by the mask to criticize the power elite.

Forms of dress were shared among people of different groups. The use of the veil, for instance, was widespread among Muslim women. Poncho styles were found in many areas, such as the *babban riga* among the Hausa, *danshiki* among the Yoruba and *mboubou* in the Senegambia. The wrapper styles could be found among coastal communities.

Marriage was a great unifier. Long-distance traders, priests, kings, and chiefs forged and cemented relationships through marriages. When a powerful person gave a daughter away, it enabled him to establish influence in another area. Lasting alliances were made possible through marriages. Intergroup marriages were not limited to the rich and powerful; ordinary folks with the opportunity to travel and interact with people of other ethnicities and locations were also involved. A study of some groups in the Cameroon shows that intergroup marriages were more extensive than has been commonly assumed.[3] When marriages involved people of different languages and religions, they also contributed to the spread of multiculturalism.

Artistic connections have been drawn between people of different regions and cultures, as in the case of Nok in the plateau and Ile-Ife in the forest, both in Nigeria. The connection between Ife and Benin in the southwest was strong, with the former establishing a dynasty in the latter and spreading the knowledge of bronze casting between the twelfth and the fourteenth centuries. The Baule of the Ivory Coast borrowed language and carving styles from the Asante of Ghana. Where connections were made, there are similarities in methods and styles.

The study of folktales has revealed the unity in diversity of these stories and their meanings. Animals were used as the protagonists, the tortoise and spider in the forest region, and the antelope and hare in the savanna. The animals were used to construct similar stories, usually told by moonlight, by an elder surrounded by children. Animals became human or supernatural beings, behaving in ways that conveyed lessons of morality and character. Studies have confirmed that stories narrated in one area were retold in others in either the same form or in a modified manner, to adapt them to the local fauna. For instance, the tortoise in a story in the forest region would be replaced by a jackal or hare in the grasslands. Mythological tales of a great man with magical abilities, endowed by a god, were common. So also were those of hunters who traveled great distances to establish new towns and dynasties. Fictional stories revealed concern for the use of wisdom to overcome problems and the necessity of avoiding anger, intrigue, jealousy, and other destructive behavior. Small animals such as the spider and tortoise, possessing great wisdom, defeated the large ones like elephants, lions, and buffalo.

Both the open and the hidden meanings of folktales were similar everywhere. The folktales revealed ideas and conceptions about history, morality, and ethics. They socialized children into society, and they constituted a rich source of knowledge with which to educate and to enrich life experiences.

To move to another genre of artistic performance, music, there are common patterns that one can point to. Octave singing characterized the music of many groups such as the Wolof, Kusasi, Dagomba, and Ganda, while homophobic parallelism was characteristic of the songs of the Baule, Akan, Konkomba, Igbo, Ijo, Bemba, and Muole.[4] Common fundamental features included speech-related

---

3. Jean-Pierre Warnier, "Noun-Classes, Lexical Stocks, Multilingualism and the History of Cameroon Grassfields," *Language and Society*, 26 (1980).

4. J.H. Nketia, *The Music of Africa* (Los Angeles: Institute of Ethnomusicology, 1965).

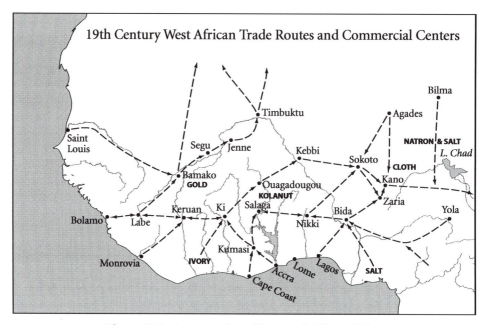

Figure 2-2. Intra-regional Routes in West Africa

melodies, audience participation, percussive techniques, and improvised variation. Cultural unity can also be discerned in the musical instruments: flutes,
horns, trumpets, gongs, and drums made from local materials such as wood, clay,
stone, rock, and animal skin and hides. Instruments were not used to produce
music, but as communication devices to praise, condemn, warn, and relay messages. Professional musicians traveled far and wide to entertain their audiences.

Foods

Archaeologists are of the view that the knowledge of animal domestication
and food cultivation grew in certain centers and spread all over the continent at
different periods before A.D. 100. They confirm that there were population
movements as well as exchanges of crops and techniques of farming. Patterns of
production were fairly similar in many areas. So too was the reliance on certain
cereals and root crops. Among the major cereals that people cultivated over a
wide region were sorghums, millets, rice, and maize. While some species of rice
and maize were introduced from outside, they quickly spread and were adapted
to local diets. As for the root crops, the major ones were yams and cassava. Cassava is believed to have been introduced by the Portuguese in the sixteenth century, and it quickly spread to many parts of the continent.

Food historians have divided Africa into zones, indicating a high level of similarity in habits within each zone. With respect to West Africa, the three major
zones were those of the sorghum-millet culture, the rice culture, and the yam culture. The sorghum-millet zone corresponds with the Western Sudan, where the
great empires of Ghana, Mali, Songhai, Kanem-Borno, and the Hausa states

flourished. Sorghum and millet were easy to cultivate in the grasslands. Grain cultivation and animal husbandry were two major occupations that were successful in sustaining large states and international commerce across the Sahara.

In the forest zone that covered most of the southern part of West Africa, rice and yam were among the key crops. Rice dominated the area from the Senegal River to the River Bandama in the Ivory Coast, while yam was the "king of the crops" elsewhere. The rice-eating groups were united by patrilineal succession, language affinity, and diets. This is not to say that rice was responsible for these common traits, but to indicate the level of similarity within a food cultural zone.

Trade

Trade was an integrative factor in African history and culture. It promoted the spread of people, goods, ideas, and institutions. Language of trade (e.g., Arabic, Hausa, and Swahili) spread widely and became important partly because of the activities of traders. Similarly, Arabic civilization reached various parts of Africa partly because of trade. Trade itself can be regarded as an integral part of culture. For instance, we can talk of currencies as part of material culture, articles of trade like manufactured objects as part of technology (which itself is an element of culture) and markets as cultural rendezvous. Indeed, some aspects of relations between the African communities constituted a seed bed of conflict. Trade, for instance, could lead to open conflicts when two societies vied for the control of a major trade route.

Trade was, perhaps, the most important form of relations between states in precolonial Africa. Trade relations were maintained both in peace and war. This is probably because no African community was fully self-sufficient in the production of agricultural and manufactured goods. Physical environments, often geographical factors, and degrees of specialization and skill acquisition, all of which varied from one region to another, were responsible for this.

Taking West Africa as an illustration of the need for trade, there were geographical differences between the north and the south. The northern part consists of a broad belt of grassland running from east to west. Geographers classify the area as belonging to three different types of savanna. These are the sahel further to the north, the Sudan in the middle, and the Guinea savanna to the south. This classification is based on rainfall and vegetation; while the Guinea savanna receives the highest rainfall and has deciduous trees and grasses, the Sahel receives scanty rainfall and has stunted thorn trees and short grasses. To the south is the tropical rain forest which merges into swamps near the coast. There are some areas which, because of their elevation, receive a fairly high rainfall and have fertile soils. One has in mind areas like the Jos and Bauchi Plateau which receives a fair share of relief rains and whose trees are taller than others within the Guinea savanna belt.

The implications of this geographical variation for trade become clear when it is realized that some crops will prosper well only under certain conditions of rainfall, humidity, and fertility. While such valuable crops like kolanuts and yams grow well in the forest region, tse-tse flies do not allow for the kind of animal husbandry that is easily supported by the open savanna belt to the north. Hence, cattle, upland rice, and millet, which were the products of the savanna region, had to be exchanged for kolanuts and palm produce, whose cultivation was well developed in the forest zone. Even within the same geographical zone, there were variations, like sub-zonal specializations in fishing, hunting, manufacturing, and mining.

To obtain goods it could not produce, a state had to establish trade relations with others. In Nigeria for instance, the Igbo maintained contacts with the Nupe in order to buy metal objects such as swords and knives, and other items such as cloth, natron, and livestock. Kano in northern Nigeria and Salaga in Ghana were friendly because of trade. In North Africa, Tripoli had to be friendly with Borno in order to obtain eunuchs and sell its own products. In East Africa, the Mrima commercial center depended considerably on the Nyika people in the hinterland for a variety of items such as ivory, gum, copper, honey, beeswax, grain, foodstuffs, and timber. The Nyika in turn sent caravans to the north and northwest to trade with the Galla and the Kamba. In Central Africa, the trade in coastal and rocksalt, copper, and iron brought the peoples of Angola and its hinterland together.

The requirements of trade, such as currencies, languages of communication, trade routes, markets and professional traders served to promote interactions among states. Traders, especially professional long-distance traders, were noted for their skill in foreign tongues. Certain languages came to dominate some exchange areas. For instance, the Hausa language was widely spoken in West Africa, and Kanuri in the Lake Chad basin. Between West and North Africa, trade was carried on in Arabic. In East Africa, Swahili was a major language of trade. From the eighteenth century onward, trade contacts spread the use of English, French, and Portuguese in the coastal areas.

Currencies had a unifying effect as well. There were various kinds of currencies: salt, livestock, gold, brass, cowries, iron, and so on. Some, like cowries, were quite widespread. Cotton strips were used among the Kanuri in Nigeria and the Wolof in Senegambia. Metal currencies such as gold, copper, and iron rods were used in different parts of Africa. Manillas, made of brass and copper, were widely used in the Niger Delta, and a variety of iron wires was in circulation on the Upper Guinea coast. Gold was the most common currency in Asante and many parts of the central forest region and also in the Western Sudan. The Arab scholars who visited West Africa reported on the use of gold as far back as the eleventh century A.D. There were two types of gold currencies. The first was gold dust normally kept in bags. The second was mithqals or dinars which were minted in large quantities at Nikki in Borgu. These two forms of gold currencies circulated widely in West and North Africa. A third variety of currency was cowry shells. These were used in virtually the whole of West Africa with the exception of eastern Nigeria and the Upper Guinea coast. The use of cowries had a long history. The cowry had a number of advantages. It made exchange possible over a wide area since it was used in many places. Its small size made it easy to carry, though it was bulky for large transactions. The cowry served as an effective measure of value and a unit of account which made it easy to know the value of each good in relation to others and to fix prices of all kinds of products. Finally, the cowry could not be forged. All kinds of currencies facilitated exchange of goods and services. Trade routes linked various parts of Africa. There were numerous water-

Figure 2-3. North African traders with camels

ways and roads. Rivers running through different states helped to promote inter-group relations. The Niger and Nile, for instance, strengthened the commercial links among the numerous people located along their banks. The West African la-goons made it possible for people from the area of the present-day Republic of Benin to navigate as far as Sapele in Nigeria.

The roads were more important than the waterways because they connected more towns and villages than the waterways. Although they were narrow foot-paths, they were adequate for traders and others who traveled on foot and with pack animals. The roads differed in importance, depending on those places which they linked together; they included local roads between one settlement and another, routes between towns and international highways passing through many territories.

The international highways of the nineteenth century are still known, and those of West Africa are used here as illustrations. One started in Wagadugu and passed through Dori, Fada N'Gourma, Say on the River Niger, on its way to Sokoto, Katsina, and Kano. From Kano it linked up with the busy Kano-Kukawa route. This route promoted relations among the peoples of Senegambia, the Niger Bend, and the entire central Sudan. Another international route started in Accra and passed through Kumasi, Salaga, and Yendi. At Yendi, the route branched into two, one branch continuing to Wagadugu to link up with the Wagadugu-Kukawa route, while the second went eastward, passed through Bussa and Zaria, and ter-minated at Kano. This route facilitated interactions among the peoples of Ghana, the Niger Bend, and Nigeria. There was yet another route from Lagos through Ibadan, Oyo, Raba, and Zaria (where it joined the Zaria-Accra road) to Kano. This highway also made it possible for the various communities in southern Nige-ria to have contacts with those in the north.

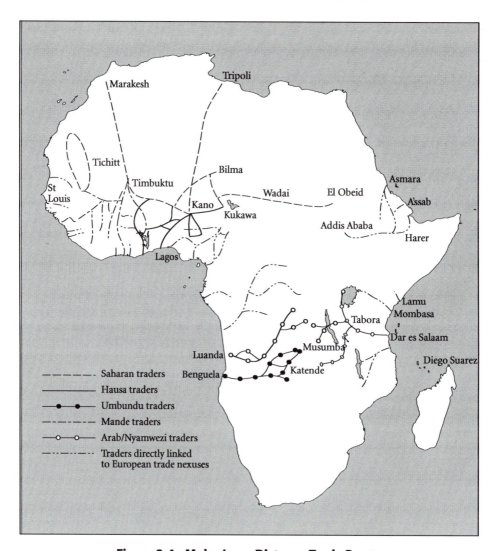

Figure 2-4. Major Long Distance Trade Routes

There were other features of the routes which promoted peaceful intergroup relations. The first was their construction and maintenance, and the second was the provision of security and safety along them: a responsibility that all states located along the routes took seriously, for their own sake and for the benefit of other neighboring states. Each town or village took care of the routes that passed through them. Neighboring states would agree on when to clear border areas, construct bridges, and placate the spirit-force of the road. For instance, the Lagos-Badagri-Whydah road was cleared by the peoples of these states and others along the route at least twice a year, both during the rainy season. Similarly, the route linking Asante with the coast was cleared by all the communities along the route almost at the same time.

As far as security and safety were concerned, many states would agree on the procedure to adopt and the extent and limits of the power of official road guards. On the Asante route to Bussa, for example, Muslim escorts were generally recognized and their orders were binding on people who were not necessarily from their state. In taking these and other measures, different states were brought together for a common cause. Indeed, it was profitable for states to cooperate in order to derive the maximum advantages from trade. If traders passed through a territory they would pay tolls and buy cooked food and other products. These payments went a long way to enrich rulers and traders in that area. Nearly all the African urban centers benefited from their relationship with others.

If the routes facilitated interstate relations, the traders who made use of them should be seen as the agents who made these cordial relationships possible. Traders were the unofficial representatives of their states, promoting peaceful coexistence. Every African state had its long-distance traders. Indeed, as the case of the Diakhanke or Dyula illustrates, long-distance traders constituted themselves into distinctive sub-cultural systems. These traders organized themselves into caravans and traveled long distances to buy and sell goods. In the process, they advertised and sold goods produced in different parts of Africa and brought various states into very close contacts. Even more importantly, it was the traders who really spread ideas from one place to another. For instance, Islam and Arabic civilization were popularized in several parts of Africa by the activities of traders. Berber traders propagated Islam in the Sahara and in sub-Saharan West Africa. The same was true of East and Central Africa, where trading contacts with the Middle East and Egypt facilitated the spread of Islam.

In attempting to overcome the various hazards of trade, traders had to build relations of trust and confidence with those they encountered on their journeys and those with whom they established trade relations. There were several methods of regulating the relationships of trade, and all these not only brought Africans together but also promoted understanding and the spread of culture. The first problem that the traders tried to overcome was that of language. A caravan trader tried to understand the language of his host. For example, the Kikuyu who traded with the Maasai tried to speak the Maasai language.

Secondly, intermarriage was encouraged. In many African communities, hospitality and trust could be more easily achieved if there were marriage ties. Marriages promoted lasting friendships, reduced cultural differences, and created strong bonds of intimacy.

Bonds were also created through blood brotherhoods. There were several examples of this. In north western Uganda during the nineteenth century, the trade in salt was flourishing. Wars were, however, prevalent in this area partly because of the struggle to control the salt trade. Salt traders traveled in armed caravans, protected one another, and established strong connections along the route. Also in the same region, the Palwo and Baluli formed a blood brotherhood with the Langi group across the Nile. Social bonds facilitated trust and enhanced commercial contacts.

Finally, traders made use of religion to promote trade. The Hausa long-distance traders, for example, used Islam to create an effective bond of unity among themselves in order to control trade. Hausa traders raised Islam to the level of an ideology in order to have a blueprint for the establishment of a powerful trade diaspora. The activities of two of the most notable trading groups—the Diakhanke and the Hausa—are briefly discussed here to illustrate how traders traversed routes and attended markets far beyond their homes.

The Diakhanke inhabited the Senegambia hinterland. They specialized in trade, carrying goods from the Upper Niger to the Senegal and Gambia rivers.

They traveled long distances, in the course of which they established many trading colonies in different parts of West Africa. From north to south, caravans often traveled up to three hundred fifty kilometers and from east to west about one thousand kilometers. A single caravan could travel from Segu to Gambia. They also formed trading networks and became prominent along particular routes and in a wide geographic area. From their homeland, they went eastwards, stopping at Sikasso or Segu, from where they also traded with the people of the Niger Valley. Their caravans also went westwards, traveling as far as the coast. Southwards they went to Futa Djallon, northwards up to the desert to exchange goods with the Moors. Just as the land area which the Diakanke covered was large, so also the commodities they traded in were diverse. They bought slaves and gold in the Sahel, especially from the Moors, in exchange for salt and textiles. They went to Bambuk and the Gambia to exchange gold and slaves for European goods up to the middle of the nineteenth century.

Like the Diakhanke, the Hausa were great long-distance traders. The Hausa-speaking peoples had their large centers in Northern Nigeria. Many Hausa were itinerant merchants. Through them, kolanuts from the places in Gonja and Yorubaland forest region were taken to the north and even across the Sahara. Hausa merchants were prominent on the caravan routes from Kano and Katsina to Tripoli and Tunis. They also went to Salaga, Dendi, Gao, Zinder Dori, Kaya and Tenkodogo in the Mossi country. Northern products such as metalwork, cloths, and cattle also found their way to many West African markets partly through the agency of these traders.

From the discussion so far, it is clear that trade between African states and peoples was widespread. Indeed, three tiers of trade can be identified. First, there was the local trade which took place in local, daily or periodic, markets. This involved the exchange of goods between people who belonged to different states or kingdoms. Regional markets were unique because of the large number of people and the wide variety of goods involved. Some regional markets were held on neutral ground or in frontier towns. There were many of these markets in every region. Among those that were well attended in West Africa up to the nineteenth century were Gao in the country of the Songhai, Kaya among the Mossi, Salaga in Ghana, Dendi in northern Dahomey, and Kano in Nigeria. Further examples can be drawn from East Africa, where peoples with different forms of production exchanged goods. There were agricultural and pastoral peoples who needed meat and milk. For instance, the Gussi, who were agriculturists, traded with the Luo who were pastoralists. Similarly, the Kikuyu sold agricultural products to the Maasai in exchange for sheep and goats. Intraregional specialization also encouraged trade. Two commodities, salt and iron, brought various states and peoples together. The deposits of high quality salt were few and the demand was widespread. High-quality salt occurred in Lake Katwe and Kasenyi and southwestern Uganda. From the seventeenth century onwards, traders from other parts of the region came to these two lakes for salt. In the case of iron, raw iron deposits were many but only a few societies had men skilled enough to produce high-quality iron goods. Samia in northwestern Kenya was one of the leading producers, and a regional iron trade between Samia and several other groups flourished.

The last tier of trade was interregional. For instance, West Africa engaged in trade with North Africa, northeastern Africa with East Africa, East Africa with

Central Africa, and Central Africa with the south. There is the well-known example of the trans-Saharan trade between the West and the North that made it possible for both regions to exchange goods and culture. Different types of centers of goods and culture exchange emerged. First, there were the southern nodal points of the routes in Kukawa, Kano, and Timbuktu serving as ports where southbound merchandise was either sold or transferred to smaller caravans going south, and where northbound goods were also packed and loaded. Second, there were halting centers in places such as Ghat, Salah, and Agades, all desert oases, where water and food could be obtained. In the third type of center, in places like Ghadames and Waryla, traders going to West Africa gathered for their journey, while those coming north unpacked their goods. The fourth type of center was the termini. While the northern termini were located mostly in Mediterranean ports such as Tripoli, Fez, Algiers, Tunis, and Mogador, from which West African goods were transported to the Middle East and Europe, the southern termini included Atlantic coastal ports such as Badagry, Lagos, and Calabar, where the goods displayed in markets and the community of traders reflected strong Saharan and Sudanic influences.

Warfare

Relations between groups were not always peaceful. Wars arose as a result of conflicting interests. War could be conducted by campaigns, battles, or skirmishes. A war could be settled by one battle. Wars were widespread all over the continent. Their major cause was the desire of powerful states to expand their territories and control their neighbors. Most attempts to build and expand empires necessitated warfare, as cases all over Africa clearly demonstrate. Wars were also fought to resist and throw off the yoke of imperialism. The history of colonies and provinces of major kingdoms show how vigorous they could be in their attempts to become independent. Wars were also fought over the ambition to control a major source of wealth, most often trade routes, fertile land, or sources of ivory, iron, salt, or gold. Other reasons for wars included the desire for tribute, slaves, and booty. With the rise of Islam, the desire to spread the religion promoted jihads (holy wars) in a number of places, such as West Africa during the nineteenth century.

As in the case of diplomacy, there were laws and regulations regarding warfare. Certain protocols had to be observed before one state declared war on another, in fighting the war and in declaring peace. A war might be decided by the complete annihilation of one of the contestants, by an agreement by the belligerents to make peace or armistice, or by the complete exhaustion of the two sides.

Among the conventions generally observed when declaring war was the practice of giving the enemy some notice of an attack and a chance to send the women, elders, and children to safety. The Hausa had a tradition of a three-day delay, during which time the soldiers were supposed to be sharpening their knives. The Igbo gave their enemies notice, often suggesting the time and place where the battle was to be fought.

After the formal declaration of war, certain traditions—religious and economic—were observed before battle actually began. Among the Yoruba, the god of iron and of war was appeased and the necessary sacrifices made to other gods before the soldiers could march out. Priests and diviners were widely consulted. Weapons were smeared with magic portions and charms and amulets were stitched into garments worn in battle. Sacred objects were taken out and carried to the battlefield, like the sacred *Mune* on which Borno depended for victory in war. Many rules and taboos were observed in order to avoid disasters.

Even war brought different groups together. War captives were used by the belligerents as domestic labor or sold into slavery. Those who were retained in the households served as agents of exchange of cultures and ideas. Because of their ability to use a foreign language, they were employed as interpreters and clerks in the courts. The victorious party in a war expected the loser to pay occasional tribute. Such payment ensured continued interaction long after the war was over.

Diplomatic Relations

All states conducted diplomatic relations, which can be defined as routine interactions among states that were not at war, in order to conduct business, solve common problems, and discuss policies. States often had agents to represent them in other places. Traders could also act as ambassadors. All large states would send residents to the provinces to supervise politics, ensure peace, collect tribute, and spy. States who engaged in trade relations usually exchanged representatives who would discuss commercial matters and resolve disputes among traders.

The major goal of diplomacy in Africa was to prevent conflict that could lead to war. This was made possible when diplomacy established some form of compromise or a treaty between two or more states. The treaties arrived at might be secret or open. The majority of treaties were, however, concluded to end hostilities, although those with the European visitors dealt mainly with trade. Treaties were entered into solemnly and were usually regarded as binding and sacred. Among the Yoruba, there was an elaborate and sacred system of oath-taking that included a penalty for its violation. Apart from oaths binding the parties of treaties, dynastic marriages were arranged to cement agreements.

The type of people appointed as ambassadors varied from one society to another. Generally, however, they were men recognized for their wealth, closeness to power, or the performance of some important religious duties. Though slaves were also used, these were palace slaves who were seen as men of rank and influence. Ambassadors had badges or insignia to differentiate them and announce their credentials. Such items could include batons, canes, whistles, fans, and swords. In the case of the Oyo Empire, which was by no means peculiar in this, a powerful chief could serve as an ambassador in critical cases. The staff of the king (the *Alaafin*) would carry embroidered leather fans in red and green. Known as the *ilari*, these men had half of their heads shaven. The names or nicknames of the *ilari* could indicate the nature of the message. Thus, an *ilari* could bear the name of *Kosija* (there is no fight), *Sunmo-Oba* (cooperate with the king) and *Magborimipete* (do not conspire against me). The recipient of the message was expected to interpret the message given by the name of the bearer. Ambassadors were generally respected and well-treated.

Protocols observed by ambassadors varied from state to state. It was common for the king to converse only indirectly with his visitors. Usually ambassadors saluted the king in the fashion practiced in their own states, except where the ambassador had stayed long enough in the land to which he was accredited to be able to pick up the local custom. Ambassadors had the reputation of being able to speak foreign tongues. Nevertheless, not all of them had that skill, often relying on interpreters. The need for the language of communication to settle disputes and negotiate treaties, again as in trade relations, necessitated the rise to importance of certain languages within a zone. Arabic was used in North Africa and Swahili in East Africa. Even when language barriers had been broken, sign language was still employed. Ambassadors and chiefs were able to interpret messages encoded in symbols and objects such as swords, cowries, and pepper. In a Yoruba example observed by a European missionary during the nineteenth century, a string of nine cowries strung together meant that "it is preferably so," six cowries strung together meant "I agree," four cowries would mean "your proposal is ridiculous," and three cowries signified "I shall have nothing more to do with you."

Review Questions

1. Discuss both the causes and the consequences of migrations.
2. Discuss the view that African societies were not "islands, isolated unto themselves."
3. In what ways did trade and war promote interstate relations in Africa?

Additional Reading

Bascom, W.R. *African Dilemma Tales*. The Hague: Mouton, 1975.
Mbiti, John S. *African Religions and Philosophies*. London: Heinemann, 1969.
Meillassoux, C., ed. *The Development of Indigenous Trade and Markets in West Africa*. Oxford: Oxford University Press, 1971.

Chapter 3

Social Institutions: Kinship Systems

Austin M. Ahanotu

Definitions

Many scholars of African social life,[1] in their formal analysis of kinship systems, have assumed the primacy of kinship as an organizing principle in preindustrial African societies. This corpus of information on African kinship generally agrees that kinship is a set of relations existing at a given moment in time which link together a number of people. Certain things emerge in the context of these relations between individuals. Social actions come out of kinship ideology, cultural behavior also comes out of kinship ideology, and, in political terms, hierarchy and political esteem are among the projects of kinship construction. Societies act in pursuit of ends, a process that involves allocation of resources within the scheme of value judgements.

During the last fifty years, the study of structures and of kinship structures in particular has been most rewarding. As African historians, we have a greater need to borrow and incorporate the findings of other disciplines and little preoccupation with maintaining sacred and impermeable interdisciplinary boundaries. Yet, as historians, we have to insist that structure and history account for each other. To neglect either one is perilous. We must keep both in sight.

All kinship is based ultimately upon relationships of consanguinity and affinity (blood and marriage), or so the argument goes (see Fig. 3-1). But each African society has stressed some genealogical links and ignored others. This process of selection gives each kinship system a distinctive shape or form. All the differentiations must be related pragmatically to the historical development of the society. African kinship concepts, then, have not stood alone, but have to be understood

---

1. A.R. Radcliffe-Brown and D. Forde, eds., *African Systems of Kinship and Marriage* (Oxford University Press, 1950, re-edited by International African Institute, London, 1987) which is a formalistic analysis of kinship system as a category. See also Claude Lévi-Strauss, *Les Structures élémentaires de le parenté* (Paris: Mouton, 1967). This massive opus made a strong plea for what he called "structure" as against the "study of events." For a rethinking of kinship systems see Rodney Needham, ed., *Rethinking Kinship and Marriage* (London: Tavistock, 1971); and Schneider, "What Is Kinship All About?" in Priscilla Reining, ed., *Kinship Studies* (Washington, D.C.: The Morgan Centennial Year, 1972).

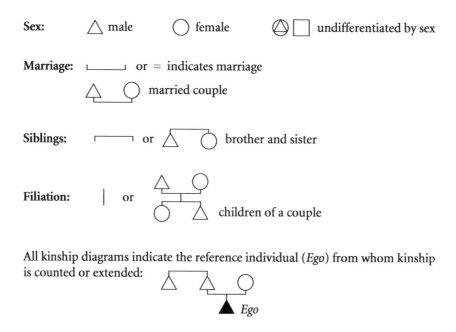

Figure 3-1. Kinship Signs

in their multitudinous relations with class and other bases of social differentiation. We can safely say that in African societies before outside interventions, kinship was often the most embracing or privileged mode of social relationship. The history of each lineage was grounded in common ancestry and this became the glue that held them together. The basic objective of the kinship ideology was to enhance the survivability of the kinship group and its physical residence. Igor Kopykoff's assertion reflects the inner core of kinship ideology:

> Traditionally, African kin groups had an almost insatiable demand for people and jealously guarded those they already had. Socially, this meant the existence of corporate groups of kinsmen, collectively holding resources, carefully enforcing their rights in membership...every newborn was legally spoken for and eagerly appropriated at birth by one or another autonomous kin group...similarly, the reproductive capacity of every woman was a resource to be appropriated at birth,...Culturally, all this had produced a variety of elaborations of systems of rights in person, so that these appropriations could be accomplished unambiguously, flexibly and with minimum of conflict.[2]

Kinship gave the individual full personhood. This is best reflected in a Yoruba proverb that says: "Ebi eni l'aso eni (your extended family members act as your closest apparel)." Scarification (*ila*) in Yorubaland was thus kinship protection

---

2. Igor Kopytoff, ed., *The African Frontier* (Indiana University Press, 1989), 43.

which said if an individual ever got lost they would find him. Other social net-works, for example, age groups, secret societies, and guilds, which were in abun-dance in African history, in certain cases supplemented kinship.

Various circumstances triggered different forms of family and kinship systems. Family and kinship ideologies were influenced by group history. Shared ances-try—the common beginning and separate histories of kin and family—was af-fected by economic forces, migrations, and internal tensions. There were attempts by individuals or the group to recreate and manipulate family and kinship ties to promote social order. We need to ask why African lineages responded to family matters in the way they did. History was largely the story of family relationships. Families interacted with each other. To cope with such interactions, various meth-ods were used. Rights and duties defined boundaries within which family members were expected to confine their behavior. A great deal of social learning in African societies was about one's duties to others and the situations in which these duties were owed.

Two questions need to be addressed as we explore the idea of kinship: Who are my relatives—how is it that an African comes to be a kinsman or kinswoman? What do my relatives and I have to do with each other? Each African group came up with answers from its own historical experience. Thus, there were great varia-tions in who qualified as a relative, in the things relatives were expected to do, and in the relatives that a given individual or group felt closest to. Kinship is a social convention. It is biological, but the biology is filtered through value systems and social usage.

Kinship Classification:
Patrilineal and Matrilineal Descent

Kinship can be classified into different categories (see Fig. 3-2). A descent group (i.e., lineage) emerges when the membership of a kinship group has grown beyond one generation. The type of descent varies from one society to another. Many African societies reckoned descent through the male-father line, a system known as patrilineal. Others reckoned relationships through the female line, a system that is described as uterine or matrilineal. In a few others, stress is put on neither patrilineal nor matrilineal; both are given equal importance. This arrange-ment is known as bilateral. For societies such as the San, Twi, and Kanuri, the double unilineal descent (in which access to high office was based on blood lin-eage) was preferred.

African societies that reckoned descent unilineally had a marked preference for patrilineal descent. Matrilineal descent occurred in societies such as the As-ante, Bemba, Tonga, and Tuareg. In Asante, for example, the *abusua*—the matri-lineage—traced relationships in the female line. The *abusua* united by common blood (*mogya*) which was passed from women to their children. The village where the *abusua* members lived was headed by a senior man or elder (*abusua panin*) and a senior woman (*obaa panin*).

The location of women after marriage was very important. So long as women left their families (and often their communities as well) to marry, they were con-sidered lost to other descent groups in many systems where residence was patrilo-

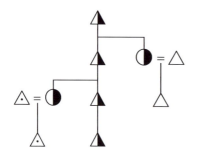

Patrilineal or agnatic descent
The daughter's children belong
to their father's group.

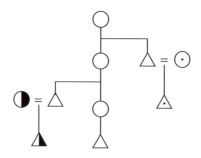

Matrilineal or uterine descent
The son's children belong
to their mother's group.

Figure 3-2. Unilineal Descent

cal. In a matrilineal system, avunculocal residence (i.e., the bride and groom moved to settle with the bride's mother's brother—the maternal uncle) was the common practice. In the case of the Asante, residence was duolocal/natolocal, that is, the bride could stay with her matrilineal relatives and the groom with his matrilineal relatives.

Kinship Obligations

The hunting and gathering period in Africa was a very challenging time.[4] Survival in the precarious environment of this period required cooperation. Forms of solidarity approximating to kinship developed. Prehistoric artists showed us this sense of solidarity in their rock paintings. In these paintings we see man the hunter, parents, families, and woman the gatherer, but more importantly, the band and community. With the emergence of agriculture came a more differentiated and complex human organization and a recognized inventory of rights and obligations. The basis for this was human relationships with others through *birth*, *marriage*, or *fictional* kinship. In each of these categories, the obligations of kinship were formalized.

The emotional side of kinship was reflected in individual's ties of affection, creating a feeling of belonging to a group in which membership was unquestioned. Studies of the kinship ideology of different African societies have shown that the sentimental attachment to families and kinsmen came out of the rein-

---

4. Peter Garlake, *The Hunters Vision: The Pre-Historic Art of Zimbabwe* (Seattle: University of Washington Press, 1996). See also T. Price and Ann Gebauer, eds., *Last Hunters-First Farmers: New Perspectives on the Prehistoric Transition to Agriculture* (Santa Fe: School of American Research Press, 1995).

forcement of *love, respect, protection,* and *identity.* Even though kinship relationships were in creative tension, a heavy emphasis on family pedigree persisted. The
kinship group had certain natural limits, such as the limitations of remembered
history. Class formation was not in competition with kinship. Large kinship
groupings usually went along with wealth and power.

Keeping track of kinship relations and connections was essential. To know
the names and relationships of many people was no mean feat. Africans knew
that kinship relations had a real existence only if the relationship was reinforced
by continued contact. This led to the following: (a) *visitations* — such as social
calls, home visits, and market-day meetings to discuss issues of common concern;
(b) festivities — important social occasions like naming ceremonies, weddings,
and funerals; and (c) *obligations* to help a kinsman. When seen as an issue of
obligations and expectations, kinsmen were naturally divided into two categories
of persons: beneficiaries and providers, that is to say, takers and givers. The obligations of kinship in most cases were formalized. There were those who benefited
from kinship and those who were expected to make sacrifices for others. This
tended to define the arena of tension in kinship ideology. Disposal of property, for
example, was rarely simple. Claims and duties were summed up in the property
relations internal to the family and kinship ideology, and at marriage certain
rights were exchanged. The dynamics of property shaped the range of relationships. A hierarchy of power distribution appeared and, in most cases, it favored
the African male. Thus patriarchal authority was the norm in the majority of
African societies. Family and kinship structures became carriers of patriarchy. The
hierarchical model of social order was heavily implicated in questions of marriage, domestic life, sexuality, and work.

There were dominants and dependents in the social ideology of kinship relations. Kinship ideology helped to produce patriarchy. It was the contrivance of
the elders, who benefited from it. The particular cultural traits of eldership were
mediated by local considerations and regional inclinations. In some areas eldership was diluted, but the social structure remained exploitative. Many African activities, values, attitudes, and beliefs were anchored to eldership. The institution
of the "elders" was one form of political contract and social arrangement.

The Nuclear Family and the Role of Elders

The primary institution at the core of the labor force was the nuclear family.
The nuclear family (i.e., a family incorporating a husband, his wife, and their children) was the basic building block for kinship systems. The matricentric unit (i.e.,
a mother and her children—the Igbo *umunne otu afo* [children of the same
womb]), a farming and eating unit, could also be central in the labor force. But
the *umunna* patricentric unit was crucial. Membership in this extended family,
which the Igbo called *umunna* (children of the same father, and in a historical and
political sense, descended from a common ancestor), was not optional but compulsory. The elder was crucial both in the nuclear family and in the extended family. He is the eldest living male descendant of the eldest son of the original founder
of the lineage. The Igbo called him *Opara* or *Okpara*. He performed all rituals demanded by custom. It was he who held the staff *ofo* that personified truth and

justice. He was at the center of family contractual arrangements. He was expected to provide structure, permanence, and continuity in family social life. The elder male thus provided the environment in which nuclear and extended families obeyed the precepts of the elders and behaved with relative decorum. Everything stemmed from the elder. In principle all powers of decision and all material resources belonged to him. He had a religious duty to ensure the survival of the kinship system. He officiated at the family shrine, and when he died he became an ancestor.

The eldest man in the patrilineal nuclear family instructed the members in the ways of loyalty and obedience. He was held responsible for his family and he was expected to keep its members within bounds, to insist upon conforming to customs, laws, and traditional observances of the kin group. He controlled the means of production and access to women, and hence political power within the kin group was in part based on gerontocracy. It was he who administered the family oath which was based on the vital potency of the ancestors. He assigned living quarters within the compound and made sacrifices to the founding ancestor of the compound. In brief, he maintained peace. The Yoruba word *bale* does not just mean "father" but "father of the house." The *bale* was the transmitter of kinship solidarity, and his job was to lead and instruct. He was distinguished by his wisdom. He was expected to be versed in folk lore, ancestral theology, and the veneration of family and kinship relics.

Although the elder held a special status, it was not a status of unqualified superiority. In some ways, he might be overruled by the council of elders, or the chief, or the king. To help the elder, other authority figures such as senior wives and oldest first daughters were put in place.[5] Senior wives were also important in the affairs of the women in the kin group, thus the *Iyale*, the senior wife in Yoruba communities, was addressed as "the mother of the house." For the Igbo, the oldest first daughters (*umuada*) who had married out of the kin group played important roles in peacemaking in their original kin group when needed. The point, then, is that the ideology of eldership was not the total picture but just part of the total system of taking care of the "children of the compound" or "house."

For a long time, Africans believed in the idea of the extended family as reflecting the continuity that bound various generations and nuclear families through lineal or horizontal networks of affinity (see Fig. 3-3). It was a cultural trait marked by geographic propinquity and the authority of the presiding elders over the component nuclear families. It was given resources and territory, power, status, and prestige. To facilitate the functions intended for extended families, African cultural innovators such as elders, titled men and women, and ritual leaders, intended the members of the extended family to have rights with respect to one another; at any given time depending on the political, economic, and social conditions of the time, these reciprocal rights could be active or dormant. Each person and each nuclear family became an actor playing roles in the network of relationships dictated by the moral sanctions of the extended family. The codes

5. For Yoruba example see Bolanle Awe, "The Iyalode in the Traditional Yoruba Political System," in Alice Schlegel, ed., *Sexual Stratification: A Cross-Cultural View* (New York: Columbia University Press, 1977), and for the Igbo see Mary Anochie, *The Igbo Woman and Consecrated Life* (Onitsha: Effective Key Publishers Limited, 1994), 14-15.

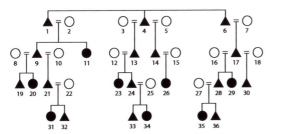 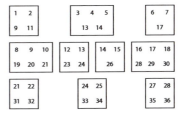

Extended families showing division into lineage members (dark) and wives who come from other lineages (uncolored)

Extended family divided into separate conjugal families

▲ male member of the patrilineal core of the extended family

● female member of the patrilineal core of the extended family

○ "Wives of the Compound" (wives who marry in from other lineages)

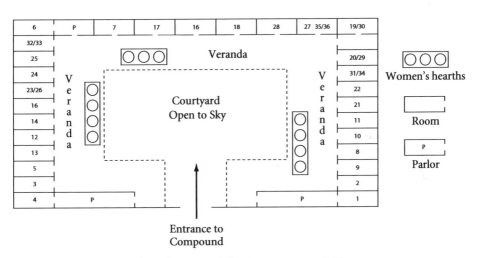

Entrance to Compound

Schematic representation of compound showing rooms occupied by members of extended family shown in kinship diagram above

Figure 3-3. Family Compound

governing extended family relationships could not be avoided, ignored or forgotten without repercussions.

The moral pretexts of extended family ideology were not static. They were constantly reinterpreted, extended into the realm of the symbolic, and constituted a kind of discourse held by members of a nuclear family. There was a dialectic between practice and ideology. The way the idea of the extended family was articulated or translated into practice was a negotiated process. This, at times, could even contradict the idea of the extended family itself. The extended family offered a wide network of security, but it also imposed the burden of extensive obligations. Victor Uchendu declared that "Ezin'ulo" (the Igbo extended family ideology) "is not just a bundle of material cultural traits, it is a people united by a bond of kin network and interlocking functions and reciprocities."[6]

Marriage

The notion of ancestral lineage singles out marriage as critical in one's life. The kinship groups constituted, formulated, and accounted for the continuance of the lineage. All African adults were expected to marry. Marriage built meaningful and enduring ties between families and kin groups. Marriage, in this sense, increased the "social capital" of the joined lineages. In African parlance, marriage created networks with social linkages and implied societal responsibilities. Since marriages were expected to strengthen families as corporate units, such issues as love, monogamy, plural marriages—polygyny and "female husbands" (literally a female master who contracted a form of marriage in which if she was barren and could afford it paid a dowry for another woman for her husband and any children from this arrangement would be regarded as the children of the barren woman for the purpose of representation in respect to estates and inheritances)—sex roles, and divorce, family and gender expectations should be seen within the context of the vested interest of the corporate group. In practical terms, for Africans, it was well-nigh impossible to get along without being married. Marriage made it possible to do the work that had to be done every day, and at least in theory only married people had a legitimate right to sexual relations.

African marriages seem to have taken varied forms: child betrothal or marriage by promise; marriage by abduction or consensual union; leviratic marriages in which a dead husband's wife or wives would be inherited by his younger brother or another family member; bride service marriage in which a wife was acquired by the prospective husband through his labor for his in-laws; marriage by exchange in which if you give someone your sister, one gives his sister in return; marriage by reimbursement in which a kinship group was expected to give a woman after taking one from another group; and finally bridewealth marriage. This means marriages for which the families arranged beforehand the amount, the composition, and payment schedule for what some call the "price of the fiancée." But it should be stressed that bridewealth carries no connotation of sale. The bridewealth paid was strongly regarded as a reflection of the honor, beauty, and righteousness of the bride, and the reputation of her natal family. Bridewealth partially determined the survivability of a marriage. Divorce, for example, was more likely to occur when fewer yams or cattle were paid. Bridewealth marriages were the most common form of marriage.

The paying and collection of bridewealth and its handing over to the bride's family was a group responsibility. This helped maintain interrelationships among

---

6. Victor Uchendu, "Ezi Na Ulo: The Extended Family in Igbo Civilization," 1995 Ahijoku Lectures, Owerri, Ministry of Information and Social Development (1995), 40.

lineage members. But a European observer of Igbo bridewealth in the 1920s noted the social and economic consequences of the practice:

> Young men find it extremely difficult to raise the ever-increasing prices now demanded, and they must either postpone marriage until well advanced in years, or contract loans. Grave evils arise from the latter course, for a man may be burdened by the incubus of debts incurred in connection with his marriage which will cripple him financially through his life... on the other hand, girls will not wait an indefinite period. Faced with almost insurmountable obstacles, the young people are much more readily disposed to cohabit without marriage.[7]

Basden, the observer, was stating the impact of capitalism on Igbo marriages when the practice of sharing the responsibility of paying the bridewealth was diminishing as well as the inability of the men in paying the bridewealth.

It is true that marriage starts a family, but a lot has to happen before marriage occurs. The members of kin groups knew that once the marriage topic was on the table it became the concern of all the kinsmen. The fortunes of the kinship group were at stake. The kin group found wives for the young men, and disposed of the girls in marriage to the advantage of the family and the kin group. Parental approval was imperative before a girl was given out for marriage, although go-betweens or marriage brokers could be used. These go-betweens were usually women because they were familiar with the behavior of the maidens. The behavior of the maiden was essential to the family of the groom. The go-betweens were those who knew the types of behavior that produce good or bad marriages. Although it was assumed that all marriages were arranged for reasons of family advantage and custom, marriage was not a cold transaction devoid of love and romance. Everyone looked out for "good" marriages. African social life, however, provided many social occasions for unmarried people to socialize and get to know each other. Public events like festivals and village market days provided such occasions, but most of the time older people were present. These occasions were opportunities to look, talk, and touch, but all were aware that the loss of virginity was considered a disaster. Mothers of girls understood that the reputation of their family was deeply involved in their daughters' premarital chastity. They did everything to maintain their daughters' chastity and to avoid scandals.

Premarital virginity was important, but good behavior and hard work were also required. With regards to premarital virginity and sexuality, customs ranged from those of the Azande of the Sudan, who permitted sexual intercourse for unmarried boys and girls (to them the attainment of physical maturity was assumed to depend upon an active sexual life), to those of the Ethiopian Kafa who, if a male had sexual intercourse with an unmarried female, might have his head or hands cut off. He was also required to pay a fine of two cows to the young woman's father and to the emperor. The girl was not punished, although she might subsequently have trouble finding a man who would marry her.[8]

---

7. G.T. Basden, *Among the Ibos of Nigeria* (London: Frank Cass, 1966, first edition 1921), 218.

8. See Gwen J. Bronde and Sarah J. Greene, "Cross-Cultural Codes on Twenty Sexual Attitudes and Practices," *Ethnology*, 15 (1976): 409-29; and Alice Schlegel, "Status, Property and the Value of Virginity," *American Ethnologist*, 18 (1991): 719-34.

It also appears that women who were voluptuous were greatly admired. The Igbo referred to *ahunwa*—a body full of children. It was no wonder, therefore, that marriage invariably carried with it the expectation of children. Childless marriages were likely to have grave repercussions, as we shall see in the section subtitled *Children*. The background of the proposed spouse was properly investigated to ensure that the the rule of endogamy, and the rule which separated people (for example among the Igbo, the *osu*, ritual slaves, from the *diala*, free-born were not broken; and that no incestuous relationship was entered into.

Marriage was a serious business, and arranging marriages was an important and time-consuming activity. Parents of the couples to-be were expected to inform you and notify the elders of the lineage about the forthcoming initiation of the marriage transaction. These elders were attentive to, and major witnesses to, all the steps in the process. The presence of these elders and their participation would subsequently legitimize the marriage. The prospective husband was expected to satisfy the demands of the women from the bride's kin group, but more importantly to satisfy the demands of the mother of the bride. The corporate significance of marriage was reflected in the fact that, whatever the details of kinship, most traditional African marriages were contracted as agreements between lineages. Yet the parental role was very important. In the eighteenth century, the traveller Mungo Park wrote about the Mande of present-day Mali:

> ... [i]f the parents agree to the [match] and eat a few kola nuts, which are presented by the suitor as an earnest of the bargain, the young lady must either have the man of their choice, or continue unmarried for she cannot afterwards be given to another.[9]

Various rites and ceremonies were used to establish the legality of marriage. Drinks and kolanuts are mentioned in many accounts of the marriage process. Victor Uchendu, the Igbo cultural scholar writing in 1965, stated:

> Before the father takes the bride wealth, he gives his daughter a cup of palm liquor and asks her to show her husband to the audience by giving him the liquor. The shy girl walks with faltering steps to her husband, sips the liquor and as she gives it to him, tells her shouting audience: "this is my husband. Father may take the bride-wealth."[10]

Describing the same situation among the Asante of Ghana, Meyer Fortes observed:

> The decisive formality for the establishment of a legal marriage is the giving of the "tirinsa" the head wine which Ashanti describe as a thanking gift (aseda) most commonly this consists of two bottles of gin or an agreed equivalent in cash. It is handed over on behalf of the husband by the head of his lineage to the head of the bride's lineage through her legal guardian in the presence of the representatives of both groups...the payment of tiri nsa gives the husband exclusive sexual rights over his wife

---

9. M. Park, *Travels in the Interior District of Africa in the Years 1795, 1796 and 1797, 1799* facsimile reprint (New York: Arno Press, 1971), 266.

10. V.C. Uchendu, *The Igbo of South Eastern Nigeria* (New York: Holt, Rinehart and Winston, 1965), 51-52.

and the legal paternity of all children born to her while the marriage lasts...tiri nsa may be paid before or at any time after the couple begin to cohabit.[11]

In these observations, drinks and kolanuts were mentioned. Drinks, especially palm wine, were poured on the ground as a libation or as a "blessing ceremony," during which elders from both the bride's and the groom's sides would pray to their ancestors. In many West African societies, such as Igbo, kolanuts symbolized unity, blessing, peace, and long life. The symbolic significance of palm-wine and kolanuts as markers to indicate the date of celebration of marriage could be revealed in the question: "In what month and year did your husband give the drink or the kola for the marriage?" This symbolism of kolanut and palm-wine rites appears to distinguish marriage that the kin groups recognize as legitimate from those that are not.[12]

Marriages were expected to be permanent and wives were expected to be faithful. The rituals of the Gusii in Kenya tended to reinforce these expectations. Here, the women underwent an elaborate wedding ritual (*enyangi*). This was a lifelong bond to the husband who gave bridewealth for her. Iron ankle-rings were then given to the married woman after another ritual (*ebitinge*) was performed.[13]

The process of contracting marriages involved meetings of whole delegations of kin groups, preceded by exploratory contacts made by family go-betweens, in formal and public circumstances. Gifts were exchanged. The quantity and quality of the gifts depended on the items valued in a given kinship group. Cattle could be held in trust by the family for the marriages of their sons. The main bride wealth payment in such societies vary according to the wealth in cattle at any given time. Among the pastoral peoples of Africa:

> the man-cattle cycle is uninterrupted. Girls marry and bring more cattle into the family. When boys marry, the family loses cattle, but these sons' wives will eventually have more girls who will bring more cattle into the family again...the more wives a person has, the more cattle—thus wealth—it is assumed he also has.[14]

Cattle were widely distributed through the bridewealth system. This same bridewealth custom of cattle exchange was so hedged about with rules and prejudice that the Tutsi in Ruanda made intermarriage difficult and prevented Bairu and Bahatu from becoming cattle owners. Among the forest peoples of Nigeria, yams and livestock were exchanged. Gift-giving was one of the most important modes of social exchange in Africa. One was obligated to give and take gifts. It was believed that gift-giving created and strengthened social kinship bonds. The

---

11. M. Fortes, "Kinship and Marriage Among the Ashanti," in Radcliffe Brown and Forde, eds., *African Systems of Kinship and Marriage*, 279-80.

12. For more accounts of marriage in Africa, see Caroline Bledsoe and Gilles Pison, *Nuptiality in Sub-Saharan Africa* (Oxford: Clarendon Press, 1994).

13. Though we have an excellent work on widows in Africa, Betty Potash, *Widows in African Societies: Choices and Constraints* (Stanford: Stanford University Press, 1986), we still need an authoritative work on African traditional marital dissolutions.

14. Aggrey Majok and Calvin W. Schwabe, *Development Among Africa's Migratory Pastoralists* (Westport, Conn: Bergin and Garvey, 1996), 51-52. See also A. Kuper, *Wives for Cattle: Bridewealth and Marriage in Southern Africa* (London: Routledge & Keegan Paul, 1982).

cultural rules that governed gift-giving were extended to weddings and marriages, burials and funerals, ancestral rites, child naming, childbirth, mutual visitation between relatives, coronations, and agricultural ritual festivities. Market days were times of gift exchanges. Grandmothers, although aged, took time to visit their grandchildren on market days with gifts of foodstuffs. Reciprocity was regarded as a way to distinguish kin from non-kin. African gift-giving was also designed to maintain the social equilibrium between potentially conflicting kin groups. Prestige items such as cattle, metal bars, and bags of cowries or money currency were also exchanged as gifts. It is important to emphasize this culture of gift-giving and exchange in Africa because it was that which bound the kinship together, whether in marriages, personal relations or family-lineage, social and political life.

Far from being a market situation or "bride purchase," the payment of bridewealth was a form of compensation to the bride's kin group for the "loss" of a daughter and her procreative capacities. The marriage contract involved gift giving that at times might continue even after the bridewealth had been paid. Symbolic acts demonstrated that one was always indebted to one's in-laws. Elaborate reciprocal exchanges of visits and services between the families of the groom and the bride continued even after the marriage had been sealed. Felicia Ekejuba has reminded us that bridewealth was a symbolic compensation for the transfer of the sexual and other services of the bride from her family to that of the groom. "These payments," she continues, "also legitimatized the marriage and defined the membership of the offspring in the patrilineal of the groom."[15]

Polygyny

Successful African farmers, traders and political leaders tended to enter into polygynous marriages. Their continued success, they believed, was dependent on the number of wives they had. Agricultural societies such as those in Africa encouraged the practice of polygyny. The number of units of agricultural production would increase as more wives were brought into the household. Wives, then, acted as a safeguard for more labor. In some parts of West Africa, polygyny was an element of social prestige, but in some areas of South Africa there was no particular barrier to a commoner becoming wealthy in stock and wives, so that the margin favoring the prominent person was not always wide. Writing about the Xhosa, a missionary observed that they had chiefs who took four or five wives.[16]

Polygyny served as a socially accepted alternative to post-partum abstinence. In some societies, for example, it was viewed as an abomination for the wife to meet her husband sexually during the long period (3-4 years) of lactation. We can

---

15. Felicia Ekejiuba, "Currency Instability and Social Payments Among the Igbo of Eastern Nigeria 1890-1990," in Jane I. Guyer, ed., *Money Matters: Instability, Values and Social Payments in the Modern History of West African Communities* (London: James Currey, 1995), 149. Cf. C. Mba, *Matrimonial Consort in Igbo Marriages* (Rome: Press, 1974).

16. J.T. Vanderkemp, "An Account of...Caffaria," in *Transaction of the [London] Missionary Society*, 1 (1795-1802): 439.

assume that polygyny was an accepted, honorable and respected form of marriage. G.T. Basden, a missionary in Igboland in the 1920s, observed that:

> A man who is able to multiply his wives rises automatically to social scale. They largely constitute his working capital. Every fresh outlay for the prevision of an additional wife is looked upon as a shrewd investment... polygyny to pristine Ibo is a worthy institution.[17]

Yet, another observer in the early twentieth century speculated that only about twenty-five percent of Igbo men were polygynous.[18] In general, however, it appeared that polygyny was a desirable form of marriage. Through polygyny, among patrilineal peoples, it was reasoned that a man could produce many sons to avoid the extinction of his name. Daughters from such marriages would also enrich the man through the acquisition of bridewealth. This would then enable him to pay bridewealth for his sons and even acquire more wives himself. The additional wives and children would further elevate his social status.

Though marriage was encouraged, in some societies sources of tension and potential cleavage appeared between the governing elders and the young men. In these societies the elders maintained tight, even oppressive, control over the younger men, monopolizing both women and cattle and thus delaying marriage and economic independence for the young. In such cases the young men occasionally migrated to escape their frustrations.[19]

Children

Marriage was only the beginning, not the whole story. The wife or wives were expected to have children. There was an abhorrence of childlessness. It was this abhorrence that encouraged the practice of a sororate system, whereby a barren woman's sister was given in marriage to the husband to procreate "on her behalf." Parenthood was always respected. Childbearing for both men and women created lifelong ties, linking kin groups into networks that were important to social and political life. An African proverb has it that: "The clan that is great in number is also great in strength." In songs and folklore, to be barren was lamented. Bethwell Ogot, an East African historian, reflected this in his reproduction of a Padhola song:

> Eee one child is not enough, One child is inadequate, Eee, when the war drum sounds "tindi! tindi!" Who will come to your rescue — one child?[20]

---

17. G.T. Basden, *Among the Ibos of Nigeria* (New York: Barnes and Nobles, 1966), 228.

18. J.P. Jordan, *Bishop Shanahan of Southern Nigeria* (Dublin, Elo Press, 1971 edition), 15.

19. See Elliot Skinner, "International Conflict among the Massai: Father and Son," *Journal of Conflict Resolution*, vol. 5, no. 1 (1961): 55-60.

20. B.A. Ogot, *History of the Southern Luo*, vol. 1 (Nairobi: East African Publishing House, 1967), 99.

Through her fertility, a married woman contributed to the growth of her husband's kin group. The Dinka position in these matters is aptly presented:

> A Dinka man's desire for more wives and more children is predicated upon knowledge that many children will not reach adulthood, so a large number are required to assure perpetuation of the family line (a major concern based partially on beliefs that it is possible to communicate with spirits of their ancestors). Also since grown children are expected to take care of the parents in old age, children are the only "pension scheme" available. In the interval children ensure the labor force essential to care for the cattle and other livestock.[21]

All daughters hoped to get married and, more importantly, become mothers. Daughters and wives became defined by motherhood. Men and husbands were proud of their wife or wives when childbirth occurred. Those from patrilineal systems expected their wives to produce especially male children. The value of sons tended to center on their obligations to the kin group and nuclear and extended families. A woman left her natal home and was only truly accepted in her new family upon the production of a male child. The ritual significance of sons to the family and to women was immense. Efforts at promoting fertility, rather than limiting it, dominated people's thought. It was not unusual for wars to be fought for the purpose of capturing women as booty so that they would in turn give birth to children to increase the size of the kin group.[22] The notion of continuity through children became a central theme in life. The ancestral geneology had to be continued. Fertility rites, ritual intercourse, and the use of fertility charms and folklore and other artistic expressions were crafted into the ideology of family procreation. African families were aware of the grim facts—stillbirths and deaths due to parturition, disease, famine, and warfare (this last especially during the wars that produced Africans for the Atlantic slave trade). All these took their toll. Infant mortality was high.

Childbirth in Africa was reserved to the world of women. Fathers were seldom participants in childbirth. But they were known to help if husband and wife were alone on the farm and the wife delivered a child. A male diviner might be called in to assist in difficult births. Both women largely depended on other women for advice about conception, pregnancy, and birth. The African midwife ritually and practically asked for a safe delivery. Mothers-in-law played a very crucial role in delivery and in what the Igbo called *omugwo* (the period of celebration of the new birth). African child mortality rates were high, so survival was a major concern during the early years. Thus, African women's high fertility may well have been based on the assumption that one could never have too many children. African husbands and wives voiced no concern over being burdened with too many children, though many complained when they had all girls or twins. African societies such as the Yoruba honor twins, but to some Africans, such as the Igbo and Efik, twin children were considered an aberration. They were

---

21. Majok and Schwabe, *Development Among Africa's Migratory Pastoralists*, 51.
22. Especially in the Khoisan wars in South Africa. See H.B. Thom ed., *Journal of Jan Van Riebeeck*, 3 vols., vol. 2 (Capetown: Published for the Van Riebleck Society by A.A. Bolkema, 1952-58), 172.

thrown into the forest where they were left to starve or be ravaged by wild animals. A mother of twin children, in this case, had to go through a cleansing ritual
to drive off the evil that had possessed her body. But other African groups honored twin children. In general, children were a source of labor, represented social
continuity, provided risk insurance, and provided a large sibling group in which
children socialized with each other. In practical terms children had three obligations to their parents: they must give them grandchildren, support them in old
age, and perform ritual respect to them after death.

The productivity of children, whether actual or ritual, guaranteed that after
death parents would be properly commemorated. The Nuer and Zulu believed
that the kinship group owed an obligation to dead kinsmen who did not have
children. A kinsman of the deceased married the dead man's betrothed and bore
children in the dead man's name. In some African societies, one had to be married
with children to qualify as an ancestor. Everyone in this environment aspired,
therefore, not to just marry at an appropriate time, but also to have an heir. This
was seen as a major reason for the institution of ghost marriages among the Nuer
and the Zulu. Due to this institution, even after death, a male kinsman was not
deprived of the opportunity of becoming an ancestor.[23]

The African mother-child household grew its own food. The mother depended on her children to help in cultivation, food processing, and household
tasks (including child care. Children were important to the household economy,
as they were required to participate in the domestic labor force.

African families and kinship groups formulated socio-religious and economic
discourses which emphasized the value of children. Women were honored for
having many children. In Igbo society, those women who had ten or more living
children were honored with a ceremony which they performed by "sacrificing a
goat on their hips." This was a mark of achievement. The husband had to buy expensive elephant tusks (*odu*) for the wife's wrist and ankles.[24] This recognition
ceremony for such women encouraged other women's aspirations for ten or more
children. It appears that early marriages for the women made this feat possible. In
the past, Igbo girls for example, married early, usually between fifteen and nine-
teen years of age.

The naming of a child was an important occasion. Its ritual significance dictated that the oldest man in the family, with the support of other male elders of
the kinship group, should preside at this occasion. This naming ceremony was observed with feasting and joy. The Asante, though their kinship descent was matrilineal, believed in a form of patrilineally inherited non-physical link. The Asante
called this *ntoro* (a kind of spiritual influence). It was due to this notion that an
Asante male acknowledged paternity by naming his child on the eighth day after
birth. This ritual infused the father's *ntro* (paternal spirit) into the child. For the
Igbo of Nigeria, the naming took place seven traditional weeks (that is, twenty-
eight days) after the birth of the child. Names given to the child could reflect the
family's experience with life, human aspirations, requests of the spiritual world,

---

23. Ghost marriages are fictive marriages by which a kinsman of a man or boy who died
before he had any legal heirs could marry a woman in the name of a deceased relative. E.E.
Evans-Pritchard, *Kinship and Marriage Among the Nuer* (New York: Oxford University
Press, 1951).

24. This ceremony is still practiced in Igboland. Cf. Anochie, *The Igbo Women*, 18.

and kinship ideals and goals. These names were highly meaningful to the child as he/she grew and developed.

Education

The learning process was a cultural activity. Kingroups devised ways to enable them to pass down their store of accumulated knowledge from one generation to another. Child-training in kingroups projected the values that the groups cherished and admired, and would like to protect and propagate. At the center of this child-training was the father. He was the center of authority and emulation, especially for sons. The father of the nuclear family disciplined the children. But the term "father" might also apply to all males of the father's generation in the lineage. These "fathers" were culturally authorized to discipline all persons called "children." Mothers were also critically important in the education of the children—especially the education of the girls. They taught them how to cook and perform domestic work. Good cooking was a recognized means for a wife to become a husband's favorite. Thus the apt observation that "the kitchen became a refuge and food then is a strong weapon in the hands of women in a culture that disparages "eating out"...women hold on jealously to their kitchen power."[25] Teaching about cooking and procreation seemed to have dominated the domestic training of girls. Oldest siblings were also involved in the training of their younger siblings. For example, among Fulani pastoralists the eldest brother taught the younger ones how to herd cattle and obey their seniors.

The education of the child in the ways of the kinship group was a collective affair. The task of socializing the child was the responsibility not only of the parents but of the extended family and the kinship group. That a child was always watched and guided by so many relatives made one scholar categorically state that : "the training of children is everybody's responsibility and every person is expected to correct a child whether they are related or not. 'Nwa bu nwa oha'—a child is the child of all."[26] Character formation was central in children's socialization. It was believed that good character was the very stuff which made family life a joy, because it was pleasing to the gods. It was also believed that a well formed character was an asset during matrimony. Child rearing was a serious communal duty: thus the dictum, "it takes a village to raise a child." The African child was made to feel deeply the debt he/she owed to the extended family, kinship group, and parents. Babs Fafunwa, the Nigerian historian of education, observed that "[t]he parent's siblings and other members of the community participate in the education of the child. Everyone wants him to be sociable, honest, courageous, humble, persevering and of good report all the time."[27] These were attributes the child had to acquire and exhibit.

---

25. Mercy Amba Oduyoye, *Daughters of Anonwa: African Women and Patriarchy* (New York: Orbis Books, 1995), especially the section, "The Power of the Kitchen," 53.

26. F.C. Ogbalu, *Igbo Institutions and Customs* (Onitsha, Nigeria: University Publishing Co., 1973), 19.

27. A. Babs Fafundwa, *History of Education in Nigeria* (George Allen and Unwin: London, 1974), 21.

The Kaguru people of Central Tanzania in East Africa had an initiation ceremony of rites of passage for girls:

> During a girl's confinement she is thought to undergo a gradual process of
> change produced by intense care from the women attending her. They
> feed or nurture the child like a novice...making her more fit to become a
> wife and mother. A well initiated girl should emerge fat, pale, soft and
> well schooled in both sexual and household matters. At the end of this
> period, the girl is brought out from the initiation house and into the vil-
> lage square to be recognized as a newly constituted woman ready to be
> wed and bear children.[28]

In certain areas of Africa the ceremony where girls undergo extensive and painful
tattooing or genital operations such as clitoridectomy and the removal of the
labia minora was performed. The circumcision of the youth in certain areas was
seen as a rite of passage. The Kukuyu, for example, say that to make a boy into a
man, the "feminine" prepuce must be removed. Clitoridectomy was performed
according to the men to satisfy their male sexual fantasies, enjoyment and desires.
African children, both girls and boys, had to be groomed to become men and
women. Manhood and womanhood are not naturally occuring conditions but
ones that must be created.[29]

Women

Much about African women in the context of African social institutions remains to be explored. At present, however, the discussion of women's lives in
African social life fall into two contested terrains. On the one hand, scholars
argue that many African societies provided opportunities for exceptional
women to lead very productive lives;[30] on the other hand, another group of

---

28. T.O. Berdelman, "Containing Time: Rites of Passage and Moral Space of Barchelor-
hood Among the Kaguru 1957-1966," *Anthropos*, 86 (1996): 453.

29. For the Kikuyu, see Carol Worthman and John Whiting, "Social Change in Adoles-
cent Sexual Behavior, Mate Selection and Premarital Pregnancy Rates in a Kikuyu Community," *Ethos*, 15 (1987): 145-65. For an Igbo community, see Ifi Amadiume, *Male Daughters,
Female Husbands: Gender and Sex in an African Society* (London: Zed Press, 1994), especially sections on "How They Made Them Men" and "Coming into Womanhood," 93-98.

30. See Kamene Okonjo, "The Dual-Sex Political System in Operation: Igbo Women and
Community Politics in Mid-Western Nigeria," in Nancy J. Hafkin and Edna G. Bay, eds.,
Women in Africa: Studies in Social and Economic Change (Stanford, California: Stanford
University Press, 1976); Amadiume, *Male Daughters, Female Husbands;* O. Muchena, "The
Changing Position of African Women in Rural Zimbabwe," *Zimbabwe Journal of Econom-
ics*, 1, 1 (1979): 50-63; S. Afonja, "Changing Modes of Production and Sexual Division of
Labor Among the Yoruba," in E. Leacock and H. Safa, eds., *Women's Work. Development
and the Division of Labor By Gender* (South Hardley: M.A. Bergin and Garney, 1986); K.O.
Poewe, *Matrilineal Ideology* (New York: Academic Press, 1981); E.C. Mandala, *Work and
Control in a Peasant Economy: A History of the Lowver Tchri Valley in Malawi* (Madison:
University of Wisconsin Press, 1990); R.S. Oboler, *Women, Power and Economic Change:
The Nindi of Kenya* (Stanford, California: Stanford University Press, 1985); Filomena
Chioma Steady, "African Feminism: A Worldview Perspective," in Rosalyn Terborg-Penn

scholars[31] argues that African patrilineal ideology prevented women from achieving autonomy. African males, they argue, sought to control the conditions under which women interacted with African males. Both arguments dig deep into African social institutions, beliefs and rituals, and history to support their contentions.

It is true that most African women were preoccupied with the home economy, and were unable to accumulate wealth outside the domestic terrain. It is also true that in hunting and gathering societies, women's domestic sphere was critical for the survival of the group. The household depended on them for their expertise in foraging and the collection of food. The interdependence of men and women was remarkable.

A queen mother often had a role in the choice of a new king. The office of the king's mother existed in many African political organizations and it was very influential in Buganda, Mwenemutapa, and Asante, and among the Ankole and Shilluk. In the kingdom of Kush, the queen mother was called "Mistress of Kush." Some queen mothers became famous and assumed political power. In Greco-Roman times, Meroe was ruled by a line of "Candaces" or queen regents. If there were no male heirs in the Egyptian ruling family, a woman could inherit the throne. Four Egyptian women became Pharaohs: Nitokris, Sebeknefru, Hatshepsut and Tanosre. In other parts of Africa one could also list women who projected their political and social presence: the queen mothers of the Asante, the Empress Menetewab of Ethiopia (1720-1771), the mother or Kabaka Mutesa of Buganda Muganzirwazza (1817-1882), Queen Nzinga of Ndongo (1582-1663), Queen Aisa Kili Ngirmaramma of the Kanuri kingdom of Borno (1563-1570) and Mamy Yako (1849-1906) of the Mende Confederacy.

After the visit of Mansa Musa,the king of Mali, to the Islamic lands of the Arabs, the domestic life of women in the Savannah Kingdoms was transformed. On his return he introduced the purdah system of secluding married women. The custom spread all over the Islamic West African Savannah Kingdoms. This innovation was institutionalized and influenced the status of women in Hausa-speaking communities.[32] Yet Hausaland produced women of influence. Queen Amina of Zaria was one of these and the history of Kano is signposted by the names of celebrated princesses. For example, madarki (queen mother) Auwa intervened energetically to save Abdullahi (1499-1509) from the hands of rebels.[33] The sarki's

---

and Andrea Benton Rushing, eds., *Women in Africa and the African Diaspora: A Reader* (Washington, D.C.: Howard University Press, 1996), 3-21; and Niara Sudarkasa, "The Status of Women in Indigenous African Societies," in Rosalyn Terborg-Penn and Andrea Benton Rushing, eds., 73-87.

31. Catherine Coquery-Vidrovitch, *African Women: A Modern History*, trans. Beth Gillian Raps (Colorado: Westview, 1997); and Onaiwu Ogbomo, *When Men and Women Mattered: A History of Gender Relations Among the Owan of Nigeria* (Rochester, New York: University of Rochester Press, 1997). For a general discussion of African women in pre-colonial Africa see: Mary E. Madupe Kolawole, *Womanism and African Consciousness* (Trenton, N.J.: Africa World Press Inc., 1997), 43-50, and Catherine Obianuju Acholonu, *Motherism: The Afriocentric Alternative to Feminism* (Oweri: Afa Publ., 1995), 24-51.

32. Cf. Beverly B. Mack, "Harem Domesticity in Kano, Nigeria," in Karen Tranberg Hansen, ed., *African Encounters with Domesticity* (New Jersey: Rutgers University Press, 1992).

33. For women in Kano history see Bawuro Barkindo, ed., *Studies in the History of Kano* (Ibadan, Nigeria: Published for the Department of History, Bayeko University, Kano, by Heinemann Education Books Nigeria, 1983) and Beverly B. Mack, "Hajya Ma'deki: A

sister, for example, played a leading political role, although she did so through the traditional form of worship. The Bori religion provided Hausa women with ritual authority which supported and legitimized the rulers of pre-Islamic Hausaland. The jihad (holy war) of Usman Dan Fodio and its aftermath at the beginning of the nineteenth century reduced the political and ritual power of the Bori religion. But there is plenty of evidence that Bori continued to be practiced as a religion although the men had appropriated women's titles.

The women of Dahomey took an active part in politics. Every officer of the state had a woman counterpart who acted as a spy, reporting to the king all the doings of the male officers. Women were recruited into the army and made up a strong fighting unit in Dahomey's military establishment; and like their counterparts in Ndenye (in present day Ivory Coast), they even acted as custodians of the history of the people. The transmission of collective memory in Africa was usually in the form of praise songs. Qualified old women such as those in Yorubaland were allowed to be the transmitters of the *oriki* (praise songs).

The commercial initiatives of African women have been well documented.[34] Through various means within kinship contexts, women were able to accumulate capital to enable them to start their career as traders—such was the origin of Yoruba women traders. The participation of Igbo women in the palm-oil, palm-kernel, and casava trade increased their usefulness and autonomy within the Igbo household. Again, G.T. Basden observed:

> Marketing is the central feature in the life of every Ibo woman and to be successful in trade is the signal for generous congratulations. By this a woman's value is calculated, it affects her position and comfort, a man considers it in the choice of a wife, and the husband's favor is bestowed or withheld largely, according to the degree of his wife's success in the market.[35]

The accumulation of wealth enabled certain Igbo women to take coveted titles. This was so in the case of Madam Nwagboka who was crowned as queen of Onitsha in 1884 by the Obi of Onitsha, Anazonwa I. Other Igbo business women also rose to fame. The life of Omu Okwei (1872-1943), the merchant queen of Ossamari, was a case in point. Women had the opportunity to become wealthy and could, therefore, acquire the things that wealth could buy.[36]

African women were also accorded politico-ritual potency. Their ritual status in kinship was so well established that, though this was an exaggeration, Nilotic women were said to be prime movers in all things except wars. In Zulu communities there existed great prophetesses, and, among the Mende, women had their own secret societies which they could manipulate to gain some political influence.

Royal Hausa Woman" in Patricia W. Romero, ed., *Life Histories of African Women* (Atlantic Highfields, N.J.: Ashfield Press, 1988), 47-77.

34. Bessie House-Midamba and Felix Ekechi, eds., *African Market Women and Economic Power: The Role of Women in African Economic Development* (Westport, CT.: Greenwood Press, 1995).

35. Basden, *Among the Ibos of Nigeria*, 194.

36. Richard N. Henderson, *The King in Everyman: Evolutionary Trends in Onitsha Igbo Society and Culture* (New Haven: Yale University Press, 1972), 464; and Felicia Ekejiuba, "Omu Okwei, The Merchant Queen of Ossomari: A Biographical Sketch," *Journal of the Historical Society of Nigeria*, 2/4 (June 1967).

The Bori religion of the Habe-Hausa accorded women great power, and in Kenya the great seer Syokimau (1840-1880) was a woman. Syokimau's ability to foretell events, to heal, and to and give protection against epidemic diseases were highly regarded. She was a military adviser both to the Kamba and to the Masai warriors.[37] The politics of women's spirituality in Africa was deep rooted. Religious innovators, ritual functionaries, and religious resisters abounded. Nehauda Nyakasikana of Mwenemutapa-Zimbabawe (1862-1898) and Kimpa Vita Dona Beatrice of the Kongo kingdom (1682-1705) were cases in point. Scholars who argue the dynamic role of African women in social institutions argue that gender in African societies essentially ran along parallel, different, and contrasting rather than along hierarchical lines. Africans thereby gave, in general terms, equal value to male and female parallel autonomy. Notions of gender relations, according to this school of thought, varied depending on the lineage ideology, the group, and the economic and political circumstances of the historical period and the moment.

African women projected their ambitions in their roles as daughters, as wives, as mothers, as queens, as priestesses, as goddesses, and even as "husbands." Some of them found prestige, honor, and power but some scholars contend that these examples were exceptions. These scholars conclude that the triumph of male ideology in African history initiated the controlling influence of patriarchy in African male-female interactions. They contend that African men employed African kinship networks, secret societies, and the appropriation of history to actualize the triumph of patriarchal values. Thus many African societies, these scholars argue, came to be organized by gender, and tasks were divided and standards set according to patriarchal values. These values were provided the social environment in which each sex was evaluated. Initiation into gendered adulthood became the political and socio-economic hegemonic theme that has dominated the history of African social systems. Yet Jack Goody's caution is apt:

> Male domination in the political or economic sphere may not simply be reflected in the family. Among the Asante of West Africa, the political system is staffed by males. The role of the Queen Mother alone reflects politically the fact that this is a matrilineal society in which women—and their brothers as distinct from their husbands—play an important part in determining the residence of men. Male authority at the political level is consistent with quite a different distribution of power in the domestic domain.[38]

Divine Kingship

Matriliny and patriliny were used in African social organization to adjust to the agrarian revolution that required a flexible mechanism for mobilizing and in-

37. Rebeka Njau and Gideon Mulaki, *Kenya Women Heroes and Their Mystical Power*, vol. 1 (Rick Publication, Nairobi, 1984), 55-59. For Bori and women, see M. Onuluejeogwu, "The Cult of Bori Spirits among the Hausa," M. Douglas and P.M. Kabry, eds., *Man in Africa* (London: Tavistock Press, 1969).

38. Jack Goody, "Women, Class and Family," *New Left Review*, 219 (Sept./Oct. 1996): 132.

corporating vast numbers of unfree laborers into an expanding agricultural society. The subsequent emergence of African state formations and increased social differentiation based on wealth and political power led the kings to appropriate certain aspects of patriliny and matriliny to consolidate kingship.

In the patrilineal kinship social system that has been examined in this chapter, it was believed that usurpation would normally not occur or be contemplated. The rules of succession to a patrilineage were usually indisputably clear and strictly adhered to, and were regulated on the basis of lineage seniority. The rules were sustained by supernatural sanctions. The ideology of kinship implied that seniority can only be claimed by one lineage at a time. This would normally rule out the possibility of competing claims. But the appearance of a "political chief" grew out of "kinship chiefs." The increased revenues in the hands of a lineage group reinforced chiefly authority, and the absorption of other lineages through the imposition of authority by force of arms attracted a growing clientele of lineages who depended on the chief for spiritual and material sustenance.

A hegemonic culture of kingship was initiated in which multiple processes of cultural and ritual renegotiation occurred and the remanipulation of mythical-political rituals, ceremonies and organized beliefs led to a new form of political and social organization—divine kingship. Once this was achieved, as in Nilotic Societies, Ogot reminded us:

> Instead of groupings based entirely on kinship relations, territorial groupings began to emerge...yet both leadership and politics were conceived largely in kinship terms...the lineages coincided with the territorial boundaries...both kinship and chiefship principles began to be applied to political organization.[39]

Two things happened. At one level, this process betrayed the inefficiency of the political system based upon kinship ties, and at another level, it portrayed the emergence of a powerful, cohesive kin group that presented a united front and well organized ideology—factors that assisted the kin group to impose its rule over other kinship groups.

Examples abound in African history to confirm this progress. The ancient Swahili custom of reckoning kinship evolved into the title and office of *mfalme* which defined the functions of property, marriage, and the transfer of ritual power. But as class formation evolved, various Swahili ethnic groups started claiming Arab or Shirazi ancestry despite their indubitably African origin—thus linking Islam to the ideology of power. Luba royalty was founded on the principle of *bulopwe* or "sacredness" inherent in the royal blood, which the Luba called *mpifo*. They insisted on "purity of blood" within the patrilineal kinship. In the kingdom of Zimbabwe, royal usurpation was based on some form of unifying faith in the powers of the divine Mwari religious catalyst that reached out to every family. It was the Ntemi in Nyamwezi who claimed the political-religious authority. The Nandi, a section of the Kalenjin, crafted and adopted a spiritual

---

39. Bethwell A. Ogot, *History of the Southern Luo V.1: Migration and Settlement 1500-1900* (Nairobi: East African Publishing House, 1967), 169-171. For matriliny and state formation see I. Wilks, "Founding the Political Kingdom: The Nature of the Akan State," in I. Wilks, ed., *Forests of Gold: Essays on the Akan and the Kingdom of the Asante* (Athens, Ohio: Ohio University Press, 1993), 91-126.

leader whom they called the orkoiyot, and by the end of the nineteenth century, this spiritual leader had transformed the Nandi polity into a theocracy with himself as the sovereign. The Maasai laibons (ritual leaders) were also beginning to claim greater political authority than their predecessors had envisaged. In Ruanda, on account of numerous taboos, certain lineage groups crafted the *buhake*—protection guaranteed to a family in exchange for increased obligations. This was used especially by the Tutsi to subjugate influential Hutu lineages. The Asante accepted the "Golden Stool" myth developed by Anokye, the chief priest, and Osei Tutu, the Asantehene. The myth of "Oduduwa" gave the Yoruba kings their rights. In Kalabari, the title of amanyanabo, "the owner of the land," emerged.

The Igbo, for a period of their history, looked towards the Nri mythology to formulate kingly culture, but some Igbo did not continue with that experiment and resorted to village-lineage gerontocracy. In Hausaland there was the sarki, whose ancestors had seized political power. In the city-states of Kano, Katsina and Zamfara, power had been wrested from the hands of a high priest, while in Kebbi it was a magaji (warrior) who rose to the rank of sarki. The warrior tradition crafted by Shaka of the Zulu also transformed Zulu kinship ideology. But, it should be noted, for centuries the incessant wrangles within dominant Xhosa clans and Nguni societies were undoubtedly encouraged by thoughtful commoners who sought to paralyze the central authority by turning it against itself. These constraints on the evolution of a despotic style of administration were not broken until the end of the 1700s when strong confederacies were formed and ultimately led to the formation of the Zulu state.

In all the examples cited the royal family or king's men used kinship ideology to consolidate their positions. The manipulation of marriage links and gifts made other clans indebted to the king. Furthermore, the ability to bestow wives, gifts, and land depended ultimately on the royal household's ability to out-produce other households and clans. Thus, members of the royal lineage usually had more wives, hence more units of production than others. But in the Great Lakes region the Kintu complex of clans and the Kimera complex of clans worked out a compromise. Each clan wanted to participate in the monarchy, and therefore there arose in Buganda the custom of clans presenting wives to the kabaka, giving each clan the opportunity to provide a successor. Thus, unlike other Great Lake states, Buganda had no royal clan, each prince belonging to the clan of his mother, although the general population followed the rules of patriliny. Any clan in Buganda had a chance to provide the monarch, but the system also encouraged each clan to give a wife to a new *kabaka* with the consequent rapid proliferation of potential royal heirs. The kings of Buganda were therefore forced to be more extravagantly polygamous than many other rulers. This contrasted with the Acholi system where, upon coronation, the king was given a wife by the elders, the heir to come from the sons of this wife only.

Conclusion

The African experience confirms the notion that kinship is itself part of the mode of production. This is significant because much of the social change in

Africa since the nineteenth century has occurred in the context of radical changes in production modes: land was being gradually privatized, and cash crops, entrepreneurial enterprises, and wage labor introduced. Kinship production has been challenged by capitalist production. Given the structural links between lineage organization and economic organization, the intrusion of capitalist forms has inevitably altered the means (and the effectiveness of these means) by which kinship was used to exert social control. Kinship descent, however, continued to be the major system that permitted the Africans to govern themselves with minimum administrative burden and tedium. Kinship relations continued to be one of the main relations of production, of juro-political and ritual significance. Kinship, thus, governed the way African communities organized and used the resources of the environment, notably the land, and spatial interaction between societal members.[40] The Vai proverb, "What belongs to me is destroyable by water or fire; what belongs to us is destroyable neither by water or fire," succinctly expresses the abiding strength of kinship in Africa. Kinship provided the anchor for people's membership, the anchor for people's identification, and the safety of effortless, secure belonging. Kinship added meaning to people's actions, which became not only acts of individual accomplishment but also part of continuous creative efforts whereby culture was made and remade. It promoted solidarity, trust, and valuable intergenerational bonds, although it also created tension. It enabled the African individual to transcend individual mortality by linking each one to an institution whose existence seemed to extend back into time immemorial and forward into the indefinite future. The endurance of kinship is explained by what it did.

Review Questions

1. How is it that an African came to be a kinsman or kinswoman? Discuss.
2. In what ways did Africans activate kinship ties? Explain.
3. Explain how African men and women came to define themselves within the kinship ideology. Were women constrained by kinship ideology? Elucidate.
4. What functions did African kinship ideology perform?
5. African kingship was an assault on the conventions of kinship. Do you agree? Explain.

Additional Readings

Coquery-Vidrovitch, Catherine. *African Women: A Modern History*. Boulder: Westview, 1995.
Das, Man Singh, ed. *The Family in Africa*. New Delhi: M.D. Publications, 1993.
Kayongo-Male, Diane and Philista Onyango, *Sociology of the African Family*. London: Longman, 1984.

---

40. Renée Ilene Pittin, "Households and Families: Sub-Saharan Africa," in *Women Studies Encyclopedia* (Hemel Hempstead, England: Harvester Wheatsheaf Press, Ltd., Paramount Publishing International, 1996).

Special Issue on the History of the Family in Africa, *Journal of African History* 24, 2 (1983).

Southhall, A. *Lineage Formation Among the Luo.* London: International African Institute, Oxford University Press, Memorandum 26, 1952.

Vuyk, Trudeke. *Children of One Womb: Descent, Marriage and Gender in Central African Societies.* Leiden, Netherlands: E.J. Brill, 1991.

Chapter 4

Education

Julius O. Adekunle

Introduction

Every society in the world has evolved a system of education to satisfy its own socio-cultural needs. Education is an integral part of human development that is both indispensable and inescapable. Its significance to the recipient as well as to the entire society is tremendous. Education is passed from one generation to the other. It is the means through which human advancement is achieved and improved upon. Among the primary functions of education are the acquisition of knowledge, the preservation of culture, the transformation of intellectual traditions, and the facilitation of interethnic relations. These functions were well discharged in the African context where education was highly valued.

The objectives of this chapter are three-fold. First, it highlights and analyzes the contents, methodologies, and values of African indigenous education. Second, it describes the subject matter of the Islamic educational system. Islamic religion and education penetrated into and flourished in several parts of Africa long before Western education. For instance, in Morocco, Islamic literacy preceded Western education by about one thousand years. Islam had a far-reaching impact on African indigenous education, especially by creating a general awareness of learning in the written fashion. Third, this chapter examines the consequences of Christian education on African peoples, in this case, taking western Africa as its example. To accomplish these objectives, this chapter will consider three educational types: the traditional, the Islamic, and the Christian (Western) systems of education in Africa.

Generally speaking, the education provided in African societies is easily understood. Although its curricula were not very specific, its purposes were explicit, and its methodologies were clear. In spite of the multiple ethnicities in Africa, there was a commonality in the essence and techniques of imparting knowledge. Where variations occurred, it was because of differences in cultural norms, expectations, and aspirations. The socio-cultural or political milieu, in most cases, determined the type of education that was transmitted. For example, a child who grew up among the Khoisan of southern Africa learned hunting, a Fulani child learned cattle rearing, an Asante child learned farming, and a Dyula child learned trading. Thus, the society formulated the curriculum and the methodology of transmission.

Most African societies did not develop the art of writing, so their education was transmitted through informal and practical methods. The lack of the ability to commit ideas to writing did not inhibit the provision of education. Although the lack of writing has been viewed as a major weakness in African culture, it should not be the only criterion with which to appraise the level of civilization. What was not committed to writing was preserved in memory.

The second type of education in Africa was introduced with the appearance of Islam and its literacy. Both the Islamic religion and Islamic education had significant results. Literacy helped in the rapid expansion of the Islamic religion. For many centuries, Islamic education offered some values and teaching methodologies which African indigenous education did not provide. In this respect, Islamic education added and supplemented African traditional education, although the two focused on different objectives. While scriptural and literary knowledge were the central themes of Islamic education, African traditional education tended to concentrate more on the attainment of moral uprightness and usefulness to the society.

Another transformation occurred when European Christian missionaries arrived with the purpose of converting Africans to Christianity. Beginning at the coast of Africa, Christian missions infiltrated the interior in the nineteenth century. One of the means of attaining the objective of the Christians' "civilizing mission" was education. Christian education was geared toward reading and memorizing Bible verses. Without a doubt, literacy was an essential ingredient for complete conversion to the Christian faith. The aims and efforts of Christian missionaries found firmer ground when colonialism gave credibility to Christian education. What traditional education and Islamic education did not provide, Western education, through the Christian missionaries, rendered. While on the one hand, Africans benefited tremendously from the transformations in education, on the other, their indigenous educational system was adversely affected.

Characteristics of Traditional Education

It is important to understand some distinctive features of African traditional education. In the first place, it was inextricably interwoven with culture and spirituality. Historical studies reveal that in every society, socio-cultural institutions express the ideals of education; and Africans, being highly culture-conscious and deeply religious peoples, amply demonstrated these aspects in the pattern of education which they evolved and perpetuated. As a consequence, education reflected, preserved, and transmitted the entire religio-cultural corpus of numerous African peoples.

Second, African education was collectively provided for the benefit of the entire society. It was an education acquired for life in the community through a continuous and consistent process and for the continuity of the society. Education was both individual and community-oriented. The parents of a child and the community conjoined in developing an intellectually and morally balanced person, as well as building a vibrant, solid, and congenial society. The Yoruba of southwestern Nigeria believed that while the procreation of a child was the responsibility of the parents, the whole community must partake in the training.

African culture and education were infused with the ideals of cooperation, societal development, and quality of life. Societies operated as commonwealths with common interests and goals, and they confronted similar problems. They were concerned with the general welfare of individuals, and therefore, shared corporate responsibility for the education of the child, realizing that the knowledge and skills imparted would be utilized to the advantage of the entire community. In other words, education included considerable sensibility to the all-embracing and multi-faceted societal needs. It exhibited African people's philosophy of life in regard to the centrality of the child, and it connected the past generations to the modern. Felix Boateng pointed out that African traditional education was an effective "vehicle for intergenerational communication."[1] It was a strong integrative force that bridged the gap between old and young.

Sociologists have also alluded to the role of education in transferring ideas from one generation to the other, thereby bringing about an unbroken chain between the present and the past. Education should also encourage the transfer of knowledge from one discipline to another. In an African framework, this challenge has been met through the transmission of education in folklore, songs, proverbs, vocations, religion, mathematics, and science. All these aspects of education are interconnected and used in everyday circumstances.

Third, African traditional education recognized progress and rewarded achievements. It was structured in stages from childhood to adulthood. For example, when a child advanced from walking to talking, the effort was rewarded. When a person proceeded from puberty to adulthood, or from one initiation to another, the occasion was usually marked with a celebration, during which rituals or rites of passage were performed. The procedure for the celebration, however, depended heavily upon the religion or custom of the people involved. For example, it was customary for the neophyte to demonstrate to the general public the mastery of the religious education, which he had received. In Yorubaland, an *Ifa* novice, had to chant long verses of the corpus which he had memorized. Through this means, he was led to develop a sense of appreciation and pride in achievement.

That Africans were spiritual has been demonstrated in various ways. Their spirituality established a profound relationship between their indigenous education and their socio-religious rituals. Participatory education was implemented in initiation ceremonies. The priest (teacher) as well as the novice (student) each had functions to perform and everything was carried out according to specifications.

As with the Yoruba, the procedure for initiation was educational among the members of the *Poro* society of Liberia, Guinea, and Sierra Leone. This is because the novice had to go through a period of education for about five years before taking vows.[2] An *Ifa* student among the Yoruba usually spent about ten years in

---

1. Felix Boateng, "African Traditional Education," in Molefi Kete Asante and Kariamu Welsh Asante, eds., *African Culture: The Rhythms of Unity* (Westport: Greenwood Press, 1985), 109-122.

2. The *Poro* (Poroh) society evolved a uniquely complex system of training young boys. The primary objective was to initiate the young boys into this society. The tradition, which has existed for centuries and remained uninfluenced by external factors, involves taking boys to a sacred forest where they remain for one to five years. Strict discipline in physical, cultural, and occupational training is given to the apprentices. While the *Poro* is for boys, the *Bundo* (or *Bondo*) is for young girls. Cooking, craft work, dyeing, spinning, beads making, and music constituted the curriculum. For both boys and girls, the completion of the training is marked by rituals. T.L.J. Forde, "Indigenous Education in Sierra Leone," in Godfrey N. Brown and Mervin Hiskett, *Conflict and Harmony in Education in Tropical Africa* (Rutherford, NJ: Fairleigh Dickson University Press, 1976), 65-75; Kenneth Blakemore and Brian

preparation, acquiring knowledge of divination, medicine, pharmacy, psychiatry, psychology, and philosophy. His ability to heal, prepare and prescribe medication, deliver babies, and foretell the future placed him above an ordinary person. Helen Callaway adds that:

> At the end of the training period, apprentices presented themselves for initiation. Sacrifices were offered to a number of gods before the trainees went into the forest with senior Ifa priests for the rituals. These included examining on different aspects of Ifa, as well as imparting further secret knowledge. The ceremony concluded with several days of feasting, dancing and singing. After this initiation the newly qualified priests began to practice their profession.[3]

After the initiation (that is, graduation), the person became recognized as a *babalawo* (healer and diviner) and his education was put into practice partly for his own benefit and partly for the members of his community. He, however, continued to seek counsel and guidance from more experienced diviners.

Fourth, African traditional education was psychologically inclined, in the sense that it was concerned with the emotional, intellectual, and physical development of the child. This conformed to the general goal of education to develop knowledge, skills, mind, and character, that is, the totality of a person. Parents and older people assisted the child to develop and utilize creative aptitudes, to gain self-esteem, and to react to situations in an intelligent manner. African education facilitated the process of building personal experience, using the support and guidance of other people. It also prepared the child for future challenges.

Emphasis of Traditional Education

Physical training for a child began at birth. The baby could be thrown up, shaken heavily, and allowed to scream with the confident assurance and belief that crying was a healthy exercise. As the child grew, jumping, climbing, balancing of loads on the head, swimming, acrobatic displays or dances constituted the primary curricular activities in physical education. Farming, the mainstay of many African economies, required strenuous work and physical fitness. In physical education, endurance was the key word.

Abdou Moumouni contends that traditional education "does not seem to emphasize the intellectual training of the child as heavily as other aspects of education," because of the "degree of economic and social development."[4] However, taking into consideration the emphasis placed on mathematical calculations, philosophy, history, geography, and scientific training, it is clear that the mind of an African child was directed towards intellectualism. This interpretation corresponds with Babs Fafunwa's line of thinking that, "if intellectualisation is the

Cooksey, *A Sociology of Education for Africa* (London: George Allen and Unwin, first published 1980, second impression 1982), 15-16.

3. Helen Callaway, "Indigenous Education in the Yoruba Society," in Brown and Hiskett, *Conflict and Harmony in Education*, 36.

4. Abdou Moumouni, *Education in Africa* (London: Deutsch, 1968), 23.

process of reasoning abstractly, traditional African education can be said to encourage intellectual growth and development."[5] As will be shown later, stories, poems, and proverbs were some of the techniques that were used.

Since African education was designed to benefit both the individual and the community, the curriculum emphasized utilitarianism in vocational and social life. It also placed emphasis on sound moral behavior. The recipients were directed to utilize their skills for the betterment and overall growth of the community. The dominant aim was to produce functioning members of the society. The process of the training was both complex and slow because of the great volume of work involved.

African education transcended mere acquisition of knowledge; it was a way of life. There were various outlets for the acquired knowledge to be utilized in everyday activities. Because education was tailored towards character-building which involved interpersonal relationships, it assisted in social acceptance. Part of moral behavior was to honor, obey, and respect elders. Maintaining a good name, honesty, diligence at work, and willingness to help others also demonstrated respectable behavior and sound education. The Asante sayings, "Din pa ye kyen ahonya" ("Good name is better than riches") and "Ntoboasee wie nkunimdie" ("Victory is the fruit of diligence") reveal the place of good behavior and hardwork.

Home education occupied a conspicuous position in the curriculum. Education began in the family circle. Active instructions from parents and older members of the family provided necessary guides for the child. Many kinds of training were offered, in dancing, games, greetings, humility, politics, economy, local history, numbers, and other areas. Specialized vocations such as blacksmithing, praise singing, and drumming were also given attention at home. According to the Yoruba people, "eko ile se koko" ("Home education is paramount"). They also say "eko ni ba ni kale" ("Education endures with a person for life"). Usually, the transmission of skills followed a gender pattern; from father to son and mother to daughter.

Elders narrated educational stories to children, especially during moonlight nights. The dual purposes of the stories were to entertain and to teach virtues such as wisdom, love, honesty, respect, and hard work. These were emphasized in order to ensure a person's moral uprightness and to build a cohesive, impressive, and trustworthy society. In addition, the stories exposed children to different ideologies, which helped to expand their thinking and broaden their world-view. Children were taught not to be self-centered but to share their knowledge or skills with their peers or others. Individualism was condemned while collectivism was the norm. Service to the community was highly promoted and cherished. Powerful, meaningful, and thought provoking poems as well as songs were performed. Dramatizations, and sex and health education also formed part of moonlight activities. The children were taught about their environment and natural physical phenomena such as rivers, mountains, the sun, the moon, and the stars. Proverbs were taught because they were the driving forces of discussion; they restored clarity.[6] All of these carried the objectives of permitting the children to socialize, de-

---

5. A.B. Fafunwa, *History of Education in Nigeria*, (London: George Allen and Unwin, 1974), 26.

6. N.A. Fadipe, *The Sociology of the Yoruba* (Ibadan: Ibadan University Press, 1970), 302.

velop their discerning ability, and acquire the power of expression. These were achieved when elders asked the children to identify and highlight the main lessons of the stories. Among the Yoruba, Helen Callaway noted that:

> *Ifiye* is often associated with evening gatherings when the father or an older member of the family told stories and posed riddles to the children of the compound. This entertainment has a direct educational intent. Children were asked to repeat the previous night's episode as a test of memory and of narrative expressiveness.[7]

The important elements to note here are the transmission of oral traditions to children for continuity of culture, intellectual training, acquisition of vocabulary, and proficiency in expression steered toward oral artistry. Voluntary self-expression was encouraged. Boldness replaced bashfulness. The children were challenged to speak out, realizing that they would occupy positions of authority in the future where their courage and expressive ability would be required. Through self-expression, children developed oratory ability.

During the moonlight stories, past heroic occurrences, which had endured in the community's oral traditions and genealogical history were similarly narrated to expose the children to their socio-cultural background. Elders remembered political events, wars, and the origins of their communities or ethnic groups. In telling the stories, kinship connections were made. Cosmogonic stories or mythology were also included. Through the historical narrations, children were inspired to develop a sense of awareness of the past and belonging to their society. Among the Asante of Ghana, the Bambara of Upper Volta, and the Yoruba of Nigeria, there were professional oral performers whose occupation was storytelling for the benefit of the society.[8] The performers were the custodians of local history and were proficient in communication skills. They often displayed their intellectual ability during special performances. The performers transmitted historical and cultural information and children tried to imitate them in order to learn the techniques of oral artistry.

Methodologies of African Education

One of the methods of imparting knowledge was memorization. For lack of writing, Africans recorded and preserved all vital information in the mind. Elders served as the repositories of knowledge. Local history, laws, traditions, ethics, and philosophies of life were conserved in memory. These were narrated and transmitted orally from generation to generation for continuity of tradition and history. Songs, proverbs, and poetry such as incantations also required exceptional recollection ability. For purposes of entertainment and demonstration of learning competence, recitations could be organized. During the installation of a king, palace historians recited names of past rulers and events, which occurred during their

---

7. Callaway, "Indigenous Education," 29.
8. Samuel Osei Boadu, "African Oral Artistry and the New Social Order," in Molefi Kete Asante and Kariamu Welsh Asante, eds., *African Culture: The Rhythms of Unity* (Westport: Greenwood Press, 1985), 83-90.

tenure. A recitation of this nature sometimes lasted for many hours, with the reciter skillfully shifting from one theme to another, and with little or no omission or repetition. Numbers and formulas were similarly memorized. In religion, long verses were committed to memory. Memorization, therefore, became a foundational and practical technique of learning that was used in all disciplines.

The *Ifa* corpus, a body of knowledge, which constitutes the sacred scripture of the Yoruba religion, provides a good example of rote learning. As mentioned above, the learning process lasted about ten years. Callaway gives a brilliant description of the divination process. Suffice it to mention that there are sixteen subdivisions of each sixteen divisions of the corpus with a grand total of 4,096 verses, which the apprentice must memorize.[9] The diviner was compelled to recite or chant with accuracy and thoroughness. Callaway adds that "it was considered sacrilegious to add or leave out any words or lines from the ritual verses; all verses were memorized as they had been preserved and transmitted from ancient times."[10]

Memorization has been particularly helpful in historical reconstruction, where oral information has been collected from palace or court historians. Family, clan and ethnic traditions were also abundant. The main obligation of court historians was to recount the genealogy of the monarch and historical occurrences. In West Africa, the palace historians were known as *arokin* in Yorubaland, *ibiota* in Benin, *ahanjito* in the Republic of Benin, and *griots* in Senegal and Mali. They existed in other societies including the Bemba, Imbangala, Lozi, Luba, Lunda of Kazembe, and Ovibundu. The regnal lists and events retrieved from them enable historians and ethnologists to present a chronological reconstruction of the past of African societies. Djeli Mamoudou Kouyaté, a Mali griot, revealed the functions and importance of griots by stating that:

> we are vessels of speech, we are the repositories which harbor secrets many centuries old... without us the names of kings would vanish into oblivion, we are the memory of mankind; by the spoken world we bring to life the deeds and exploits of kings for younger generations....I teach kings the history of their ancestors so that the lives of the ancients might serve as an example, for the world is old, but the future springs from the past.[11]

Before a person could acquire or perfect enough skills to empower him to become a functional member of the society, an extended period of apprenticeship was required. Since functionalism was one of the main goals of education, it was not uncommon to find adults still working under the supervision of more experienced and skilful elders. Although the theoretical aspect was taken care of, it was

---

9. Callaway, "Indigenous Education," 34-36.

10. Ibid., 35; Wande Abimbola, "Ifa as a Body of Knowledge and as an Academic Discipline," *Lagos Notes and Records*, 2, 1 (1968): 37. For further reading on *Ifa* divination, see W.R. Bascom, *Ifa Divination, Communication Between Gods and Man in West Africa* (Bloomington: Indiana University Press, 1969).

11. Richard W. Hull, *Munyakare: African Civilization Before the Batuuree* (New York: John Wiley & Sons, 1972), 191-192, quoting from D.T. Niane, *Sundiata: An Epic of Old Mali* (London: Longmans, 1965), 7.

emphatically an education of "do as I do." At home, parents were very watchful of their words and conduct; they avoided bad behavior, realizing that their children would imitate such actions. Children lived by imitating their parents and other adults. For instance, speech training was carried out through imitation for correctness and fluency. Using information garnered from A. Fajana, Callaway pointed out that "in Yoruba education theory, two elements of learning were specified: *awoko*, by imitation of older youth and adults; *afiye*, by active instruction given by adults."[12] Among the Asante and Akan of Ghana, as in other societies of Africa, children "learnt by listening [theory], by watching [observation], by doing [practice]."[13] African education included both theory and practice, but emphasis was placed on the latter.

In occupational training, such as farming, hunting, fishing, blacksmithing, drumming, trading, and the like, the child was required to follow the directions and actions of the instructor. Instructions should be carried out correctly to derive the desired results. This is what the Yoruba people describe as *awokose* ("learning by doing"). In East Africa, the concept of imitation was expressed in Swahili as *kufuata* ("to follow"). In Kenya, among the Maasai and Kamba, children learnt cattle rearing by following their parents. The Akan of modern-day Ghana usually involved children in seasonal occupations such as ploughing, sowing, and harvesting. Attached to an elder for guidance, they were assigned to a defined small area to ensure their active participation. As he grew, a boy would be given "a gun for hunting as well as for playing his part in the local force, the *Asafo* (friends in arms)." Henceforth he became a member of the military (*Asekamb fo*).[14] This formed part of the training in traditional values (*ntetee*) which the Asante gave to their youth. By emphasizing a practical approach to learning, African indigenous education has produced successful people who have contributed in a functional manner (economically, militarily, politically, and socially) to the development of their communities.

A high degree of pragmatism was similarly applied in religious practices. Normally, initiates were trained in both theoretical and practical aspects of the religion. But ritual and initiation ceremonial procedures often involved collective and active participation of all members of the religion. The trainees not only observed, they also participated as directed by experienced priests, to enable them to put into practice what they had learned and to facilitate their ultimate attainment of autonomy.

Traditional education encouraged social activities as a useful method of training the children. This was done mostly through the age-grade system. By the operation of the age-grade system, it was possible for children within the same age-group to receive a similar education from different teachers (parents or other adults). Learning in groups facilitated cooperation and fostered inter-personal and community relationships. The age-grade system as applied in education produced successful results presumably because Africans lived in close-knit societies. In addition,

---

12. Callaway, "Indigenous Education," quoting from A. Fajana, "Some Aspects of Yoruba Traditional Education," *Od: University of Ife Journal of African Studies*, 3, 1 (1966): 16-28.

13. K.A. Busia, *Purposeful Education for Africa* (The Hague: Mouton, 1969), 13.

14. F.L. Bartels, "Akan Indigenous Education," in Brown and Hiskett, *Conflict and Harmony*, 50-51.

age-grade associations stimulated self-expression, the interchange of ideas, and teamwork. It has been pointed out that: "It is through socialization with a diversity of peers in main-stream settings that children may learn, find meaning and purpose, and gain a greater understanding of many of the subject areas covered in school."[15] Three distinct age-groups existed in Kenya — the *watoto* (children's group), the *vijana* (youth's group), and the *wazee* (group of elders). Not all societies developed the concept of age-grades. But where they existed, they functioned as schools for politics, socialization, and educational competition. They provided a cheap source of community labor. For example, they were useful for construction of roads and bridges and renovation of palaces, for physical education, and social entertainment.

The concept of teamwork through age-grades or guilds was epitomized in the Yoruba saying, "ajeje owo kan ko gberu d'ori" ("One cannot accomplish with single-handed effort"). Teamwork was an expedient educational technique because of its high degree of cross-vocational transfer of ideas and skills, which improved the quality, effectiveness, and speed of performance. Utilizing their different specialized skills in the collective discharge of community responsibilities, members of the team became more efficient and more useful to society. Cooperative work was an integral part of African culture from time immemorial. Numerous economic, occupational, and social thrift or guild organizations were formed to serve as credit unions for members and to inculcate the sense of collective responsibility. Members made regular monetary contributions and the disbursement was rotated. Usually, the money was ploughed back into individual businesses or expended on house construction. This made it possible for every member not only to accept financial responsibility, but also to maintain their credit worthiness and to prove that they were reliable.

In addition, members of the association worked by rotational arrangement to clear farmlands, plant seeds, or harvest crops. The integrative cooperative work (whereby people with different skills pooled them together) was applied to communal assignments such as road and bridge construction. Through this means, interpersonal relations were strengthened, members learned from one another, and acquired a better knowledge of the work in process. As demonstrated in traditional education, teamwork teaches tolerance, respect for others, and cooperation with others. It permits recognition and appreciation of educational, cultural, and ethnic values and differences. It allows members to develop a strong sense of self-esteem because the expertise and contributions of each member are properly recognized. Clearly, problems were more easily resolved in groups through the exchange of ideas and joint action. The lessons learned from cooperative work or regular monetary contributions were transferred and used in other human endeavors.

Another functional technique in African indigenous education was the application of words or expressions, which were specific to social life, rituals, or worship. For example, in greetings, commercial bargaining, proverbs, and folklore, specific terms were to be used. During social activities such as naming, wedding, funeral, and installation ceremonies, Africans employed explicit and appropriate words. During worship or when sending petitions to their venerated objects, spe-

15. S. Stainback and Moravec, "Using Curriculum to Build Inclusive Classrooms," in Susan Stainback and William Stainback, *Curriculum Considerations in Inclusive Classrooms: Facilitating Learning for all Students* (Baltimore: Paul H. Brooks, 1992), 68.

cific, clear, and emphatic expressions were required.[16] When recounting incantations or communicating with the ancestors or gods, precise words were used. In divination, special words were utilized to curry the favor of the gods.

It was usual in most African religions to perform sacrifices or hold initiation ceremonies at specified times. An early morning sacrifice was not to be performed in the afternoon. Furthermore, each of the gods required special sacrificial food items. In some cases, a priest of specific gender was required to perform the worship, sacrifice, or initiation. Among the Yoruba, only the priest and one or two attendants were permitted to enter the sacred building (shrine) ostensibly because of the small size of the temple, but more importantly because there were some "emblems which only the consecrated persons [were] allowed to see."[17] If these rules were violated, the devotee(s) would incur the wrath of the god, the consequences of which might be catastrophic. To a child or neophyte, the specific words were taught. This method facilitated comprehension of the subject matter, promoted clarity of purpose, and permitted lucidity of self-expression.

Values of Traditional Education

African traditional education had much intrinsic value. Although given in an informal setting, it was well structured for the understanding of the child. The authoritative and disciplinary nature of the education should not be seen as a serious obstacle to sound training. It was, in reality, an advantage because it empowered the child to confront difficult situations. An African adage states that "the words of elders are the words of wisdom," and since education was transmitted by elders, the recipients were equipped with a web of guidance and wisdom to see them through hard times. It was generally expected that well-educated people would demonstrate high levels of self-control, intellectualism, and understanding of their circumstances. They would handle situations with a mature and positive outlook.

African education prepared the individual for industrial and commercial occupations. In certain societies such as those of Akan of Ghana, the Maasai and Kikuyu of Kenya, and the Zulu of southern Africa, education was geared toward military leadership. Furthermore, it prepared males to assume the duties of husbands and fathers and females to become competent wives and mothers.

Islamic Education

The introduction of Islam provided the means by which Islamic education and Arabic culture penetrated Africa. Taking West Africa as an example, in Borno, a Muslim dynasty was established. By the twelfth century, Muslim schol-

---

16. E. Bolaji Idowu, *Olodumare: God in Yoruba Belief* (New York: A & B Books Publishers, reprinted 1994), 116-117

17. Ibid., 128.

ars ("*ulama*") and missionaries were establishing Qur'anic schools in the urban centers of the Western and Central Sudan. Islamic books from North Africa and Saudi Arabia were sold. Timbuktu, Djenne, Gao, Futa Djallon, Kano, Katsina, and Borno emerged as centers of Islamic education at various times before the nineteenth century. Before the end of the nineteenth century, Islamic literacy had spread as far south as Yorubaland. Through the numerous Muslim scholars and their educational activities, the Western Sudan became an intellectual part of the wider Muslim world.

Islamic literacy was more narrowly focused than traditional education. It taught mainly Islamic law, theology, philosophy, Qur'anic exegesis, and Arabic language and literature. Unlike the traditional system where education followed the age-grade structure, Islamic education did not take age into cognizance. The cooperative (within the entire community) and competitive (usually within the age-grades) frameworks, which existed in traditional education were lacking in Islamic education. The attainment of a certain level of education in both systems often culminated in celebrations. Like traditional education, Islamic literacy recognized moral and participatory education.

As early as the fourteenth century, aristocrats in the Western and Central Sudan sent scholars to Egypt and Tripoli for further Islamic studies. When rulers fulfilled the Islamic requirement of the pilgrimage to Mecca, they often returned with scholars as a means of promoting Islam. Mansa Musa of the Mali Empire who went on pilgrimage to Mecca in the early fourteenth century was a good example.

Islamic education was formal in structure. The general pattern was that every day, children and adults receiving Islamic education sat in classes and in circles, usually under a tree (in some cases in a mosque) on mats or animal skins, receiving instruction from a *mallam* (teacher). They chanted together words or sentences in a monotone, and in a rhythmic fashion. Through a systematic process of rote-learning combined with constant repetition, students gradually grasped the essence of the verses of the Qur'an and the Arabic language. Beginning with short verses because they were easier to learn, students proceeded to longer and more difficult ones. The older the students were, the longer the verses they memorized. In addition, they wrote verses of the Qur'an and notes or commentaries from the teacher on slates. Thus, reading and writing went hand-in-hand with memorization. Rote-learning seems to have been an integral part of Islam since its inception and it remained the primary pattern of transmitting education in all the centers of Islamic learning throughout Africa. It was also common in the Islamic world for a student to go from one teacher to another as demonstrated by Usman dan Fodio and his brother, Abdullah.

Although women also received Muslim education, those who advanced to higher learning were few and far between. A major cause was the belief in seclusion, which prevented women from participating on an equal basis with men. From ages past, the role of women transcended procreation. Like men, they were astute traders, preservers of morality, and propagators of culture. And to successfully carry out these responsibilities, they needed to be well-equipped educationally. In neither traditional nor Western education was the practice of educational gender discrimination as pronounced as in Islamic education. Women in the Islamic world were generally dependent upon their husbands and their roles and services were restricted to the family and compound surroundings. This limited their participation in public affairs.

Christian or Western Education

From the African perspective, Islamic religion and education were identified with Arabic culture, while Christianity and Western education were associated with Western civilization. What the Arabic language was to Islamic education, English was to Western education. In both educational systems, Africans were not only introduced to new languages and cultures, but traditional ones were to be replaced. The resistance of Africans to the proliferation of these new cultures and then education did not, however, last. The persistence of Islamic and Western education coupled with the ancillary benefits derived from them lessened the resistance, eventually leaving only fragments of traditional systems remaining.

The inauguration of Western education in West and West-central Africa antedated the era of colonialism by about four centuries. It began with the Portuguese. During the second half of the fifteenth century, two notable and powerful African kingdoms—Benin and Kongo (in West and West-Central Africa respectively)—permitted missionaries and teachers to operate within their territories. The commercial revolution resulting from the increased demand for slaves extended Portuguese activities on the west and east coasts of Africa. The Portuguese arrived in the Benin kingdom in 1515 and offered to train the king's son in some elementary aspects of Christian education. But the Portuguese Christian influence in Benin did not last long.

For political, economic, and educational purposes, the relationship between Kongo and Portugal remained crucial, especially between 1520 and 1539. Afonso, the Kongo king, cooperated closely with the Portuguese, agreeing that his people would convert to Catholicism in order to receive education, although this arrangement did not work out. While a recipient of Portuguese education became Afonso's secretary, "one of the most successful students in Portugal was Afonso's own son, Dom Henrique, who was delegated to Rome and was consecrated a bishop."[18] After Afonso's death in 1541, the Portuguese increased their commercial activities and paid little attention to education. Thus Kongo-Portuguese relations soured. Subsequent rulers continued to befriend foreigners in order to pursue educational programs for the people of Kongo. Eventually, Diogo I struck a deal with four Jesuits who arrived in Kongo in 1548. When a school was established, six hundred students attended and the king funded the program.[19] But rancor between Diogo and the Jesuits did not permit Christian education to thrive. Although Diogo wanted commerce and education for his people, the Jesuits concentrated on commerce and conversion without paying much attention to education because they did not fund it.

Early Christian enterprises in West Africa were initially restricted to the coast and its immediate hinterland. Noticeable educational programs did not begin until the nineteenth century when there was a proliferation of Christian missions in West Africa. For instance, the Church Missionary Society (CMS) founded Fourah Bay College in Sierra Leone in 1827. By 1841 there were twenty-one elementary and two secondary schools in Sierra Leone. There were few secondary

---

18. Jan Vansina, *Kingdoms of the Savanna* (Madison, The University of Wisconsin Press, first published 1966, second printing 1968), 56.
19. Ibid., 61.

schools at the middle of the nineteenth century simply because the CMS was opposed to the idea of educating Africans at that level. African public opinion for quality Western education altered that position. Thus in 1849 the CMS was forced into opening a secondary school in Lagos under the leadership of T.B. Macaulay. Following that, the Catholic Mission opened St. Gregory's College in Lagos in 1881, and the Baptist Academy began in 1883.[20]

For reasons including the difficulty of penetrating the forest and the problem of malaria fever, expansion into the West African interior was slow. However, schools began to be established, for example in Yorubaland in the mid-nineteenth century. Through the influence of the numerous evangelical missions and their literacy programs, a unique educated elite class began to emerge along the coast, particularly in Sierra Leone, the Gold Coast (now Ghana), and Nigeria. The liberated slaves who were settled in Liberia and Sierra Leone formed the core of the educated class. They scattered throughout West Africa, spreading Western culture and education.

The pervasive influence of the Catholic missionaries made the enterprise of the French relatively simple in providing education for their colonies in West Africa. Between 1880 and 1900 when the French finally occupied Senegal, some elementary schools were founded to spread French culture and education. In addition, a teacher-training college was opened in Gorée. Similarly, in the Ivory Coast, French Catholics founded a school in 1887. In spite of a long history of trading connections, the French did not become actively involved in educating the people of Dahomey (Republic of Benin) until the last decade of the nineteenth century.

Conclusion

This chapter has analyzed the characteristics, contents, and methodologies of traditional education in Africa. Every society in Africa was conscious of education, valued it, and provided it for its people. With the advent of Islamic literacy and Christian education, indigenous education became vulnerable to foreign influences. For instance, Islam displaced the priesthood and initiation ceremonies in African religions, and it gave rise to some changes in African cultural philosophy.

Africans evolved a well-defined system of education long before their contact with Islam or Christianity. Encountering other educational systems meant shifting from and adjusting to one experience or the other. Formerly, the determination of the curriculum and its administration was the prerogative of the parents and older members of the family and community, the biological parents playing a dominant role in the education of their children. But responsibility shifted to Islamic scholars (in Islamic education) and Missions or Educational Boards and teachers

---

20. The growth of education and the establishment of schools by Christian missions throughout Africa had a lot to do with the roles that Africans themselves played. The educated ones were forceful in their efforts to close the gap between traditional, Islam, and Western education. They played significant roles in shaping educational policies. Edward H. Berman, *African Reactions to Missionary Education* (New York: Teachers College Press, 1975), 1-53.

(under Western education). From the time the Arabs penetrated Africa in the seventh century through the nineteenth century, Islamic religion and Islamic education had been interwoven together. The same thing happened with Christianity and Christian education. For both Islam and Christianity, education was considered a necessity for evangelical expansion. In spite of the remarkable transformations, traditional education persisted in certain vocational and religious aspects where foreign influence failed to make an impact.

Review Questions

1. Discuss the role of education in the preservation and propagation of African history and culture.
2. Describe the traditional techniques of transmitting knowledge among African peoples.
3. How did Islamic education affect traditional education?
4. Compare and contrast the curricula of traditional, Islamic, and Western education.
5. What role did the missionaries play in the introduction and transmission of Western education?

Additional Reading

Berman, Edward H. *African Reactions to Missionary Education.* New York: Teachers College Press, 1975.

Fafunwa, A. Babs and J.U. Aisiku, eds. *Education in Africa: A Comparative Survey.* London: George Allen and Unwin, 1982.

Foster, Phillip. *Education and Social Change in Ghana.* Chicago: University of Chicago Press, 1965.

Lewis, L.J. *Society, Schools, and Progress in Nigeria.* Oxford: Pergamon Press, 1965.

Scanlon, David G., ed., *Church, State, and Education in Africa.* New York: Teachers College Press, 1966.

Sloan, Ruth and Helen Kitchen. *The Educated African.* New York: Frederick A. Praeger, 1962.

Wilson, John. *Education and Changing West African Culture.* New York: Bureau of Publication, 1963.

Chapter 5

Indigenous Religions

Joel E. Tishken

African indigenous religions are the ethnic-based religions of Africa that were original cultural creations of African peoples. In Africa, religious structure was an integral component of the way in which a people defined itself. Religion was part of and reinforced the social and political structure and vice versa. In this way, identity, ethnicity and culture were partially empowered by religion. This chapter has three main intentions. The first and primary aim is to explore African indigenous religions, including their foundations, underlying cosmologies, beliefs, practices, and types. The second is to dispel misconceptions that have plagued scholarship concerning African indigenous religions since the time outsiders first observed them. Third, the chapter provides evidence of the diversity and variety of African indigenous religions.

Origin Myths[1]

Like all religions, African religions had a cosmogony, or a way of explaining the way the universe came to be. Non-Africans often have difficulty in understanding how Africans can truly have believed such creation myths. However, African origin myths were little different than those found in other religions, including Christianity. It is merely one's own cultural upbringing that may make some origin myths seem more plausible than others. All people attempted to answer the same questions and often came up with similar explanations. African origin myths have been called myth-history. While scholars regarded them as myths, the people regarded them as history.

Most origin myths fall into one of three categories regarding the creation of the physical universe. The first type attributed the creation of the universe to a primordial creator god who formed the earth. For instance, the Bushoong of Central Africa, claimed that all that existed in the beginning was darkness, water and Bumba, the creator god. One day, Bumba felt a pain in his stomach and suddenly vomited up the sun. The sun shone on the water for so long that the water began to dry, leaving land. Bumba again vomited, this time bringing forth the moon, the stars, and the animals, with man coming forth last. Bumba's three sons also created beings to inhabit the earth. Thus was the earth created. According to the

---

1. The origin myths were adapted from David Leeming with Margaret Leeming, *A Dictionary of Origin Myths* (Oxford: Oxford University Press, 1994).

73

Mande, in the beginning, Mangala made the *balaza* seed. This seed did not work well so he made other seeds that became the four directions, the four elements, and all the things that organized the universe. There were also seeds for two pairs of twins, each set a male and female; these would become the first people. All the seeds existed in Mangala's egg, the world egg. One of the male twins, Pemba, thought he could seize control of creation so he broke out of his egg early. He fell through space to earth where part of his placenta became the earth and the other half became the sun. Pemba's twin, Faro, was sacrificed to atone for Pemba's sin and then resurrected. Mangala then sent Faro to earth with an ark carrying the original eight ancestors and all the first animals and plants. All were in balance, each with a male and female. Faro created the world as we know it from Mangala's original seeds containing the male and female life forces.

Myths of the second type posited that the earth was primordial and a creator god sprang from it. The Fulani said that first there was a drop of milk. From the milk emerged Doondari who made stone. The stone made iron, the iron made fire, fire made water, and water made air. Man was not created until Doondari came to earth a second time. Thus, for the Fulani, the creator god was born and was not held to be timeless and without birth. The Zulu claimed that Unkulunkulu broke off from the reeds. He broke people off from the reeds as well as cattle and the other animals. Next he broke off medicinemen and dreams. Then he created the mountains and streams. He taught the Zulu how to hunt, how to make fire and how to eat corn. No one knows where Unkulunkulu is now. For the Zulu, reeds (*uthlanga*), which also means "the source," existed before the creator god Unkulunkulu.

Myths of the third type regarded both the earth and the gods as primordial. The Ijo of the Niger Delta hold that once upon a time a field existed with a giant *iroko* tree. Into that field suddenly descended a table with a huge pile of dirt on it, a chair and a very large creation stone. Then Woyengi, a female deity, descended to the earth, sat in the chair, rested her feet on the stone and created humans out of the dirt. She held them and breathed life into them. She ordered them to choose their gender, which they did. She also told them to decide how to live and how to die. That is why people all live different lives and leave the earth in different ways. The creation myth of the Nandi of East Africa declared that earth, gods and man were all primordial. One day God decided to arrange the earth. When he arrived he found thunder, elephant, and man. Thunder was afraid of man and retreated to the sky. Elephant teased thunder because of thunder's fear. Yet when man created a poison arrow and began to kill elephant, elephant begged to be taken into the sky. Thunder refused to take elephant into the sky, so man continues to hunt elephant to this day. Man reproduced and took power over the world.

A number of themes can be identified in African origin myths. First of all, many, if not most of them, involve more than one agent in the act of creation. Some involve a single creator god but most include other gods or human actors. Second, origin myths vary greatly throughout the continent, with some assuming a primordial and pre-existing universe while others begin with a near empty universe. Third, many strike a balance between the sexes with men and women coming to earth at the same time, unlike the Judeo-Christian myth in which the man is the first human being. Last, and perhaps most importantly, the tales explain the way the universe was made and why it works the way it does, but they do not provide a code of conduct for the living. In other words, African origin tales do not, normally, contain laws of morality and proper conduct.

Because African creation myths were not written down for most of the history of their people, it is certain that many of them have changed over time. It seems obvious that Christianity has influenced some myths. For instance, the Efe of Central Africa tell this story. With help from the moon, the creator god made a man, Baatsi, out of clay, covered it with skin and filled it with blood. Then a woman was made and she and Baatsi were told to make children. They were given one rule, "Do not eat of the *tahu* tree." So they produced many children who grew old and happily went to heaven when they died. Everything went this way until a pregnant woman with a craving for *tahu* fruit convinced her husband to break some off for her. The moon saw this happen and told the creator god. Because of what they did, now we all must suffer death, said the tale. There are many commonalities between this story and that of Genesis in the Bible; however, it seems obvious that the story was superimposed on an older legend of the Efe. Some ethnic groups have also borrowed from one another.

Origin myths played a considerable role in defining identity. A Yoruba myth states that Obatala created the earth and the first people, who became the Igbo. But then Obatala became drunk on palm wine so Olorun encouraged Oduduwa to make more people instead. Oduduwa fashioned the Yoruba people. He founded the kingdom of Ile-Ife, from which all Yoruba kingdoms derive. Jealous of Oduduwa, Obatala organized his people, the Igbo, in a failed attempt to gain the kingdom. Obatala and Oduduwa were eventually reconciled and Obatala returned to Ile-Ife to become its fourth oni (king). The story of Obatala and Oduduwa was regularly reenacted. Thus, Yoruba myths reinforced their separate identity, as the Yoruba believed they were created by Oduduwa and were therefore different from their neighbors. Also internal cooperation among the Yoruba was encouraged through the belief that all Yoruba came from one place (Ile-Ife) and time. The same could be said of the myths of other ethnic groups, as most defined their own group as somehow special of different from their neighbors.

Time and Space

Many scholars of religion have paid little attention to African conceptions of time and space, arguing that African religions were nothing more than an amalgam of rites and rituals and can not therefore be viewed as coherent theological or cosmological systems. In fact, African religions were every bit as sophisticated as any other religion. Varied and complex notions of space and time supported African religions. It is important to understand these notions because they underlay the rituals and practices. This section will first explore some African notions of space, including both earthly and metaphysical space. Then, notions of time will be examined.

Space

African religions had varied conceptions of space. Among the Venda of Southern Africa, the universe was conceived as a large flat disk floating in water. It was covered by the dome of the sky, *makholi*, that was identical in circumference to the earth. The sun, *duvha*, traveled across the dome from east to west. Some held that it went under the disk of earth reappearing in the east, while others maintained that the sun retreated back east across the dome under the cover of night. The moon, *nwedzi*, was king of the stars but was always in a losing race with the sun. The stars were believed to be suspended from the sky-dome and were invisible by day due to the brightness of the sun. The ancestors inhabited the same earth as the living. Sacred groves and lakes were common abodes of the dead. Spirits often possessed enough power to exist alone in a tree, river, or other features of the land. The sacredness of these locations was reinforced by supernatural events such as strange behaviors in animals, abnormal weather, visions, and the like. Some lakes were so hallowed that they were not used for any purpose for fear of angering the dead who lived there. If you entered the lake to drink or wash, the dead could pull you into the lake to join them. Royal ancestors had the greatest power to affect the land of the living. If angered, it was thought that the ancestors of the royal family could hurl rocks at the villages of the living. In Venda religion, the supernatural and material realms existed in the same physical space despite their separation in metaphysical space.

For other groups, the land of the dead and the land of the living existed in separate physical spaces as well as separate metaphysical spaces. In Kongo religion, *nsi a bafwa* (the land of the dead) existed as a mountain of land under the mountain that was *nza yazi* (the land of the living). They were separated by *nlangu* (water) and the sun and moon traveled around them both. When it was day for the living it was night for the dead and vice versa. The dead lived lives similar to those of the living, except that everything was done in reverse. As with the Venda, the dead were still able to affect the land of the living; they just did so from a separate physical realm. All African indigenous religions, whatever their spatial conceptions, believed that the dead could affect the land of the living.

Time

For nearly all African cultures, time is something to be lived, not measured. With few exceptions, no African cultures in precolonial Africa, unless Muslim or Christian, were concerned with measuring time in precise mathematical units. This is not to say that African cultures did not have calendars or were not concerned about reckoning time. But African calendars were based on phenomena. That is, time was reckoned according to specific events. A farmer counted the number of days it took to plant his fields, a pregnant mother counted the number of lunar months in her pregnancy, and the community counted the number of generations since the foundation of the village. It was valuable for a traveler to know that the sun would rise and set three times if he walked from town X to town Y, but the same traveler was not concerned with the exact number of minutes or hours within those days. To further illustrate this point, let us consider one more example. In most African societies a period of rest occurred around midday when the sun was directly overhead. Whether the sun reached its apex at 12 noon, 1 p.m. or precisely at 12:08 and 32 seconds was not of importance. What was of importance was that the sun reached its apex, and when it did, one rested.[2]

---

2. John S. Mbiti, *African Religions and Philosophy* (London: Heinemann, 1989), 17-19.

African notions of the past and future were entwined with beliefs about the life cycle. All African cultures believed in an ancient mythic past. No one knew precisely when this mythic past existed or when creation occurred. If one could have asked a Bushoong of the past, "When did Bumba vomit the sun?" one would likely have been met with the response, "A long time ago." That Bumba vomited the sun was important; exactly when he did was inconsequential.

The past was located between the mythic past and the present. Because no-one knew when the mythic past occurred, no-one knew how long the past had lasted. The most important thing about the past was that it was the time in which the ancestors lived. The ancestors that died most recently were among the most important. This was because they had relatives still living who remembered them and because they had the greatest ability to interfere in the present. So, those that died in the past were still existing in the present. They did not live in the same form as they once had nor as those living currently did, but they existed all the same. This was one way in which African concepts of time differed greatly from the Judeo-Christian concept of linear time. It is difficult to understand how African cultures held simultaneous beliefs in linear and circular time, so let us examine this further.

It was well-known that the ancestors inhabited the land of the living before those currently in existence. In this sense, African time was held to be quite linear. A Bushoong of the past understood that her grandmother had died before her mother, who had died before herself. However, the Bushoong also believed that while she was surviving in the land of the living, her mother and grandmother were simultaneously existing, either in the land of the dead or on earth just as she was. In this sense, African concepts of time were circular. People of the past and people of the present were believed to be existing in the same moment. This was how the dead could affect the land of the living. Thus, if the ancestors were not honored, they would remind those in the land of the living to honor their memories and accomplishments.

Some scholars have called the combination of linear and circular time a spiral conception of time. Imagine stretching a spring. If one traced the spring, one would be simultaneously rotating in circles as well as moving from one end of the spring to another. Thus, in African conceptions of time, one was part of a chain of human ancestors which existed in the past and will exist in the future (linear) as well as being part of a universe inhabited by all human beings: living, dead, and yet to be born (circular).

But time was not seen as a perfect spiral. An ancestor was able to exist in the land of the dead so long as he or she was honored and could be named by someone living. After a number of generations, when those alive no longer remembered the name, the ancestor in the land of the dead died there as well. For some, their spirit dissipated entirely. Others could become noteworthy parts of the environment like a rock or tree. Still others would be reborn into the land of the living as an infant. This was why elders and children had close ties in African cultures; they were both seen as being near the land of the dead. Thus, the future (children) was tied to the past (ancestors).

Even the not too distant past (five or six generations) could perhaps be considered mythic time, as little was known of it. One noteworthy exception to this rule concerned royal lineages. Some large states took great pride in being able to recite the entire king list from the founder of the state to the present. In some cases these lineages could be recounted for fifteen or twenty generations, perhaps

Figure 5-1. Zebola initiate outlined in white to aid purification

more. The royal lineage of the state of Buganda, for instance, was thirty individuals long (although some of these individuals likely existed in myth only). Thus, royalty and other significant community leaders such as priests were thought to survive in the land of the dead much longer than the average person because they were remembered by many. Also, some leaders were so significant that they became deified upon death and never entered the land of the dead at all. Such was the case for Sango the fourth alaafin of Oyo (a Yoruba state) who, it was asserted, was deified upon his death.

Polytheism or Monotheism?

One of the greatest debates among scholars of African religions relates to the existence and importance of a supreme being and whether or not this means that African religions were monotheistic. Some scholars, most of them Christian and a significant number of them ministers, assert that African indigenous religions were clearly monotheistic. They highlight those religions that believed in a supreme being and ignore those that did not as evidence that African religions were monotheistic. Many times, these scholars are interested in claiming that Christianity is a universal religion and a part of the spirituality of all peoples. Other scholars have asserted that African religions were the total and unique cultural creation of African peoples that owes nothing at all to Christianity and bears no commonalities. They argue that African religions were very clearly polytheistic and as a result quite different, and in fact theologically opposed to, Christianity.

The scholars interested in making African religions look Christian-like pointed to the fact that many indigenous religions believed in a creator god. Indeed many did believe that a god created the universe. However, some ethnic groups believed the universe to be primordial and not created by anyone. Also, some creation myths included not just one creator god but several. Thus, beliefs about the existence and activity of a creator god or gods were highly varied. The idea that *all* African religions believed in a single creator god analogous to the Christian idea of God is false. Moreover, where an African religion claimed that the entire universe was created by a single god, that god always removed him/herself from their creation after the act of creation was finished. Virtually no African religion worshiped the creator god; this is further evidence that African creator gods were not conceived of in the same way as the Christian God. At best, where a single creator god exists, one could claim that the concept was analogous to the Deist conception of God during the Enlightenment era of Europe.[3]

African indigenous religions were unlike Christianity in a number of other ways. They were polytheistic. Scholars do not know for sure how many gods or spirits any specific religion believed in but estimates have ranged from four hundred to several thousand. Normally the number of gods related to a number of ritual significance or a multiple of a sacred number such as 400, 401, 800, 801, or 1000. A religious song of the Yoruba claimed there were 3200 gods and goddesses. The emphasis placed on polytheism within African religions also makes it difficult to see how these religions can be like Christianity with its stress on monotheism. Many scholars have claimed that the saints in Catholicism served the same purposes as the multiple gods in African religions. However, Catholicism does not argue that God was just one of many saints. The supernatural hierarchy in Catholicism was well-defined and the power differential between God and the sainthood vast. This was not the case in African religions.

Another important way in which African religions differed from Christianity related to their beliefs concerning who should belong. In Christianity, the scripture stated that the religion should be spread to everyone (Romans 10:12, Matthew 28:19-20). Christianity was, and remains, an evangelical religion whose mission was to convert the world. This was certainly not the case among African religions. Rather than evangelically based, African religions were ethnically based. That is, only members of a particular ethnic group practiced a specific religion. Members of other groups were not interested in converting.

---

3. Deist theologians posited that there was a god who created the universe. But, after creating the universe, the god retreated to the heavens and left the earth to operate on its own. This explained why imperfections existed in the world.

As the ethnic nature of African indigenous religions is an important point, let us examine it in further detail. For example, if one was an ethnic Mang'anja living in the Lower Shire Valley of Malawi then one believed in the gods of the Mang'anja and practiced Mang'anja rituals. If one were a member of the Sena ethnic group, neighbors of the Mang'anja, then one followed Sena ritual and believed in Sena gods. One's religion was defined according to one's notions of ethnicity. However, this is not to say that African religions were primordial and constant. As notions of ethnicity changed, so too did the corresponding religious systems. Ideas were also often interchanged among ethnic groups due to trade, diplomacy, or other contacts. African religious history is also replete with prophets, oracles, and gods that possessed so much supernatural power that they had multiethnic appeal. In southern Malawi, both the Mang'anja and Sena, and other groups like the Tonga and Lundu, all worshiped the territorial god Mbona. Mbona protected the land. Since all the ethnic groups inhabited the same region, all relied on Mbona to protect the land and to ensure rain and plentiful harvests.

While multiethnic gods like Mbona were common, this does not negate the fact that African religions were ethnically based. This is true for two reasons. First, multiethnic gods normally derived from within the pantheon of a particular ethnic group. Mbona was first a god of the Mang'anja before he became a land guardian for other ethnic groups. It was because Mbona demonstrated great power over the land and the elements that his fame spread and others began to worship him as well. Second, other ethnic groups still maintained their own pantheon of gods and goddesses even while worshipping Mbona. New religious knowledge was placed upon old. Worshipping Mbona did not necessitate rejecting one's previous religion and embracing a new religious system.

However, this is not to say that conversion never occurred. It was not solely religious, however, but more a general ethnic and cultural conversion. Those who most commonly converted were women and slaves. Women often converted to a new religion because it was customary in many societies for them to marry into another ethnic group. Thus, women were forced to join a foreign society, practice its culture, and raise their children in it. Adhering to the new culture meant practicing its religion and ensuring that the children were versed in it. Slaves were also common converts. This was because they were normally purchased from another ethnic group and, like many wives, were also foreigners in the community. As slaves earned their freedom and became part of their new community it was expected that they would shed their old identity in favor of the norms and precepts of their adopted community. Part of this involved religious adherence. While conversion occurred in African religions, it was not however, the policy of any religions to actively seek converts nor was the conversion separated from general cultural conversion. In addition, it took place on an individual level and did not involve the wholesale absorption of neighboring groups.

Gods and Goddesses

Most African cosmological systems held that the gods were divided into two general realms, those above and those below. The existence of these two realms also explained the dual nature of the universe. For instance, the realm above was associated with masculinity, virility, lightning, fire, heat, fierce animals, birds of prey, sickness, and the color red. The realm below was associated with all the op-

Figure 5-2. Sango wand, Yoruba (Nigeria), wood

posites: femininity, fertility, earth, water, cold, domestic animals, healing, and the color white. Despite the realm above's association with men, deities of both genders can be found in both realms, although male deities do predominate above while female deities predominate below. Patronage from human beings was not gender restricted either; both men and women worshiped both male and female deities. Thus the categories of above and below were not conceived as a means of splitting the universe in two; rather they were seen as ordering the universe into complementary halves. Just as men complemented women and the sky complemented the earth, so too did the parts of the universe complement each other. Neither realm could exist without the other.

Some groups believed in only the realms, above and below, and attributed each god's power to one of these realms. Other religions believed in the realm of divination and prophecy, the realm of trade and diplomacy, and the realm of sex and procreation. For some pastoral groups relying on cattle, the gods of cattle and their well-being were sometimes conceived of as inhabiting a separate realm. Even in those religions with three or more realms of gods, the dual conception of the universe still held true. That is, the dual conceptions of male-female, virility-fertility, sky-earth, red-white, and wild-domestic held true even in systems with many realms of gods.

Let us examine two gods of the Yoruba in order to explore the nature of the realms of above and below. These two gods (*orisa*) of the Yoruba have been selected because of their prominence in Africa and the Americas today. Osun was a very prominent member of the Yoruba pantheon and was known throughout Yorubaland. She was said to be the guardian of the city of Osogbo and it was her protection that spared the city from being conquered during the Sokoto jihad. She was the goddess of the Osogbo River and of healing waters in general. In addition, Osun's fertility was greatly admired and women looked to her for children. She was the most beautiful and sensual of all the *orisas* and the epitome of female sexual power. Yellow was her favorite color and could often be found within her shrines and altars. While most patrons of Osun were women, male devotees were not unknown. Osun was considered a goddess of the realm below because she controlled terrestrial waters, was concerned with fertility and motherhood, and her favorite color was yellow (similar to white and a color of the realm below).

Sango was a typical god of the realm above. He was the fourth king of the state of Oyo, and was deified upon his death. Sango was the god of thunder and lightning. He used lightning to remind humans of his power and to punish the wicked. Those struck by lightning were not greatly mourned, as it was believed that they deserved their punishment from Sango. Tales of Sango were filled with stories of his virility and womanizing. One famous myth of the Yoruba told of how Sango stole Oya, the goddess of the Niger River, from Ogun, the god of iron. Sango's favorite color was red. Thus, he was associated with the typical features of the above.

While Osun and Sango may seem different in every way, they were not viewed as opposing figures in Yoruba mythology. In fact, Osun was Sango's second wife. Sango found a complement to himself in his wife Osun; his great enemy was Ogun, the equally virile and powerful god of iron. The importance of complementarity can not be overstated. Both parts were needed for the universe to function properly. Some have seen complementarity as dominance. Just as the sky was over the earth, so too were gods of the realm above (often male) over the gods of the realm below (often female). While it often worked this way in practice as a reflection of the social hierarchy, in purely cosmological terms both parts were seen as equal. In addition, as stated earlier, the gender of a deity did not dictate his or her inclusion in one realm or the other, rather it was the deity's sphere of control that did so.

Gods for every aspect of the universe could be found in African religions. Deities of agriculture, domestic animals, weather, health, the home, the forest, the hunt, the earth, and the heavens were common. Most ethnic groups had gods and goddesses that were common to the entire group and were part of the basis for their ethnic identity. Often these were creation deities from a mythic past or ancestral deities who had founded the group's initial settlement, defeated their enemies, or founded their state. Other ethnic deities were based on topography. Groups which lived near major rivers, lakes, or mountains often had gods known to all parts of the group, such as Osun among the Yoruba. The Kikuyu near Mount Kenya believed that the creator god Mwene-Nyaga sometimes dwelt on the mountain. However, the gods known to the entire group were normally only a small percentage of the total pantheon and could be seen as a sort of deitic elite.

The majority of deities in African pantheons were local. They may have been gods of local features of the topography such as smaller rivers, ancient trees, large rocks, and so on. Others were ancestors and founders of smaller towns, while still others might be newer deities that had simply not taken on great prominence. On occasion, new deities were discovered whose previously hidden powers became apparent. The gods of other ethnic groups were also sometimes added, but very rarely gained the "elite" status. Local deities and deities of the whole ethnic group were equally important to their African worshipers. Which god was patronized at which time depended on one's needs and the perceived power necessary to resolve one's concerns. One could not always approach the most powerful gods, it was believed, or they would become annoyed. Thus, more minor gods were patronized when possible.

Ancestors

As we have seen, the ancestors were linked to those living. Though dead, they continued to affect the land of the living. The most recently deceased ancestors held the greatest power while those who died long ago faded out of existence, became deified, or re-entered the land of the living. A cult of the ancestors existed in all African religions for two reasons. First, ancestors were honored out of reverence for their accomplishments while alive. For the recently deceased, there were still people living who loved them and could pay homage to their memory. Second, because the dead did have the power to affect the land of the living, those alive wished to keep the ancestors happy and content. The movement or loss of objects and minor misfortunes were often attributed to the activity of saddened ancestors. These could become angry and might kill livestock, spoil a hunt, or destroy buildings. It was important to honor the ancestors so that they did not become angry and spiteful toward the living. Despite occasional acts of malice, the ancestors were generally believed to hold no ill-will towards the living. Harmful acts were merely intended to alert the living to their laxness in honoring the ancestors.

Evil, Witchcraft, and Society[4]

African religions defined evil differently than Western religions. In Western religions, evil was defined theologically. Satan or a host of evil beings were responsible for the existence of evil in the world and were often believed to be the source

---

4. Information on witchcraft has been synthesized using John Middleton, *Lugbara Religion: Ritual and Authority among an East African People* (Washington, D.C.: Smithsonian Institution Press, 1987); E.E. Evans-Pritchard, *Witchcraft, Oracles, and Magic among the Azande* (Oxford: Clarendon Press, 1976); Berglund Axel-Ivart, *Zulu Thought- Patterns and Symbolism* (London: C. Hurst, 1976); Herbert Bucher, *Spirits and Power: An Analysis of Shona Cosmology* (Cape Town: Oxford University Press, 1980); and T.O. Beidelman, *Moral Imagination in Kaguru Modes of Thought* (Bloomington: Indiana University Press, 1986).

of evil deeds. Evil took shape through the actions of these beings or by their influence on humans. Evil was everything that was contrary to God's word. When humans committed evil they were rejecting God and accepting his enemies.

In African religions, however, evil had a sociological definition. Evil was that which destroyed the social fabric or brought harm upon others. Individuals who worked only for their own good and cared nothing for the community were defined as evil. Evil deeds would have included hoarding food while others starved, allowing the livestock of a community member to be killed by a predator when one could have prevented it, or betraying the group to invaders. Human beings were held to be agents of free will who chose whether or not to do evil. They were not prodded into evil action by evil supernatural beings. Those that the evil deed offended were not the gods but the community of which one was a part. A person was not held to be evil if he went against the wishes of a deity. The community would likely believe that person to be stupid as they would soon be the victim of the deity's wrath, but he was not necessarily doing evil.

Acts such as betrayal were overt actions of evil that could be readily identified and affected the entire group. However, some actions of evil were not recognized as easily and may only have affected a few members of the community. Because of this, even general aloofness and arrogance could be viewed as evil. If one preferred to remain separate from the community than one must have something to hide; those who had nothing to hide would certainly wish to be part of the greater community. In preferring to live alone, one was making a statement against the community and one's behavior could not be monitored. Outsiders and loners were commonly suspected of witchcraft because of their anti-social tendencies. Because women were often outsiders in the community whose customs might be seen as alien and incomprehensible, they were also often commonly suspected of witchcraft. While women predominated among those accused, witchcraft was not limited by gender, however. Among the Zulu an *abathakathi* (witch) could be a woman, a man, or even a child. In some ethnic groups only men were witches. Among the Lugbara a witch was known as a *ba oleberi*, or "a man with indignation." One who possessed indignation (*ole*) in his heart was a witch. *Ole* could be fostered by jealousy, hatred, or a desire for personal aggrandizement. Whatever the reason, a *ba oleberi* always acted in his own interest at the expense of others.

Highly successful individuals were also commonly suspected of witchcraft. If an individual enjoyed success it might be because he or she was harnessing supernatural power to suit his or her own desires and ends. After all, if one person's cattle died while another's thrived, perhaps the other person was stealing the life force of the cattle. If a person was suddenly struck by a peculiar illness, perhaps this had been caused by another person. If someone had a large number of slaves, pawns, and other retainers, perhaps he or she gained the power to harness this labor through supernatural means. Again, too much success could be seen as an indication of acting selfishly against society. Yet, power and status in most African communities was gauged by accumulation whether in cattle, wives, slaves, or a large labor force under one's control. Individuals who enjoyed the respect of society because of their power as evidenced through accumulation were known as "big men." "Big people" would perhaps be a better term, as women were not excluded from this status even though men predominated. It is indeed paradoxical that African societies valued communal desires over those of the individual, and yet simultaneously held ideas of status that encouraged the gaining of more resources than one's fellow community members. Indeed, scholars claim that in some societies "big people" harnessed the same supernatural power as witches. However, their power was even greater than that of witches because they had the ability to disguise themselves better.

While successful members of the community were often suspected of witchcraft, they were rarely accused. They were often part of the socio-political elite and could harness greater power and resources in their defense than outsiders, common people, or many women could harness. In addition, because they had greater resources they were also in a position to redistribute some of their wealth. While these individuals certainly amassed more resources than they gave out, so long as they redistributed some of their wealth they could maintain a veneer of being pro-society. Many would view a witchcraft accusation against them as false because of their generosity. Thus, while a witchcraft accusation could be leveled at nearly any member of an ethnic group, it was the powerless who were the most often accused and convicted.

Types of Witchcraft

While scholarship knows of no African culture that did not believe in witchcraft, the types of witchcraft varied. In Lugbara culture, witchcraft was practiced exclusively by men and occurred because of *ole*. *Ole* was an antisocial sentiment or feeling that all men housed in their hearts. Men who had no reason to be jealous or envious or who were otherwise powerful enough to deny their *ole* did not practice witchcraft. Yet, some men enjoyed acting antisocially and listened to their *ole* feelings. Such men could enter your homes by night or day. They could set traps to make you ill, break your bones so that they ached in the morning or ruin your property.

To the Azande, witchcraft was a physical substance found within the body. They believed that witchcraft derived from a small, black, oval organ near the liver that secreted a substance that induced a person to behave as a witch. (Evans-Pritchard claimed the organ to be the small intestine in certain digestive periods.) Not only could biology make one a witch but so could genetics. The daughters of female witches and the sons of male witches (but not the daughters of male witches or sons of female witches) were also witches. While possessing a witchcraft organ or having witch ancestry made one a witch by definition, it did not necessarily cause one to act like a witch. It was possible to have witchcraft substance in your body that remained "cool" and inert. Witches choose to act as witches even if they had the biology or genealogy that made them witches. Active witches consumed the souls and organs of people over a long period of time and slow lingering deaths were attributed to them.[5]

In Shona culture, witchcraft was attributed to *shavi* (pl. *mashavi*), or the stranger- spirit. *Shavi* were spirits of deceased people that were unknown in the community in which they had selected a host. Shavi had the ability to possess people and to grant power to their living companions. Malevolent *mashavi* were the stranger-spirits of witches (*varoyi*) who encouraged their companions to do

---

5. E.E. Evans-Pritchard, *Witchcraft, Oracles, and Magic among the Azande* (Oxford: Clarendon Press, 1976), 1-3, 13-14.

evil and to crave human flesh. *Mashavi* encouraged this activity in witches either to increase their own power or purely for the pleasure of doing evil. The *shavi* of a witch was also believed to be inherited, especially among women. While men could also have a malevolent *shavi* and become a witch, it was most often women in Shona society who were thought to be witches.

Thus, we have here three highly diverse types of witchcraft beliefs. To the Lugbara, witchcraft was a male-only activity and derived entirely from sentiment (*ole*). In Azande culture, witchcraft was due to both biology (witchcraft substance) and also sentiment through the will to do evil. Witches could be women or men. Among the Shona, witches behaved as witches through the actions of outside parties, the *shavi*, who motivated people to do evil. Witches in Shona culture were most commonly women.

Some scholars have asserted that African religions differentiated between witchcraft and sorcery. Witchcraft was an exclusively psychic power, common among women, while sorcery was based on the use of physical objects for witchcraft purposes, primarily among men. However, little effort should be wasted in attempting to discriminate between these two concepts. Sorcery still demanded the use of psychic power and witchcraft demanded the use of physical objects. The end result was the same regardless of which witchcraft method was employed.

Combating Evil

African cultures had many ingenious ways to combat evil. The most basic way was the use of what could generically be called charms or medicines. Charms came in as many shapes and varieties as there were perceived needs for them. They were worn, hung in homes, buried under the entryways to homes or compounds, strapped to trees, hung on the necks of cattle, or placed anywhere it was thought a witch might go. Charms normally contained dried or ground plant or animal material, earth, shells, or for particularly powerful charms, even human bones. Some charms even used witches' tools in their making, such as grave dirt, snakes, owls or bats, in order to use the witches' power against themselves. Not all charms were designed to combat witchcraft, however. Charms were used for all sorts of protective and healing purposes such as: protection in war or during a hunt; healing individual ailments or endemic ones; or even attempting to conceive a child. While witches performed the majority of evil deeds, one never knew if a mischievous ancestor or spirit might also cause one harm. Thus charms protected from evil, whatever the source.

Some charms were created for generic purposes while others served specific ones. A religious specialist created all charms, however. For general purposes, the priest made charms for protection. Charms might be made for an entire army without knowing the specific dangers they might face, or might be placed in a home to ward off evil without knowing the specific circumstances of that evil. Charms created for a particular purpose were often more potent. If one was struck by a particular ailment or felt that a witch was preying on one's family, a priest was sought. The priest assessed one's condition and then prepared a charm precisely designed to fit the particular needs.

Ritual cleansing was another means of combating evil. If witchcraft was suspected in a village or among a band, a priest or priests gathered everyone together and ritually cleansed the community. Often, this involved each community member walking between some charms or ingesting some medicine. If the problems still persisted, more drastic measures would be taken but purification often worked in those societies that utilized this technique. Cultures that practiced ritual cleansing to combat witchcraft were normally those that believed in witchcraft as sentiment, such as the Lugbara. Those cultures that held that witchcraft was genetic or the result of possession by malevolent spirits, like the Azande or Shona, did not normally have ritual cleansing ceremonies.

Cultures with genetic or spirit-based witchcraft beliefs customarily had a more severe means of combating witchcraft known as the poison ordeal. In some religions the ordeal could take on a number of forms and depended on the circumstances of the accusation and the priest who was officiating. Among the Kaguru of East Africa, a suspect accused of witchcraft took an oath and was then subjected to a test. This might involve drawing a stone from boiling sheep fat or water without being burned. It might involve having one's ear lobe pierced with a twig by the priest. If it hurt, it was an indication of guilt. Sometimes the suspect was questioned after drinking medicine; a lie would make the suspect sick. Those convicted through the ordeal were known as *muhai kalakala* (burned witches) and were clubbed to death in the bush outside the village.[6] In many cultures, though, the poison ordeal was uniform and highly ritualized. Among the Kuba, the poison ordeal was always executed in the same way. To identify a witch, a piece of bark was cut from the *ipweemy* tree. The way the bark fell determined whether or not the suspect might be a witch. If a possible positive response was achieved, the suspect was given poison derived from the bark of the *ipweemy* tree. If suspects survived, they were innocent and were paid restitution. If they died, it was a sign of their guilt and their body was burned to prevent rebirth. The entire ordeal was surrounded by elaborate ritual that almost made the suspect appear as a sacrificial offering.[7] In societies that practiced the capital punishment of witches, it was very common for the body to be burned after execution. In this way the witch could not become a ghost (malevolent ancestor) and haunt the community or be reborn in another body.

Supernatural Creatures

Not only were the universes of African religions filled with a host of gods and goddesses, ancestors, and witches but most included yet other supernatural creatures. The Akan held beliefs in *mmoatia*, or "little people" who stood a foot tall with their feet on backwards. Some were thought to be harmful but most were simply mischievous. They also believed in the *sasabonsam*, a huge hairy forest monster with long legs and backward- pointing feet. The *sasabonsam*, who often worked with witches, waited in silk-cotton trees to catch unwary travelers and bore a special hatred for priests. The Kpelle believed in the *nyai nenu* (water women or mermaids) who entered the sexual dreams of men, and the *kakelee* who intruded upon the dreams of both men and women. *Kakelee* promised success in the person's waking life if they gave the spirit of one of their relatives to the

---

6. T.O. Beidelman, *Moral Imagination in Kaguru Modes of Thought* (Bloomington: Indiana University Press, 1986), 144-145.

7. Jan Vansina, *The Children of Woot: A History of the Kuba Peoples* (Madison: University of Wisconsin Press, 1978), 202.

kakelee. In Venda culture, the *turi* were greatly feared for their ability to become invisible, enter the body and cause a mortal illness. If a *turi* crossed a person's path, he or she went to a priest to obtain charms for protection. While many more examples could be given, these cases make the point that Africans believed in a variety of supernatural creatures, or ordinary creatures with supernatural powers. Many of these creatures could cause harm to humans if care was not taken.

Augury and Sacrifice

Because the universe was filled with such a variety of supernatural beings, it was important to understand the behavior and wishes of such beings, whoever they might be. The simplest way of knowing was to consult a priest. The supernatural power of priests not only permitted them to locate and combat witches, it also gave them the ability to deduce the wishes of the gods, spirits, or ancestors. Consultation with a priest most often solved a problem existing at the present time. If one had lost some livestock, perhaps an angry ancestor wished to be remembered. If crops were failing from drought, perhaps a god needed appeasement.

Prediction of the future most often involved some form of divination, as also discussed in this volume's chapter on divination. People consulted a diviner-priest concerning their future, family, success, or the wish for blessing or protection. Divination in most cases involved the casting of bones, dice, stones, or shells that were then read and interpreted by the diviner. Many cultures, especially pastoral ones, also had diviners who could predict the future by the reading the entrails of particular animals, especially cattle. Not all of the future could be seen, and the unfolding of future events nearly always involved the rectification of events in the present. If a woman consulted a diviner to ask about her future as a mother, she might be told: "You will bear no children until you make peace with your co-wives." Town elders consulting a diviner about a drought might be met with the response: "There will be no rain until Rain God X is appeased with a sacrifice. Sacrificing two black cows will bring rain."

Another means of augury was oracles. Oracles can be distinguished from diviners. While divination could be practiced anywhere by anyone with the ability, oracles were located in a particular place. The oracles were either immortal, supernatural beings or humans in hereditary positions. In general, oracles were the mouthpieces of the major deities and answered more serious concerns rather then dealing with merely personal matters. Also, while diviners generally acted only within their own ethnic group, oracles often attracted patrons from numerous groups. Among the most famous African oracles was the Igbo oracle of Arochukwu, near the Cross River in eastern Nigeria. Aro traders and slave dealers spread word of the oracle far and wide and patrons could be found among the Ibibio, Efik, and Ijo as well as the Igbo people. So famed was the Arochukwu oracle that a number of pilgrimage routes wound their way to it. However, as it was difficult to know the minds of the most powerful deities, oracles were fairly rare. Many ethnic groups did not have an oracle and those that did usually had only one. In addition, most people could not afford to patronize an oracle because of travel costs and religious fees.

The results of an augury, whether through some means of divination or by an oracle, usually pointed to something that was out of balance in the universe. The proper ancestors were not being honored, worship to a particular deity was being neglected, or a deity had been offended. In some cases the enactment of a ritual could restore the balance and assuage the ill-feeling of the ancestor or deity. Often, it was declared that a sacrifice of some sort was needed, the type depending upon the situation. A sacrifice of drink (a libation) or food (grain, agricultural products, gathered or prepared foods) sometimes served to pacify the ancestors. More important ancestors, especially royal ones, and most deities demanded blood sacrifices. Blood sacrifices most often consisted of the ritualistic killing of domestic animals. Blood would be poured on the ground, a tree, or a shrine to honor the gods and goddesses or ancestors demanding appeasement. The animal was normally cooked and eaten and a portion of the cooked flesh was sacrificed as well.

While it was not common, human sacrifice was not unknown in Africa. The most well known cases were in the militaristic states of Benin, Old Calabar, Dahomey, and Asante in West Africa during the sixteenth-nineteenth centuries. After the death of a monarch (who then became a royal ancestor), humans were sometimes sacrificed to act as attendants in the afterlife. Associates of the king, slaves, and criminals were sacrificed in these situations and most human sacrifice was conducted for these purposes. Some deities, however, did demand human sacrifices. In nearly all cases, these deities were of three types: deities of war, deities of war materials (such as iron), or guardians of the royal line (hence appeasing these gods guaranteed the security and well-being of the state). Humans sacrificed to the deities were almost exclusively war captives. Unlike animal sacrifices, there is no evidence that human sacrifices were consumed.

Religious Leaders

There were various types of religious leaders. While all priests were imbued with supernatural power, their skills varied and addressed the different religious needs of their respective communities. This section maps out the types and duties of religious leaders. In some ways, this outline is artificial as the types of leaders often overlapped. For instance, being a diviner did not mean that one only engaged in divination; nor was divination under the exclusive control of diviners. Two main groups of religious leaders can be distinguished in African religions, however, those that operated solely within their own ethnic group and those that operated at a multiethnic level.

Ethnic-Based Leaders

The most numerous priests were those who operated at the level of the village, band, family or other societal units in the ethnic group. They were responsible for the health and well-being of their ethnic group, at the individual and group levels. Some have called these leaders "medicinemen" or "witchdoctors," but calling them "local priests" is much less ethnocentric and value laden.

Local priests included both men and women. The type and length of their training depended upon the culture, although all underwent some form of ap-

Figure 5-3. Nganga Botoli Laiem, a priest

prenticeship. Some priests received a call from the gods. Among the Ndembu, all priests were selected by Kayong'u, the god of divination, who called them by giving them a serious illness. When diagnosing an illness, a priest could tell whether or not it came from Kayong'u. If so, one had to become a priest, as not heeding the call could mean death. Students had to learn to identify plants and animals; to create medicines and charms; to provide diagnoses and cures for personal ailments; to identify witches; to understand the nature and handling of the supernatural world; and to adhere to numerous sexual and dietary prohibitions. Much of the training might be "on-the-job." Some local priests were primarily devoted to the maintenance of a temple dedicated to a particular god or goddess. For particularly powerful deities, this could be a full-time occupation. The most important deities of an ethnic group might even have a host of priests consisting of several dozen members.

It was the local priests who aided in childbirth, cured the sick, inducted the chiefs, eradicated evil, and buried the dead, in addition to a host of other responsibilities. In sum, they met all the daily religious needs of their community. While some of the duties varied between cultures, the duties were largely the same whether the group was sedentary villagers, pastoralists, hunter-gatherers, or some combination of these lifestyles. The duties of priests were not solely religious, as they overlapped with the social and political realms. Diviners were another kind of ethnically based leader, and diviners also acted in the role of local priest. In very few cases did a diviner act only as a seer of the future.

An important type of religious leader was the prophet. Prophets were ordinary local priests or diviners who, as in other religious traditions, brought new religious knowledge to the community. Most often, this knowledge was given to the prophet in a vision from some supernatural being. The contents of the visions could have a number of purposes including a new deity telling the community to worship him or her; a forgotten ancestor regaining power; or the provision of a recipe for a new, more powerful medicine for witchcraft combating. The prophet might be told to steer the entire community down a different course. The success of the prophet's message depended upon his or her communication skills and the believability and strength of the message. The believability of the prophet's message hinged on proof. If the signs a prophet predicted were coming true, the community often took the prophet's preaching seriously. If proof was not forthcoming, the vision was seen as delusional or a lie. Depending upon the success and popularity of the vision, it was not uncommon for the new item to be integrated into the group's established religion. In most cases, prophets acted within their own ethnic groups, but very powerful visions often gained adherents from other groups. This was particularly the case with new anti-witchcraft medicines that had proven especially powerful.

Rulers, in those societies that had them, were also seen as religious leaders, as they were the mystical and religious heads of their people in addition to the political heads. Kings, queens, and chiefs also possessed supernatural power enabling them to rule. Just like priests, rulers were surrounded by proscriptive behaviors. In some societies (the Shilluk, and Baganda, for instance) no mention of the ruler's human needs could be made. No one could mention that the ruler ate, slept and had sexual intercourse because that would be an acknowledgement of the ruler's humanity. In some societies (notably Baganda and Nyamwezi) the king's feet were not allowed to touch the ground. Rulers were seen as powerful individuals. Because of their power, they oversaw numerous religious ceremonies.

Leaders with Multiethnic Followers

Mention has already been made of oracles that had patrons from numerous ethnic groups. Land guardians also often attracted multiethnic adherents. Some have called these leaders "rainmakers" but "land guardian" is more accurate as rain was not their only responsibility. Land guardians protected the land of a particular environment and attended to the needs of the land's spiritual entity, whether a god or a former ancestor. While it was common for many trees, rocks, and waterways to have spiritual entities, only the most powerful were significant enough to attract a shrine and a land guardian-priest.

Let us examine Mbona as an example. The multiethnic nature of the Mbona shrine in southern Malawi has already been discussed in a previous section. Mbona began as a deified ancestor of the Mang'anja but eventually spread to neighboring peoples in Malawi and Mozambique including the Sena, Tonga, and Lundu. A handful of land guardians oversaw the maintenance of the shrine (and rebuilt it every year), conducted the rituals, and saw to the needs of Mbona's worshipers. Mbona saw to the well-being of the land. Alleviating droughts and floods, exterminating locusts (or other crop-destroying pests), and ridding the land of epidemics were among the main responsibilities of Mbona. Rain, and its regulation during the wet season, were always central concerns for Mbona worshippers. The land guardians heard the pleas of the worshipers and brought their problems to Mbona for solution. The cause of the land's problems was normally moral misconduct by the region's inhabitants. It was the duty of the land guardians to communicate the nature of these misdeeds from Mbona to the fol-lowers.[8] For instance, drought could be due to a pretender being on the throne, a lapse in the honoring of ancestors, or a resurgence of witchcraft. Land guardians were largely intermediaries between the inhabitants of the region who wished for a healthy land and the powerful spirit(s) that dwelled there.

Interaction with Islam and Christianity: The Resilience of Indigenous Religions

Africa was intimately linked with the early history of both Islam and Chris-tianity. Islam entered the lower Nile Delta in 640 A.D., just two decades after the foundation of the religion. The spread of Islam across North Africa was rapid. Numerous important religious centers developed, including Fez, Tunis, and Cairo; and a number of significant poets, philosophers, and theologians hailed from Africa, including Ibn Khaldun. Traders and wandering holy men eventually spread Islam to the northern portions of West Africa and the coastal areas of East Africa. Many religious and cultural centers emerged, such as Gao, Timbuktu, and Jenne, and large numbers of Africans were converted.

Alexandria was among the most important centers of Christianity in the first century A.D. Significant early theologians, including Origen, Athanasius, and Cyril of Alexandria, Tertullian and Cyprian of Carthage, and Augustine of Hippo, all came from Africa. These theologians helped to outline early Christian theology. Numerous Berbers converted to Christianity, and North Africa became a critical part of early Christianity. However, with the arrival of Islam in North Africa, most Berbers converted to Islam. Christianity retreated from most parts of Africa with the exception of the distinctively African Christian Coptic Church in Egypt and the Ethiopian Church in Nubia. Christianity would be reintroduced with the establishment of trade linkages between Europeans and Africans from the fifteenth century onwards.

Many scholars have noted the accommodating way in which Islam tended to deal with the indigenous religions it encountered. Even the central shrine of Islam, the Ka'ba ("the navel of the earth"), was once a pre-Islamic site of pilgrimage and sanctuary throughout central Arabia. Thus, some of the success of Islam has been attributed to a process of conversion that allowed for the simultaneous practice of indigenous traditions alongside Islamic practice. This was the case in Africa. Islam entered Hausaland in the fourteenth century and many converts were gained. However, indigenous spirit possession, called *bori*, continued to be prac-ticed and sacrifices were still made to the deities and ancestors inhabiting the land. The rituals of indigenous religions continue throughout Muslim Africa. Yam and other seasonal festivals are conducted, the ancestors are honored, charms are used to ward off evil, and local priests act as healers.

European traders brought Christianity to many parts of West and Central Africa from the fifteenth century onwards. The Portuguese were among the earli-

---

8. J. Matthew Schoffeleers, *River of Blood: The Genesis of a Martyr Cult in Southern Malawi, c. A.D. 1600* (Madison: University of Wisconsin Press, 1992), 49-52, 71.

est, and Catholic missionaries came to a number of African states. In Kongo, the king was baptized in 1491. Despite the conversion of the monarch and a portion of its noble class, indigenous religious beliefs and rituals remained. Ancestors were still honored, initiation rites conducted, protective medicines produced, and deities and ancestors appealed in order to heal the land. Moreover, Kongo Catholic priests called themselves *nganga*, the KiKongo word for local priest. To call themselves by the same name as the priests of the indigenous religion, rather than by a new or foreign name, suggests that they perceived continuities between their current duties and the Kongo religious past. The rituals and beliefs of Kongo indigenous religion pervade Kongo Christianity to this day. While many Africans have converted to Islam and Christianity in recent times, the ways of indigenous religions are still maintained.

Review Questions

1. How did origin myths relate to African notions of identity? How did they relate to religion?
2. What was the relationship between African indigenous religions and conceptions of time and space? What was spiral time?
3. In what ways did African indigenous religions differ from Christianity? Can it be said that African indigenous religions had a notion of a monotheistic God?
4. What was the relationship between ethnicity and African indigenous religions? What was the role of class?
5. How was evil defined in African indigenous religions? How was it combated?
6. What were some types of African religious leaders? What were their roles and duties?
7. In African religious life, what role did the ancestors play?
8. A number of misconceptions have plagued scholarship concerning African indigenous religions. What were those misconceptions and how do we understand them now?
9. What role did women play in African indigenous religions?
10. Were African indigenous religions static or fluid? How and why did they change? What effects did the introduction of Islam and Christianity have on them?

Additional Reading:

Fernandez, James W. *Fang Architectonics*. Philadelphia: Institute for the Study of Human Issues, 1977.

Herbert, Eugenia W. *Iron, Gender and Power: Rituals of Transformation in African Societies*. Bloomington: Indiana University Press, 1993.

Macgaffey, Wyatt and Michael D. Harris. *Astonishment and Power: Kongo Minkisi and the Art of Renee Stout*. Washington D.C.: Smithsonian Institution Press, 1993.

Mbiti, John S. *Introduction to African Religion*. London: Heinemann, 1975.

Ray, Benjamin C. *African Religions: Symbol, Ritual and Community*. Englewood Cliffs, N.J.: Prentice-Hall, Inc., 1976.

Turner, Victor. *The Forest of Symbols: Aspects of Ndembu Ritual*. Ithaca: Cornell University Press, 1967.

Zuesse, Evan M. *Ritual Cosmos: The Sanctification of Life in African Religions*. Athens: Ohio University Press, 1979.

Chapter 6

Talking to God: Divination Systems

Kathleen O'Connor

This chapter discusses a variety of divination systems in Africa. It examines divination systems as historical records and as poetic statements on the societies that generated them. Religious systems can be seen to reflect the societies in which they were created and developed, through an analysis of the discrete spiritual and moral needs and concerns addressed by those systems. Divination and related techniques, literatures, and interpretive decisions illustrate the poetics of social structure. It should be noted that divination remains a vital part of African religious systems both in Africa and in the African Diaspora. The systems highlighted in this chapter are still in use today, although I will be discussing them as part of Africa's history.

Overview

Although Africa is a huge area with many peoples and ethnic groups, and wide diversity in religious practices, one of the most common methods of regulating activities and assisting with decision-making, both individual and societal, has been the use of one or more systems of divination. The purpose of divination was to access information not available through ordinary empirical means. The source of this information was generally either one or more god-figures or the ancestors. Through divination, people and communities found solutions to problems and guidance for the future. This chapter examines a variety of systems that were used in Africa. Most are centuries old and still in current use, although due to the nature of oral traditions, their origins are difficult to determine with complete accuracy.

Many religious traditions have also used mediumship, a type of divination, to access information. Mediums are people who relay messages from entities not in the temporal world. In many traditions these entities were deceased ancestors. Mediums generally accessed their informants while in an altered state of consciousness (trance) and often but not always with the help of musical systems used for this specific purpose. Shona mediums of Zimbabwe were an excellent example of this type of divination. Their function has remained relevant in contemporary society; they played an active role in the guerrilla war for liberation.[1] A va-

---

1. David Lan, *Guns and Rain: Guerrillas and Spirit Mediums in Zimbabwe* (Berkeley, California: University of California Press, 1985).

riety of mediums interpreted messages in dreams; these included Zulu diviners, who considered dreaming essential; not dreaming was unhealthy.[2]

Other systems of divination employed tools which were manipulated and interpreted by the diviner, such as animals or special shells or stones, and it is this type of divination that will be featured in this chapter. Because divination has not been adequately studied, the chapter will highlight those systems that have been best known, leaving others for future research.

Among the systems to be examined, the Dogon, the Mambila, and the Banen made use of animal oracles reflecting the poetics of each society. The Mambila and Banen of Cameroon used spiders and land crabs. The Dogon of Mali engaged the services of the fox, which also played an important role in Dogon creation myths. Through divination, the fox continued his eternal dialogue with humans using the only means of communication left to him. Thus he perpetuated through myth the ever-renewing creation, the continuance of the world. The fox retained his undependable, ambiguous nature, just as the answers he gave were open to interpretation. His reduced status and limited communicative ability emphasized the importance to the Dogon of words and communication through speech. Spiders and crabs, on the other hand,[3] were independent tools whose activities assisted the diviner in interpreting a situation whose solution was not clearcut. Spiders represented wisdom in mythology and iconography. The use of spider divination was banned for private use because the spiders were thought to be able to disclose state secrets such as the health of the king; the punishment for private use was death. Although spiders were used as tools by diviners, they were the sources of wisdom and they did not lie. Therefore, they were used judiciously.

The divination systems of the Yoruba and some Muslim societies made greater use of inanimate tools. Both the Yoruba and the Muslims used a cowry shell system and a random binary system employing a tray covered with sand or dust on which marks were made and a sacred literature to interpret the marks. Muslim sand diviners used verses of the Qur'an, and the Yoruba people used the verses of *Ifa*, also a body of sacred literature. The Yoruba also used a simple system with *obi*, or kola nuts, which carried only five possible answers for bipartite questions.

Diviners themselves have played important roles in the social structure of their cultures. Kings of Yorubaland retained cadres of diviners to assist with important state decisions. Cameroon spider divination was essentially the property of the ruling class and of the judiciary; the Mambila used divination as the primary evidence against witches, and the Banen used it to diagnose and treat illness. Among the Turkana, Lokario, a famous and powerful diviner, led his people in their military expansion in the first half of the nineteenth century. Lokario, a charismatic leader with universal social power, centralized authority while strengthening Turkana ethnicity. After his death in 1880, power struggles among the remaining diviners ended Turkana expansion. The example of Lokario illustrates how an appropriately-placed diviner who is not only adept at his work but also charismatic can enjoy enormous social and political power.

---

2. Axel-Ivar Berlund, *Zulu Thought-Patterns and Symbolism* (Bloomington and Indianapolis: Indiana University Press, 1989, 1976), 97.

3. David Zeitlyn, "Spiders In and Out of Court, or, 'The Long Legs of the Law': Styles of Spider Divination in their Sociological Contexts," *Africa*, 63, 2 (1993).

The feature which all systems of divination had and have in common is that the action of divination was only one part of a general process. The process began with a problem, question, or desire on the part of the "client," who might have been an individual, a family group, an entire community, or the society as a whole. The client sought out a diviner and asked for his or her services to resolve the issue. The diviner looked at the issue, defined the problem, and determined the solution. The diviner then prescribed the appropriate action to be taken. Sometimes the solution was an offering or sacrifice (in which case the process ended with a meal), sometimes a medical remedy, and sometimes merely a change in behavior. Divination was employed for such diverse issues as the need for rain, the healing of an illness or wound, solving marital or legal problems, determining the succession of kings, and so forth.

A second generalization that can be made is that diviners who became most successful had some observable measure of talent at their craft. By this is meant that a diviner whose remedies, recommendations, predictions, and spells accomplished the desired ends for his or her clients developed a reputation of competency and as a result enjoyed respect and often fame as well. Such a reputation resulted in greater wealth or social status. In this chapter, when we speak of talent, this concept should be understood as culturally determined and recognized, and accepted as real to the people who practice these religions.

Divination Systems of the Yoruba

Among those systems which have been very well documented, probably the most famous of all was the *Ifa* system of the Yoruba people of West Africa. The Yoruba religious tradition venerated numerous nature deities called *orisas* while acknowledging one Supreme God, Olodumare. Two of the most important *orisas*, worshiped and propiated universally among traditional Yoruba, were Orunmila and Esu, and these controlled divination. Ifa divination, which was the domain of Orunmila, relied on an immense body of literature, the *odu* corpus or verses of *Ifa*. The texts were similar to poetry and contained stories and parables illustrating all the values of Yoruba culture. It was through the *odu* that the *orisa* Orunmila spoke. According to the myth detailing the creation of this system, Orunmila suffered an insult of disrespect from his youngest son and returned to heaven, refusing to return but leaving in his place the *Ifa* system of divination in the form of sixteen palm nuts. Orunmila, therefore, although a remote father, can always be accessed through the sacred palm nuts, the divination system of *Ifa*.

Ifa divination represented an impressive preliterate academic system[4] due to the volume of its literature, which has been preserved through oral tradition. In *Ifa*, there were sixteen main *odu*, or signs, which were randomly combined to produce a total of 256 *odu*. The priest of the *Ifa* tradition, the *babalawo* or father of secrets, memorized at least sixteen verses pertaining to each of the 256 *odu*. Different *babalawos* memorized different verses; the literature was so vast that no

---

4. Wande Abimbola, *Sixteen Great Poems of Ifá* (Paris: UNESCO, 1975).

one *babalawo* memorized them all. The literature was contained in sixteen (oral) "books," each of which contained more than 800 verses.

Contrary to popular opinion, particularly in Diaspora areas to which *Ifa* divination traveled, women could be diviners and evidence of women diviners appears in the literature.[5] However, *babalawo* training was arduous and took years to complete; social structure in Africa was such that it was rare for women to undertake it. The bearing and raising of children, who were considered to be a form of wealth among the Yoruba,[6] took precedence for many women, and even the *Ifa* literature reflected the value placed on children, wives (both having a wife and being one), and family as indicators of prosperity and happiness.

Typically, a *babalawo* began studying the system at a very early age, often learning from his own father. He passed through several stages of initiation, learning herbal remedies and at least sixteen verses of each of the sixteen *odu*, which he had to be able to recite by heart before being ordained to practice on his own. After ordination, he continued to study and discuss and debate the verses with other *babalawos*. The intelligence and rigorous discipline required has excluded all but those who are absolutely committed to the tradition.

In the *Ifa* divination process, the *babalawo* was typically approached by a client who had a problem, a question, or a decision to make, which he whispered to a coin or cowry shell placed in front of the *babalawo*. The *babalawo* sat on a mat on the ground with his legs apart and a wooden tray *(opon Ifa)* in front of him. He spread a special wood dust *(iyerosun)* on the tray. He then took sixteen nuts from the palm tree *(ikin)* and rolled them between his hands. Leaving the nuts in his left hand, he attempted to grasp them and pull them away with his right. Usually one or two remained in his left hand. If one remained, he made two parallel vertical marks in the dust on the tray, and if two nuts remained, he made one mark. He repeated this process eight times until he had two rows of marks on the tray, making the marks in turn from left to right until he had two vertical lines of four each. This pattern was the "signature" of the *odu*, and the *babalawo* then began to recite the verses that pertained to this particular *odu*. For example, two rows of single lines referred to *Eji Ogbe*, the first of the major *odus*. Each column of marks referred to a major *odu*, and two columns were made to give the signature of the *odu* .

As the *babalawo* began to chant the verses, the client listened attentively and stopped the chanting when he recognized his problem or question in the verses. At this point, further divination and interpretation was needed to determine how to solve the problem at hand. To assist in interpreting the verses, the diviner used several other tools for yes and no answers. These could be a piece of bone, a shell, a pottery shard, and so forth. One was held in each of the client's hands. A question was asked, and the nuts were manipulated again. If the second *odu* was more important than the first, then the client was asked to open his right hand. The bone meant "no"; the shell "yes" and so forth.

A faster method employed the *opele* chain, to which were attached eight seed halves or metal disks, each having a concave and convex side. There was an empty space in the middle of the chain, where the diviner grasped it. The diviner

---

5. Bernard Maupoil, *La Géomancie a L'Ancienne Côte des Esclaves* (Paris: Institut D'Etnologie, 1943).

6. Roland Hallgren, *The Good Things in Life* (Löberöd, Sweden: Bokförlaget Plus Ultra, 1988).

cast the *opele* away from him, allowing the disks to land while holding on to the chain. The disks fell on one side or another, giving with one toss the same *odu* signature as eight manipulations of the palm nuts. Use of the *opele* was more common and thought to be for everyday use, whereas the palm nuts were used for occasions with greater ritual significance such as determining the destiny of the client, a ritual that was usually performed for a newborn.

Once the appropriate verse of the *odu* had been identified, the *Ifa* literature contained a prescription for the solution of the problem. This usually involved making an *ebo*, or offering. Often the *ebo* involved the sacrifice of a fowl or other animal in more serious cases, but could also be as simple as a special bath or the presentation of fruit or flowers to one of the *orisas* or to an ancestor *(egun)*. It should be noted that the *ebo* was a process rather than simply the act of sacrifice, and that the final part of the process was the consumption of the sacrificed animal by either the diviner himself as payment for his services, or by the client and his family. The sacrifice of an animal in this context reinforced the sense of community between the diviner, the client, and the *orisas* in the form of a shared, life-giving meal.

Cowry Shell Divination Systems

The cowry shell system was also extensively used by the Yoruba. A form of cowry shell divination was also employed by the Anufo Muslims of North Ghana, although Muslim sacred literature specifically prohibited divination, as did that of Christianity.[7] In the cowry system of the Yoruba, the *babalorisa* (priest, father of *orisa)* or *iyalorisa* (priestess, mother of *orisa*) threw sixteen cowries down onto a mat, and counted how many fell with the open side up. The cowries were specially prepared by slicing the rounded back off so that when they fell they would not automatically roll over onto the "mouth," or "up," side. To obtain the *odu* signature, the cowries were thrown again and the counting process was repeated. The names of the *odu* were the same, but in the cowry system they were assigned to different *odu* than in *Ifa*. For this reason, one was not allowed to be a priest of *Ifa* *(babalawo)* and also read the cowry shells, as one would become easily confused and give incorrect readings. One could "graduate" from the cowries to *Ifa*, but in the *babalawo* initiation neophytes took an oath never to use the cowries again.[8]

In the Ghanaian Muslim system, ten cowry shells were used. The diviner acted merely as a diagnostician, and his pronouncements therefore tended to be pessimistic as the client generally came with a problem. According to Jon P. Kirby,[9] the diviner spoke little as the process was guided by the spirit of divination. This implies that both diviner and client were familiar with the system, and in fact all heads of households were able to divine with the cowrie shells if necessary, although most preferred to go to someone with socially recognized talent.

7. E. Dada Adelowo, "A Comparative look at the Phenomenon of Divination as an Aspect of Healing Processes in the Major Religions in Nigeria," paper presented at the Ife First Annual Religious Studies Conference, University of Ife, Ile-Ife (1986), 3.

8. Abimbola, personal communication, February 1997, Boston.

9. Jon P. Kirby, "The Islamic Dialogue with African Traditional Religion: Divination and Health Care," *Social Science and Medicine,* vol. 36, no. 3 (1993): 237-247.

The cowries fell in certain specific patterns which needed no interpretation. Repeated casting of the cowries identified certain symbols which represented common concepts such as life, death, fertility, and so forth, as well as common misfortunes such as a court case, woman trouble, loss, and illness. Problem areas such as neglect of shrines or impersonal natural forces such as lightning striking the home compound, therefore polluting the family and its associates, were also identified in the same way, letting the client know that work or propitiation was needed to resolve the problem.

Muslims and Divination

Also used by Muslims throughout West Africa was sand divination which resembles *Ifa* in its use of a "rosary" *(tasbih)* or string of beads (the *opele* was often referred to as a rosary since it resembled a necklace and was used for a religious purpose). The Muslim diviner used sand from Mecca in which to make the divining mark on a tray similar to that of the *babalawo*. After reciting an invocation to the beads and placing them on a carpet, the diviner asked the client to pick a bead. Then the diviner recited "good" and "bad" for each bead up the string until he arrived at the large beads that divided the rosary into three parts. At this point, depending on whether he had arrived at a good or a bad bead, he interpreted for the client, using verses from the Qur'an as references. The diviner made various marks in the sand, ending with writing in Arabic. Where *Ifa* and the *tasbih* system interconnected was in the random binary form, using sixteen possibilities. The literature was quite different, as *Ifa* literature reflected Yoruba mores, and Muslim sand divination used passages from the Qur'an to address the problems of the client. In this way, Muslim sand divination reinforced Muslim values, emphasizing social issues important enough to appear in Qur'anic verses, and providing a culturally acceptable means of ameliorating common problems, just as the *Ifa* literature, developed over centuries, performed the same function for the Yoruba people whether Christian, Muslim, or traditionalists.

There is disagreement as to whether the Muslim system predated *Ifa*. According to nineteenth-century historian and Christian clergyman Samuel Johnson the *Ifa* system came from Nupe in the eighteenth century, carried by a certain Setilu who was exiled from Nupe for corrupting Muslims with his divination system.[10] *Ifa* certainly was present in Yorubaland prior to the years of jihad in the nineteenth century. *Ifa* divination literature itself contains the history of its origin, along with stories of the beginnings of Yoruba culture. These stories contain no mention of Islam. In his discussion of Muslim cowry divination and sand divination, Kirby[11] documents a shift in technique in Muslim divination away from the pessimism of the cowries to greater use of sacred texts for solutions of the problems identified in the divination session, both in the cowry shell technique and that of sand divination which resembles *Ifa*. This shift likely illustrates the imposition of a newer world view (that of the Muslims) on an older system, as does the introduction of the use of sacred texts, possibly modeled on the *Ifa* system.

---

10. Fela Sowande, *Ifa* (published by author, n.d.).
11. Kirby, "Islamic Dialogue."

A third system used by the Yoruba employed *obi*, or kola nuts. This simple technique was also used in Diaspora areas (particularly in Cuba and the U.S.), where kola nuts were replaced by coconuts. In *dida obi*, as the technique is called, two kola nuts were split in half, giving four pieces which each had a concave and convex side (using coconuts, a white and a dark side). Asking a yes or no question, the kola was thrown on the ground and the pattern read. If all fell with the convex side up, the answer was no, and a problem or bad fortune was indicated. All concave meant good fortune *(alafia)*. Three concave kolas indicated uncertainty and the diviner threw the kola again; three convex was no. Two concave and two convex was definitely yes. *Dida obi* was primarily used to determine if an *orisa* was pleased with a particular *ebo* that had been offered or if more propitiation was required.

Spider Divination

In Cameroon, spiders and land crabs were used as tools in divination. A spider or crab hole was located and all the surrounding brush was cleared. An old pot with the bottom knocked out was placed around the hole, and cards made from palm leaves with certain possibilities marked on them, were arranged around the spider or crab hole. A question was asked, and the spider was left to its own devices, often overnight. When the spider emerged from its hole, it disturbed the cards, providing the answer to the question by the way it rearranged them. For example, markers representing male and female enemy and male and female friend might have been placed over the hole. As the spider emerged, perhaps he moved the male friend marker so that it crossed the enemy markers, thus indicating that the enemies would be vanquished. A marker showing a palm tree which was disturbed possibly indicated that the client should not climb palm trees because it was dangerous for him. Obviously, the markers and the images appearing on them were referents to important cultural issues or factors which impacted the lives of the client and the diviner.

Spider divination among the Mambila was often used to detect witches. The testimony of the spider was used in court cases against persons accused of being witches. Although the divination itself was not performed in court, the diviner went to testify. This divination, among others, was used in the continued social control of men over women, who were not allowed to divine but were usually the accused witches as well as being required to obey any pronouncements made by male diviners.[12] Spider divination among the neighboring Banen, however, was used to detect and treat illness and never for the identification and prosecution of witches.

Dogon Fox Divination

In the Dogon society of West Africa (in present-day Mali), divination was linked with the creation myth of Ogo. In this myth, which was as bloody and vio-

---

12. Zeitlyn, "Spiders," 225.

lent as birth itself, Amma the creator made eight primordial beings called the *nommo,* each a composite of all elements. The first seven were androgynous creatures who were to help Amma create the world, but the eighth, Ogo, was missing the element of water and could not reproduce independently. The myth details Ogo's tragic and unceasing efforts to complete himself, a desperate struggle of life and death, in which his increasingly drastic and violent actions met with more and more severe punishment from Amma, until finally he was doomed to crawling on all fours in the body of the fox. The myth emphasizes Dogon philosophy which privileges communication, especially the spoken word, for each of Ogo's punishments further limited his ability to communicate verbally. Yet even in his debased form as a fox, he was still permitted to communicate through divination.

Divination by the fox included the interpretation of dreams and the reading of tossed cowries and stones, but particularly the reading of fox tracks left across a divining table drawn in the sand. Generally, fox divination was undertaken for the benefit of the community when forces such as those of nature threatened the existence or order of the social group. In the process, a diviner drew a four-cornered table in the sand in the functionally neutral area at the outskirts of the village, between the inhabited space and the cultivated space. The table was divided into six squares with images representing Ogo's travels through time and space and the upper and lower worlds. A circle representing the world was traced in the sand next to the table, and an altar to the fox was erected next to the table with a spider drawn at its highest point. The diviner made offerings of food to the fox and placed them in a calabash which he put on the altar. The next day, the pawprints left by the fox were interpreted according to which way they faced and which images on the table they crossed or avoided. Marks left by other animals or a confusing excess of tracks were considered to be ambiguities representative of the fox's unreliable character, and by extension, the intrinsic unreliability of the divination system itself. Dogon fox divination, therefore, built ambiguity into its structure, and according to Laura Grillo, "in refuting the possibility of certainty in its predictions, [it] is also affirming the primacy of human freedom in ultimately determining the course of events."[13]

Social Issues and Divination

As noted above, divination and its literature and interpretations could be and were used as forms of social control. Divination dealt strictly with human beings and their problems and failings and therefore carried the burden of directing individuals to appropriate courses of action. The key word, of course, is "appropriate." Appropriate behavior and problem-solving is culturally determined; behavior that is required or expected in one culture is likely to be meaningless elsewhere. Therefore, a closer analysis of divination reveals a great deal about the nature of the people using the system. For example, as noted above, women rarely learned to be Ifa diviners because of the time required to learn the system. Yet women diviners did and do exist. Interestingly, in the transposition to Diaspora areas, this infrequency has

---

13. Laura Kétékou Grillo, "Dogon Divination as an Ethic of Nature," *Journal of Religious Ethics.*

been translated into a strict prohibition against women learning the *Ifa* divination system. Diviners in the Diaspora insist that women simply do not become *Ifa* diviners even though there is concrete evidence to the contrary in the literature.

The *Ifa* literature frequently referred to wives as a form of wealth and good fortune. In this way, it was a guide to both men and women in their relationships with one another. The *Ifa* literature also talked of losing a wife or husband through ill-treatment or neglect, as well as through infertility. For the Yoruba, family was of paramount importance; a man was nothing if he had no offspring, particularly sons, for when he died he would cease to exist if he had no children to care for his memory. Therefore, the Ifa literature taught Yoruba traditionalists to respect their relationships with their spouses and to care for their children, thus reinforcing deeply-held values within the culture.

Also reflecting gendered social control is Muslim sand divination, which had as its primary focuses wealth, illness, and sex or control of the reproductive capabilities of women.[14] The lessons from Muslim sand divination primarily contained warnings of evil that could be avoided by living according to Qur'anic texts, rather than any sort of pessimistic pronouncements such as can be found in the Muslim cowry shell system. According to Kirby, "[this] method functions less as a utilitarian method of solving problems than as an idealistic new way to perceive them."[15] Without including a study of the Qur'an's admonitions regarding women, which is beyond the scope of this chapter, a glance at this literature's emphasis on obedience to men, particularly the husband, proper behavior including the covering of the entire body, the death penalty for adulterers, and other rules for women, shows that a divination system based on these verses would certainly include a heavy measure of social control over women. Since divination was thought to be a direct means of communicating with God or divine agents, pronouncements by any divination system were taken very seriously.

The influence of Christianity and Islam had a serious effect on traditional religion in Africa, especially divination, particularly in areas such as Nigeria where these religions made major inroads among indigenous populations. However, Christianity and Islam failed to address deeply held beliefs about social factors such as witchcraft, which was thought to cause a variety of illnesses unresponsive to Western medicine. Fear of witchcraft among the Yoruba began to increase during the colonial period, coinciding with the advance of Christianity and Islam which in turn attacked the very built-in social restraints on witchcraft, such as identification through divination, that had once kept these fears at bay. The advance of the so-called "world" religions failed to quell or even speak to centuries-old cultural beliefs; therefore, those beliefs remained active. African methods of dealing with fear were deliberately expunged from daily use by colonial religions, leaving only the prospect of an afterlife following a life of fear. As a consequence, traditional religion was still practiced, even if clandestinely, for relief from traditional problems and fears. All of the systems discussed above with the exception of the Muslim systems addressed the possibility of external spiritual forces as the cause of a client's problem, including witchcraft. Traditional divination systems therefore continued to provide a means to address and ameliorate deeply-rooted social concerns.

---

14. Kirby, "Islamic Dialogues," 14.
15. Ibid.

Conclusion

We have seen that divination systems reflect and reinforce the values and poetics of the societies that create and employ them, and that divination systems can thus be seen as mirrors of these societies. For the Dogon, the ambiguity of existence, communication through speech, and human freedom of choice were the ideas most represented by fox divination. For the Mambila and the Banen, truth and its consequences were illustrated by the spider of wisdom. The Yoruba valued human relationships and family unity as indicators of personal wealth. Muslim divination depended on the sacred words and teachings of the Qur'an. Questions asked and problems presented to the diviner carried all of the history of the questioner. The answers as well were contained in those same questions, and also within the diviner's tools and his skill at interpreting their message.

Divination continues to flourish in Africa and the African Diaspora as a vital part of both religious worship and daily living, functioning as primary medical care as well as fulfilling the roles of Western service providers such as legal and marital counselors. Therefore, divination and related activities link the traditional and contemporary worlds by serving both; treating illnesses caused by witchcraft as easily as solving legal problems caused by life in an increasingly urban society. Divination inhabits the liminal space between spiritual faith and empirical results; between human and extra-human; between the past and the present, and extending into the future. A greater understanding of divination systems through concentrated research will provide a wealth of information about their corresponding social systems, and the histories of the peoples who belong to those systems.

Review Questions

1. Discuss the differences between Muslim and Yoruba divination systems.
2. What is the significance of Dogon fox divination in describing what is important to the Dogon?
3. How are the spiders used in court?
4. What are the major social issues highlighted by divination? What other possibilities can you think of?

Additional Reading

Apter, Andrew. *Black Critics and Kings: The Hermeneutics of Power in Yoruba Society.* Chicago and London: University of Chicago Press, 1992.

Barnes, Sandra T. *Africa's Ogun: Old World and New.* Bloomington: Indiana Univerity Press, 1989.

Bascom, William. *Ifa Divination: Communication Between Gods and Men in West Africa.* Bloomington and Indianapolis: Indiana University Press, 1991 (1969).

———. *Sixteen Cowries: Yoruba Divination from Africa to the New World.* Bloomington and Indianapolis: Indiana University Press, 1980.

Griaule, Marcel. *Conversations with Ogotemmeli: An Introduction to Dogon Religious Ideas*. London: Oxford University Press, 1965.

Laitin, David D. *Hegemony and Culture: Politis and Religious Change among the Yoruba*. Chicago and London: The University of Chicago Press, 1986.

Mbiti, John S. *African Religions and Philosophy*. New York and Washington: Praeger Publications, 1969.

MacGaffey, Wyatt. *Religion and Society in Central Africa: The BaKongo of Lower Zaire*. Chicago and London: University of Chicago Press, 1986.

Sawyerr, Harry. *God: Ancestor or Creator? Aspects of Traditional Belief in Ghana, Nigeria and Sierra Leone*. London: Longman, 1970.

Simpson, George E. *Yoruba Religion and Medicine in Ibadan*. Ibadan: Ibadan University Press, 1980.

Chapter 7

Islam

Toyin Falola and Steven J. Salm

The relationship between Africa and Islam dates back to the first years of the Islamic religion. Only a decade after the death of the Prophet Mohammed, Islam was already making inroads into Egypt and establishing a base for its movement into other areas of the continent. After establishing a presence across North Africa during the seventh century, Islam moved far south into West Africa and also made an impact on societies in Northeast and East Africa. It is difficult to discuss the history of a large part of the continent without including the introduction, spread, and impact of Islam. Islam is truly a world religion and it helped to bring Africans into a closer relationship with a larger part of the world than before. In this chapter, we shall touch upon the following issues: the beginnings of Islam, its spread to different regions of Africa, and its religious, political, social, economic, and cultural consequences for African societies.

The Beginning and Spread of Islam

The Prophet Mohammed was the founder of the Islamic religion. He was born in Mecca towards the end of the sixth century A.D. (ca.570 or 571 A.D.). He saw himself as a savior ordained and sent by God to redeem his people, the Arabs, from the hands of their "pagan" rulers. Around A.D. 610, after one of his solitary retreats to a cave in Mecca, he emerged to proclaim that he had received the words of God through the Angel Gabriel. Thereafter, he began to preach the new religion in and around Mecca. Prophet Mohammed explained to the people that though there had been many prophets before him, people had corrupted their messages and God was now making use of him as the last prophet to seal the faith.

Many people in Mecca, especially the rulers, ignored his message. However, his popularity increased tremendously and he succeeded in gaining many converts who looked on him as their leader. He was popular because of his revolutionary preaching which condemned many of the social practices of his time, especially the oppression of the poor by the rich. Prophet Mohammed's popularity posed a threat to the Meccan leaders and they started to persecute him in the fear that he could usurp their powers. Under the pressure of this persecution, he fled from Mecca to Al-Medina (formerly called Yathrib), a small town two hundred miles north of Mecca. This flight, known as the *hijra*, is one of the important tenets of Islam.

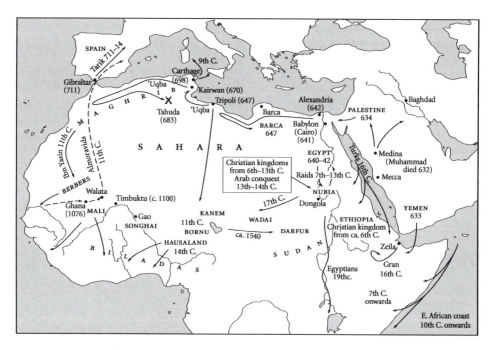

Figure 7-1. The penetration of Islam into Africa

While in Medina he consolidated his power and strengthened the belief of his followers. In fact, he became so popular that many people in this town accepted him as their leader. With this relatively strong base he embarked on a number of holy wars (jihads) beginning in A.D. 625. The jihad is a practice of Islam that began in Medina. There are many different ways to perform what can be loosely defined as "striving in the path of Allah."[1] These include: the jihad of the heart, which involves purifying the heart and soul of evil thoughts; the jihad of the tongue, which involves making pleas to others to do what is right; the jihad of the hand which involves administering discipline according to Islamic customs; and, lastly, the jihad of the sword, which asks believers to use force to defend, reform, or spread Islam to nonbelievers. The last is the type most commonly referred to when using the term jihad. It is seen as an obligation for the whole community and, by employing this tenet, Mohammed succeeded in overthrowing the "pagan" rulers of Mecca by 630 A.D.

Prophet Mohammed returned to Mecca and received many revelations over a period of years which later formed the basis of the Holy Qur'an. By the time of his death in A.D. 630 at the age of 60, Islam had been firmly established in Arabia. The Holy Qur'an was produced fifteen years after his death, during the caliphate of Uthman (644-661). For Muslims the Qur'an is the Word of God revealed to them through the Prophet Mohammed. In the Qur'an the Prophet is set next only to God as deserving of moral and legal obedience, and thus his sayings and deeds, along with the Qur'an, serve as a basis for the beliefs and practice of Islam. The Qur'an is a book of holy scripture concerned with the relationship of

---

1. Peter B. Clarke, *West Africa and Islam: A Study of Religious Development from the 8th to the 20th Century* (London: Edward Arnold, 1982), 4.

one person to another, and people to God, with laws on marriage and inheritance, and with other matters. The Qur'an also deals with how to establish an Islamic state which would remove oppression, fraud, deceit, and other forms of corruption from society.

The Qur'an, however, is not the only book of Islam. In fact, it is a small book, and the need for others was felt soon after the Prophet's death. His followers compiled many books based on his teachings, preaching, and deeds. One of these books contains the Sharia, the "canon law" of Islam. The various writings are collectively known as the *sunna*, meaning the practices laid down by Prophet Mohammed which all Muslims are enjoined to follow. From these books and the activities of the early Muslims, five important practices, often called the Five Pillars of Islam, emerged:

(i)   The belief that "There is no god but God (Allah) and Mohammed is the Prophet of God." This statement is known as the *shahada*;
(ii) The duty of all Muslims to perform ritual prayer (*salat*) five times per day;
(iii) The duty of fasting (*saum*) from dawn to sunset during the month of Ramadan, the tenth month of the lunar year;
(iv) The necessity of alms-giving (*zakat*) to the poor and the needy; and
(v)   The performance of a pilgrimage to the holy city of Mecca (hajj) if one has the physical and financial means.

The adherence to these beliefs and practices defines a true Muslim.

The death of Prophet Mohammed did not put an end to the expansion of this new religion. His followers and disciples carried it to other places. The Arabs, following the footsteps of the founder, strove to expand the religion beyond the boundaries of their territories, and in the process spread Islam to parts of Europe and many places in Africa. The spread of the religion also meant the establishment of Islamic government and the introduction of Arabic culture to various parts of the world.

Prophet Mohammed himself had already laid down the tradition of overthrowing a government, removing the "pagan" rulers, and putting believers in their place. Thus, when the Arab proselytisers infiltrated any community they either overthrew the existing government or made sure that the members of the ruling class were devout Muslims. Islam was not to be just a religion but a total socio-economic and political system. In Africa, as we will see, this was truer in some regions than in others.

The Expansion of Islam in North Africa

Because the followers of Prophet Mohammed were very eager to propagate the new religion and because the Arabs were by that time also looking for more fertile lands to settle, they embarked on a vigorous and rapid conquest of many places close to their homeland and in Africa. They conquered areas such as Syria, Persia, Central Asia, Iraq, and North Africa. They set up Islamic governments and gradually Islamic and Arabic civilization replaced or mixed with the indigenous

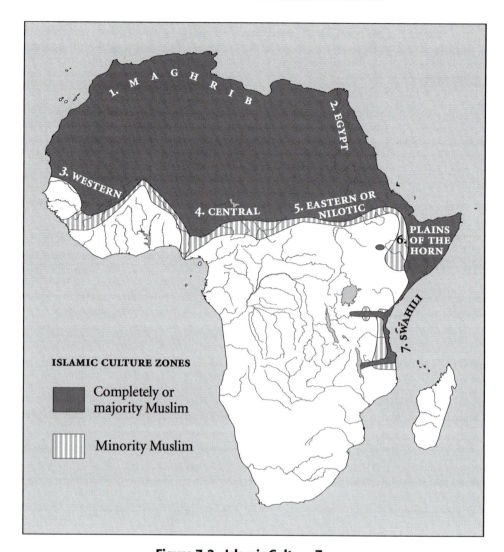

Figure 7-2. Islamic Culture Zones

cultures of the people. What is remarkable is the speed of the early conquests. By A.D. 640, just about ten years after the death of Prophet Mohammed, Islam had begun to make inroads into Egypt and some parts of North Africa.

Shortly after the death of Prophet Mohammed, the Arabs conquered Syria and imposed their authority on it. From Syria they launched an attack on Egypt and subdued it by A.D. 642. In fact, they had little or no problem in conquering Egypt because the Egyptians saw them as liberators who could deliver them from the oppression of their Byzantine overlords. Some Egyptian soldiers even joined the Arabs. Egypt became a permanent base for the Arab army and there was the great desire to expand westwards and conquer the Berbers who were the predominant inhabitants of North Africa.

The Arabs wanted to conquer North Africa for three main reasons. To start with, their success thus far in such places as Syria and Egypt demonstrated and convinced them of the necessity for holy wars in order to convert more people to

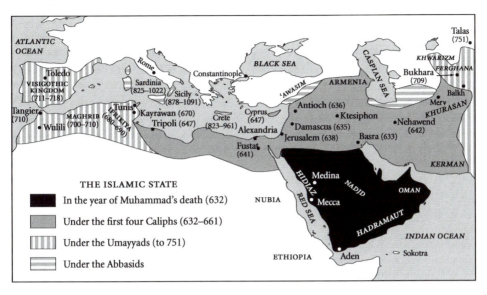

Figure 7-3. Islamic State Expansion

Islam. Second, the Arab soldiers, and a few Egyptians too, had a thirst for more wars because of the likelihood of securing booty. And third, some Arab soldiers thought that the conquest of North Africa would bring them military prestige.

Unlike the ease with which they conquered other places, the Arab army found it difficult to take control of North Africa, and the conquest took many years. The caliphs had to send powerful generals to raid parts of the area. For example, Caliph Muawiya sent the famous Ugba Ibn Nafi to conquer the region. Ibn Nafi commanded the Arab army that occupied Tunisia in A.D. 675 and founded the town of Al-Qayrawan (Kairouan, in present day Tunisia), which became the first center of Arab administration in the region. He was determined to assert Arab rule across North Africa and succeeded in conquering parts of present day Algeria and Morocco, reaching all the way to the Atlantic Ocean by A.D. 682. But his success proved to be only temporary. He was attacked by the Berbers and killed before he could assert full control over the region. It was not until the reign of the determined Caliph Abd al-Malik b. Marwan that Hassan b. an-Numa was able to conquer the Berbers between A.D. 701 and 708.

It was difficult for the Arabs to conquer North Africa in part because of an internal struggle for power and leadership which lasted from 644 to 661 A.D. The dynastic conflict was between the popular Umayyad family in Mecca and Prophet Mohammed's son-in-law, Ali. The Umayyads gained the upper hand and in A.D. 661 transferred the capital of the Islamic empire from Medina to Damascus. The dynastic struggle diverted the energy of the Arabs from their expansionist wars. In addition, the Byzantine army still held a number of strategic places and prevented the Arabs from capturing many of the coastal towns and villages. The most important factor, however, was the resistance of the North African Berbers. A well known Berber chief who resisted the incursion of the Arabs was Kusaila. Kusaila was the one responsible for the death of Ibn Nafi. He forced the Arabs to abandon most of what they had initially conquered, and many of the new converts to Islam reverted to their old religion. It took many decades, but the

Arabs did eventually succeed in subduing the Berbers and began the process of establishing a stronger Islamic presence throughout North Africa.

Many Berbers eventually converted to the new religion. The following factors contributed to the spread of Islam among the Berbers: many Islamic missionaries preached the religion; many Berbers were recruited into the Arab army and there became Muslims; and some Berber soldiers were even interested in fighting to gain war booty. Furthermore, the Berbers had never been strong, serious Christians and their attachment to Latin civilization was very weak. The Christian religion, rather than uniting the Berbers, had created divisions among them which made the spread of Islam much easier.

The Arabs, attempting to win more converts to Islam, imposed special taxation on the Christians with the result that many people were forced to abandon the Christian religion to avoid payment. In addition, only Muslims were allowed to assume leadership positions, and thus many prominent citizens had no alternative but to convert. Though many Berbers of North Africa did convert, they still continued to resist the Arabs, but the second stage in their resistance was based on their newly accepted Islamic principles. This opposition, which combined political with religious issues, is known as the Kharijite resistance. The Berbers used Islam to press for socio-economic changes. They wanted the men of their group to be chosen for high offices such as the caliph, which was a monopoly of the Arabs. The imposition by the Arabs of excessive taxation including the *jizya* (poll tax) and *kharaj* (land tax) also contributed to the wide spread of Kharijism. Wars broke out in Morocco and Tunisia between 739 and 740 A.D. and many Arabs were killed. By A.D. 771, the Kharijites were in full control of the central part of North Africa. Though the Arabs later triumphed in the struggle, the Kharijite movement furthered the spread of the religion to places remote from the Arab-dominated capital cities. The Kharijites seized the opportunity to establish Berber theocratic or Islamic states in places like Sijilmasa, and converted their own people to the new religion.

It was not until the eleventh century A.D., however, that Islam could be said to have been firmly established in North Africa. The region was invaded by thousands of Arabs known as the Banu Hilal and Banu Sulaim between A.D. 1050 and 1056. These two groups of nomads had been looking for places to settle and the power struggle in North Africa provided them with an opportunity to invade the region. The Banu Hilal and Banu Sulaim came to North Africa and inflicted a heavy defeat on the Berbers. "Like an army of grasshoppers, they destroyed everything in their path," concluded one scholar.

This second invasion of North Africa by the Arabs in the eleventh century had major consequences. Further Islamization followed and within a very short time the Christian religion had virtually disappeared from the region. Along with the religion of Islam, Arabic culture was also extended to many parts of North Africa and became more popular as the Arabs penetrated into virtually all the important places in the region. The Arabic language became widespread and it gradually displaced the Berber language. But, the Arabs did more than lend their language and culture to North Africa, they migrated to the region as colonizers and brought their families along. They took over some of the most fertile lands to graze their animals and forced the regrouping and dislocation of many Berbers, who were left with little choice but to move further south into the Sahara. These Berbers in turn carried Islam into their new homes and helped spread Islam to other parts of Africa.

The Spread of Islam in West Africa

Islam began to spread to West Africa from the North by the ninth century, but the new religion penetrated to various places at different times and to varying degrees. The Sudanese states were introduced to Islam before the forest dwellers farther south, and there were usually various stages of conversion. The first to convert were the trading and ruling classes, especially those in urban centers, and only later did the general population begin to follow suit. This section will address the many factors that contributed to the spread of Islam and the processes which facilitated that spread.

In the first place, the spread of the religion to North Africa led to the Islamization of the Berbers who in turn carried Islam to West Africa. Until the eleventh century and after, there are no records to show that the Arabs crossed the Sahara into West Africa with the sole purpose of propagating their religion. Prior to this it was the Berbers who carried Islam southwards. The earliest attempt to introduce Islam into the Sudan was made by a group of nomadic Berbers known as the Sanhaja. The Sanhaja had, by the ninth century A.D., started to use the religion as a means of pursuing their commercial interest in gaining control over the trans-Saharan trade routes and its two important terminals, Zanata in the north and Ghana in the south. The Sanhaja Berbers were involved in serious military struggles with other groups in the Sahara and on the northern fringes of the Sudan. The Berbers won most of these encounters and they captured the famous commercial city of Awdaghost. They imposed their authority over the whole of the western Sahara and pushed many groups towards the Senegal region. Their control over societies in Mauritania was also firm. The Sanhaja Berbers, who had just converted to Islam, tried to set up theocratic states and forced many more people to convert. Those who refused were forced to pay the *jizya* (poll tax). Awdaghost maintained its commercial importance, but it also became a Muslim town from which a Sanhaja chief, Tarsina, went on the pilgrimage to Mecca around 1020 A.D.

Apart from the Sanhaja Berbers, other Islamized pastoral groups inhabiting the Sahara also moved southwards to live among the indigenous groups and often intermarriage occurred. When the nomadic Banu Hilal and Banu Sulaim Arabs invaded North Africa and the northern fringes of the Sahara in the eleventh century, the movement of the Islamized Berbers to the Western Sudan increased. Because of the invasion, many Berbers were forced to move south to escape from the Arabs and became active and effective missionaries bringing many souls into the Islamic fold in the Sudan.

A second important factor in the spread of Islam to West Africa was the trans-Saharan trade, which facilitated the introduction of new ideas. Traders from North Africa were Muslims and they practiced their religion wherever they carried on their trade. Many Arabs and Berbers were interested in West Africa because of the trade in gold. Muslims from various parts of North Africa could be found in many markets in the Sudan. Many of these traders settled in the region and peacefully converted some of their customers. The trans-Saharan trade was the single most important factor in the early stages of Islamic penetration into West Africa and more will be said about it below.

Finally, the jihads contributed in no small measure to the spread of Islam in West Africa, but their greatest impact was not felt until the eighteenth and nineteenth centuries. The Senegambian region was probably the first in West Africa to be exposed to Islam. War Dyabi, a king of Takrur, is believed to be the first ruler in the Western Sudan to have converted to Islam, probably by A.D. 1040. Other evidence shows the existence of Muslims in the Sudan before the Almoravid invasion, but they were very few and most of them were foreigners. The Almoravid movement was the first major jihad in West Africa. The Almoravids, a group of Berbers from North Africa, had a more rigid conception of Islam and saw the need to spread the religion to nonbelievers by conquest, if necessary. During their movement into the Western Sudan, there was an upsurge of conversions among the ruling, trading, and merchant classes, but the impact of the Almoravid movement on these conversions has often been exaggerated. It has been said that the conversion of the Ghana rulers to Islam was a result of an Almoravid conquest in 1076, but as we have seen there was already an Islamic presence before that time. In addition, it now appears that the rulers of ancient Ghana had a more friendly relationship with their northern neighbors and such a conquest never took place. Though the influence of the Almoravid movement in the region as a whole must be acknowledged, it seems probable that their impact on Islam in ancient Ghana was not as substantial as previously believed. The time immediately following the Almoravid movement did, however, mark a period of increased Islamic activity in the region, and by the end of the eleventh century, Islam had gained a foothold in Takrur, Ghana, and Kanem to the east.

However, most of the earliest conversions occurred only within the traders and ruling classes in the major cities; the religious beliefs of the majority of the population in the villages remained unchanged until much later. The nature of these early conversions in urban enclaves where trade and political power were established, emphasizes the importance of the trans-Saharan trade in the spread of Islam.

Islam and the Trans-Saharan Connection

Contact between West Africa and the rest of the world had been going on long before the Christian Era. The great Sahara Desert was not an insuperable barrier to inter-regional contacts; in fact, it served as the link for the flourishing trans-Saharan trade. The introduction of camel transportation intensified the development of the trans-Saharan trade. By the eleventh century, many Islamic merchants from North Africa could be found at Kumbi Saleh, the capital of ancient Ghana. The Saharan trade attained its peak between 1490 and 1590, a period which neatly corresponded with the golden age of the Songhai and Kanem-Borno empires. There were three main routes linking West and North Africa:

(i) The western route: This started in Morocco and passed through Taghaza and Taodeni before terminating in Timbuktu. It also had a branch that ran from Mabruk to Tuat.

(ii) The central route: One branch started in Ghadames and passed through Air to Kano, while the other began in Tripoli and ended in Borno.

(iii) The eastern route: This started in Cyrenaica and passed through Kufra to Wadai and Darfur.

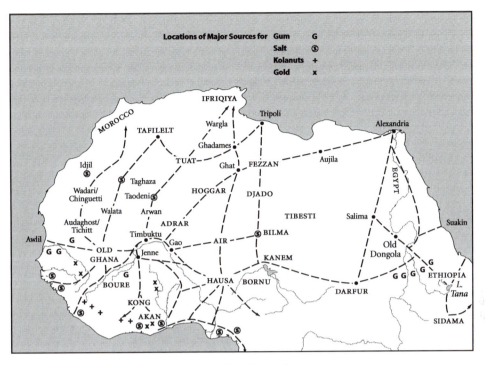

Figure 7-4. Islamic Trade Routes

Many articles of trade were carried along these routes. The Western Sudan exported gold and slaves, kolanuts, ivory, honey, corn, and skins. Slavery was a recognized institution within Islamic beliefs, but some restrictions were applied. Slaves were kindly treated, and allowed to marry, but they could not be Muslims. In exchange for slaves and other goods, the Western Sudan imported brass vessels, cloths, copper, glass beads, horses, armor and firearms, dried figs and dates, leather works, and books. Gold remained for a long time the most desired of all the articles of trade with rich gold mines in the upper Volta, upper Senegal and upper Niger areas. The gold was brought from the forest region of West Africa to the savanna from which it was exported to North Africa and Europe where it found a ready market. Further east, slaves were the most valued commodity. They were procured in Borno and Hausaland and taken to Islamic countries in Southwest Asia and North Africa.

The trade was conducted both by barter and by metal and other currencies. For example, slaves could be exchanged for salt. Other goods were paid for in gold, iron, and cowries. The large amount of capital needed to finance the trade was provided largely by wealthy North African merchants who also organized the caravans. The traders normally took off from the northern terminals of Fez and Marrakech in Morocco, Constantine in Algeria, Tunis in Tunisia, or Tripoli in Libya. The traders would use camels to cross the desert and reach the southern terminals in the cities of Djenne, Timbuktu, Gao, Kano, Katsina, and Kukawa. The trans-Saharan traffic, however, started to decline in importance beginning in the latter part of the sixteenth century, due to the collapse of the Songhai Empire. By the end of the nineteenth century, the trade routes had lost their former glory. The western trade lost its importance first, followed closely by the eastern route; the central route, however, was active until much later when it was affected by the warfare associated with the Sokoto jihad of the early nineteenth century. Still, the central route with its terminus in Kano, was partially protected by the Fulani jihadists and maintained a considerable degree of activity until the advent of European colonialism.

The decline in the trade overall was not without its consequences. It badly affected the means of livelihood of Sahara dwellers like the Tuaregs who were forced to look elsewhere (e.g., on the fringes of the desert) to maintain themselves. Second, it removed the major tie connecting West and North Africa and limited further penetration of North African Islam. Finally, the decline contributed indirectly to the ascendancy of Western culture in the Sudan by redirecting the main routes of trade from the Sahara to the Atlantic coast. The trans-Saharan trade had been important for West Africa and its decline marked a change for both economic and religious reasons.

The Sudanese empires rose to prominence in part because of their participation in this lucrative trade; because of the many advantages derived, and the religious and commercial links with the outside world that it provided. The old empire of Ghana, for example, controlled the areas west of the Middle Niger where gold merchants met to transact their business in the major markets of the kingdom. This enabled the kings of Ghana to gain immense wealth from the trade through various measures. They obtained market dues from the traders that attended their markets. They exercised a monopoly over gold nuggets and only allowed others to deal in gold dust, thus preventing fluctuations in the gold trade. The empire also controlled trade in copper and desert salt. Other Sudanese empires derived immense wealth from the trans-Saharan trade as well by controlling the exportation of articles of trade derived from their territories. Famous West African towns like Djenne, Timbuktu, Gao, Kano, and others owed their fame to their position as middlemen in the trade. These cities started as small settlements, but expanded as commerce grew and traders arrived in large numbers.

Most important in our context, the trans-Saharan trade routes were highways by which the Islamic religion and Arabic culture was carried to West Africa. As the Berbers became Islam's main missionaries and agents of transmission to the Sudan, trading and commercial cities gradually assumed the character of Islamic centers. Unlike North Africa where the soldiers opened the way for religion, farther south it was the traders who became the main carriers. Traders from North Africa carried Islam with them and endeavored to convert other traders and merchants. Islam and commerce were closely linked because the religious ideology also offered ethical and practical precepts that could help control and steer business transactions in a more efficient manner. The second social group to convert to Islam was the ruling class and other members of the royal court. Again, this was sometimes done to advance trading relationships and, hence, bring more wealth into the kingdom. It was done also to facilitate political rule over a larger area; by converting the heads of different African societies to Islam, even if on a superficial basis only, the king was able to establish a common religious bond and, therefore, make subjection less difficult.

The routes also linked the Muslim communities in West Africa with their counterparts in North Africa and Asia. Islamic students and scholars made use of the routes for further studies or teaching. Scholars like Muhammad al-Maghili found their way to West Africa along these routes. Other religious groups such as the *tariqas*, or Islamic brotherhoods, established their settlements along the routes and influenced the religious lives of many people. Invaders also made use of the routes: the Almoravids, for example, were active in and around the old empire of Ghana and attempted not only to control the trade in gold, but to spread the Islamic faith as well.

Without the trade routes, it would have been very difficult for West African pilgrims to visit the holy land. The famous pilgrimages of such notables as Mansa Musa, Askiya Mohammed, and Mai Idris Aloma were made possible by these routes. Finally, the routes also facilitated the spread of Islamic learning and culture and enabled some aspects of the Sharia, the system of Islamic law, to be introduced into West Africa.

Islam and West Africa in the Eighteenth and Nineteenth Centuries

Islam was not always accepted readily by African societies. In the latter part of the fifteenth century, for example, an anti-Muslim offensive arose. The relationship between Sunni Ali and the Muslim-dominated urban centers, such as Timbuktu and Djenne, was filled with tension. This was partly a result of economic and strategic conflicts, but just as important was the fact that Ali's power

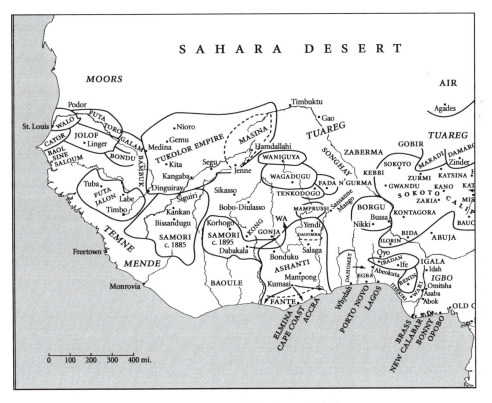

Figure 7-5. States of Sudan and Guinea

was upheld by his subjects' adherence to African traditional religions, which were being challenged by the urban Muslim scholars.

The decline in the trans-Saharan trade routes after the fall of the Songhai Empire did not result in an equivalent decline in the importance of Islam. Until the eighteenth century, Muslims in West Africa constituted a minority in the areas where they lived and worked, but there were many changes in the eighteenth and nineteenth centuries that led to the further proliferation of Islam. These changes were largely a result of a new Islamic spirit and the jihads that arose out of this spirit. Religious proselytisers felt a new "exclusive, legalistic, intolerant, and militant"[2] reaction against previous accommodation and began an era of jihads. The significance of this period is that Islam was brought from the periphery of cultural and social life to its center.

There were two main reasons for the increased presence of Islam in West Africa. The first, a socio- economic factor, involved the Fulani, members of a pastoralist society who were scattered throughout the Sudanic region. Islamic scholars from this group began to organize; they captured power in Futa Djallon and Futo Toro in the eighteenth century, then followed that by asserting their control in the Hausa region during the next century, and forming a military and religious aristocracy in the areas under their control.

The second, a politico-religious factor, was the emergence of religious brotherhoods.[3] Under the leadership of a sheikh, these brotherhoods had existed as hierarchical societies and as secret organizations in Sunni Islam since the twelfth century. There were two prominent brotherhoods in West Africa. The Quadiriyya arrived in the southern Sahara in the early sixteenth century and by the eighteenth century began to flourish more widely because of its mysticism and as a support for the economic and political power of the Fulani. In the latter half of the nineteenth century another brotherhood, the Tijaniyya, spread from Futo Toro and Futa Djallon to Timbuktu and, sometimes forcibly, converted many more people to Islam.

The jihads included those in Futa Djallon in the 1720s and in Futa Toro during the 1760s and 1770s. These jihads, led by Muslim scholars turned militant reformers, helped to establish a strong Islamic presence in communities where it had previously not existed at all or had only superficially been adopted. The most significant of all the jihads of this era was led by Usman dan Fodio and began in 1804 in Hausaland. Since the fifteenth century, religious specialists, known in Hausaland as Toronkawa, had moved to the region from Senegambia. Dan Fodio belonged to this class of specialists. He did not accept those who mixed Islam with their indigenous religions. He saw himself as one who was chosen by God to purify the religion. He relied on mysticism and was a member of the Quadiriyya brotherhood whose members believed that God would make his will known to chosen people through their dreams. It was the mission of the jihadists to establish a stable and just society that was organized and administered in strict accordance with the laws of Islam. Dan Fodio's jihad had major consequences not only for Hausaland but for West Africa as a whole. Politically, it led to the establish-

---

2. J. Spencer Trimingham, "The Expansion of Islam," in James Kritzeck and William H. Lewis, eds., *Islam in Africa* (New York: Van Nostrand-Reinhold, 1969), 24-25.

3. For Islamic brotherhoods, see D.B. Cruise, O'Brien and C. Coulon, eds., *Charisma and Brotherhood in African Islam* (Oxford: Clarendon Press, 1988).

ment of a widespread empire, the Sokoto Caliphate, that replaced what had previously been many smaller states. It also provided the opportunity for the important political offices to be open to Muslim scholars instead of solely to members of the nobility. Finally, the jihad contributed to the downfall of other empires such as Oyo to the south, and to the outbreak of another great jihad led by Al-Hajj Umar Tall in Futa Djallon in 1851.

Islam in Northeast and East Africa

Islam also recorded progress in these parts of the continent. In the case of the Nilotic Sudan and the Horn of Africa, Islam spread from Egypt, principally along the Nile, and also through direct contacts with Arabic Muslims across the Red Sea. In terms of the emphasis on trading relationships, it resembled the spread of the religion in West Africa, but there were also many differences.

Islamic influence from Egypt dated back to the seventh century when Egypt attacked Nubia without success. Nevertheless, Islam penetrated largely through a gradual process of interactions with Arab immigrants and nomads from Egypt. Over time, the region was heavily influenced, to the extent that by the fourteenth century Arab culture and Islam had displaced Christianity in Nubia. In the sixteenth century, Arab teachers went to this region, particularly to the present-day Sudan. Most of the teachers belonged to either the Shadhiliyya or Mirghaniyya *tariqas*, brotherhoods which emphasized proselytisation. So great was the influence of these teachers that in contemporary northern Sudan it might be said that there are closer links with the Arabs than with other Africans. Islam was used later to reform the Sudan during the Mahdist era (the second coming of the prophet to reform the world, 1881-1898) which witnessed the emergence of the Sudanese reformer, Muhammed Ahmed, the mahdi.

In the Horn (Somalia, Eritrea, and Ethiopia), the Qadiriyya, Salihiyya, and Ahmadiyya groups played a dominant role. They came from among the Persian traders and Muslim Arabs who had well-established trading posts on the Indian Ocean and the Red Sea. From the eighth to the tenth century, a number of Muslim settlements were established on the coast. Areas like Zeila and Mogadishu and their immediate neighborhoods became Islamic zones. Islam did not establish a presence far into Ethiopia, however, because of strong resistance from Christians.

In East and Central Africa, Islamic influence was a result of the long history of trade links with Arabia and Egypt. But in this region, the penetration of Islam was very different from that in West Africa. Between the tenth and sixteenth century settlements were established in Kilwa, Mogadishu and Zanzibar which attracted Arab traders who dealt in gold, ivory, timber, iron, copper, slaves, and hides and skins. During this early period, however, the activities of Muslims were restricted to the coast because the hinterland offered only limited economic opportunities for them. Nevertheless, successes were recorded on the off-shore islands of Pemba, Zanzibar, and the Comoros, and in the coastal town of Mombasa. Because of the strong presence of Muslim culture and intermarriage between Arab settlers and African women, an Afro-Arab culture emerged that gave rise to the Swahili language, an admixture of Arabic and Bantu, now widely spoken in East Africa and parts of Central Africa.

Figure 7-6. Seyyid Said

Early in the sixteenth century, the Portuguese made a successful incursion into East Africa. Led by Vasco da Gama in 1502, they succeeded in forcing Kilwa to pay tribute to Portugal. Portugal later extended its influence to areas in the Indian Ocean as well. One impact of this was the ruination of Muslim trading posts and economic stagnation for almost two hundred years. The Arabs, however, later re-established their influence, thanks in part to Portuguese misrule. In the second half of the seventeenth century, Oman invaded Zanzibar, Pate, and various coastal settlements. By the early eighteenth century, Omani influence had been established in a number of coastal towns and islands. Omani hegemony facilitated rapid conversion (or re-conversion) to Islam. The well-known Omani leader, Sultan Seyyid Said (1804-1856), encouraged Arab domination of trade as well as the proselytizing activities of mystics.

Conversions in Central Africa were due to the trade that originated at the coast or in Zanzibar and was carried by Swahili merchants who advanced into the interior in search of ivory and slaves in the nineteenth century. Inland from the coast of East Africa, however, there were only scattered cases of conversion of

Africans to Islam, particularly in Uganda. The British later discouraged Islamic encroachment by traders, Sudanese Mahdists, and Egyptian preachers in an attempt to curtail radical preaching.

The Impact of Islam

There were several reasons why the people of sub-Saharan Africa accepted the new religion of Islam. In the first place, the religion gave some benefits to converts. For example, they could learn how to read and write and become members of the trading community. Many sub-Saharan African rulers used the religion to establish diplomatic links with North Africa, to secure favorable terms of trade, and to win friends. Individual conversion was a way of protecting oneself against being captured and sold into slavery, especially along the trans-Saharan and East African caravan routes. Second, Islam allowed converts to continue with some of their old practices. For example, converts could still marry more than one wife, wear charms, and live with their relatives. Many African customs and institutions adapted themselves to the teachings of Islam, but Islamic institutions also showed adaptability within African social structures, resulting in religious dualism. Third, there was the attraction of something new. Many people converted because their close relations or friends had already done so. Finally, some people were forced to convert because of religious wars or the difficulties of living with Muslim rulers without becoming Muslims. Such difficulties included the imposition of heavy taxes and tributes. The advent and acceptance of Islam had profound consequences, both positive and negative, on African societies. The following discussion will focus on those consequences by looking at changes that were brought about in the religious, cultural, political, economic, and international sectors.

Religious and Cultural Impact

Since the introduction of Islam to Africa, it has had to exist side by side with traditional religions. Rarely did Islam completely usurp indigenous religions or mean the abandonment of non-Islamic customs or rituals. The process of introducing the Muslim social system was a long and slow one. Islam first emerged amongst the traders and the ruling classes, then in other urban classes, and lastly in the larger population. In the long run, however, it had many different effects on the social, cultural, and religious structures of African societies.

In West Africa, Islamic cities such as Timbuktu and Djenne, and later Gao and the Hausa towns of Katsina and Kano emerged and became important trading and religious cities. These commercial and Islamic cities attracted many immigrants. Among them were lawyers, scholars, doctors, and scientists. This was the beginning of the development of a Muslim intellectual elite in West Africa. The children of this group became theologians, lawyers, writers, astronomers, and mathematicians, and a vibrant Islamic-African culture emerged. This is clearly shown by Ahmad Baba, a product of one of the Islamic schools in West Africa, who wrote biographical sketches of many members of the Timbuktu elite in his book, *Nayl al-ibtihaj*. With the growth of urban Islamic culture also came a change in dress, mainly the wearing of white or colored cotton robes and the turban.

But Islamic and Arabic influence was not limited to West Africa alone. Just as Arabic influences led to the development of a new language along the East Coast, so did it influence the social and cultural systems there, especially among the Swahili. African customs prevailed in most cases but they were mingled with Arabic and Islamic features. This can be seen in patterns of dress and in some architectural elements. A Dutch sailor described the island of Kilwa in 1583: "These inhabitants are all dressed in white silk or cotton; their wives wear gold bracelets and precious stones around their necks and arms. They have quantities of silver jewels... their houses are usually built of stone, lime and wood, with pleasant gardens where many kinds of fruit and sweet flowers grow."[4]

Islam was very important in much of Africa by the sixteenth century, especially in the Western Sudan, and was sending missionaries into the forest lands and along the Guinea Coast. But it was still largely a religion of the cities, towns, and economic centers, while outside of these areas it had not taken root. Most inhabitants of the rural areas remained attached to their own religious value systems but, nonetheless, a base was established for Islam.

In the rural areas, Islam gained ground through the activities of certain rulers and through the extension of trade. Askiya Mohammed, with the help of his marabouts, attacked fetishes and attempted to remove "bad" Muslims through various means, including jihads. Traders and merchants also helped to take Islam into the rural areas and further south than it had been before. Over time, Islamic concepts and rituals became more prevalent among the larger population and a sort of religious "dualism" came into play. There was little feeling of incompatibility with African religious life. In some cases, Islamic characteristics that would be a challenge to traditional life and customs were largely neutralized.

While Islam might have been visible in activities such as daily prayers, in other areas it was much less so. For example, the bride-price system remained as the basis for the acceptance of prospective suitors, but the Islamic system of payment to the bride *(sadaq* or *mahr)* might be incorporated into it as well. The idea of marriage as a rite of passage also remained important in most societies, as did the importance of the naming ceremony for newborns; in some cases, the traditional naming ceremony for a newborn was held alongside the Muslim *'aqipa* and a Muslim name was added to the other names of the child.

For many people, conversion to Islam did not entail massive changes in daily religious practice because Islamic practices often existed side by side with traditional religious beliefs. Islam was acceptable to many Africans because it was adaptable to some traditional African beliefs. For example, Islam, like most African religions, believes in the existence of a supreme being, and the Qur'an allows a Muslim man to have up to four wives, easily acceptable in African societies that practiced polygamy. But the acceptance of Islam also meant the introduction of new religious practices that are essential tenets of Islam: fasting, praying five times daily, and going on pilgrimage.

---

4. J.H. Van Linschoten, *Voyages to the East Indies*, 2 vols., vol. 1 (London: Hakluyt Society, 1885), 29-31. Quoted in James Kritzeck and William H. Lewis, eds., *Islam in Africa* (New York: Van Nostrand-Reinhold, 1969), 68.

The Islamization of African societies was a long, slow process. Take the example of the blacksmiths' relationship with the ruling class. Blacksmiths were associated with certain powers and the *marabouts*, bearers of Muslim law, wanted to undermine their influence. As societies became more Islamized the relationship between the rulers and the smiths began to change and the latter lost much of their influence in political matters, though they maintained much of their economic importance. As their religious and social isolation grew over the centuries, a blacksmith caste developed.[5] From this example, we can see that Islamic practices were not imposed directly or instantly, but over a long period of time and helped to change but not eliminate certain aspects of traditional African social systems.

The Introduction of a New Language

Another impact was the introduction and creation of new languages where Islamic and Arab culture made an impact. Arabic was introduced in Islamic areas of Africa because, for Muslims, it was compulsory to memorize passages from the Qur'an. Without the knowledge of Arabic one could not access the holy book.

Swahili, found among the people of the East Coast and Central Africa, also was heavily influenced by contacts with Arabic-speaking Muslims. The spread of Islam along the coast and to nearby islands as early as the seventh and eighth centuries brought Arab merchants, fleeing from religious and dynastic conflicts, there to settle. Through intermarriage and trade, Swahili, an African-Arabic language and culture, developed. Swahili has a mainly Bantu language structure and base but with a large percentage of Arabic words and expressions. In addition, the Arabic alphabet served as the main script until the use of the Roman script became more prevalent in the nineteenth and twentieth centuries.

Educational Impact

In the cities where Islam was widely accepted, Islamic institutions of learning first appeared in Africa. Islam placed great emphasis on the training of clerics, as well as lawyers, doctors, and administrators. Missionaries appeared as early as the tenth century in the city of Gao, and by the eleventh century there were many Muslim missionaries at work throughout the Western Sudan. Formal Islamic schools developed during the fourteenth century in the empire of Mali and in the Songhai cities during the fifteenth century. By the sixteenth century, Timbuktu had some 180 Qur'anic schools and thousands of students from all over the Sudan and sahel regions.[6] Islamic universities taught a wide variety of subjects such as the humanities,

---

5. See Z. Dramani-Issifou, "Islam as a Social System in Africa since the Seventh Century," in M. Elfasi, ed., *Africa from the Seventh to the Eleventh Century*, UNESCO General History of Africa, vol. 3 (London: Heinemann, 1988), 102-103.

6. S.I. Cissoko, "The Songhay from the 12th to the 16th Century," in D.T. Niane, ed., *Africa from the Twelfth to the Sixteenth Century*, UNESCO General History of Africa, vol. 4 (London: Heinemann, 1984), 209.

Figure 7-7. Sankore Mosque, exterior

which included theology *(tawhid)*, traditions *(hadith)*, and jurisprudence *(fikh)*, as well as grammar, rhetoric, logic, astronomy, history, geography, science, and mathematics.[7] West African scholars thus became versed in a wide range of subjects. The mosque of Sankore, part of the university in Timbuktu, became a famous center of learning and produced many great scholars. Two great historians, for example, emerged from it. They were Abderahman al-Sadi, the author of *Tarikh al-Sudan*, and Mahmud Ka'ti, who wrote *Ta'rikh al-fattash*.[8] These two books, as well as numerous accounts by Islamic geographers and other historians, have been important in helping historians to reconstruct the history of the Western Sudan.

The educational system included several stages. The first was the elementary stage, usually taught in Qur'anic schools. Emphasis was placed on reading, writing, and memorizing the Qur'an. Students did not pay heavy tuition because their teachers often combined other duties with teaching to make a living, but parents provided all the materials needed. In the second stage the training became more rigorous and subjects such as Arabic grammar, literature, law, elementary science, and medicine were introduced. In the last stage, the advanced, students could specialize in any branch of knowledge and they might travel far from home to study under specialists. Before the sixteenth century, students had to travel to places like Agades to study advanced subjects, but when many more universities were established during the Songhai empire, many Sudanese went to these institutions in-

7. S.I. Cissoko, "The Songhay from the 12th to the 16th Century," in D.T. Niane, ed., *Africa from the Twelfth to the Sixteenth Century*, 209.

8. See *Ta'rikh al-Sudan*, ed. and French trans. O. Houdas (Paris: Leroux, 1900) and *Ta'rîkh al-fattash*, ed. and French trans. O Houdas and M. Delafosse (Paris: Publications de l'Ecole des Langues Orientales Vivantes, 1913).

stead. Islamic education was limited for many years to the offspring of the elite, but this changed as the religion began to spread to new regions. One of the effects of the reform movement of dan Fodio in the nineteenth century was to spread Arabic literacy to a much wider range of people than before. More people became familiar with the Qur'an and the history of Islam.

Economic and Political Impact

Islam also had an important impact on the economic and political development of Africa. It served as a unifying factor because it linked many peoples into Islamic states and also provided contacts with other Islamic regions. Such associations arose because of the fundamental and idealistic political philosophy in the Muslim world that the whole world is divided into two: *Dar-al- Islam* (home of Islam) and *Dar-al-harb* (home of war). There were diplomatic, political, and commercial relationships among Muslim states. All members of Dar-al-Islam co-operated with one another and had little in common with those in Dar-al-harb. All Muslims are linked together because Islam is not just a religion but a political, economic, and social system. The contacts and relationships that were derived from Islam helped to strengthen the political and commercial links between many states and led to changes in African political systems. The importance of the trans-Saharan trade has been discussed, but it should be reiterated that Islam promoted internal and long-distance trade by providing a common cultural basis and a language of communication. The Dyula and Hausa long-distance traders, for example, used the Arabic language as a means of facilitating trading relationships. Also, because the trade covered vast areas and many different peoples, a common religion provided a familiarity, trust, and understanding that could not have otherwise been attained.

In the political realm, the coming of Islam promoted centralization and large administrative bureaucracies. As a politico-religious system, it provided a commonly accepted basis of authority for African societies. In the Western Sudanese empires, the rulers employed the services of Islamic scholars as secretaries, advisers, jurists, and governors to make administration more efficient. Sudanese rulers, such as Mansa Musa of Mali, Askiya Mohammed of Songhai, and Idris Aloma of Borno, commissioned Islamic scholars to provide them with information on administration and effective ways to organize and govern large territories. At the request of the king of Kano, one such scholar, Muhammad al-Maghili, wrote the treatise, *Obligations of the Princes*, which describes the nature of Islamic government and offers a code of conduct for Muslim rulers.[9] Many of the strict Islamic practices advised by al-Maghili were not put into effect until the jihad of Usman dan Fodio.

In the Islamic administration set up by Usman dan Fodio during the Sokoto Caliphate, the sultan of Sokoto became the leader of all the Muslims in Hausaland. Emirs were in charge of governance at the provincial level, and a chief judge was in charge of administering justice according to Islamic principles. Though dan Fodio was trying to purify the practice and beliefs of Muslims, the system of

9. Muhammad al-Maghili, *The Obligations of Princes: An Essay of Moslem Kingship* trans. T.H. Baldwin (Beirut: Imprimerie Catholique, 1932).

governance retained some indigenous elements as well. The office of the Kofa, for example, retained its responsibility for the collection of taxes. After the jihads in Futa Toro and Futa Djallon an Islamic framework was also established there. The Islamic leaders took control of the land in the name of Islam. As the accepted political and religious leaders, they held the land; but it was their duty to distribute it and assign plots to the people for agriculture. By refusing to distribute the land until tax was paid, the leaders ensured that administration would remain within an Islamic framework.

When Islamic law was first carried into Africa, each society already had its own set of customary laws. Islam was carried into these societies by merchants, clerics, or jihads; often only individual conversions took place, making it impossible to enforce the Sharia over the whole society. At other times, if it was adopted by the ruling class, it might be imposed on an entire society, but it was still difficult to enforce; many Africans who had embraced Islam continued to follow traditional laws in their everyday lives. Often, Islamic law was implemented only in serious cases. For example, under the Sharia the head of the judicial organization was the Muslim judge, but in many Islamized African societies only serious cases reached his court, while traditional institutions continued to deal with most litigation and disputes. The judge, nonetheless, received a salary, had a number of clerics and judges to assist him, and was seen as a very powerful man in society. This is another example of the combination of Islamic customs and practices with indigenous African ones to produce, in this case, dualism within a legal system.

Contact with the Outside World

Africa became part of the "Islamic world." The pilgrimage, one of the five pillars of Islam, helped to spread knowledge of Africa and increase the reputation of African leaders in the outside world, while pilgrims brought new ideas and knowledge back home. People went on pilgrimage for various reasons: religious devotion, imitation of others, curiosity, trade, diplomacy, pleasure, and prestige.

Mansa Musa's pilgrimage to Mecca in 1325 was one of the highest profile pilgrimages and had important consequences for the Western Sudan. Musa carried a great deal of gold to Egypt and Mecca, and created an interest in the land of its origins through his extreme generosity. Because of this pilgrimage, outside influences in architecture became more prominent in the Western Sudan. Musa, impressed by the palaces he saw in places such as Cairo, brought with him on his return a well-known architect who designed the mosques at Gao and Timbuktu.[10]

Negative Results

However, the introduction of Islam had some negative results as well. It challenged the traditional basis of authority and led to the ultimate demise of king-

---

10. D.T. Niane, "Mali and the Second Mandingo Expansion," in D.T. Niane, ed., *Africa from the Twelfth to the Sixteenth Century*, 149.

doms such as ancient Ghana. It also divided African societies into two groups—Muslims and non-Muslims—and introduced a source of conflict. One example was mentioned earlier, that of Sunni Ali (1464-1492), the leader of Songhai, who killed many of the Islamic clerics and scholars of Timbuktu because he saw them as close friends of the Tuaregs. Because of this, he had difficulties with the *ulama*, the Muslim aristocracy, and was seen as someone who was not a "good" Muslim. Though he laid the foundation for his successor to establish a Muslim state, he never gave up his own traditional religious beliefs.

The desire to spread Islam throughout Africa in general, and in West Africa in particular, also resulted in many jihads. Many people, therefore, were displaced while others lost their lives. Such wars led to instability and destruction and the sale of many Africans into the Atlantic and trans-Saharan slave trades. Some lost positions of power and authority which were based on traditional systems. In other cases, non-Muslim rulers were overthrown, their lands were seized and given to others who were Muslims.

Conclusion

Islam first arrived in and spread over Africa partly because of economic factors. In the Mediterranean regions of North Africa and along the Atlantic coast, African societies were incorporated into the Islamic world. The Islamization of North Africa provided the gateway to the expansion of Islam into West Africa and beyond. The trans-Saharan trade network linked the Sahara and the Sudan to the Islamic economic sphere. Islam, as a religion and culture, penetrated into West Africa through these trade routes and was incorporated to different degrees into African ways of life. In East Africa, the role of Islamic traders was similar. International traders initially restricted their activities to the coastal areas, but as Arab interests expanded into the interior, Islam made some inroads, albeit small, into that region.

Although the impact of Islam was substantial because of its contribution to the rise and fall of large states and kingdoms, to trade, urbanization, education, language, and change in African social structures, until the eighteenth century it still remained predominantly a religion of the ruling classes, traders, and other urban dwellers. Its impact on the life and culture of the large majority of Africans was not great until the jihads of the eighteenth and nineteenth centuries.

Review Questions

1. Trace the historical development of the spread of Islam to the different regions of Africa.
2. What was the significance of the trans-Saharan trade in relation to the spread and development of Islam in West Africa?
3. How did the "jihad of the sword" further the development of African Islam, especially in the eighteenth and nineteenth centuries?
4. Discuss the religious and cultural impact of Islam on African societies.

5. How did Islam contribute to the expansion of economic and political systems within African societies?

Additional Reading

Clarke, P.B. *West Africa and Islam: A Study of Religious Development from the 8th to the 20th Centuries.* London: Edward Arnold, 1982.

Esposito, J.L. *Islam: The Straight Path.* New York: Oxford University Press, 1988.

Hiskett, M. *The Course of Islam in Africa.* Edinburgh: Edinburgh University Press, 1994.

Lewis, I.M., ed. *Islam in Tropical Africa.* Oxford: Oxford University Press, 1964.

Sanneh, L. *The Crown and the Turban: Muslims and West African Pluralism.* Boulder, CO: Westview, 1997.

Trimingham, J.S. *The Influence of Islam Upon Africa.* 2nd edition. London: Longman, 1980.

Chapter 8

Christianity

Felix Ekechi

Christianity, like Islam, is a religion alien to Africa. Yet, as will be shown below, Christianity has flourished in parts of Africa, and, for better or worse, has become an integral part of the African religious heritage. It has been a potent force in the transformation of African cultural, social, and political life.

Parenthetically, while Europe, from which Christianity historically penetrated into Africa, is no longer "the heartland of the Church," modern Africa, on the other hand, appears to be the region of an ever-increasing religious/Christian reawakening. Peter Gifford's study, for example, clearly points to the rapidity with which Christianity is currently sweeping over Africa.[1] Others note that whereas every day in the West thousands of people cease to be Christians, the reverse is the case in Africa, Latin America, and parts of Asia.[2]

African Christian Antecedents

Christianity has been around in Africa from antiquity. For example, North Africa and Ethiopia were once the early centers of Christianity. In fact, until the Arab conquest of Egypt and the Maghrib in the seventh century A. D, Christianity predominated in the region, starting in Egypt. Exactly how the Christian religion first came to Egypt we do not know. But from the available literature on the early Church, there were Christians in Egypt by the second century, if not earlier.[3] Equally intriguing is why the Egyptians who had their own religion and worshiped numerous gods, embraced a new God and a new religion. It has been sug-

---

1. Paul Gifford, *Christianity and Politics in Doe's Liberia* (Cambridge: Cambridge University Press, 1993), ch. 4; c.f. Rosalind I.J. Hackett, ed., *New Religious Movements in Nigeria: African Studies Volume 5* (Lewiston, NY: Edwin Mellen Press, 1987).

2. Explanations for the remarkable Christian movement, particularly in contemporary Africa, vary, but they lie outside the purview of this chapter. For discussions on the Christian movements in the non-Western world, see Terence Ranger quoting Paul Gifford, "New Approaches to the History of Mission Christianity," in Toyin Falola, ed., *African Historiography: Essays in Honour of Jacob Ade Ajayi* (London: Longman, 1993), 191; Elizabeth Isichei, *A History of Christianity in Africa: From Antiquity to Present* (Grand Rapids, MI: William B. Berdmans, 1995), 1; and Lamin Sanneh, *West African Christianity: The Religious Impact* (Maryknoll, NY: Orbis Books, 1983), 1.

3. Philip Hughes, *Popular History of the Catholic Church* (New York: Image Books, 1954), 19.

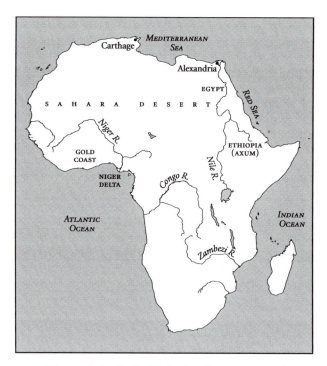

Figure 8-1. Early Christian Centers in Africa

gested that the adoption of the Christian God was possibly due to the decline of the power of ancestral gods. Thus, S. Donadoni suggests that "there was a crisis in the pagan world, whose traditional religion no longer satisfied the spiritual needs of the people."[4]

Whatever their reasons, the Egyptians adopted the Christian religion after the Roman conquest of North Africa in the first century. In time, Egypt and the Maghrib (especially Carthage and Cyrenaica) became centers of the Christian faith. Northern Africa, and especially Egypt, provided some of the foremost Christian intellectuals and apologists. These included Clement (c. 145-210) and Origen (185-253) from Alexandria (Egypt) and Tertullian (c.150-225) and Augustine of Hippo (354-430) who came from Carthage in the Maghrib. Origen, for instance, popularly acclaimed as "the greatest mind" that the Catholic Church has ever known, was one of the greatest defenders of the Church. It was while he was the bishop of Alexandria, in fact, that "philosophical speculations...reached their summit" throughout Christendom.

Monastic life was a major development in the Alexandrian Church. Monasticism emphasized teachings such as prayer, self-denial, poverty, and purity. One of the early Alexandrian monks was Anthony (251-356), who sold all his possessions, "endowed the poor and abandoned society for a life of solitary retreat in an old fort." [5] Alexandria remained for several centuries a seat of Christian con-

---

4. S. Donadoni, "Egypt Under Roman Domination," in G. Mokhtar, ed., *Ancient Civilizations of Africa*, UNESCO General History of Africa, vol. 2 (Paris: UNESO, 1981), 217.

5. Sanneh, *West African Christianity*, 7; Isichei, *History of Christianity*, 28.

troversy, as reflected in the debates on the two natures of Jesus Christ, as God and as man. This controversy, and others, seriously divided the Alexandrian Church, and heralded the birth of the monophysite church in Alexandria. Although the Council of Chalcedon affirmed the duality of Christ as both God and man, the controversy persisted. Thus, the Coptic Christians continued to uphold the doctrine of Christ as man, not God, as the only "acceptable theological truth."[6]

Christianity in Egypt, as elsewhere in tropical Africa, did not go unchallenged. Indeed, "a long-enduring contest took place between Christian teachings and indigenous religious traditions." In other words, although Christian altars eventually "displaced the traditional altars on which sacrifices were made," the old religious habits survived. But the spread of Christianity into the rural areas in Egypt "precipitated a crisis within the ranks of the adherents of local religions."[7] Thus, as elsewhere, Christianity brought with it a fundamental ideological cleavage that lasted for generations. In any case, the conquest of Egypt by the Arabs about 640 A.D. marked a new era in Egyptian religious and political history. Islam replaced Christianity as the dominant religion, both in Egypt and the Maghrib. Thus, with the exception of Ethiopia, the Christianity of North Africa can be said to have "virtually disappeared" by the eleventh century.

Christianity in Ethiopia

Christianity in Ethiopia (Aksum), it is commonly believed, came from Alexandria, some time in the fourth century. Its acceptance as a national religion is generally dated from the conversion of King Ezana (c.333 A. D.), even though there were certainly Christians among the foreign residents in Ethiopia prior to King Ezana's conversion.[8] He was converted by two young Syrian Christian brothers, Frumentius and Aedesius. His reign was marked by the introduction and expansion of the Christian religion, as well as the expansion and unification of the Aksumite Empire. The religious and political expansion "culminated in the formation of the Ethiopian nation, whose endowment was its remarkable individuality in the annals of history."[9] By the sixth century, under King Kaleb, the Christian religion had, in fact, gained a strong foothold in the country, as reflected in the numerous churches that were established almost everywhere. In addition, the sixth century was characterized by the spread of the Christian religion throughout the whole of the Red Sea area.

Christianity in Ethiopia had (and still has) a number of distinctive elements. "In its observances and ritual," writes Lester Brooks, "it follows the Coptic Church...under the Patriarch at Alexandria." Thus Ethiopian bishops, until

---

6. S. Donadoni, "Egypt Under Roman Domination," 220.

7. Sanneh, *West African Christianity*, 6-7.

8. Taddesse Tamrat, *Church and State in Ethiopia, 1270-1527* (Oxford: Clarendon Press, 1972), xxi, 23. Also see Jean Doresse, *Ethiopia*, trans. from French Elsa Coult (New York: Frederick Ungar, 1959), 30.

9. Doresse, *Ethiopia*, 31.

1950, were always Egyptian Copts. "Other special aspects of the Ethiopian Christian observances include vigorous dances and highly sophisticated drumming as central features of the liturgy on some of the high holy days."[10]

Other versions of Christianity spread steadily in Ethiopia in the nineteenth century, largely because of the arrival of European Catholic and Protestant missionaries. The first Protestant mission was established in Tigre about 1830, following the arrival of the Anglican missionary Samuel Gobat (later Anglican Bishop of Jerusalem). Gobat reportedly established friendly relations with Ethiopian Christians, and, at times, engaged them in theological debates. Gobat himself reported that the young aristocrat Habta Sellase, "put several questions to me, on the nature of God—on the manner of the Union of the Divinity with the humanity in the person of Christ, etc." However, these questions seemed too "obscure for me to be able satisfactorily to reply to them."[11]

Like other African monarchs, Ethiopian rulers welcomed Christian missionaries for national or personal reasons. Indeed, as Elizabeth Isichei informs us, Ethiopian princes welcomed missionaries partly "because of a genuine interest in theological dialogue," and partly because "they also hoped for access to western technology, and, especially, firearms." Ethiopian rulers desperately needed firearms not only in their internal struggles, but also to defend their country from the military expeditions of Mohammed Ali, the expansionist ruler of Egypt (1805-1848). According to one missionary, the ruler of Shoa welcomed missionaries precisely because he "wishe[d] to make use of us as physicians, architects, artists, etc."[12] But, as elsewhere, difficulties arose between Ethiopian rulers and the missionaries. Ethiopian-missionary relations were particularly strained during the reign of Emperor Tewodros II (1855-1868). Though a deeply religious man, Emperor Tewodros wanted to use the Ethiopian Church and the western missionaries as vital instruments of his modernizing domestic policy. Clashes with the church and the missionaries ultimately ruptured his relations with both agencies and led to his downfall. The conflicts arose when the emperor expropriated church lands and imprisoned British missionaries. In 1860, Emperor Tewodros attempted to reduce the number of Ethiopian clergy, and, in the process, "give the surplus land to his tax-paying peasants." In doing so, he inevitably alienated the clergy, and thus lost the support of the Church for his modernizing programs. His imprisonment of British missionaries, in 1868, due to the lack of response from the Queen of England to his requests for materials for economic development, provoked a British invasion of Ethiopia. This British military expedition of 1868 resulted in the Tewodros' death.[13]

But despite domestic and foreign problems, the Ethiopian Church continued to grow, as exemplified by the ever-increasing number of churches and clergymen. In sharp contrast to other parts of Africa, the Ethiopian Church developed a solid program for the training of indigenous clergy. Thus, by the 1970s, the Ethiopian

---

10. Lester Brooks, *Great Civilizations of Ancient Africa* (New York: Four Winds Press, 1971), 216-217.

11. Isichei, *History of Christianity*, 211.

12. Ibid., 212.

13. Ibid., 214. For discussions of Emperor Tewodros' policy and his imbroglio with England see Richard Pankhurst, *Economic History of Ethiopia 1800-1935* (Addis Ababa: Haile Selassie I University Press, 1968), 7-16.

Church reportedly had about 250,000 clergymen, (priests, deacons, and cantors), and fifteen thousand monks in eight hundred monasteries.

Christianity in Sub-Saharan Africa

While Christianity penetrated into North and northeastern Africa relatively early, sub-Saharan Africa remained virtually free from Christian influences until the fifteenth century. Indeed, Christianity made very little visible impact until the nineteenth and twentieth centuries. Attempts to convert Africans to Christianity, especially on the West Coast, were made first by the Portuguese, and later by other European missionaries, between the fifteenth and the eighteenth centuries. But hopes of mass conversion were "shattered on the unyielding rock of African resistance."[14] Targeted areas included the Benin Kingdom and Warri (in Nigeria), the Gold Coast (Ghana), Kongo, and the Zambezi valley. With the possible exception of Kongo, where Christianity became the national religion under King Afonso I (1506-1545), the evangelization schemes failed, precisely because the Africans saw little value in the new religion. Thus, in places like modern Ghana, where, in the eighteenth century, Protestant missions labored for decades, not much was achieved. Frustrated with his unproductive work there, the missionary Philip Quaque (Kweku), a Fante, exclaimed, "All my hopes, I am afraid, are in vain." And he later added, "this unsuccessful mission...at present on the face of things bears but an indifferent aspect."[15] Early missionary activity in Africa yielded very little result, partly because traditional African religions "exerted a powerful counter pressure against [missionary propaganda]," and partly, because of European blunders. The missionaries' expectations that the "native religious life" of the Africans would soon be in their hands were unrealistic.[16]

Hence, it was not until the nineteenth century that the Christian missionaries found "open doors" in sub-Saharan Africa. The nineteenth century was, of course, a revolutionary period, an era of dramatic and visible change throughout the African continent. First and foremost, nineteenth-century missionary enterprise in Africa accompanied the abolition of the Atlantic slave trade and European political and commercial expansion. Thus the missionary movement of the period must be seen in the context of the economic and political changes in Europe. It is inextricably linked to the economic and political changes in Europe itself. Briefly, the European quests for raw materials (instead of slaves) and colonies provided the impulse for missionary activity.

The Christian missionaries themselves saw the introduction of Christianity into Africa as essentially an altruistic and humanitarian venture. Hence missionary work, as they saw it, was a clear manifestation of European humanistic concern for "the cruel wrongs which the slave trade had inflicted upon [the African

---

14. Sanneh, *West African Christianity*, 52

15. Quoted in Philip D. Curtin, ed., *Africa Remembered* (Madison: University of Wisconsin Press, 1968), 109. For a discussion of Portuguese early mission work in West Africa see Sanneh, *West African Christianity*, chs. 2 and 3; Alan Ryder, *Benin and the Europeans 1485-1897* (London: Humanities Press, 1969), ch. 4.

16. Sanneh, *West African Christianity*, 52.

people]." [17] In this sense, the Christian evangelization of Africa was perceived as a "civilizing mission." Put differently, the missionaries interpreted the planting of Christianity in Africa as essentially the liberation of Africa from the "bondage" of sin, fear, and superstition. Said the Rev. A. L. Kitching of the Church Missionary Society (CMS):

> In the evangelization of the animist we find frequent illustrations of the words of our Lord: "Ye shall know the truth, and the truth shall make you free." The African has always been in bondage to the fear of spirits, and to the pretensions of practitioners in the supernatural. Christianity makes him a free man.[18]

Pruned of its humanitarian pretensions, however, missionary enterprise in Africa must be seen for what it actually is: a classic example of European cultural and political imperialism. For, as T. O. Beidelman has aptly pointed out, the *raison d'etre* of mission work is "the undermining of a traditional way of life." In this, continued Biedelman,

> the missionary represents the most extreme, thoroughgoing, and self-conscious protagonist of cultural innovation and change.... The missionary, at least in the past, was unashamedly ethnocentric, though he saw the struggle to impose his values as loving and altruistic. He was cruel to be kind. His ethnocentrism and proselytization represent a blend of exclusion and inclusion, domination and brotherhood, and exploitation and sacrifice.[19]

Similarly, Mortimer Arias, a Methodist Bishop in Bolivia, describes the work of Western missionaries as being essentially "a...colonizing evangelization...more successful in transplanting culture than in transplanting the Gospel. *Europeanization* (emphasis added) was the context and intent of Western evangelization."[20] Indeed, the missionaries' claims of altruism and humanitarianism have been widely challenged. An African critic, Godfrey Z. Kapenzi, asserts that "the missionary always gave the colonial set-up an aura of humanitarianism [and] anointed the European as the superior custodian of values, morals and ethics and as the soul measurer of culture, civilization and history." In doing so, Kapenzi argues, the missionary sought to make imperialism "look like humanitarian responsibilities."[21]

---

17. F.K. Ekechi, *Missionary Enterprise and Rivalry in Igboland, 1857-1914* (London: Frank Cass, 1972), 1.

18. "Christianity and Native Government of Uganda," *The Church Missionary Review*, 72 (1921): 306.

19. T.O. Beidelman, *Colonial Evangelism: A Socio-Historical Study of an East African Mission at the Grassroots* (Bloomington: Indiana University Press, 1982), 212.

20. Quoted in E.M. Uka, *Missionaries Go Home? A Sociological Interpretation of an African Response to Christian Missions. A Study in Sociology of Knowledge* (New York: Peter Lang, 1989), 191.

21. Godfrey Z. Kapenzi, *The Clash of Cultures: Christian Missionaries and the Shona of Rhodesia* (Washington DC: University Press of America, 1979), 2-3.

Early African Responses to Missionary Propaganda

The pioneer Christian missionaries were not only culturally arrogant, they also had an abounding optimism. For example, they seemed to believe that Africans would readily embrace the Christian religion, essentially because they had no knowledge of God. Africa, therefore, appeared to the missionaries and to their supporters at home as a virgin land to be conquered and one where Christianity would readily be accepted. This assumption, of course, proved to be false. The fact of the matter is that Africans had their own religions, and believed in the existence of a Supreme Being, known by various names in different places. Asked by a pioneer missionary who they worshiped, the Igbo replied unequivocally, "Chukwu," or "Chineke," meaning the Almighty or the Creator. Not surprisingly, the Igbo initially responded to missionary proselytization with either suspicion or indifference.[22] In fact, almost everywhere, the Christian missionaries lamented their inability to win converts, precisely because of the influence of a deeply entrenched traditional African religion, which was integral to their social and political structure. "You preach of the blessedness of the Christian [life], or the regenerating power of Christianity," lamented John C. Taylor, the pioneer missionary among the Igbo, but "none are elated."[23] In East Africa, the pioneer missionary Johann Ludwig Krapf expressed despair: "I often prayed fervently for the preservation of my life, at least until one soul should be saved."[24] Clearly, resistance to Christianity was "an affirmation of the legitimacy of traditional religion, necessary for the continuation of custom."[25]

Missionaries' problems with conversions stemmed from a variety of factors, among them misguided mission strategy. For example, the early missionaries directed their missionary activities towards the conversion of African rulers and notables—kings, chiefs, and nobility. The reasoning behind this approach was that if the leaders were converted, then their subjects would naturally follow. But this never materialized. Reasons for the failure abound, but there is no question that the African perception of their traditional religion as being "good enough for them," was an important factor. In short, African leaders expressed no hunger for the Christian religion, even though they welcomed missionaries. Said one missionary of Nigerian leaders' primary interests, "they want us without our religion.... They want us [for] trade and [to] be well supplied with guns and powder for sale or war as may be required."[26] In essence, African rulers welcomed missionaries for the material benefits that derived from their presence, such as the building of schools, hospitals, maternity clinics, and so on.

---

22. Ekechi, *Missionary Enterprise*, 10-14; James F. Schon and Samuel Crowther, *Journals of the Expedition Up the Niger in 1841* (London: Frank Cass, 1970), 33.

23. The Church Missionary Society Archives, London, CA3/037, John C. Taylor's Journal, entry for June 25, 1863.

24. Isichei, *History of Christianity*, 128. Also see Robert Rotbert, *Christian Missions and the Creation of Northern Rhodesia, 1820-1924* (Princeton, NJ: Princeton University Press, 1965).

25. Sanneh, *West African Christianity*.

26. J.A. Ajayi, *Christian Missions in Nigeria* (Evanston: Northeastern University Press, 1965), 100. See ch. 4.

In fact, Africans viewed their ancestral religion as being not only adequate for their needs, but also even more "nobler" than Christianity, as the Rev. Solomon Perry of the CMS found out in his encounter with the Nri priests in Nigeria. Nri, an ancient center of civilization, is at times described as the spiritual capital of Igboland. Its priests were perhaps the most famous and conservative in the Igbo country. When in 1878, Perry confronted them, and, in the missionary tradition, excoriated traditional African religion, the priests quickly called his bluff. "I . . . informed them," said Perry, "[that I came] to preach the Gospel of the Kingdom of God, [and] to tell them of the One only true God, to explain the folly and sinfulness of idolatry." But he adds, "As regards my talk about their idols, they in turn tried to argue me out of my belief in Christianity, pointing out how theirs was the nobler religion. . . ." Indeed, "My talk with them was long, and I tried to impress on them the foolishness and sinfulness of their idolatry . . . [but] a number of them [strongly] objected."[27]

Several other factors militated against the conversion of African notables, chief among them being polygamy. To the African, having many wives and many children was an index of social standing. A polygamous household was a symbol of affluence. Thus among the Igbo, a man with many wives and children is regarded as an *Ogaranya*, a wealthy and powerful man. Missionary condemnation of polygamy, as well as criticisms of traditional African religion, social customs, and institutions, obviously alienated polygamists from Christianism. To the Africans, the missionary's view of monogamy as the only Christian marriage seemed odd and quite contrary to their cultural values. Polygamists once told the Anglican bishop, Samuel Crowther, that monogamy "is not God's Law [made] for man's benefit."[28] Besides, to ask a polygamist to drive away all his wives except one, as the condition for conversion, was tantamount to social and political suicide.

Unable, therefore, to convert African leaders of thought, and especially polygamists (though some were eventually converted), the missionaries turned their attention elsewhere — to the younger generation and the lower classes. Hence it was that most of the early converts to Christianity were young boys and girls, as well as the so-called *nde efulefu*, or outcasts (including slaves). Thus, the early church congregations were not from the mainstream of the society. In some places, such as Asaba, Nigeria, the association of missions with outcasts (slaves) significantly hampered the growth of the church. The freeborn stayed away from both church and school, essentially because of the presence of slaves, whom they despised.

At any event, neither the children nor the slaves knew anything about Christianity; they often congregated at the mission out of curiosity, and because of the gifts of food, toys, and clothes they received from the missionaries. Of the attitude of the children towards the new religion, one pioneer CMS missionary reported in 1858, "They laughed when we knelt down to pray."[29] Most of the early converts embraced the new religion simply because of the material benefits they derived from their association with the missionaries. They were called "rice Christians."

27. CMS: CA3/030-36, Solomon Perry's Letter Journals, entry for November 4, 1878.

28. Felix K. Ekechi, *Tradition and Transformation in Eastern Nigeria: A Sociopolitical History of Owerri and Its Hinterland, 1902-1947* (Kent, OH.: Kent State University Press, 1989), 63.

29. CMS: CA3/037, Taylor to Venn, 26 August, 1859. See also Ekechi, *Missionary Enterprise*, 15.

There was, also, the bandwagon effect: "I want to become a Christian," young boys often told the missionaries, "because everybody is becoming a Christian." Thus, when one's peers embraced the new religion, the tendency was to follow. Whatever attracted the early Christians, they nevertheless faced a variety of problems, including persecution and ostracism. This was the reason for the establishment of the so-called Christian villages, where the early converts, as well as redeemed slaves, lived. One such village was established in Aguleri, Nigeria, by Chief Idigo, in 1891. Chief Idigo was reportedly the first Igbo chief to be converted to Christianity. Being poor, the villages depended almost entirely on the charity of the missions. In return for the economic and social security they received from the missions, the residents virtually surrendered all "control over every detail of their lives, including their marriages."[30] With particular reference to marriages in the Christian villages, a Roman Catholic missionary in Nigeria wrote:

> The families are well constituted, and what we rarely find elsewhere, are irrevocably constituted. Not one divorce has yet been heard of. What a consolation for me, who have so much cried and lamented in reviews and newspapers upon the instability of our marriages in Gabon and the Congo. I believe with many others that the future success of a Mission depends on Christian marriages. We have them...at Onitsha and especially at Aguleri.[31]

It was against this background that the Catholic missionaries encouraged the continuation of Christian villages, regardless of the financial burden these entailed.

There were other considerations, especially the attitude of the missionaries towards African culture and society. The establishment of Christian villages "often reflected the [missionaries'] belief that Africans could not practice a Christian life in a traditional environment." It was therefore necessary, they contended, "to make a clean break." Thus, as was the case even in the twentieth century, "mission boarding schools embodied something of the same attitude. It was rooted in an understanding of Africa as...an 'unfathomable abyss of corruption and degradation.'"[32]

As already noted, conversions to Christianity came very slowly. African parents were initially reluctant to send their children to church or to school, as in East Africa, partly for fear that the children would be stolen and sold into slavery. Others were reluctant to welcome missionaries because of local suspicion of missionaries' motives. In fact, the missionaries were at times perceived as harbingers of war. Said an Igbo chief to a Protestant missionary, who made overtures to him: "But people...say that if a man receives Oibos [whites] in his country they will soon bring war upon him; this makes me somewhat afraid of you."[33] Similarly, the Mijikenda elders of the Kikuyu coast feared that, if they allowed their children to embrace Christianity, the ancestors would not only become angry, but they also would "withhold the rain, and send disease." Furthermore, "If we give you our children to teach, your words will steal their hearts; they will grow up cowards, and refuse to fight for us when we are old." And for Rwandan elders, the concern was that "there would be no one left to conserve our customs and our

30. Isichei, *History of Christianity*, 135.
31. Ekechi, *Missionary Enterprise*, 90.
32. Isichei, *History of Christianity*, 135.
33. *Niger & Yoruba Notes* (1894-1896), 31.

cult to the ancestors."[34] Thus, resistance to missionary work was almost universal. In some places, such resistance involved military action against the missions and their political allies. The Ekumeku movements against the Roman Catholic Society of African Missions and the Royal Niger Company in southern Nigeria are classic examples. Whatever form the resistance took, the fact of the matter is that Africans sought to preserve their ancestral religions and traditional ways of life.

Christian Conversions and Sociocultural Change

In time, of course, conversions were made, and, as would be expected, the missionaries were delighted. Thus, from almost every mission field, especially from about the 1890s, missionary reports were replete with optimistic predictions of "conquest," or expressions like an "open door," "an avalanche," "overflowing churches," or "extraordinary progress." Writing with understandable excitement about the new developments in the Nigerian Niger Mission, Miss A. L. Wilson of the CMS noted, "Doors stand wide open on every side."[35] Judging from missionary reports, therefore, one could easily conclude that a "Christian fever" had swept all across Africa. This report, by a CMS missionary in West Africa, is typical:

> There has been a remarkable increase in the attendance of Divine Services in most of our churches lately. Our Sunday *morning* averages...up to 22,000. I cannot account for this sudden advance....Whatever may be the cause or causes our churches are filled to overflowing, and we pray for grace to buy up the opportunity thus afforded.[36]

Missionaries, of course, had the tendency to exaggerate; hence mission statistics are often misleading. Nevertheless, there were, in fact, noticeable changes in African attitudes towards missionary work. It is against this background that one can actually explain the persistent demand for reinforcements from virtually all mission areas. Now that the people "welcome us," apparently showing their receptivity to the Gospel message, noted one Protestant missionary in West Africa, reinforcements ought, therefore, to follow as a matter of course. Said Archdeacon Dennis, "*We must have* reinforcements, if the ground already possessed is to be held; *we must have reinforcements* if any advance is to be made." In East Africa, another missionary put it in more dramatic terms, reminding his homefolks that:

> It should never be forgotten that war is a costly employment, and if the Church of Christ means to win the world for Him, she will have to pay a heavy price in lives and treasure to do it....The people of God must realize that they are called upon for sacrifice and strenuous effort in their

---

34. Isichei, *History of Christianity*, 134. Ian Linden, *Church and Revolution in Rwanda* (Manchester: Manchester University Press, 1977), 172.

35. *The Church Missionary Review*, 5 (1905): 277.

36. CMS: ACC/89/F1, Archdeacon Dennis' Letter Journal, entry for March 5, 1916. Hereafter Dennis' "Letter Journal."

greater warfare with the powers of darkness. The earth is the Lord's if we dare to establish His claim to Suzerainty. It will cost us much but let us not begrudge the cost for so great and glorious an end.[37]

Politics, Education, Medicine, and Conversion

Africans actually embraced Christianity in large numbers during the colonial era. Why did this happen? Explanations for the so-called Christian revolution in Africa are complex and multiple. For convenience, only a few examples will be cited here to illustrate the dynamics of socio-religious change. First, it would indeed appear that the violence of colonial conquest played a critical role in the spread of Christianity. In an attempt to escape the disastrous colonial wars, and the colonial exploitation that followed, many African communities, which had earlier opposed missionary penetration, actually began to invite missionaries to open churches and schools. In addition, the preferential treatment given to Christians, especially with regard to forced labor, and exactions by colonial chiefs, helped to drive people towards the missionary orbit. "[Our neophytes]," reported an Anglican missionary in Nigeria, "know very little about Christianity, and seem to think that [coming to church] would mean immunity from Government Expedition." Furthermore, "There are plenty of palavers between certain sections in each town and their head chief, and one cannot help thinking that part of the desire for teachers from the different towns is due to a desire for freedom from chiefs, rather than from a sense of the burden of sin."[38]

Clearly, some communities believed that association with the missionaries via the establishment of churches and schools was, indeed, a good policy. Again, consider this report from a Protestant missionary:

> The people at Ogwa [in present Imo State of Nigeria] are very persistent. They have been here four times...to take me and my things....I wonder why they want us to come so much. It is a bit puzzling to me and I wonder if it is because they have palavers with other villages and I am a sort of strength to them, making the other villages afraid to quarrel too much with them. I believe there is something of that in it.[39]

Western education was particularly instrumental in the spread of Christianity. This was largely because it provided a new opportunity for socioeconomic advancement, either for individuals or for the community. Desirous of a better life for their children, or, for that matter, for their communities, even arch-defenders of traditional African religion welcomed missionaries who came to open schools. The attitude of one Osu, "a medicine man" from the Western Igbo town of Issele

---

37. CMS: G3/A30, Dennis to Baylis, March 11, 1898; *The Church Missionary Intelligencer* (1899), 1001.

38. Quoted in Ekechi, *Missionary Enterprise*, 148, 217.

39. CMS: ACC/4/F2, vol. 5 (1907), Frances Hensley's Letter Journal, entry for June 13, 1907.

Ukwu, is a case in point. According to the Anglican missionary, Frances Hensley, Osu was a medicine man of great repute, and one of the "bitterest opponents of the Gospel." But "strangely enough," she writes, "this very man has been *the* one to bring the Gospel to his town (by asking evangelist Abraham to stay). It is strange and hard to understand that the man more than any other to whom our Message must bring loss of faith of people should be the very one to bring it there."[40] Unaware, of course, of the fact that the school, that is, education, was the most effective instrument of religious indoctrination, and hence the source of cultural alienation, African rulers and others welcomed missionary schools. The missions, eager to ensure "the collapse of paganism," and the demise of traditional African culture, naturally accepted the invitations wholeheartedly. Here is the explanation:

> *Christian* schools are of unquestionable importance in missionary labours....They afford the best opportunities of communicating divine truths to those whose minds are freest from hostile prejudices, and most likely to receive them with docility....Their consciences are more easily awakened to a sense of sin...than those of adults, and their hearts more easily touched with good affections. How important for a Christian to win...the young hearts of children around him, who in a few years more will be the men and women, the fathers and mothers of the country![41]

Education was the prime agent of denationalization, cultural destruction, and social disintegration. It was missionary education, for instance, that transformed Africans into "Black Europeans"; and it was missionary education which sowed the seeds of social and political dissension between the young and the old, a cleavage that continues to haunt Africa to the present day. More specifically, it was Western education, which ultimately led to the overthrow of the power of the old oligarchy, the elders, by the emergent educated elite. Yet, education opened up new vistas of opportunity in the colonial society. It was, among other things, the passport to economic, social, and political mobility. Hence, it was the utilitarian value of education, rather than the Christian religion *per se*, that significantly influenced African attitudes towards missionary work. That Christianity and Western education are inextricably linked can certainly be discerned from the poignant words of a Roman Catholic missionary: "without schools, there would be no church."[42] In short, education was the handmaid of Christian conversion.

There were, of course, other factors that significantly promoted the acceptance of Christianity. These include medical missionary work, which acted as a powerful bait. From all accounts, medical work served as a diplomatic weapon, insofar as it helped to break down local prejudice against missionary propaganda. "It is a means to an end," conceded a missionary, because it helped to win the affection and confidence of the people perhaps far more than any other agency. In the Igbo town of Awka, as Rev. G. T. Basden informs us, CMS medical aid provided to the wounded during a civil disturbance "won [us] the confidence of our neighbours, and [so we] were able to establish ourselves in a place where, up to

---

40. CMS: ACC/4/F1-2, Frances Hensley's Letter Journal, entry for January 9, 1902.
41. Rev. Hope Masterton Waddell, *Twenty-Nine Years in the West Indies and Central Africa, 1829-1858* (London: Frank Cass & Co., 1970), 540.
42. Ekechi, *Missionary Enterprise*, 176

that date, our tenure had been more precarious than we comprehended at the time. From being merely tolerated we were accepted as friends, and the relationship thus established has remained a cordial one ever since."[43]

Illustrations of how western medicine won converts abound. Its efficacy in promoting missionary evangelism induced the various missions, Protestant and Roman Catholic alike, to seriously embark upon medical work, both in Africa and elsewhere in the Third World. But it should be emphasized that this preoccupation with medical work was almost an afterthought. Most missionary agencies initially rejected the idea of medical missionary work, believing that faith and prayer were sufficient to ensure native health.[44] Thus, the missionaries "sought primarily to propagate the Gospel, without a commitment or obligation to systematically attend to the health needs of their African hosts." But once it became clear that medical work could win converts, virtually all missions embraced it. Hence the growth of hospitals, dispensaries, maternity centers, and other medical facilities.

Quite typically, of course, the missionaries viewed medical work as a humanitarian act, arguing that the provision of medical services derived purely from altruistic motives. Thus, the alleviation of human suffering is often given as the explanation for the adoption of medical work. Indeed, insists the Protestant Bishop Hoare, even "if we saw no converts brought out by medical missions, it would still be the bounden duty of Christian people to do what they can with this western science which God has given, to alleviate misery, wretchedness, pain and disease wherever it may be found."[45]

In addition to providing relief of sickness and misery, and advancing Christian evangelism, missionary medicine also enabled the missionaries to establish cordial relations with African rulers and notables. For example, it was missionary medical care, given to the king of Onitsha, in Nigeria, that enabled CMS missionaries to forge friendly relations with him. In 1864, the king, Obi Akenzua, was reported to have been very sick, and so solicited medical aid from the missionaries to alleviate his rheumatic pains. Considering this a special honor, since it was "a rare thing to [even] hear that the king is ill," the missionaries provided him some medication, which reportedly enabled him to get better. Not only did the king express gratitude for the medical help, but henceforth, we are told, the missionaries enjoyed the king's favor and patronage. Specifically, Obi Akenzua is said to have become more favorably disposed towards the missionaries and their work, as reflected in his intervention on their behalf whenever troubles arose between them and the local people. His warnings to the chiefs and others regarding the missionaries and their converts illustrate the point. "Not one of you my subjects, nor my underchiefs should molest the *Oibos* for they are helping me to make my country good; neither must [you] on no account molest the Christians."[46]

---

43. G.T. Basden, *Among the Ibos of Nigeria* (London: Frank Cass & Co., 1966), 204. Jan Harm Boer, *Missionary Messengers of Liberation in a Colonial Context: A Case Study of the Sudan United Mission* (Amsterdam: Rodopi, 1979), 455; see Felix K. Ekechi, "The Medical Factor in Christian Conversion in Africa: Observations from Southeastern Nigeria," in *Missiology. An International Review*, 21, 5 (July 1993): 291.

44. Charles M. Good, "Pioneer Medical Missions in Colonial Africa," *Social Science and Medicine*, 32, 1 (1991): 1.

45. *The Church Missionary Review*, 72 (1921): 27.

46. CMS: CA3/037, Taylor's Journal, entry for August 10, 1864, also entry for January 14, 1863.

Interestingly, friendship played a significant role in the conversion of African notables. The case of Chief Ubochi from Issele Ukwu, Nigeria, is an illustration of this. His friendship with the missionaries of the Society of African Missions (SMA) resulted in his conversion to Roman Catholicism in 1899. Ubochi (spelled "Oboutche" in mission records), was a prominent chief, a *dibia*, and a polygamist. Like most *dibias*, he viewed the missionaries as nuisances in the land. But, as we learn from the Roman Catholic missionary Superior, "a fortuitous circumstance" brought him and the SMA missionaries together. Briefly, Chief Ubochi's nephew was reportedly involved in a fight at school, which resulted in his breaking the lip of his antagonist. Since the shedding of blood was "a very serious matter" in the town, the boy's father was asked to pay a fine of five goats. It was at this juncture that Chief Ubochi's "Christian friends" reportedly advised him to seek the assistance of the SMA missionaries, "who might help to arrange things" on his behalf. The missionaries' mediation led to the "annulment of the penalty," and the beginning of cordial relations between Chief Ubochi and themselves. Capitalizing on their successful intervention, the missionaries visited the chief regularly, and seized the opportunity to instruct Ubochi in the fundamentals of the Catholic religion. Their teaching about hell, we are told, so captivated Ubochi's imagination that he opted for baptism. "You have told us," he reportedly said, "that the sinner who has not been baptized goes to hell.... I don't want to go to hell; I want baptism. Please give it to me." Accordingly, Chief Ubochi was baptized, and given the name Alexander, after he had agreed to retain only one of his five wives.[47] Whether his conversion actually stemmed from fear of eternal damnation is hard to determine, but whatever the case might have been, the SMA missionaries were understandably overwhelmed with joy. In their view, the chief's conversion was "a miracle of grace." Being the first chief to become a Christian at Issele Ukwu, Alexander, in the words of the Father Superior, thus became "a powerful right arm of the Mission." In other words, he would be the inspiration for others. On this, Alexander did not disappoint them. In fact, his daily attendance at Mass made people view him as an exemplary Christian. Indeed, many thereafter followed in his footsteps. Alexander had become a real catalyst. It is no wonder that the missionaries fondly described him as the "right arm of the Mission" and "the pillar of Issele Church."

However, Alexander paid a high price for his conversion. Having obviously abandoned his ancestral religion and traditional responsibilities, he found that his erstwhile associates could hardly tolerate his apparent betrayal. Here is how the Catholic Superior explained Alexander's "many tribulations":

> Following his baptism...his trials began. When he reached home he found the house empty save for his wife (now his only wife). Brothers, sisters, uncles, and his pagan friends, all had turned their backs on him. He could not expect pardon for his abandonment of local traditions. The fetishists (dibias), likewise, pursued him slyly and secretively with their hatred. He was obliged from the start to relinquish all his titles and privileges.... The village sought to dispossess him. The hours of religious services were especially chosen to despoil him of his belongings. Now a fowl, which he lost when he returned from Mass; then a goat; at other times the fruits and vegetables in his garden were stolen.... None of his

---

47. *L'Echo des Missions Africaines* (January-February 1905), 21-22.

fowls and goats were left to him after his baptism. The tribulations of Job were upon him.[48]

The African Factor in Christian Evangelization

In discussing the planting of Christianity in Africa, it would be a serious mistake to ignore the critical role that Africans, both clergy and lay people, played. In fact, African catechists, teachers, interpreters, and others were, in the words of European missionaries, "the cornerstone of the African church." In short, the Africans were, for all practical purposes, the real missionaries to their people. Certainly, without them, there would be no church, as we know it today. They were essentially responsible for the dissemination of the Christian message; and they did everything almost "entirely for God." Most of these Africans were poorly paid, and were unable to even buy a bicycle until after many years of service. Thus, despite the fact that some missionaries were unashamedly racist, many of them nonetheless, held the African catechists, teachers, and pastors in very high esteem. "The African clergy have shown considerable initiative and capacity as superintendents of large districts, and they have been able in a number of instances to discover and develop the capacities of their fellow workers in a way that few Europeans could do."[49]

The Africans saw themselves as the logical messengers of the Gospel. "If Ethiopia must hear the untold mysteries," they asked, "by whom must they hear them?" Surely, they answered, it must come from their own "sons and daughters." Not only did the Africans view the "theology of mission" as too Eurocentric, but they also deplored the "colonizing mentality" and the airs of superiority of Euro-American missionaries. "There is something wrong," Africans say, "when spreading the gospel leaves one community feeling culturally superior, while the other feels inferior!"[50]

It is no wonder, therefore, that Africans now talk about the liberation of the African, as well as the African church, from missionary "humiliation and domination." Indeed, nationalistic African churchmen now demand the redefinition of the theology of mission, insisting that it must no longer be arrogant, and should, for all practical purposes, be home-grown. In specific terms, Africans contend that, as missionaries to themselves, they should define the parameters of Christian teaching and worship.

European racism and cultural arrogance not only poisoned Afro-European relations, but also led to the "Ethiopian" movements, or the establishment of African independent churches. Euro-American domination of churches in Africa, as well as in the Third World in general, prompted the call for a missionary moratorium, implying that Euro-American missionaries must go home. After all, the "idea of invading and conquering other cultures is alien in God's mission."[51] Third World

---

48. Ibid.,24-25.

49. *The Church Missionary Review* (1927), 37.

50. Gwinyai Henry Muzorewa, *An African Theology of Mission: Studies in History of Missions, Volume 5* (Lewiston, NY: The Edwin Mellen Press, 1990), iv, 4.

51. Ibid., 24

peoples believe that the problem of missionary domination has made a moratorium imperative. As they say, "the present structure of modern missions is dead." Perhaps the best thing to do, they contend, is "to eulogize it and bury it, no matter how painful and expensive it is to bury the dead."[52] Hence, liberation has become the watchword of African and other Third World Christian leaders. The declaration of the All African Conference in Lusaka, Zambia, in 1974, is illuminating:

> The African Church, as a vital part of the African Society, is called to the struggle of liberating the African people. The African Church, as part of the world community, must also share in the redeeming work of Christ in our world. But our contribution must be African.... Thus, as a matter of policy,... our option has to be A MORATORIUM on the receiving of money and personnel [from outside].[53]

Impact of Christianity on African Culture

Criticisms of missionary enterprise in Africa abound. But these do not stem principally from the fact that Christianity is incompatible with traditional African religion. On the contrary, many scholars have argued that traditional African religion is not, in fact, essentially different from Christianity, especially as reflected in the teachings of Jesus Christ.[54] Rather, the problem arises from the teaching and iconoclastic proclivities of the Christian missionaries, whose raison d'etre, as noted at the beginning of the chapter, was to undermine African culture and replace it with European culture. Hence, as some say, it was not Christianity *per se* that the missionaries brought, but European-ness. James Coleman's catalogue of missionary iconoclasm is worth repeating here.

> The early missionaries were inclined to feel that the African was in the grip of a cruel and irrational system from which he ought to be liberated.... In their eyes ritual murder, human sacrifice, and cannibalism were sufficient to condemn the whole system.... [Hence] they included among the preconditions for entry into the Christian fold the abandonment of such customs as initiation ceremonies..., dancing..., marriage payment..., polygyny..., secret societies..., not to mention...African names, and traditional funeral ceremonies. Renunciation of the old order was a prerequisite to acceptance of the new.[55]

There is no question that Christian missionaries deliberately propagated an ugly image of Africa, to serve their own specific needs. To be sure, they had to jus-

---

52. Uka, *Missionaries Go Home?*, 196-7.
53. Ibid., 207.
54. See Emmanuel Asante, *Toward an African Theology of the Kingdom of God. The Kingship of Onyama* (Lewiston, NY: Edwin Mellen Press, 1996); J.E. Casely Hayford, *Ethiopia Unbound* (London: Frank Cass & Co., 1969).
55. James S. Coleman, *Nigeria. Background to Nationalism* (Berkeley: University of California Press, 1958), 97.

tify their presence in Africa. Hence, "the darker the picture of the African barbarism, the more necessary the work of the missionaries."[56] Indeed, by showing the deplorable conditions of things in Africa, the missionaries obviously sought to arouse not only sympathy, but also increased contributions. It is indeed regrettable that missionary descriptions of African society as depraved, barbarous, and uncivilized, shaped and influenced European thought and action in Africa. The propagation of this image is perhaps the most enduring legacy of missionary enterprise in Africa.

While some missionaries have expressed remorse for the wholesale condemnation of African society and culture, others, however, insist that they, in fact are justified in such condemnation. Thus in the eyes of missionary apologists, Christianity served as "an efficient instrument for the upliftment of the African." For this reason, missionaries perceived themselves as "messengers of liberation." Since Christianity is seen as a liberating force, missionary work thus becomes a "civilizing" mission. Writing in a popular British missionary journal in 1915, a CMS missionary defended both missionary work and colonialism, noting that, when "a civilized nation" encounters "a primitive people," "it is inevitable that changes must come." The encounter may lead to the "disintegration of laws and customs which have operated for generations, (but) it is folly to imagine that it could be otherwise." He continued:

> There may be many genuine reasons for regret, but [to] cavil at what must be, is unreasonable and displays ignorance of the actual condition of affairs [in Africa]. The tide of progress must flow on, and its course obliterate much of the past.... The death-blow has been struck at the very foundations of many ancient institutions, and out of the *debris* a fabric is rising of an altogether different pattern. The moulding of the pattern should be our great objective.[57]

In destroying, or undermining African religion, its rituals, and beliefs, the missionary, as an anthropologist put it, "was at the same time, and unwittingly, destroying all that gave coherence and meaning to the social fabric, and was depriving the people of many interests besides those the destruction of which he had willed."[58] Yet there were missionaries who cautioned against indiscriminate condemnation of African society and culture. "We must study (native religions, customs and institutions)," noted one missionary, "in order to conserve the best elements in the institutions, and we must beware of premature destruction."[59]

Nevertheless, many missionaries took special pride in the transformation of Africa, essentially through missionary education. It was through this means that the missionaries succeeded in colonizing the mind of the Africans. Africans were induced to imbibe European values, embrace European culture, and reject their own heritage. For example, African dances and songs were replaced with European dances and church music. In regions where Irish priests and nuns predominated, the Irish jig displaced the traditional forms of dance in schools. Indeed,

---

56. Philip Curtin, *The Image of Africa: Ideas and Action, 1780-1850* (Madison, Wisconsin: University of Wisconsin Press, 1964), 326.

57. *The Church Missionary Review*, 66 (1915): 597-598.

58. *The Church Missionary Review* (1917), 210.

59. *The Church Missionary Review* (1917), 210.

missionary zealots extolled the ideals of Western society, as seen in the emphasis on school discipline, order and obedience, the wearing of uniforms, and so on. In the process, missionary education became a powerful instrument of deculturation and denationalization.

However, Africans also acknowledge the contributions of the missionaries to the emergence of the educated elite. Thus African missionary enthusiasts express appreciation for the missionaries' efforts and in the establishment of schools and colleges. Throughout Africa, they say, "leaders in Church and State, in business and education, owe their training in whole, or in part to the missionary enterprise."[60] But critics also point to the decline of African languages as part of the pernicious effects of missionary education. With the exception of the lower grades, in which local languages were taught, foreign languages formed the basic medium of instruction. The result was the neglect of local languages in the education systems. In my own secondary school days, for instance, we were not allowed to carry on conversations in the local language. A student caught speaking the Igbo language on campus, for example, was made to wear an ornament made of cardboard, on which was written, in Latin, DO SIGNUM ("I bear a sign"). This was degrading. Since no student wanted to be associated with this degrading sign, every effort was made to speak English at all times. Thus, students (including myself) hardly learned to read or write their own languages.

Also, while modern medical services—hospitals, maternity centers, clinics, and so on— owe their origin to the advent of the Christian missionaries, it must be pointed out that Western medicine was also a colonizing force. By encouraging Africans to patronize hospitals and health clinics, both the missionaries and the colonial authorities consciously sought to promote Western medicine, and, in the process, devalue traditional African therapeutic techniques. This contributed to a decline in traditional African medical services. However, many Africans resisted European medical technology, preferring instead the services of diviners, medicinemen, and oracles. They argue that there are diseases, which European medicine cannot cure, but African medicine can.

Many educated Africans resented the imperializing work of the Christian missionaries, and particularly the habit of giving Africans foreign names at baptism. "I am fully convinced," wrote the West African nationalist John Mensah Sarba, "that it [is] better to be called one's own name than be known by a foreign one."[61] Indeed, Africans wrote with great pride in defense of African culture, as be seen in Edward Blyden, *African Life and Customs* (1908), J. E. Casely Hayford, *Ethiopia Unbound* (1911), John Mensah Sarbah, *Fanti National Constitution* (1968), Chinua Achebe, *Things Fall Apart* (1958), and Jomo Kenyatta, *Facing Mount Kenya* (1938), to name but a few. The Igbo nationalist and patriot, Mazi Mbonu Ojike, in his book *My Africa* (1946), issued a clarion call to Africans to "boycott all boycottables," including European names and clothes, body bleaches, and so on, which tend to denationalize the African. He adds:

For the African to seek modernism in shameful foreign names is equally disgraceful. His language is one vital mode of expressing his culture and

---

60. Quoted in S.N. *Nwabara, Iboland: A Century of Contact with Britain 1860-1960* (Atlantic Highlands, N.J.: Humanities Press, 1978), 76.
61. Mensah Sarbah, *Fanti National Institution*, xiii.

remaining honorably African. Christian missions and not Christianity have no one else to blame for this uncultural practice. A man can be as good as anyone else intellectually, financially, politically, and religiously whether he is called James or Ikoli, Churchill or Stalin... Some Africans are so miseducated by the Christian missions that they do not know this truth....[62]

Ojike admonished Africans to be themselves, arguing that Africans would certainly be respected by "the world," if they lived in accordance with their culture. He further warned that Africans should not be mere imitators of others; for this, he insisted, would expose them to ridicule. Ojike was not a xenophobist. On the contrary, he was an internationalist, as exemplified in his entreaty that Africans need "to enrich and strengthen" what they already have by borrowing useful ideas from other cultures.[63]

Africans, including Christians, still consult oracles and diviners. The fact that they do this suggests that traditional religious beliefs still have a strong hold. Thus, while Africans take their Christianity seriously, many have not, in fact, jettisoned their belief in traditional religion and its rituals. This is probably because traditional religion tends to satisfy the emotional, psychological, and other needs of the people better than the Christian religion. The persistence of African culture and religious practices, after conversion, implies that Africans have not, after all, completely "forsaken" their traditional religion and belief systems, as some scholars would have us believe. Put differently, to argue that Christianity has totally eclipsed traditional religion would be a gross exaggeration.

Review Questions

1. Summarize the history of Christianity in North Africa before the advent of Islam.
2. Examine missionary efforts to convert Africans to Christianity before the nineteenth century. Why did missionary efforts fail?
3. How and why did Christianity spread in sub-Saharan Africa?
4. Critically examine the role of Western medicine and technology in the spread of Christianity in Africa.
5. In your view, is missionary Christianity a blessing or curse for Africa?

---

62. Mbonu Ojike, *My Africa* (New York: The John Day Company, 1946), 108-109. African nationalists were particularly concerned (agitated?) about the imposition of foreign names on Africans. On this matter Mensah Sarbah writes in *Fanti National Constitution* (xiii): "I am fully convinced that it be better to be called one's own name than be known by a foreign one, that it is possible to acquire Western learning and be expert in scientific attainments without neglecting one's mother tongue, (and) that the African's dress... should not be thrown aside."

63. Ojike, *My Africa*, 106-107.

Additional Readings

Ajayi, J.A. *Christian Missions in Nigeria, 1841-1891: The Making of a New Elite.* Evanston: Northwestern University Press, 1965.

Baeta, C.G., ed. *Christianity in Tropical Africa.* London: Oxford University Press, 1968.

Gray, Richard. "Christianity and Religious Change in Africa," *African Affairs,* 77 (January 1978): 96-98.

Hastings, Adrian. *African Christianity.* London: Geoffrey Chapman, 1976.

———. "Christianity and Revolution," *African Affairs,* 74 (July 1975): 347-361.

Horton, Robert. "African Conversion," *Africa,* 41, 2 (April 1971): 87-108.

Ilogu, Edmund. *Christianity and Igbo Culture.* New York: Nok Publishers, 1974.

Kalu, O.U. *The History of Christianity in West Africa.* London: Heinemann, 1980.

Oliver, Roland. *The Missionary Factor in East Africa.* London: Oxford University Press, 1952.

Ranger, T.O. and J. Weller, eds. *Themes in the Christian History of Central Africa.* London: Heinemann, 1975.

Sindima, Harvery J. *Drums of Redemption: An Introduction to African Christianity.* New York: Praeger Publishers, 1999.

Chapter 9

Politics and Government

Saheed A. Adejumobi

Traditional African social and political institutions included many different patterns of philosophy and culture. These cultures evolved over thousands of years and represent successful attempts of African societies to integrate themselves with their environment. African institutions were also marked by inter-related yet diverse institutions, many of which suffered in the throes of the modernization process. It is, however, remarkable that in spite of all the changes on the continent, traditional ways of life still hold sway as traditions continue to contribute to the survival of many polities in spite of changes from within and from outside. This chapter is divided into three segments, namely: (i) political philosophy, (ii) mechanisms of social control and legal systems, and (iii) ethnicity. These categories are both fluid and interconnected.

In ancient Africa, there were elements which both encourage and discouraged generalizations. Africa is a continent of over one thousand groups each with its own set of beliefs about the world, although similar world views and cultural and political philosophies produced a degree of uniformity. These beliefs meshed together to form a coherent thought system. There was, in many parts of Africa, a uniformity of metaphysics and epistemology, in beliefs about the origins and nature of the state, the authority of the ruler, the rights of the citizens, and the social structure, to mention only a few.[1]

Political Philosophy

Many African societies located their origins in a traumatic supernatural phenomenon. Many traced their origins to the benevolence of an all-powerful god or to the abilities of a mythical or super-human ancestor. These myths had consequences for social relationships, the exercise of authority, and notions of political obligation. They also indicate that "state" or society in Africa involved a supernatural or super-ordinary juxtaposition of events. The modern idea of state, with its impersonal institutions and primary emphasis on geographical contiguity, did not exist in the traditional African political imaginations.[2] Common descent was the underlying force and justification for all social existence.

---

1. Zaccheus Sunday Ali, John A.A. Ayoade, and Adigun A.B. Agbaje, *African Traditional Political Thought and Institutions* (Lagos, Nigeria: Civiletis International, 1989), 6.
2. Ibid., 8.

From at least the fourth century A.D. onwards, various African empires and kingdoms have flourished. For these kingdoms and also for the non-centralized political systems of the Tallensi, Igbo, or Luo, an underlying thread was the link between divinity and power. The thread that bound these societies together was the belief that the supernatural provided the legitimization of power.

Indigenous African societies may be classified into two general groups. The first group consisted of societies with a centralized authority, administrative machinery, and judicial institutions. The second are societies with no strong centralized authority, administrative machinery, or judicial institutions. The societies of the former group were culturally heterogeneous communities of units bound together by common interests and loyalty to a political superior, usually a paramount chief or king-in-council. Examples include the Zulu, the Ngwato, the Bemba, the Bayankole, and the Kede. The latter societies, on the other hand, had no single centralized authority enjoying a concentration of political, judicial, or military power that was capable of enforcing control by decree over the activities of its members. Examples of this group include the Logoli, the Tellensi, and the Nuer.

One feature identified with the centralized society was the existence of "organized force" as the principal sanction. This feature corresponded with distinctions of wealth, privilege and status. This type of society was also usually an amalgam of different ethnic groups since there was a limit to the size and diversity of the population that could hold together without some kind of centralized government. On the other hand, the decentralized society lacked what is usually called formal government, and exhibited cultural and ethnic homogeneity.

The question of establishing a useful and valid typology of traditional political structures in Africa has received considerable attention ever since the publication in 1940 of Evans-Pritchard and Meyer Fortes' *The Nuer* and *African Political Systems*. Historians and anthropologists have encountered numerous problems in the classification of African political systems. The simplest classification lies in Evans-Pritchard's and Fortes dichotomy between centralized and non-centralized political structures.[3] In the first group, central political authority and organization existed in the form of centralized and formal governments and a hierarchy of administrative offices. Amongst the second group, political activity took place within the sub-groups of society and through their interaction within social relations.[4] I.M. Smith also identifies a linear typology of four main categories of political systems. The classification includes: (i) states, (ii) segmentary states, (iii) "tribal polities" with some degree of hierarchy, and (iv) decentralized societies. These categories are often fluid. Some political systems can be classified as sub-systems or variants within a dominant category.

---

3. M. Fortes and E.E. Evans-Pritchard, eds., *African Political Systems* (Oxford University Press, 1962 edition), 5.

4. S.N. Eisenstadt, *From Generation to Generation: Age Groups and Societal Structures* (Glencoe, IL: Free Press, 1956), 186-193.

Centralized Political Systems

Modifications in the level of centralization and development of hierarchy led to transitions from a small polity to state. On the other hand, groups of petty chiefdoms could also become segmentary states. This occurred when one cheifdom assumed control over the others. A wide range of possible political and governmental arrangements also existed within each category.

In sub-Saharan Africa, one could find some of the world's most simple political systems, as well as some of its most complex and sophisticated. The full range of complexity in political organization could be found even within relatively small areas. Political systems varied from nomadic bands to intermediate forms to complex, hierarchical kingdoms.[5] Fortes and Evans-Pritchard produced a classification of African political systems which was subsequently adopted by many anthropologists and historians of African politics. Many scholars have merely attempted to seek a common origin to explain the structural similarities between many societies and kingdoms. They argue that the spread of a Sudanic civilization across Africa encouraged the incorporation of various African societies into states with similar institutions, and thus they ultimately came from a common source. This group of scholars stress that the formation of states was a process that involved the deployment of common political ideas.[6] Many, for example, attribute the cultural similarities between African kingdoms to a common origin in the Nile Valley or the Near East, especially in the context of divine kingship.

Many African kingdoms have been characterized as "divine kingships," a concept that is based upon the assumption that the king was the actual embodiment of the kingdom. The supernatural provided more than an explanation of descent in most African states. It also provided the legitimization of power. The right to rule in most instances was located in the commonly accepted myth of descent. Rulers derived their mandate from the same divine source from which society emerged. In the centralized political systems, this divine source was also the inspiration for the identification of the ruler. In many societies, rulers were selected from the lineage which could trace its origins to the society's "first" family.[7]

There was a tacit belief in a mystical union of the king and his kingdom. This, in many societies, was revealed in two major characteristics. First, the king was often regarded as a symbol of fertility. In this situation, the future growth of each year's crops was dependent on his actions. In essence, a good performance by the king resulted in a good harvest. The second major characteristics was the possibility of regicide. Divine kingship sanctioned killing the king when he became disabled or unable to govern. Similar fates also awaited him if the fortunes of his kingdoms dwindled.

---

5. Phyllis Martin and Martin O'Meara, eds., *Africa* (Bloomington, Indiana: Indiana University Press, 1977), 44.

6. B.G. Trigger, "The Rise of Civilization in Egypt," in J.D. Fage and Roland Oliver, eds., *The Cambridge History of Africa* (London: Cambridge University Press, 1975), 523-525.

7. Sunday Zaccheus Ali, et al. *African Traditional Political Thought and Insititutions,* 181.

An example of divine kingship is the Luba-Lunda political system which affected a large region of Africa. The differences between the Luba and Lunda states reflected not so much ethnic distinctions as they did two varying political and cultural systems. It was because of these systems that references to ethnic identity emerged. Early territorial organizations comprised small chiefdoms, each governing one settlement. The Luba-Lunda system, incorporated the fishing and farming chiefdoms of Kalunduwe, Kanyok, Kanincin, Nsanga, Mpinin, Rund, and Hemba. The political ideology of these states can be traced to the main Luba kingdom which operated according to two interlocked *bulopwe* or principles, the sacred character of kingship and rule through a closed association. In the kingdom's heartland often witnessed a balance between the two. But in general, the overwhelming political principle was the sacred character of kingship.

Variants of the Luba political structure were found in its spheres of influence. In the south, in Shila and Kanyok counties, the political organization was either limited to the village and its land, or higher office given for life or for a limited period to the highest bidder. The Luba State was organized in a pyramidal hierarchical fashion. A pyramidal system was one that consisted of different levels of segmental groupings that were not entirely autonomous; the groups were usually based on kinship and each one had a chief, a paramount chief, or a king. The levels of the pyramidal system were based on seniority of the political figures.

The kingdom was ruled from the capital where royal and titled officials of both sexes held quarters, and at the center was the *bulopwe*, or the royal office. Households were linked at the village level by patrilineal connections. Although the king was not supposed to have a lineage or clan, as the office was handed from father to son, the Luba saw the succession system as a rotation in office of different lineages, i.e., of the king's mother. Marriage between the king and women of various districts forged a link of kinship between the king and many of the district heads. Another example of a pyramidal-hierarchical system is found among the Yoruba of West Africa.

For many African rulers, the king's family played an important part in the decision making process which often served as a restraining force upon the given ruler. Many African societies featured an individual designated as the "kinsman', who was sometimes genealogically related to the king, but he or she behaved towards the king in an informal rather than political manner. For example, the Swazi recognized the title of "mother" and the Lozi, the king's "sister" who related to the king in a familiar manner. In Ankole, the king's mother's brother had the right to collect tribute, and the royal ladies of Ankole had the "right to demand cattle from whomsoever they pleased."[8] Among the Asante, possession of the royal stool symbolized both temporal and spiritual power. The failure to accept the guidance of the councilors, which included the Queen mother, was a legitimate cause for destoolment. These kinsmen were able to criticize or deflate the king's ego and they also provided sanctuary to anyone believed to be unjustly abused by the king.

The African political model had an in-built protection against absolutism or tyranny. While the symbolic power of African kings was exceedingly great, in practice they were circumscribed by other controls and their absolutism was often more apparent than real. Africans expected their rulers to uphold their traditions,

---

8. Ibid., 28.

defend their territory from aggressors, and expand, if possible, their wealth through wars, but they also expected them to be just, considerate and conscious of the conventions and interests of the people at all times. The king was expected to work, in almost all cases, within a structure characterized by several layers of chieftaincy groups, secret religious groups, which exercised great powers of control, and age grade associations. All these groups were sources of pressure and acted as checks on the rulers' use of the powers granted him or her by society. In many instances, African political systems are related to other aspects of the society, one being the clear relationship between population and political complexity. In essence, it could be said that the higher the population density of the political unit, the greater the tendency for it to have a relatively complex form of government to exist.

Segmentary Political Systems

Traditional African political systems also included societies without centralized government. In these communities, the largest political unit might be a group of people united with one another by ties of kinship. The political structure and kinship organization were parallel in scope, and in many instances they were completely fused. Cultural and ethnic homogenity was usual in these societies. There was also a decentralized system of government involving permanent, unilateral descent groups, and in addition, a kinship system which consisted of a set of relationships linking an individual to other persons and to particular social units through the transient, bilateral family. The only step in the direction of an organized judicial system under the kinship system was the recognition of certain elders as traditionally qualified and entitled to participate in the adjuration of disputes; such recognition was usually based on their seniority as members of the social unit.[9]

The Igbo of West Africa were acephalous and organized on the basis of descent. The descent units were lineages of unequal size and power, associated with local villages, which sometimes incorporated unrelated people. Although no single individual was recognized as chief, there were well-defined councils of chiefs or ruling elders corresponding to different levels of lineage structure who are responsible for enforcing ritual and moral values.[10] Distinct from the genealogical validation of positions of influence was the recognition of achieved power by the personal qualities of an ambitious individual-a "big man," *onye uku*. These "big men" were men of wealth or ability or both, who could bypass lineage alignment to manipulate the system and influence decisions. They were, however, restrained from being too arbitrary as they were vulnerable to the same local opinion that had brought them into prominence. Each village was segmented into lineages and each lineage was further divided into sub-lineages. A lineage occupied a certain area that was divided into compounds. Within

---

9. T. Olawale Elias, *The Nature of African Customary Law* (Manchester: Manchester University Press, 1956), 11-12.

10. Hilda and Leo Kuper, *African Law: Adaption and Development* (Los Angeles: University of California Press, 1965), 8.

each compound were several households. The compound, the lineage, and the village each had a head. The political structure at the village level included a legislative assembly. "Interest groups," such as secret societies, priestly associations, title societies, and age-grade associations, played important roles. The legislative assembly held open air meetings at which extensive discussions took place. Everyone was free to contribute to the debate, after which the elders retreated to a separate meeting to consider all the views presented and to reach a decision, usually by consensus.

The Gusii of East Africa consisted of a number of clans with no central authority and no clan hierarchy; they were autonomous, discrete units characterized by equality in structure. Political and legal situations were scarcely differentiated. As there were no recognized agents for the settlement of disputes, appeals were made to individual men who were sufficiently recognized to be specifically designated. These men were known as *etureti*. Among the Yako also of East Africa, the political system was founded on 'authoritative associations' and kinship groups. Among the Nilo-Hamites, political functions were vested in an age-set system.

The absence of centralized power in segmentary societies elevated the role of religion in the maintenance of social order. Among the Tallensi, religion in the form of ancestor cult, the supreme sanction of kinship ties, is described as the great stabilizing force counteracting the centrifugal tendencies inherent in the lineage system. There was usually an absence of autocracy and authoritarianism in decentralized societies. Here, power was diffused and shared by numerous institutions. Although there were hierarchies determined by age or sacredness, no institution or person was ever considered to be the repository of all power. Power was collectively shared and administered by many, operating, in most cases, within a council of elders. While the judicial, political, and ecclesiastical powers of the society were sometimes vested in this council, the opportunity for tyranny was forestalled by the representative quality of its members. In such a context, the only tyranny that was possible was that of religious or moral obligation, which was hardly ever resented.

In most segmentary or decentralized societies, individuals within a group shared the same rights, but these rights were generally far from equal. It was primarily kinship terms or relations that determined one's rights vis-a-vis others. Some rights were passed on only at a certain age. Puberty rites, the ceremony which ushers in adulthood, conferred on all individuals certain new rights. As they came of age, candidates became full members of their group and "inherited" new rights. Even among nomadic groups, hunters and gatherers, there were traditional rights with regards to exploitation of resources.

Mechanisms of Social Control
and Legal System

Studies of societies in different parts of the world indicate that many did not have separate lawmaking bodies, courts, or any specific legal machinery for enforcing rules. Nevertheless, these societies carried on a regulated existence and were able to cope with disputes without self-annihilation, because they continued to operate effectively through other types of organization and control. The legal systems of traditional African societies were extremely diverse and in some cases there were no units or offices that coincided with the Western concept of a judiciary. Sometimes, only the religious aspect of power was institutionalized, thus it provided the main sanction for public activities. There were also societies with elaborately conceptualized and verbally defined distinctions, creating a separation of the legal institution from other institutions.

All African societies operated within the context of myths which provided the ideological framework for the relationship between the ruler and the ruled. Acceptance of the myth of descent and the superintending role of the supernatural world involved the disposition to obey. This was also related to a general belief in the organic nature of the society. The society was a system of interlocking, familiar relationships and destinies. There was, therefore, a common good which was in the interest of all to protect and enhance. To do otherwise was to invoke the wrath of the god(s) or ancestors whose existence provided an essential ingredient of social order.

It is, however, important to emphasize that not all laws in Africa were enveloped in a mystical aura. There was a clear recognition of the distinction between the secular and the sacred, and between crimes against the society and crimes against the person. Crimes against society often weighted more and called for a greater retribution. Murder was often included in this category because of its dislocative and destructive impact on the society. Crimes in this category often called for atonement, propitiation of gods or ancestors and punishment which was as severe as banishment or even the death sentence. Crimes against person hardly ever lead to such severe measures. Such crimes or disputes were usually resolved by arbitration. In cases such as adultery or theft, atonement was often necessary. Retributive actions were the exception rather than the rule.

In chiefly societies, the central authority of the king or chief was usually buttressed by factors such as his control of the national regiment, his powers of appointment and removal, and the mystical qualities attributed to his office in the popular imagination. To prevent monarchical absolutism and political tyranny, there evolved mechanisms like the king's council of chiefs, the queen mother's courts, sacerdotal or sacred officials with a decisive voice in the king's investiture, powerful secret societies in which the king was only first among equals, and devolution of authority to regional and local chiefs. All of these coupled with the intangible but effective factor of public opinion, served to protect law and custom by controlling the arrogation of royal power.

Circumstances in which the chief abused his power were usually met with a response from the subordinate chiefs who had the right to secede from the commonwealth, or alternatively depose him. In Yorubaland, the king would be requested by his chiefs to "open the calabash," i.e., to commit suicide by voluntarily taking poison. In a similar vein, if subordinate chiefs became tyrannical to their people or insubordinate to their overlords, the latter could, with the co-operation of other subordinate chiefs, remove them from office. Thus, government in a traditional African state implied a delicate balance between power and authority, on the one hand, and obligation and responsibility on the other.

Generally, laws in Africa may be divided into two classes: legal interdictions promulgated by rulers or arising from general disapproval, and taboos which depended on a magico-religious sanction. Thus, besides civil prohibitions, there were also religious and ecclesiastical inhibitions. But because there was no hard and fast division between the two, it is difficult to say where the former ended and the latter began. Some prohibited acts, such as certain sexual bans, were included under both.

A very strong sense of justice prevailed among all ethnic groups, perhaps because the mystical connection between kings and their people meant that their prosperity depended on justice and due observance of the laws and taboos. No difference was made between the executive and judicial powers, as they were combined in the chief ruler, or rulers, of the people. In all large states or populous towns, the right of trying minor cases and of settling disputes of lesser importance was deputed to the sub-, or provincial chiefs. Still the final word in those crimes which were punishable by death invariably remained with the chief or king.

In places where the administration was carried out by a secret society, the judicial power was also kept in its hands. Elders were always present; even when they were not allowed to rise and give their opinion, their advice was generally sought. The court was open to all, and proceedings were conducted in public, usually in the market place, in "play grounds," or in the chief's compound, in the presence of any members of the community who wished to attend.

There appears, with most societies, to have been strictly state crime, such as treason, but many offenses, including taboos, were regarded as a transgression against the entire community. Anybody in the community could call a public meeting to state his or her complaint. Assemblies were generally summoned by the chief or by his representative who called out the news or orders around town by ringing special bells or drums. The role of prosecutor was played by the injured party. If the case was at all doubtful, the accused could demand an ordeal, one of the greatest safeguards of justice. The success of this process was dependent on the unquestioning belief in the just government of the world by the gods and the people; thus, they had no hesitation in submitting to this test. In fact, they often demanded it of their own accord.

There were many kinds of ordeals. The most common one was the appeal to a god or some supernatural force to kill the criminal, or send them serious illness or misfortune, if they made a false statement or were guilty of the charge. A period of three months to a year would be set by the judges, within which time the appeal should take effect. If nothing happened during this time, the accusation was considered false and the person who made it was severely dealt with; often he or she was awarded the same penalty as his or her victim might have suffered.

In many cases, the word of a diviner was accepted as final. Ignorance of the law was not accepted as an excuse. Capital punishment was only exacted for witchcraft, and among some groups for murder and theft. Penalties varied considerably, especially those for theft, perhaps due to the special circumstances prevailing in a particular region.

Islamic Law

Attention to Islamic law is relevant here. Islam was one of the major sources of external influence, even though indigenous laws prevailed almost everywhere in sub-Saharan Africa. The principles of Islamic law never wholly ousted indigenous law, but rather fused the two in a distinct amalgam. Muslims had their own system of law that was an integral part of their religion. As Allah's Prophet and Messenger, Mohammed simultaneously proselytized, organized the Muslim community, and delivered Allah's pronouncements. The Quran became the unquestioned basis of Islam, together with a system of law divinely ordained both to regulate and to protect the faithful.

In one place after another in Africa, the principles of Islamic law spread through the influence of holy men and women, merchants and traders. In some cases, a Muslim ruler would profess to accept and impose Islamic law in its purity and entirety. Although Islamic law, or the Shari'a, as expounded in the handbooks of the schools of law could not in theory be modified by contact with indigenous law, in practice, the decisions of the Muslim courts represented a fusion of Islamic law and local customary law, varying according to the relative orthodoxy of the court concerned. Indigenous laws either coexisted with the Sharia as a separate and distinct system, each applied in suitable circumstances, or else fused with it into an amalgam. An example of this could be seen in the Wa-Digo, near Mombasa in Kenya, many of whom were only nominal Muslims and still followed their customary law, which was entirely matrilineal; at the coast were those who embraced Swahili culture and were governed by Islamic law in comparative purity; and, in between, there were people who adopted Islamic law only partially. The courts gave decisions according to the levels of the respondent's acceptance of Islam. These patterns were typical of varying regions of the continent, as conflicts were avoided with the recognition of differing customs regarding inheritance, marriage, divorces, etc.

African societies of the past were largely theocracies. Myths and religion pointed the way, mobilized action and defined strategies yet, the societies of traditional Africa were also democratic in the sense of pluralistic decision making and in the opportunities which existed for dialogue with and control of rulers. As the Tswana were wont to say, "a chief is chief by grace of his people." Most states in contemporary Africa have departed from the ways of the past; they have become secular either because of the historical exigency of colonialism or the expediency of religious pluralism. Today, there is confusion and suffering in many African societies, as areas which were sacred within the framework of society's conventions and interests are ignored by arbitrary rulers. Thus, the weakening of the grip of myths and religions is accompanied by an ideological vacuum, and confusion about the nature and purpose of the state. This often leads to anarchy, and purposeless polities entrenched by force.

Ethnicity and Politics:
The Nature of Ethnicity

Ethnic traditions portray the distant past as a story of movements of groups of outsiders into their communities and subsequent expansion of their descendants. Ethnic units, or communities, have come to be regarded as stable entities. But, in reality many of the so-called "tribal" groups were creations of the colonial period. There is a pressing need to move beyond such oversimplified approaches where inter-ethnic relationships in Africa are concerned. In Kenya for example, the fact that people have for centuries recognized the existence of populations corresponding roughly to the present day Gikuyu, Kamba, Embu, Mbeere and Meru ethnic groups should not be taken as evidence that even during the nineteenth century Kamba speaking peoples, for examples, possessed a clear notion of ethnic identity, let alone any sense of common experience or destiny. In early nineteenth century Kenya, there was a great deal of population movement and local social formation. People identified themselves as residents of their local societies, not as members of any monolithic ethnic group. In an area such as Migwani in central Kenya, local identity was expressed on the surface in distinctive traits such as styles of dress and decorations, hairstyles, popular songs and dances, and nuances of language. In other areas, particular patterns of body tattoos or marks, styles of detrition, or techniques of male circumcision set people apart. Identity is sometimes determined by relation to the environment either directly, as in the case of the Shambaa people of northeastern Tanganyika who lived in a mountainous environment. Identity can also be determined indirectly as in the case of people who are defined or define themselves by reference to their mode of subsistence. This kind of occupation or situational identity could be used as a means of controlling scarce resources, by delimiting the group that had access to them.[11] Natural dichotomies are sometimes implicit in the notion of identity, and especially in the definition of boundaries between groups. Since identity can be situational, it could change frequently as groups and individuals changed their mode of life.

Ethnicity in African history is a reaction to both internal and external forces. The process of fusion and fission is a continual one; it is not erased with the formation of new political units. Examples of the changing nature of ethnicity are found in all parts of Africa. One example can be witnessed in the experience of the Hausa of northern Nigeria. With the introduction of Islam in Hausaland during the fifteenth century, the people who accepted Islam assumed the name "Hausa," and those who did not remained "Maguzawa." This process of fission essentially divided the community into two distinct ethnic societies. On the other hand, in the nineteenth century, after the Fulani conquered the area, there was a merger of the urban Hausa and Fulani into a new group called "Hausa-Fulani." This new group absorbed many other groups, and all these together are now referred to as the "Hausa" of the north by people in the south when there is confrontation or competition.

Other forms of changing inter-ethnic contact, especially in the context of the socio-political changes associated with colonial rule, include: (i) Peripheral Con-

11. Richard Waller, "Ecology, Migration, and Expansion in East Africa," *African Affairs*, 23 (1985): 349.

tact: people exchanging goods without much interaction; (ii) Institutional Contact: a mostly peripheral contact based upon some institutionalized meeting point such as trade or conflict; (iii) Acculturation: a partial merging, where the weaker society makes more adjustments than the stronger and accepts some of the outward manifestations of identity of the dominant group; (iv) Domination: a single society with two categories distinguished primarily by non-ethnic characteristics such as income, education and religion; (v) Paternalism: a specialized form of institutional contact which, unlike domination, involves the retention of distinctiveness among the interactive societies; (vi) Integration: a reduction of identifying with ethnic group and instead, the establishment of a larger unity based upon associational ties, and (vii) Pluralism: similar to an integrated situation, but the distinction being the existence of a larger order without the clear dominant-subordinate relation.[12]

Conclusion

This chapter has discussed the means by which politics and government is coordinated in African societies. To better understand the dynamic nature of African institutions, heavy reliance has to be placed on examples from a trans-regional perspective. In spite of the changes which occurred over centuries of interaction with the outside world, African governmental institutions have withstood the penetration of external ideas. Many would argue that it is these institutions that hold the various societies of the continent together in the face of the unstable and ever-shifting identity politics and government of the modern era.

Review Questions

1. Identify the major characteristics of any one centralized political system in pre-colonial Africa.
2. Compare and contrast centralized and decentralized political systems in traditional Africa.
3. Discuss the mechanisms for maintaining social order and civility in traditional Africa.
4. What are some of the ways in which ethnic groups change their boundaries in pre-colonial Africa?
5. Explain the interaction of politics, religion, and law in traditional African societies.

---

12. John Paden and Edward Soja, eds., *The African Experience, Vol. II* (Evanston: Northwestern University Press, 1970), 26.

Additional Reading

Basil Davidson, *The African Genius, an Introduction to African Cultural and Social History*. Boston: Little Brown and Company, 1970.

————. *The African Past: Chronicles from Antiquity to Modern Times*. Hammondsworth, UK: Penguin, 1966.

Fortes, M. and E.E. Evans-Pritchard. *African Political Systems*. London: Oxford University Press, 1962.

July, Robert. *A History of African People*. New York: Charles Scribner's Sons, 1974.

Chapter 10

Pastoralism in Africa

John Lamphear

African pastoral societies are complex, and because of this, they often have been misunderstood. Even a satisfactory definition of them has been difficult to achieve. Typically, some definitions have stressed economic and ecological factors. In these, pastoralists are described as highly nomadic peoples who derive their livelihoods exclusively from domestic livestock—cattle, sheep, goats, donkeys and camels—which they herd in semi-arid regions unsuitable for agriculture. These definitions certainly fit many pastoral groups, and there is general agreement that it is in the drier grasslands of Africa that pastoralism is the most efficient form of subsistence. But, as this chapter will show, the definitions do not cover others who not only live in areas suitable for agricultural activity, but actually combine herding with intensive cultivation. In many cases, pastoral communities are not in any sense nomadic; in some of them only the most limited movements take place. Moreover, it is highly doubtful that any pastoralists ever derived their entire subsistence from their herds.

Other definitions have focused on political aspects, depicting pastoral communities as decentralized and egalitarian. At the same time, these definitions suggest that pastoral societies were essentially exclusive and closed, as well as naturally expansive, warlike, and resistant to change. But again as we shall see below, African pastoralists historically had many different types of political organization. While some were indeed egalitarian, others were decidedly stratified and hierarchical or even strongly centralized under hereditary chiefs and kings. Again, while the history of African pastoralism did sometimes involve dramatic military expansionism, the normal movement involved in herding activities did not necessarily involve expansion or conflict. Widespread peaceful interactions were at least as common as aggressive expansion. Finally, far from being exclusive and tradition bound, pastoralists time and again showed themselves to be open and adaptive. As we shall see, much of the image of pastoral communities as closed, self-sufficient, and hostile derives from the distortions of the colonial period in Africa when romanticized, though deeply paternalistic, portraits of pastoralists as consummate "noble savages" were common.

Perhaps it is another definition focusing on the question of self-image that provides us with our most valuable clue in determining what constitutes a pastoral society. By this definition, societies who call themselves pastoralists do so because of a deep commitment to a certain cultural identity. In some cases this commitment may be only an idealistic one, but all such societies who themselves claim a pastoral identity should probably be defined as such, regardless of other factors.

It is evident, then, that African pastoralists are by no means monolithic in terms of their economic and socio-political structures. Rather, they represent a wide range of dynamic communities successfully adapted to a variety of ecological niches and historical circumstances throughout Africa. Beneath their diversity, however, is a fundamental subscription to a way of life in which the struggle to raise domestic animals is a central focus, economically, socially, and even psychologically.

To understand something of these complex peoples I shall first trace their historical evolution, and then turn to specific cultural aspects of pastoral communities themselves.

Pastoralism and Pastoralists
in African History

The first African pastoralists apparently lived in what is now the Sahara Desert, which was then a much wetter environment. As early as perhaps 7000 B.C. they began combining the herding of "small stock" (sheep and goats) with fishing and gathering activities. Within three thousand years they were also herding long-horned, humpless cattle possibly descended from wild bovines native to the region. After about 3000 B.C., some of them also began cultivating grain. Vivid rock paintings have survived which depict their camps and villages, their

**Figure 10-1. Pastoralist scene with cattle, huts, and women
and children working from a cave painting at Tassili n'Ajjer**

herding activities, and their religious ceremonies. Sometimes the paintings bear uncanny similarities to current pastoral practices. But then, around 2500 B.C., the Saharan region entered a severe dry phase. Desiccation forced pastoral groups to move rapidly to the south with their livestock into the sahelian grasslands beyond the edge of the rapidly forming desert.

A serious barrier to pastoral expansion in many places, however, was the presence of tsetse flies. These insects, which feed on blood, transmit sleeping sickness, a disease fatal both to humans and to cattle. They infest shady, humid areas of wetter woodland, but avoid drier, open grasslands. The desiccation after 2500 B.C. had the effect of transforming some moist woodlands into drier savannas, reducing the tsetse habitats and allowing the spread of herds into areas formerly inhospitable to them. In addition, the herdsmen pushing down into the Sahel apparently developed a strain of tsetse-resistant cattle, the N'dama, as they moved further into the wetter southern environments.

Simultaneously, or perhaps even earlier, a similar process was occurring further east. Here herdsmen impelled by the desiccation of the Nile Valley and parts of Ethiopia moved down into East Africa. The first arrivals may have spoken Kushitic languages. Fashioning stone tools, pottery, and distinctive stone bowls, these early groups established themselves in the areas near Lake Turkana and then in upland regions further south. Some of them buried their dead under stone cairns and constructed circles of upright stones that served as remarkably accurate stellar calendars. They apparently experienced close contacts and cultural exchanges with communities of fishermen and hunters, and the herders themselves routinely engaged in fishing, hunting, gathering, and sometimes cultivation to augment their pastoral pursuits. Indeed, in many instances there was probably no clear distinction between pastoral, agricultural and hunting/gathering ways of life during this period.

By perhaps 2,500 years ago, livestock was spreading much further to the south. By then Khoisan-speaking peoples throughout much of southern Africa were herding sheep, and by a few centuries later cattle also had arrived, though the exact route by which they did so remains unclear.

By now, some groups were becoming more and more specialized in their pastoral activities. Fundamental to this was apparently a profound psychological adjustment. Instead of viewing animals as an immediate source of food to be slaughtered for their meat as hunters do, some began to see their domestic animals as providers of renewable resources of milk, blood, and offspring. They also began to accept constraints on their own freedom of movement, due to the availability of grazing or waterholes. As animals thus came to be preserved and developed as breeding stock, they increasingly came to be revered for their social, religious and aesthetic worth.

Another factor also contributing to increased specialization was the appearance of new types of livestock in many parts of Africa. By the sixth century B.C., the camel, an animal originally from Arabia, had spread throughout much of the Horn of Africa, into North Africa and down into the still desiccating Sahara. Admirably suited to the driest conditions, camels permitted herdsmen to utilize even desert areas. Another important newcomer was a type of humped cattle known as the Zebu which had originated in India. Able to stand high temperatures and long drives with relatively little water, they were ideal animals for arid grasslands. By perhaps 2,000 years ago, various strains of a hybrid animal, the Sanga, apparently descended from admixtures of the earlier humpless longhorns and the later Zebus began to appear as the most common cattle throughout many parts of Africa.

Another profound impact on the development of African pastoralism was the appearance of iron technology. At Meroe in what is now the Sudan, blacksmiths were smelting iron by the fifth century B.C. and others were doing the same at Nok in West Africa by a century later. Iron technology may have appeared even earlier in the interlacustrine area (the region between the great lakes) of East Africa. It was not until the early centuries A.D., however, that iron working began to spread widely throughout the continent.

In much of eastern, central and southern Africa those responsible for the spread were people speaking Bantu languages. Entering eastern Africa from areas essentially unsuitable for pastoralism, they originally were farmers who lived in small communities in the wetter regions, leaving the dry grasslands of East Africa to earlier populations of Stone Age herders and hunters. But in clearing forest and bush lands for their farms with their iron tools, the Bantu sometimes created new tsetse-free pastures and some began to place more emphasis on livestock. It seems that this was sometimes a factor in the emergence of chiefs who unified small-scale societies into larger political units based on the need to regulate the distribution of animals and their products throughout the community.

Apparently these processes began to intensify after about 1000 A.D. as a more sophisticated stage of iron technology, the Later Iron Age, began in many parts of Africa. In East Africa a rather mysterious people called the Chwezi amalgamated smaller kingdoms into the large Kitara state in parts of what is now Uganda. We are uncertain whether these Chwezi were immigrants who moved to East Africa from elsewhere or simply an outgrowth of the established Bantu populations who began placing even more emphasis on herding.

It is more certain, however, that people speaking Nilotic languages were migrants who soon began arriving from the north. They quickly introduced a more intensive and specialized focus on pastoralism into many parts of East Africa, and, with improved herding practices and access to iron weapons and tools, began to absorb or displace earlier populations of the grasslands. The first of these Nilotes were probably the ancestors of Kalenjin-speaking groups who settled mainly in upland areas where they mixed with earlier Kushitic-speakers. Later, by about 1500, the Luo branch of the Nilotes appeared in some of the wetter regions inhabited by Bantu farmers. Apparently few in number, these Luo were largely absorbed by the Bantu and adopted their languages, but in the interlacustrine region they were still able to oust the Chwezi, replacing them with their own Bito dynasty and founding the kingdom of Bunyoro as a successor to Kitara. Other dynasties established among societies such as the Nkore and Rwanda again may be attributable to Luo immigrants.

In every instance, it was the possession of large herds that provided the key to the establishment of these dynasties. But in time, the pastoralists, who apparently had developed more effective military techniques, began to offer protection to farmers and to lend them animals so they could use manure to fertilize their crops, in exchange for agricultural produce and various services. In some communities pastoral and agricultural elements tended to blend, but in others, where intermarriage between herding elements and farming elements was rarer, stratification along economic, and, to an extent, socio-political lines, began to develop. In the Rwanda kingdom, for instance, the Tutsi clans of "aristocratic" herdsmen remained rather distinct from Hutu farmers, although there was probably always room for some fluidity and social mobility.

Other groups of Nilotic immigrants also began moving into the drier East African grasslands, often in significant numbers. Most of the earlier herding and hunting populations were now absorbed by the newcomers. Unlike the situation in some of the wetter interlacustrine regions, however, these Nilotic societies retained their own languages and cultural features, and most developed as egalitarian communities without hereditary rulers. Many, such as the Maasai group, practiced elaborate initiation rites and developed age-class systems. These systems cut across families, giving people a range of interaction wider than just their own kinsmen, and provided these decentralized societies with their main source of corporate identity. Many of them engaged in grain agriculture, in conjunction with their pastoral activities, wherever they could.

Other Nilotic-speakers who remained in parts of the Sudan and northern Uganda experienced similar developments, retaining their languages and cultural features and having a livelihood in which both pastoral and agricultural products were vital. But while some, such as the Dinka and Nuer, were decentralized, others, including the Shilluk, Bari, and Acholi formed chiefdoms or kingdoms.

Further to the north in the Sudan, clans of Arab pastoralists had been moving south and southwest. Part of an earlier Arab migration into North Africa which brought with it the Islamic faith, they intermixed with indigenous Nubian populations in the Sudan, many of whom had converted to the new religion by the fourteenth century. Between these areas and those of the Nilotic-speakers to the south, still another pastoral people, the Funj, managed large herds which included horses. They, too, eventually converted to Islam and with an efficient cavalry army established a centralized state.

Eastwards from them, in the area below the Ethiopian highlands, lived another group of herdsmen, the Oromo. Attracted by the good grazing in the hills and plateaus to their north, they began to move steadily in that direction until, by about 1600, they had gained control of most of southern Ethiopia. In the process, many converted to Islam or Christianity (the state religion of Ethiopia), and some, after arriving in fertile areas, began to abandon their pastoral lifestyle for that of the sedentary agriculturist.

Adjacent to the Oromo to the east, Somali pastoralists herded small stock, cattle, and camels. Apparently they or similar societies had been established here for quite a long time, for a Chinese document of the ninth century A.D. tells of herdsmen living on the milk and blood of their livestock. While many Somalis were decentralized, other formed kingdoms that converted to Islam by the twelfth century. Some of these Somali Muslims came into conflict with Christian Ethiopians and others pushed south into coastal regions of East Africa where they encountered Bantu populations.

By now, Bantu-speaking groups were also inhabiting many ports of central and southern Africa as well, and were often responsible for introducing a new emphasis on herding to these areas. As we have seen, sheep and cattle had arrived in some places well before this and were kept by Stone Age populations. By at least 1000 A.D., iron-using cattle herders were living in some places, too. One of these groups, the Toutswe culture, succumbed to droughts not long after, but others, such as the Leopard's Kopje culture of Zimbabwe, developed thriving mixed

Figure 10-2. Longhorn Cow

economies based on herding, cultivation, and mining. In many of these societies, the ownership of cattle became a symbol of wealth and power, and was concentrated in the hands of those in positions of authority. A prime example of such a civilization was that of Great Zimbabwe which featured impressive stone wall enclosures, apparently constructed around 1400 A.D., by Bantu-speaking Shona people. Developed in an area with excellent pasture for cattle, fertile soils for crops, abundant wild animals for hunting, rich deposits of minerals, and a prime location from which to control the flow of commerce, Great Zimbabwe became a prosperous, powerful state. While its economy included many elements, there was a special focus on livestock. The Shona also established several other states in the same general region, including Torwa, Changamire, and Mutapa. Huge herds of cattle controlled by elite elements provided a fundamental economic basis for all of them. By at least the seventeenth century, some had developed a practice whereby young men were awarded cattle in return for military service, allowing a somewhat broader distribution of animals, but also affording rulers large armies with which to capture even more livestock and other resources. One such state was Changamire whose *rozvi* armed forces became a virtually professional standing army.

South of the Limpopo River, other Bantu communities with a similarly increasing emphasis on pastoralism also were coming into being. Here, in a manner similar to processes further north, clans who had amassed large herds extended their patronage and protection over others and established themselves as chiefs over small but vibrant Later Iron Age states. The Nguni-speaking group of these southern Bantu were typical of the process. Included in their number were the Zulu, who, as we shall see, would use their resources, especially large herds of cattle, to make sweeping changes through a wide area.

As these iron-using communities developed and expanded, earlier populations of Khoisan-speaking hunters and herdsmen were absorbed into the new
Bantu communities, contributing the distinctive click sounds of their languages to
Bantu speech. Others maintained their own ways of life by moving off into peripheral areas and/or forming symbiotic relations with the Bantu. In some regions, such as parts of Nambia and into the Cape region at Africa's southern tip,
Khoisan pastoralists remained the dominant population. They, too, eventually
came under severe pressures, not from Bantu immigrants, but from Dutch settlers
who began arriving at the Cape by sea by about 1650. Rapidly expanding into the
interior, the Europeans seized lands from the Khoisan to establish their own herds
and farms.

As all this was transpiring, thriving iron-age societies were also developing
throughout the wetter savannas and forests of western Africa, but the presence of
tsetse and other environmental factors precluded much pastoral activity, and their
focus was on sedentary agriculture. Further north, however, in the dramatically
drier conditions of the Sahara and sahel were many groups of Berber-speaking nomads who followed a strongly pastoral lifestyle. Most of them kept large numbers
of camels, small stock, and horses, often augmented by dates gathered at desert
oases by client populations. Some of these desert herdsmen also participated in
long distance trade, leading camel caravans across the Sahara to provide vital
commercial links between their agricultural neighbours to the south and the peoples of the Mediterranean coast to the north. In drier years, however, these pastoralists might push into southern savannas, employing their horses and mobile
lifestyles to their advantage in raiding farming communities and sometimes even
taking control of lands suitable for grazing.

Probably it was partly in response to such pressures that sedentary savanna
populations began to organize themselves into stronger political groupings, and,
wherever they could, adopt war-horses of their own to neutralize the military efficiency of their nomadic neighbours. Exemplifying this process was the kingdom
of Ghana in the borderlands of what is now Mauritania and Mali, which, by as
early as the fifth century, had developed into a powerful state capable, not just of
containing pastoralists' raids but of dominating some of the Saharan trade
routes.

From about the ninth century, Islam began to expand along these same trade
routes from northern Africa. Berber nomads were among the first converts. They
derived from their new religion a greater sense of unity, and it also strengthened
their trading links with fellow Muslims to the north. In the western Sahara,
Berber pastoralists formed the Almoravid movement in the eleventh century,
preaching a stricter adherence to Islam. Fired by religious zeal, the Almoravids
embarked on an era of dramatic expansion. A northern branch captured much of
northwestern Africa, and from there undertook the conquest of Iberia, bringing
many Europeans under their domination. In the process, many of the Berbers
gave up their nomadic lives for a more settled existence. To the south, another Almoravid branch extended its influence, if not control, over the kingdom of
Ghana, inducing its rulers to accept the Islamic faith.

Other kingdoms which eventually succeeded Ghana in the western Sudanic
belt, including Mali and Songhai, also adhered to Islam. Agriculture and trade,
rather than pastoralism, was the dominant economic activity of these societies,
but just to their north a strong pastoral tradition persisted, as it had done for cen-

turies. Some of these pastoralists were Berber-speaking groups, such as the Tuaregs, but in time they included other peoples, such as the Mossi. Although sometimes pushed back into arid environments by the sedentary southern kingdoms, the herdsmen frequently turned the tables and pushed their own raids into the regions of the agriculturists. In the fifteenth century the Tuaregs grew strong enough temporarily to capture the great city of Timbuktu and they did so again in the eighteenth century.

Sometimes pastoral groups themselves formed large centralized states in the region. Kanuri nomads, for example, established the kingdom of Kanem in the region of Lake Chad. Raiding and taxing agricultural populations, Kanem controlled some of the most important trans-Saharan trade routes.

While all this was happening, another West African pastoral group, the Fulbe or Fulani, who first lived in the area of Senegambia, were gradually expanding throughout much of the Sudanic belt. In general, they lived peacefully with farming peoples, trading with them and sometimes even surrendering their own pastoral ways to live amongst them. Among the region's first converts to Islam, some Fulani settled in urban areas where they became a respected class of Islamic scholars and clerics. In all instances, however, they retained a strong sense of their own cultural identity. Fulbe clerics in the eighteenth and nineteenth centuries led a series of religious jihads, often mobilizing their pastoral brethren as their main fighting forces. As a result, Islam spread more widely and effectively through much of West Africa.

It is abundantly clear, then, that far from being in any way peripheral to the main currents of the African historical experience, herding peoples played vastly important roles in key historical developments literally throughout the continent. By the nineteenth century, most of the present-day pastoral societies had taken shape, representing a wide spectrum of economic, social, cultural, political, and military forms. It is to these aspects of pastoralism that I now turn.

Economic, Social, Cultural, Political, and Military Aspects of Pastoral Societies

Economic Aspects

Taking their inspiration from the influential anthropologist, M.J. Herskovits, some studies of African pastoralists used to stress the concept of the "cattle complex" of these societies, in which the social and cultural aspects of livestock ownership were seen as rather more important than the economic one. Recently, however, scholars have begun to re-emphasize the fundamental economic significance of herding, while still acknowledging its importance in other areas of pastoral life. Indeed, it is evident that under reasonably favorable conditions even a few herdsmen could manage large numbers of livestock effectively, and extract from them abundant resources. In addition to providing food supplies, livestock provided hides, leather, wool, horns, bones, and sinews that were used for a wide variety of implements and utilitarian objects. Even dung could be mixed with clay and used as a construction material for a house, and of course could be used to fertilize crops. In many societies, livestock, especially donkeys, were also used as beasts of burden. In much of northern Africa, camels were used both for riding and to transport goods, and in southern Africa oxen were trained for the same purposes.

It is important to emphasize, however, that unless they were old or sick, animals were seldom slaughtered for meat by pastoral peoples, and even when they were it was usually in conjunction with an important religious or social observance. Rather, it was the products of the livestock—their milk, and, in some communities, blood drawn from living animals, that provided the most important foods. Often the milk was curdled and consumed as sour milk cheese, and some societies made butter and ghee.

The actual number of animals herded could vary greatly from one society to another. Those which followed a more specialized pastoral lifestyle would often own numbers of livestock many times greater than the human population, while those who engaged in some agriculture might herd far fewer animals—perhaps only about one beast per person. Nevertheless, pastoralists usually tried to possess as much livestock as possible, not just as a source of livelihood, but as we shall see, for other purposes as well.

Production typically was based on individual family groups, with clear divisions of labor between men and women. In some societies women might play vital roles in livestock management itself, often being the ones in charge of daily milking routines and being assigned specific animals from the family herd to feed their own children. In other cases, females might not deal directly with the herds at all. In most instances, younger men performed such tasks as guarding and watering the animals, typically under the direction of elders. Women commonly were responsible for the construction of houses, granaries, fences, and palisades, and they usually were the ones who tanned leather and manufactured many of the family's utensils.

There was once a notion that some herding societies were "pure pastoralists" who were entirely self-sufficient and lived exclusively on a diet of animal protein provided by the herds. Scholars now doubt that this ever was so. Rather, it is clear that all pastoralists were also dependent on grains and were closely linked with peoples producing these and other forms of subsistence. It would be incorrect to imagine any pastoral group existing in isolation from all others.

As we saw in the preceding historical survey, many pastoralists combined herding and farming activities where conditions permitted. Among these "agropastoralists," as they are sometimes termed, it was often the women who concentrated on cultivation while the men had charge of the livestock. In many cases, a society's livelihood might be derived equally from each of the two components of its mixed economy. Typical of this were the Nilotic-speaking Jie of Uganda, who expressed the economic importance of the two activities by saying that "God created cattle and sorghum [their main grain crop] on the same day." Even in inhospitable conditions where extensive agriculture was impossible, a pastoral community could practice "casual" horticulture by digging small gardens close to a reliable water source.

In other circumstances, pastoralists might depend on a separate cultivating people to supply their agricultural foods. This arrangement could take a variety of forms. As we saw in the previous section, pastoralists would sometimes extend a certain domination over their neighbours, as with the Tuaregs of the Sahara who collected produce from sedentary populations. Another example was the way in which "aristocratic" Tutsi cattle owners in East Africa marshaled the labor of agricultural Hutu in exchange for military protection.

More often, though, a pastoral society would establish symbiotic commercial links with their neighbors. In, for example, the highly varied ecological conditions of East Africa, these might develop into extensive regional networks including communities of pastoralists, farmers, and hunters. They could even develop into multi-ethnic communities where cultural and economic forms might blend so closely as to blur distinctions between the three categories of livelihood. Similarly, in West Africa, regular markets featured the exchange of pastoral products, agricultural produce, game products, fish, and salt, and featured close social and cultural interactions between the various producers. In many instances, pastoral communities devoted considerable attention to long-distance trade, and often controlled important commercial routes.

In some places, such as parts of the central Sudan, pastoralists and agriculturists might even share the same lands, with the herdsmen moving their animals into the cultivated fields of the farmers after the harvests had been gathered in. In yet other cases, pastoralists might establish reciprocal relations with their neighbors by which farmers borrowed some animals from pastoralists to utilize their manure as fertilizer. Conversely, a prosperous farmer who had collected some animals of his own might lend them out to a pastoral friend whose mobile lifestyle allowed him access to much more pasture land and therefore the ability to manage larger numbers of livestock.

Indeed, mobility and movement were implicit in herding activities. Only very rarely did African pastoralists use fodder crops to feed their herds; rather, livestock mainly foraged on natural pasturelands which were held communally by the society. Because in most of Africa's grasslands rainfall is seasonal, with alternating wet and dry seasons, herds had to be moved frequently to take advantage of local vegetation as it appeared. Pastoralists also understood the benefits of regularly moving their animals from one location to another, as different pasturelands featured different sorts of grasses containing a variety of nutrients and minerals.

The actual movements could take many forms. In those societies which also practiced agriculture, there was often a division of the community into two main sections for much of the year. One part, typically comprising older people, women, and children, would remain in established villages tending the crops. As conditions permitted, some livestock, especially milking animals whose products were an important food source, would stay nearby. Most of the herds, under the care of younger people, would be moved from pasture to pasture in areas far from the settlements. In those regions, only temporary stock camps would be built. Such was the system of many Nilotic-speakers in eastern Africa, including the Ateker group of Uganda, and also many Bantu-speaking communities in Central and southern Africa.

In those societies where agriculture was not practiced, the entire population might regularly move. Sometimes such movement would be confined to a well-defined region, following definite seasonal patterns. This we term "transhumance," and an excellent example was provided by the Fulbe of West Africa who followed an annual north-south movement, following the rains across the savanna. Likewise, Khoisan populations living in the Cape region of southern Africa followed a pattern whereby they wintered along the seacoasts, harvesting maritime resources, and then moved to inland pastures with their herds during the rainy summers.

Other societies followed a more truly nomadic pattern of fairly constant movement throughout vast areas. Frequently such movement was a feature of Africa's direst environments, including even parts of the Sahara. Here Tuareg communities would become widely dispersed over a huge region during the dry season, then they congregated in the better pasturelands when rain fell.

The types of livestock herded might also contribute to the sort of movement practiced. Small stock, for example, could browse (that is, live off the leaves of bushes) and therefore could be moved into bush country where there was little grazing. Similarly, camels could be kept in environments too harsh for cattle, and, because they needed far less water, could be driven further away from watering points. Thus, among the Turkana of Kenya, who herded all three varieties of stock, families would divide into sections, one of which would move considerable distances with small stock and camels across semi-arid plains, while other sections would graze cattle in upland pastures close to permanent springs.

Sometimes demographic, ecological, or other pressures could cause a community to move beyond the area they normally used. Such wider movement could take many forms, as we shall see below, but typically it was a gradual peaceful process of "migratory drift." Frequently, for instance, a part of the community—perhaps some of the younger people out at the distant stock camps—might split off from the rest to push into a new area, perhaps absorbing, mixing with, or themselves being absorbed by the people they found living there.

Social and Cultural Aspects

While livestock was thus vital to the economies of pastoral peoples, it was of key importance in other areas, too. To begin with, animals were vital in establish-

Figure 10-3. Young Oxherds in Kenya

ing, defining, and maintaining social relations between members of the community. Thus, in most pastoral societies a man with large herds was reckoned to be a very important person, not merely because he was wealthy, but because he could use his animals to construct social networks with many other people. He might, for example, provide animals or their products to neighbors who had lost their own herds. At the very least he thus would earn their indebtedness and support, and they could even become his dependent clients. Or, on ceremonial occasions, a rich man could earn the respect and admiration of his entire society by providing animals for ritual sacrifice. Indeed, generosity was seen as a great virtue by pastoral peoples. Even less affluent men typically sought to establish "bond friendships" with as many other herdsmen as possible through the constant reciprocal exchange of livestock. In patrilineal societies (that is, those who trace their descent through the father's family), animals contributed by kinsmen and friends of the groom were given to the family of the bride as bridewealth at the time of marriage. It was this constant "flow" of livestock throughout a pastoral society that gave it its very cohesion and identity. And in most instances, the greater the flow, the greater the degree of egalitarianism within the community.

This essential egalitarianism helps us to understand the relatively high social status of women among many herding peoples. Sometimes, as with the Tuaregs of the Sahara, women could even be the heads of families. In matrilineal systems (ones tracing descent through the mother's line), such as the Herero of southwestern Africa, children inherited livestock from their mother. As we have seen, women frequently controlled important aspects of economic life, and they could have great religious powers as well. In many societies, women had much more sexual freedom than was generally the case with sedentary agriculturists.

On a more personal and psychological level, there was often a close identity between herdsmen and their animals. Because the lives of people and animals were so intimately intermeshed, it is hardly surprising that herders should have been utterly engrossed with their livestock. In many eastern African societies, fathers commonly presented their sons with special animals, sometimes referred to as "bell oxen." A young man would spend long hours composing poems and songs to this ox; he would hammer its horns into distinctive shapes and imitate those shapes with his hands to gain courage in battle; he would even take the name of the ox as one of his own; and, when the ox died, he would mourn it as though a close kinsman.

Livestock also played vital roles in the spiritual life of a pastoral community. Animals often provided vivid religious symbols and were at the very heart of belief systems, linking divinity with human populations. So important was their link to the supernatural that the breeds of animal to be herded, their colors, and their markings were sometimes dictated by religious considerations. Very often they served as sacrificial offerings used in such important rituals as making rain, ensuring fertility, conferring initiation, reconciliation of feuds, and funeral transitions from life to death. In the centralized pastoral states, livestock symbolized royal power and the divine authority of the rulers. In some, the king was regarded as the ultimate "owner" of all the cattle, and by granting them to his subjects he formed vital links which bound the kingdom together.

In terms of material culture, the mobility of many pastoral groups meant that heavy items, such as large drums, grinding stones, or weaving looms commonly found among sedentary peoples, were often absent. Instead, light, portable items which could easily be transported from place to place were the rule. This was also true of art forms, where, instead of the bulky carvings, masks, and metal castings of many agriculturists, the artistic expression of pastoralists often meant ornamenting portable items of daily life. Thus, such things as milk gourds, headrests, tobacco containers, articles of clothing, leather bags, and weapons were often richly decorated with beads, cowry shells, paint, or toolings. Even the human body was frequently ornamented with elaborate jewelry, clays, ochres, paints, or tattoos.

In West Africa, the Fulbe revered beautifully fashioned domestic utensils and women proudly displayed them outside their homes. Among the Maasai of East Africa, young men went on cattle raids carrying hide shields painted with intricate heraldic designs and wearing splendid headdresses of lions' manes or ostrich plumes. Among these and many other communities, performing arts, including oration and the spirited rendering of traditions and stories, together with many types of musical expression, were also highly developed.

Political and Military Aspects

As we saw in the earlier part of this chapter, African pastoralists had a great variety of political structures. Many were decentralized, without hereditary rulers, and often featured age-class systems where authority was vested in a council of older men (known as a "gerontocracy"). Many of the pastoralists of eastern Africa conformed to this pattern. Others, including the Bantu-speaking kingdoms of the interlacustrine region and Central Africa, had strongly centralized systems led by hereditary divine kings. Still others, such as the Tuaregs, had complex hier-

Figure 10-4. The Great Zimbabwe, Excavations of the Enclosure

Figure 10-5. View of the Conical Tower of the Great Zimbabwe

archical structures which divided the society into virtual castes. As we saw, political forms were directly derived from the ownership of livestock, and in many instances political centralization may have initially been dictated by the need to distribute herds and their resources.

No matter what their political form, however, all pastoral communities had to be concerned with the difficult tasks of protecting and maintaining their vulnerable livestock. Droughts, livestock diseases, the attacks of wild animals, and the raids of rival groups could wipe out herds very rapidly. To counter the first two problems, pastoralists might frequently rely on their mobility to move away from affected areas. To protect their herds from animal or human predators, pastoralists traditionally became well-skilled in the use of weapons and sometimes developed elaborate military structures. Among many of the decentralized peoples of eastern and southern Africa, these were based on the age-class systems. Here, the consolidation of young men into a corporate grade of "warriors" assigned to defend the community, could, coupled with the rugged self-reliance of the pastoral lifestyle, translate into a particularly aggressive sense of masculinity. And, because they derived a strong notion of corporate identity from performing a variety of collective activities, age-sets of young men by their nature closely resembled military units. Sometimes age-sets could indeed provide the basis for a society's expansion. Such was apparently the case with the Oromo, whose Gada age-class system provided a constant source of aggressive, newly initiated young men who each year drove the herds further and further northwards into Ethiopia and raided the populations living there. Because of all this, the pastoralists of eastern Africa have frequently been regarded by outsiders as particularly warlike people. Similarly, in West Africa, where, as we have seen, conflict between pastoralists and agriculturists sometimes occurred, there has been a tendency to view animosity between herders and farmers as a constant, inevitable phenomenon. In fact many have concluded that by its very nature pastoralism equals predatory expansion.

More recently, however, we have formed a different assessment of pastoralists. First of all, it is important to distinguish between the day-to-day transhumant or nomadic movement of herding peoples and more aggressive forms of movement. The first sort of movement usually did not involve expansion at all, and, even when it did, it was typically a gradual, peaceful process. Occasionally, however, environmental or political problems might cause an entire community to move suddenly and dramatically into a new region. But even here conflict did not necessarily occur. In many East African cases, for example, migration helped to construct wide commercial and social networks among fluid, constantly evolving groups of herdsmen, farmers, and hunters. Similarly, migrating Fulbe in West Africa often lived in harmony with agricultural populations; and shifting economic outlooks and identities were a typical feature of historical interactions throughout much of that same region.

Beyond this, it is clear that powerful forces in many pastoral societies tended to *limit*, rather than encourage, military activity. For example, the "segmentary" organizations (that is, individual, independent, stock-owning families making up the society) of some peoples, such as the Somali, which might sometimes foster oppositions and feuds, could just as easily ensure reconciliation and alliance. Even age-class systems, which in some respects could facilitate military organization, were more basically a means by which elders could control truculent young men and prevent the escalation of violence. Very often pastoralists followed a stylized form of warfare known as "reciprocal raiding" regulated by almost chivalric codes. Far from causing social unrest and disintegration, this sort of raiding was a balanced arrangement in which few people were killed or injured. In a fundamental sense, it insured the smooth flow and redistribution of animals between communities.

Mainly, it was only when a centralizing authority gave a pastoral society some wider sense of political, or sometimes religious, purpose that expansion became co-ordinated and aggressive. Prime cases are provided by the Fulani jihads in West Africa. Perhaps the most dramatic example of all, however, took place when the great king Shaka revamped the Zulu military system in South Africa and set off a dramatic, far-ranging series of expansions known as the *Mfecane*.

However, the image of truculent, overbearing, and exclusive pastoral societies was born largely during the era of colonialism. Colonial administrations sharply curtailed free interaction between African communities and accentuated differences between them. Such was certainly the case, for example, in interlacustrine East Africa, where colonial policies strengthened the domination of Tutsi pastoral "aristocrats" over Hutu agriculturists with cataclysmic results. In many other cases, colonial boundaries and "closed districts" sealed pastoralists off from major political and economic developments, making them seem exclusive and resistant to change.

Review Questions

1. How would you define an African pastoral society?
2. What impact did iron technology have on the development of African pastoralism?
3. Describe the interactions between pastoralists and agriculturalists in West Africa.
4. What are the various forms of movement and migration practiced by African pastoralists?
5. What is the social significance of the "flow" of livestock through a pastoral community?
6. What role does livestock play in the spiritual life of pastoral societies?

Additional Reading

Fukui, Katsuyoshi and David Turton, eds. *Warfare Among East African Herders.* Osaka: Senri Ethnological Studies, No. 3, 1977.

Galaty, John G. and Pierre Bonte, eds. *Herders, Warriors and Traders: Pastoralism in Africa.* Boulder, CO: Westview Press, 1991.

Monad, T., ed. *Pastoralism in Tropical Africa.* London: International African Institute, 1976.

Smith, Andrew B. *Pastoralism in Africa: Origins and Development Ecology.* Athens: Ohio University Press, 1992.

Spear, Thomas, and Richard Waller, eds. *Being Maasai.* London: James Currey, 1993.

Chapter 11

Agriculture, Trade and Industries

Toyin Falola

There are at least two major constraints in reconstructing the history of the domestic economy of precolonial Africa. The first is the paucity of source materials. Though the literature on economic history is growing, information on different parts of Africa is very uneven; there is more on West than on East Africa, and more on the post-fifteenth century era than on the centuries preceding it. As a result of this, generalizations and unsubstantiated statements abound. Furthermore, it is difficult to quantify the level of production and exchange of goods in that period. This makes it hard to measure economic change and growth. The modern economic methods for measuring change and rate of growth are hardly useful in examining indigenous economies. Therefore, it is scarcely possible to calculate production, national income, foreign exchange earnings, annual growth rate, and other sectors in production and exchange in most precolonial African economies. What is clear from the sources is that the economy was dynamic, changing in many sectors, and moving toward a monetized market economy. The second constraint relates to chronology. While it is possible to identify the major revolutionary changes in the domestic economy, it is often difficult to give exact dates. This difficulty is partly due to the inadequacy of source materials.

These two constraints do not, however, prevent a reconstruction of the basic features of the domestic economy, and some of the most profound aspects of it are now understood. In this chapter, the distinguishing features of the production and distributive systems are presented, starting with the most essential factors of the former. Readers should note the interaction of social and religious elements with the economic system.

Factors of Production

By the first century A.D., when most African communities had established an agricultural and commercial economy, four factors of production and exchange had become distinct; these were land, capital, tools, and labor.

The most important factor was land. Generally, land was not scarce though there were regions with poor soil conditions or with inadequate land to support large populations. By the nineteenth century, such regions included the Sahara, the Kalahari, and the Ethiopian desert, parts of eastern Nigeria, western Cameroon, North Africa, East Africa, and southern Africa.

The organization of land tenure for economic activities was regulated by laws and customs enforced by communities or their leaders. While the laws varied from one state to another, they shared certain common features. First, land was corporately owned and its administration was vested in the community leaders or rulers. As trustees, they defended and upheld the people's rights to their land. Throughout much of precolonial Africa, the idea of corporate land ownership remained unthreatened despite the infiltration of Islamic and Western ideas.

Second, all descent groups in a community had rights to land. Such rights remained inviolate except in cases of external conquest. Therefore, an individual possessed rights to land for any legitimate economic activity only through membership in a descent group. Third, a stranger could, after satisfying certain conditions which included payment of a token gift such as kolanuts, obtain land from his host family or community. This gift, whether in cash or kind, was not regarded as payment for the land but rather as an acknowledgment that the stranger recognized the rights of the hosts who gave him the land to use. Among the Kikuyu in Kenya, the stranger worked for the ruler or the leader of the descent group who gave out land. Over time, the land could become the permanent possession of the stranger who could then transfer it to his children.

Finally, the descent group, the individual, and the stranger were forbidden from alienating the land. Strong religious beliefs and sanctions backed up this rule. Almost all communities deified the land and regarded the earth deity as the guardian of public morality and the fountain of fertility, both human and agricultural. It was universally believed that land belonged not only to the living but also to both the ancestors whose wrath could be incurred if land was sold, and to the yet unborn who could only come into the world and survive if there was land for them.

Capital was another factor of production. It was organized at the individual level by those who needed it for economic or other purposes. Capital was raised in several ways: through savings, loans, gifts, and proceeds from the sales of goods. It is not always realized that many African states had indigenous credit and banking institutions. One notable example in many communities was the co-operative savings club, like the *esusu* among the Yoruba. The members of these clubs agreed on how much to save within a specified period, and the rules to guide loans and withdrawals. There were also money lenders in most communities, despite religious rules which tended to forbid their operations.

The last factor of production was labor. An extended family unit constituted the main operative economic entity and was therefore central in production. Family labor was competent, effective, efficient, and well-organized to engage in desired economic activities. There was the family mode of production in which a man organized all his unmarried children, wife or wives, and relatives living with him for production purposes. Though the man did not pay any wages, he was solely responsible for all the basic needs of those working for him. Since the quantity of goods that could be produced was largely determined by the size of the family, a man tried to have as many wives as possible, thus making large families the norm in many African societies.

There were, however, other ways to secure additional labor, and this suggests that the African labor force was more varied than it is generally assumed. A first source was through co-operative work groups which involved employing many able-bodied men (and sometimes women) within a community for a specific as-signment. It was not usual for the beneficiary to pay any wages, but he provided drinks and food.

A second source of labor supply was through peonage or patron-client rela-tionships whereby a debtor would work for his creditor or allow his son or rela-tion to do so until the debt was repaid. The labor represented the collateral secu-rity and the interest on the loan. Among the Kanuri and the Baganda, there existed a patron-client relationship between members of the aristocracy and the commoners. In Rwanda, it was called *buhake,* literally meaning "to pay one's re-spect to a superior in his court." The client offered his services to the "superior" in return for protection and gifts of milk, cows, or land.

Finally, there was the institution of domestic slavery which provided chiefs, warriors, and wealthy traders with labor for diverse economic activities, espe-cially those activities considered odious by the freeborn. The use of slaves indi-cated the existence of social and economic inequalities and of a labor market in Africa. Domestic slavery probably grew out of the desire to solve shortages of labor in a booming economy.

To ensure their loyalty and maximize their labor, slaves were often integrated into their owners' families and thus into the community. They were usually promised redemption as soon as they could buy their freedom—a difficult task considering the fact that many slaves had little or no time to work for themselves. In most centralized states, the use of slaves on a large scale gave rise to an embry-onic "slave mode of production," an arrangement which created a few rich slave owners as entrepreneurs and slaves as the labor force. This occurred in parts of West Africa during the nineteenth century, including the Sokoto Caliphate, Borno, Ibadan, and Dahomey where chiefs and warriors had large farms worked by slaves who had the right to only a small part of the harvests to keep them alive. It also existed in the Omani Empire in East Africa in the nineteenth century where slaves worked in large clove plantations. During the nineteenth century, areas that were integrated with the international economy as suppliers of raw materials used slaves in large numbers, the more so as the trans-Atlantic slave trade was nearing its end and slaves were diverted to large-scale domestic production.

Production of Goods and Services

The production system was characterized by remarkable changes and innova-tions, regional diversities, and complex organizations resulting in the production of a diverse range of goods. The sectors in the production system comprised agri-culture, mining, manufacturing, and the provision of essential services.

Agriculture, which embraced farming, animal husbandry, and fishing, was the leading sector in the economy. The history of agriculture in Africa has been one of monumental changes, though it has not been possible to document all the signifi-cant phases.

In the Stone Age period (ca. 3m. B.C.-5000 B.C.), human communities in Africa went through a very long and slow pace of economic development. Progress was slowest during the Early and Middle Stone Ages (ca. 3m. B.C.-15,000 B.C.) when communities lived a mainly migratory life, gathering fruits and hunting wild animals with crude stone tools. From ca. 15,000 B.C., which marked the beginning of the Later Stone Age, improvement became more noticeable and remarkable. Climatic changes led to vegetational differentiation between grasslands and forests. By ca. 7000 B.C., human fishing communities had emerged at Baringo on Lake Turkana and Ishango on Lake Mobutu, and later along the Zambezi River and at Diama in Nigeria. These communities began using barbed harpoons, net weights and other fishing-specific equipment. Production of surplus food led to more permanent human settlements; this created changes in socio-political structure that eventually led to the evolution of full-fledged descent groups and succession laws.

On the other hand, human communities who inhabited the grasslands and forests continued their migratory lives as hunters and gatherers, but began to use refined stone tools. The Gwisho hunters near the Kafue River in Zambia typified the height of this development. By 2300 B.C., these hunters led a communal life and hunted with dogs, bows, and arrows. They, like the fishing groups, now produced enough food for larger populations, leading to similar socio-political developments. Relics of the hunting and gathering groups are the San in Southwest Africa, the people of the Zaire basin, the Ndorobo of Kenya, and the Mahalbi between Chad and the Nile. All these groups except the San and the Gorate (Teda-Danza) hunters in northern Chad lived harmoniously with their agricultural or pastoral neighbors.

The evolution of human settlements and of descent groups, therefore, occurred before the domestication of animals and crops, but both of these were important phases in the agricultural revolution. Between 6000 B.C. and 5000 B.C., human communities in the Sahara, then a grassland area, kept cattle, sheep, and goats. By 5000 B.C., they had begun to experiment with a variety of crops. As barley and wheat were not suitable for the soil, new crops were domesticated in the tropical and sub-tropical regions north of the equator between 5000 B.C. and 500 B.C.: sorghum (guinea corn) between the Sahara and the Western Sudan; pearl and finger millets in the Sahara (from where they diffused to Ethiopia and the Horn of Africa); the *ansete* (banana family) and cowpea in the Ethiopian highlands; rice in the inland delta of the Niger River; and yam varieties and the oil palm in the forest region of West Africa.

The desiccation of the Sahara from about 2000 B.C. led to the diffusion of some of the crops to Egypt and to sub-tropical Africa north of the equator. Early farming communities existed at various times from 1100 B.C. to the first century A.D. at Dartichitt in southern Mauritania, Karusakata and Diama in Borno, Kintampo in modern Ghana, and Djenne.

The diffusion of domesticated crops in sub-equatorial Africa is associated with the Bantu migrations. From their homeland in the Cameroons, the Bantu migrated about 500 B.C. north of the Zaire forest to the Lake Victoria region where they introduced the finger millet and yams and herded cattle and goats. Another Bantu group migrated into the forest region on the border of Zaire and Angola and introduced yams. From these two subsidiary centers, the Bantu migrated into East and southern Africa introducing the new crops and animals as they went. Between the first and the eighth centuries A.D., bananas, cocoyams, and plantains were adopted from Asia. After the fifteenth century, cassava, maize, peanuts, tobacco, and a variety of fruits were adopted from South America, and, in the nineteenth century, cocoa was also introduced from South America.

By the first century A.D., a virile agricultural system, adapted to specific environments, had emerged in most parts of Africa, and the agricultural year followed a regular pattern: the bush was cleared in the dry season, ridging and planting were done during the earliest rains, weeding at intervals, and harvesting before the dry season returned. The harvest, a time of plenty, was usually a season of festivals and religious ceremonies during which sacrifices were offered to the gods of fertility.

The crops grown depended largely on the suitability of the soil. In the tropical rain forest, staple root crops, varieties of yams, melons, pumpkins, and cowpeas were cultivated while tree crops like oil and raffia palms, kolanut, bitter kola, locust beans, and *akee* (apple) were domesticated. In the savanna, the emphasis was on cereals (e.g., rice, millet, and sorghum), cotton, indigo, and peanuts. The introduction of Asiatic and South American crops enriched the agricultural economy. Each African community integrated the crops into its domestic economy at different periods, the new crops could solve problems of food shortages because of their high yields. The introduction of new crops, therefore, diversified the agricultural economy, improved nutrition, facilitated the support of large populations, and reduced the risk of famine.

The major systems of agriculture were shifting cultivation, irrigation, permanent cultivation, rotational bush fallow, and mixed cropping. The choice of any of these systems depended largely on the availability of land, the land tenure system, and physiographic factors. Shifting cultivation was the most widespread. It was practicable where there was abundant land because it involved a temporary abandonment of over-used land to allow it to regain its fertility. Shifting cultivation helped to reduce the spread and danger of insects and weeds, and restored the fertility of farmland without the application of fertilizers.

Farming had three other features. First, it was intensive, though the tools used were simple. Second, it was very efficient, and production not only met the needs of the local population but also provided a considerable surplus that was exchanged for other goods and services. Finally, agriculture was ritualized—sacrifices were made at the beginning and end of the farming year to appease the spirits, forces, or gods who were believed to control agricultural fertility.

Animal husbandry is another agricultural sector. This was practiced by pastoralists who lived in the grassland and savanna areas where there were no tsetse flies. The animals were kept for hides, manure, milk, and meat, and the pastoralists lived a migratory life in search of water and pasture for their herds and in order to trade their products in exchange for food items produced by farmers.

Another major agricultural sector in precolonial Africa was fishing and hunting. The economy of riverine and coastal areas was often dominated by fishing and allied activities such as canoe building, ferrying, and repairing of fishing tools. Various types of nets, traps, and hooks were employed in fishing. Fishermen also migrated in search of fish, the availability of which depended on flood periods and tidal movements. For instance, the Sorkawa and Bozo of the Middle Niger travelled thousands of kilometers annually along the River Niger. Similarly, the Fante of Ghana moved periodically both to the west as far as the Ivory Coast and to the east as far as Nigeria. In their migrations, the fishermen often established fishing settlements which later grew into large towns (e.g., Lagos in Nigeria). They also engaged in trade with inland groups, exchanging fish for other products. Furthermore, by conveying goods from one place to another, they provided links among different hinterland communities and contributed to the diffusion of ideas and urbanization.

Hunting is an age-old occupation which was important in the forest region where meat was in short supply. Hunting was intensified during the dry season when farm work was light and the bush was dry and easier to burn, thereby facilitating hunting expeditions. Hunters were specialists and the occupation was restricted to men who were believed to have the charms to overcome physical and spiritual dangers. They used traps, clubs, bows and arrows, and later guns.

Two other major sectors in the production systems were mining and manufacturing. Mining activities revolved around the working of iron, gold, salt, silver, tin, and copper. Of these, iron was the most significant. The knowledge of ironworking was spreading by the first millennium B.C. For example, iron had been worked in Nok, in present day Nigeria, by about 500 B.C., and by the 4th century A.D. it had spread to most parts of Africa.

Ironworking included complex and integrated segments. There were miners, smelters, and smiths. Usually, the miners were smelters, while the smelters could also be smiths who fashioned the iron into different tools and implements. The production of pig iron involved a laborious search for iron stones in pits, and quarries, and these were melted in the furnaces at a temperature of about 1500 degrees centigrade to separate the pig iron from the slag. In the smitheries, iron was further smelted, cut into smaller sizes, and processed into such tools as hoes, javelins, cutlasses, sickles, adzes, arrows, hairpins, daggers, knives, and various types of swords, which revolutionized agriculture, warfare, and trade. To ensure occupational secrecy, the smithing process was ritualized.

Salt was produced for domestic consumption and for external trade in two ways: in the sahelian region, it was produced by mining, and along the coast by boiling sea water or allowing sea water to evaporate in the sun.

Gold was also important, not only as an article of trade but also because gold mining and smithing were lucrative and prestigious. It was also a source of wealth to rulers of gold producing states. Gold mining in Africa probably began in about 500 B.C. but large-scale production, especially in West Africa, began after the seventh century A.D. when there was a high demand for gold in Europe, North Africa, and Asia. The leading production centers were Bambuk, Noure, Lobi, and Asante, all in West Africa, the Ethiopian foothills, and the Zimbabwean plateau south of the Zambezi River.

There were only a few tin producing areas, such as Nigeria and Chad. In the Jos and Bauchi plateau of Nigeria, for example, tin occurred in shallow deposits usually covered by varying depths of barren ground called the "overburden." The "overburden" was removed by the use of pickaxes and hoes. The tinbearing earth was then washed in a river or stream to obtain the raw tin which was later smelted by a process similar to that of iron. Thereafter, tin smiths mixed the smelted tin with copper or lead to produce alloys that were used to manufacture cooking utensils, plates, and statues.

Manufacturing was more diverse than mining. Manufactured goods were made from plants, minerals, and animal products in the form of processed foodstuffs, cloth, leather, wood, and ceramics. Leather production involved many specialists who cured, tanned, and dyed animal skins which were in turn used to manufacture bags, cushions, aprons, saddles, etc. The ceramic industry was limited to areas with clay, and the workers exhibited great skill in the making of kitchen utensils, as well as ritual and decorative items. The cloth industry, one of the oldest in Africa, was the most widespread and engaged a large number of people in the production of yarns, threads, cloth, and dyestuff. Before the discovery of cotton, raffia and the bark of trees had been used. Cotton technology, however, revolutionized the weaving industry.

One important feature in manufacturing in precolonial Africa was that it depended essentially on local raw materials, though these were supplemented with imported materials. Another is that the production of various goods was restricted to certain households. Sometimes, however, children from other households were recruited as apprentices and given thorough training in a specific skill. In some communities, miners and manufacturers formed themselves into highly organized guilds, while in other communities only loose associations existed. Guilds regulated occupational practices, controlled prices, and united to defend their interests within their community.

Other workers such as masons, diviners and doctors, barbers, singers, drummers, and other artists provided specialist services either on a full or part-time basis.

Exchange of Goods and Services

A number of factors gave rise to, and promoted, the exchange of goods and services in precolonial African societies. First, because production of goods had gone above subsistence level, the surpluses had to be sold. Second, there was specialization of economic activities in every community and one occupational group often needed the products of another. For instance, craftsmen and farmers often exchanged their products to meet their individual and family needs. Indeed, no African community was self-sufficient in all its requirements. Physiographic factors, and degrees of specialization and skill acquisition varied from one state to another and, therefore, promoted economic interdependence among states. For example the savanna area of West Africa has been classified into three separate zones of vegetation: the Sahel furthermost to the north, the Sudan in the middle, and the Guinea zone to the south. Further south is the tropical rain forest which merges into the fresh water and mangrove swamps that lead to the coast. The implication for trade of this geographical variation on trade becomes clear when it is realized that some crops prospered only in certain conditions of rainfall, soil fertility, and humidity. While kola nuts and yams grew well in the forest region, tsetse flies disallowed pastoralism in this environment. Hence cattle, upland rice, and millet, the products of the savanna region, had to be exchanged for the kolanuts and palm produce of the forest zone. Even within the same geographical zone, there were obvious variations, like the sub-zonal specializations of fishing, hunting, and manufacturing.

Exchange probably started through non-market institutions such as gifts, inheritance, bride-wealth, payment of tribute and taxes, and the routine allotment of goods and other commodities by heads of households to their members. Thus, large quantities of goods were exchanged in all communities without the use of currency in order to maintain social relationships.

Exchange based on social relations limited the flow of goods to a few people and a few areas; but this eventually developed into exchange based on rudimentary market principles. For a long time, exchange by barter predominated, but it promoted imbalance and inequality in exchange and, to a great extent, restricted trade in area. The inadequacies of the barter system facilitate the development of the infrastructure of commerce including currencies, markets, trading conventions, language(s) of communication, trade routes, and professional traders.

Commercial systems had some common features. Trade operated at two main levels: internal and external. Internal or local trade operated within the community, while all towns and large villages had daily or periodic markets which served as the local exchange points where producers, traders, and consumers met to transact business. One characteristic of these markets is that they were often sited in open spaces close to the residences of the leading community members, with trees, stalls or tents providing shade. Sellers of similar commodities sat in groups, an arrangement which helped buyers to easily locate the commodities they wanted.

The markets provided a central place where various craftsmen, barbers, and other occupational groups offered their services. Singers, poets, and drummers also performed there. Political and judicial activities occasionally took place there. Markets were also centers for rapid dissemination of information and the circulation of news and rumors about current events in the society.

The markets were organized and trading went on in such a peaceful atmosphere that one nineteenth-century European observer remarked: "that such immense crowds should meet day after day in perfect harmony and order [in West African markets] and transact their affairs like one great family without fighting and bloodshed is more wonderful because it stands out in such bold contrasts to what is seen in lands boasted for civilization and good government." This orderliness was achieved through the agency of market officials, trade guilds, and customary laws prohibiting attacks on defenseless traders.

Periodic markets attracted large numbers of people from two or more communities and a larger volume of trade and served as centers for the distribution of raw materials, processed food items, imported goods, and craft products. They were often in places which were convenient for people in different communities to attend, and individual markets in an area were arranged to fall on different days of the week to avoid clashes and encourage maximum participation.

Trading also went on outside the market places, notably in compounds, private houses of chiefs and brokers, in farms, and along routes. In Muslim areas, considerable trade was carried on in the compounds of women kept in purdah. In addition, there were hawkers and itinerant traders.

The commodities of trade can be divided into three groups. Food crops, usually the food grown in a locality, were common items in all markets. Related to these were agro-allied commodities processed from basic foods. Staple food items as millet, maize, and yams and products derived from them were common trade items. A third group of goods included mined and manufactured items, such as gold, copper, iron, salt, and ceramic products. There were, of course, many other items difficult to classify into groups, such as slaves, luxury materials (e.g., books and clothes) from distant lands, and textiles.

At least three types of currencies were used in trade transactions before the colonial period. The first type was produce currency (i.e., exchange units based on the key products of the region). Slaves, salt, cloth, horses, and cattle fall within this category. Cotton strips were used in the Sudan, the Central African Republic, Borno, and Senegambia, cattle in parts of East Africa, and salt in the Sahara and parts of North Africa. In the Niger-Benue area, an *agi*, a standard calabash of corn, was reckoned as a standard of value which was equivalent to a large manilla which, in turn, was equivalent to five cup measures of salt.

The second type was metal currency including iron, gold, copper, and brass objects. Iron plates were used in Nigeria, Niger, and the Cameroons, manillas along the West African coast, and gold in Asante and the Western Sudan. Gold currency was either in gold dust put in small bags or in coins known in West Africa as *mithqals* or *dinars*.

The cowry (*cyprae moneta*), the third type of currency, was more widespread than the others. Imported from the Maldive Islands, it first reached North Africa and the Middle East before 1000 A.D. It spread to other parts of Africa and remained in circulation till the early twentieth century. From the sixteenth century onwards, European traders imported huge quantities of cowries to Africa, extending their circulation and importance. The cowry had some advantages which accounted for its wide acceptability. First, its units of counting were uniform in many states: it was usually counted singly or in multiples of tens and twenties. Second, it was suitable and efficient for small transactions, and, third, it could not be counterfeited.

Most African currencies shared characteristics of a general purpose money — contrary to the view that they were primitive and special purpose currencies that failed to assist liquidity and could not be exchanged for all goods and services. Like modern and general purpose currencies, precolonial African currencies acted as a medium of exchange, a common measure of value, a store of wealth, and a recognized standard of deferred payment.

The price of commodities in many markets was arrived at by haggling. The seller would demand the highest price possible by stressing the quality and scarcity of the goods. Decrying the merchandise, the buyer would then offer a very low price. Both would eventually agree on a price which might be up to two thousand percent lower than that originally quoted. However, goods such as pepper, vegetables, and drinks measured in pots, calabashes, and skin containers sometimes had fixed prices.

External trade was carried out at two levels. The first was regional, involving societies within the same geographical region. The second was international, linking one state with others far away. Egypt, for instance, had commercial contacts with East Africa. The trade could also be between two sub-regions, the trans-Saharan trade between West Africa and North Africa being an example. International trade also linked Africa with other continents, notably Asia, southern Europe, and the Americas.

The organization of external trade called for a complex network of routes, a well-developed transport system, a highly organized merchant group, efficient credit institutions, and languages of commerce. Transportation by land and water was well-developed and largely by human porterage, pack animals, and canoe. Trade routes linked villages and towns in localles, states, and regions. Porterage — the carriage of goods by people also transporting themselves at the same time — was the oldest and the most common. A person could carry a load of sixty-five lbs. in weight. While porterage contributed to the massive movement of goods, its drawback was that the labor could have been used for other productive enterprises. Where they could survive, pack animals such as camels, donkeys, and mules provided a faster and more efficient means of transportation than porterage. Pack animals carried more luggage and allowed the transportation of bulk and heavy items. However, they were limited to the desert and savanna regions from which tsetse flies were absent. Also, pack animals were less useful during the rainy season because of the difficulty of crossing swollen streams and muddy terrain. Different vessels, such as reed canoes and dugouts, were constructed to navigate all sorts of waterways. Canoes carried more goods than human beings and animals, and provided shelter and comfort at the same time.

The various African societies also had long-distance traders who specialized in carrying goods from one market place to another. They included the target traders who traded beyond their states during the dry seasons; regular traders who sold what they produced; professional and specialized traders such as the Dyula, Hausa, and Arabs who dealt in high value goods which they did not produce themselves; and official traders transacting businesses on behalf of rulers.

Long distance trade was organized in caravans, some of which could involve as many as a thousand traders, with guards, porters, guides, and leaders. Travelling in caravans enlivened the journey and reduced the risks of becoming lost or being attacked by marauders. It was usually a slow journey, traveling five or more hours daily, with rest and sleep stops in places established along the routes. The traders paid tolls or custom duties to state officials at the various borders through which they passed. The amount paid depended on the policy of the state, the commodities involved (slaves, cloth, and horses attracted more duties than foodstuffs), and the whims and caprices of toll collectors.

External trade among states and regions assured the distribution of goods between areas of surplus production and areas of scarcity. As a result, trade became an important factor of interstate relations, even in times of war. The existence of external trade also encouraged regional specialization and consequent large-scale production of goods. Trade brought wealth which in turn enhanced the prestige of individuals, rulers, and the states they governed.

Conclusion

The precolonial African domestic economy was diversified and included agriculture, mining, manufacturing, and commerce. Essential services were offered by specialists and professionals in various fields. Farm and industrial products were produced in large quantities, well above the subsistence level. Local and long-distance traders distributed the surpluses.

The domestic economy developed over time and always responded to changes, internal as well as external. Among the internal dynamics of change were population increases, occasional technical innovations, and expansion in the market. Among the external contacts were contacts with the Middle East, Europe, and the Americas. Finally, the economy provided the necessary basis for political systems and the emergence and survival of states.

Review Questions

1. What would you regard as the most important aspects of farming in Africa?
2. Discuss various aspects of trade and evaluate their significance in the development of African societies.

Additional Reading

Akinjogbin, I.A. and S.O. Osoba. *Topics on Nigerian Economic and Social History.* Ile-Ife: University of Ife Press, 1980.

Austin, R. *African Economic History.* London: James Currey, 1987.

Birmingham, D., ed. *Pre-colonial African Trade.* Oxford: O.U.P., 1970.

Curtin, P.D. *Economic Change in Pre-colonial Africa: Senegambian in the Era of the Slave Trade.* 2 vols. Madison: The University of Wisconsin Press, 1975.

Goody, Jack. *Technology, Tradition and the State in Africa.* London: O.U.P., 1972.

Gray, Richard and David Birmingham, eds., *Pre-colonial African Trade: Essays on Trade in Central and Easter Africa Before 1900.* Oxford: O.U.P., 1970.

Hopkins, A.G. *An Economic History of West Africa.* London: Longman, 1973.

Shaw, T. "Early Agriculture in Africa," *Journal of the Historical Society of Nigeria* (June 1972): 143-191.

Wickins, P.L. *An Economic History of Africa from Earliest Times to Partition.* Cape Town: O.U.P., 1981.

Zeleza, T. *A Modern Economic History of Africa: Vol. 1 The Nineteenth Century.* Dakar, Senegal: CODESRIA, 1993.

Chapter 12

Medicine, Science, and Technology

William C. Barnett

Introduction

Principal Arguments

Africa has a rich history of profound achievements in medicine, science, and technology during the long period before colonization. The diverse peoples of the African continent have been responsible for many of the most fundamental advances in human history. Over the course of thousands of years, Africans steadily made innovations that made human life easier in Africa and elsewhere. Unfortunately, these achievements have often been forgotten, ignored, or attributed to non-Africans. Most people outside Africa are unaware of Africa's proud legacy of innovation, and some have even argued that the continent's people have made no significant contributions to the human understanding of medicine, science, and technology.[1]

The goals of this chapter are to explain the roots of this contradiction, to correct the mistaken views, and to demonstrate some of the ways in which Africans have made crucial medical, scientific, and technological advances. This introduction will outline these arguments, and suggest ways to analyze these areas of human knowledge within an African context. The introduction will be followed by an examination of the crucial role of technological change during four basic periods: the prehistoric period, the ancient civilization of Egypt, the age of Islam and the great kingdoms, and the era of slavery and colonization. Following this short chronological analysis of the centrality of technology in Africa's history, ad-

---

1. John Iliffe, *Africans: The History of a Continent* (New York: Cambridge University Press, 1995), 1-5; Ali A. Mazrui, *The Africans: A Triple Heritage* (Boston: Little, Brown and Company, 1986), 11-38; Ivan Van Sertima, ed., *Blacks in Science: Ancient and Modern* (London: Transaction Books, 1983), 5-6; M. Akin Makinde, *African Philosophy, Culture, and Traditional Medicine* (Athens: Ohio University Center for International Studies, 1988), 91-92, 97-98; Robert W. July, *Precolonial Africa: An Economic and Social History* (New York: Scribner Books, 1975), 285-288; Harold K. Schneider, *The Africans: An Ethnological Account* (Englewood Cliffs, NJ: Prentice-Hall, 1981), 8-11; Roland Oliver and J.D. Fage, *A Short History of Africa*, 6th ed. (New York: Penguin Books, 1990), 1-2.

vances in the fields of medicine, science, and technology will be examined individually and in greater depth.

Viewing Africa's history in a specifically African context is the key to understanding these precolonial innovations. This shift in perspective requires some knowledge of African cultural values and of the unique challenges of Africa's ecology. Adopting an appropriate perspective or viewpoint is quite difficult because precolonial Africa is a world apart from modern society in the year 2000 A.D. Those who have argued against any progress by Africans have not been viewing Africa within its own context, and they have been using very limited definitions of medicine, science, and technology. Such views of these fields are based only on their meaning in today's industrial nations, not what they signified in precolonial times. In order to evaluate thousands of years of human history, we must explore these three fields from a broad perspective, and understand their meanings within African societies.[2]

Medicine, science, and technology have been part of human life throughout our history. Evaluating the African role in these fields requires a conceptual journey across time and space, and a broad appreciation of the human experience. All people have worked to protect their health, to understand the world around them, and to increase their power to change that world by developing tools. Africa was the birthplace of humanity, so these efforts, and the resultant developments, have been occurring on the continent for several million years. The profound advances that make us human, like language, society, and religion, were first developed in Africa. The very idea of making tools defined early humans, and fundamental technology like cutting blades, projectiles, and fire originated in Africa. The continent was also the site of the great civilization of ancient Egypt, and this society's remarkable medical, scientific, and technological advances continue to amaze people today. The African civilizations of the two thousand years since the end of the Egyptian dynasties are not nearly as well known. The leading African kingdoms since the ancient era include Mali, Songhai, and Zimbabwe, and these societies also developed complex technology. Only during the era of the slave trade and European colonization did Africa's sophistication in medicine, science, and technology fail to equal or surpass European achievements.[3]

Africans possess a proud history of adapting to the natural world to make human life better, and it is impossible to do justice to this complex story of technological change in one chapter. We can only analyze the advances in very broad terms, since the topic encompasses the story of the human experience on a diverse continent over a massive span of time. More research is needed on medicine, science, and technology in early Africa, but it is clear that an amazing diversity of

---

2. Makinde, *African Philosophy, Culture, and Traditional Medicine*, 91-92, 97-98; Van Sertima, ed., *Blacks in Science*, 5-9; Schneider, *The Africans*, 8-11; July, *Precolonial Africa*, 285-288; David W. Phillipson, *African Archaeology*, 2nd ed. (New York: Cambridge University Press, 1993), 8-10.

3. James L. Newman, *The Peopling of Africa: A Geographic Interpretation* (New Haven: Yale University Press, 1995), 1-8, 202-205; Van Sertima, ed., *Blacks in Science*, 5-9; Iliffe, *Africans*, 1-26; Oliver and Fage, *A Short History of Africa*, 1-9; Thomas Spear, *Kenya's Past: An Introduction to Historical Method in Africa* (New York: Longman, 1981), 1-10; Basil Davidson, *Modern Africa: A Social and Political History*, 3rd ed. (New York: Longman, 1994), 3-4.

African societies and kingdoms flourished in precolonial times, and that each used tools and ideas and adapted to the environment in unique ways.[4]

Conflicting Perspectives on Africa

Those people who have tried to argue that Africa has no medicine, science, or technology have ignored all the achievements. They often refuse to acknowledge that Egypt was part of Africa, and they attempt to claim the glories of this ancient civilization as part of a European world. There is an underlying element of racism and ethnocentrism in such arguments, as the implication is that no Africans could have built a society as remarkable as Egypt. Similar ideas led to the more obviously racist arguments of the colonial era, when it was commonly held that the impressive stone structures of Great Zimbabwe could only have been built by unknown visitors to Africa. Scientific research has demonstrated that both Egypt and Zimbabwe's ancient societies were African achievements, but continuing research is needed in this effort to reverse centuries of misinformation and stereotypes.[5]

It is absurd to claim that Africa has no medicine, science, and technology in the face of so much evidence to the contrary. Despite the evidence of African innovation, the belief that Africa lacks any technological sophistication has been prevalent outside the continent for over a century. The roots of these misconceived views of Africa lie in the colonial era. Europeans sought to justify their scramble to take over Africa and its resources. They claimed that their presence was not based on self-interest, and argued that they enriched Africans not only with Christianity, but with superior medicine, science, and technology. Their views on Africa's supposed lack of technology were based on the continent's situation in the late 1800s, when the ravages of the slave trade had left African societies in a state of decline.[6]

When Europeans began colonizing Africa in the late nineteenth century, they had very little understanding of the continent's history. Many of the great kingdoms had collapsed during the centuries of the slave trade, and much knowledge of Africa's past was lost. A significant problem stems from the lack of written documents. Few societies outside North Africa kept written records, as most cultures used oral traditions to preserve their history. Rather than working to use these methods to understand the continent's past, European colonizers asserted that Africa *had* no history. This paralleled the claim that Africa had no science, and it was just as false. However, it became a commonly held belief in Europe because it helped justify colonial efforts to dominate Africa and Africans. These stereotypes are still difficult to overcome because they are deeply embedded in the views of many non-Africans. The colonial era may be over, but these stereotypes

---

4. Iliffe, *Africans*, 1-26; Newman, *The Peopling of Africa*, 202-205; Oliver and Fage, *A Short History of Africa*, 1-9.

5. Mazrui, *The Africans*, 11-38; Van Sertima, ed., *Blacks in Science*, 67-91; Fred Burke, *Africa: World Regional Studies* (Boston: Houghton Mifflin Company, 1991), 122-123; Joel Samoff, "Triumphalism, Tarzan, and Other Influences: Teaching About Africa in the 1990s," in Patricia Alden, et al., *African Studies and the Undergraduate Curriculum* (Boulder: Lynne Rienner Publishers, 1994), 35-80.

6. Mazrui, *The Africans*, 11-21; Ieuan Ll. Griffiths, *An Atlas of African Affairs* (New York: Methuen & Co., 1984), 49-51; Van Sertima, ed., *Blacks in Science*, 5-9.

still play a role in justifying outside interventions in independent Africa and mis-treatment of people of African heritage.[7]

Most scholars have recognized the blatant racism beneath the assertion that Africa had no history before the arrival of Europeans, and they have revised their thinking. African history is now a thriving and respected field, but the same can-not be said for the study of African science. Despite recent advances, many acade-mics still view Africa as a continent without technology. This view is most preva-lent among those who limit their study of Africa to the last century or so, from the colonial era to the present. With these starting and ending points, it is no sur-prise that the analysis of Africa's technological contributions leads to the conclu-sion that Africa has little to offer. The problem is that any true narrative of African achievements must start much further back in time, and trace the long rise of medicine, science, and technology. Some scholars have analyzed these fields in a search for the reasons why Africa has lagged behind Europe, but in defining their questions in this manner, these researchers are committing major errors.[8]

The scholars who approach the gap between recent African and European de-velopment levels by searching for reasons why Africa fell behind are making sev-eral questionable assumptions. First, their efforts to explain this difference by ar-guing that Africa was isolated from outside influences are often mistaken. The Sahara Desert did present a formidable barrier to contact between sub-Saharan Africa and the rest of the world, but it never completely blocked the movement of ideas and tools. Furthermore, beneath this search for a barrier is the assumption that innovations were occurring outside Africa that Africans would adopt if they could. This leads to a second presumption, which is the idea that the direction Eu-rope took was preferable and desirable within African cultures. In fact, Africans were aware of other technologies, but often they could not fit these systems to the challenges of their environment.[9]

The plow and the wheel are two of the innovations that were not readily adopted in Africa. Viewing these tools from an African perspective illustrates the problems with much writing on this subject. Some authors assert that these two technological innovations were crucial steps toward human progress, and suggest that Africans must have been isolated from them. The plow and the wheel were not adopted by early Africans, but the reason is not that they never learned of these devices. Instead, these inventions, important in Europe and Asia, did not transfer well to Africa's challenging climate and geography. Africa's arid regions and its wet, dense forests were completely unsuitable for wheeled travel, and Eu-ropean colonizers eventually realized that human porters and pack animals pro-vided more appropriate means of transport. Plows did not work in Africa either, as they caused major erosion problems in the broad expanses of Africa with thin soils, and the livestock needed to pull plows often could not survive in the tsetse fly belts.[10]

---

7. Makinde, *African Philosophy, Culture, and Traditional Medicine*, 1-2; Van Sertima, ed., *Blacks in Science*, 5-6.

8. July, *Precolonial Africa*, 285-288; Van Sertima, ed., *Blacks in Science*, 5-6.

9. Schneider, *The Africans*, 8-10, 32-33, 43-44; Iliffe, *Africans*, 49-55; Kevin Shillington, *History of Africa* (New York: St. Martin's Press, 1989), 46-48.

10. Schneider, *The Africans*, 8-10, 32-33, 43-44; Iliffe, *Africans*, 81-82; Phillipson, *African Archaeology*, 8-10; July, *Precolonial Africa*, 285-288;

African Technology in an African Context

The examples of the wheel and the plow suggest the need to understand medicine, science, and technology in an African context. We must avoid making the assumption that other technologies are preferable, and we must refrain from judging Africans from outsiders' perspectives. Comparing Africa's developments to those of other continents should not be the goal, and it will not be the emphasis of this chapter. However, it should be noted that if such a comparative approach is taken, Africa performs very well. Africa was far ahead of all other continents during the long prehistoric period in which humans populated the globe, as these pioneers all originated in Africa. In comparing the earliest ancient civilizations, there are persuasive arguments that Egypt's achievements surpassed its Asian rivals in Mesopotamia, India, and China. There was certainly nothing comparable in Europe, North America, or Australia five thousand years ago, and the achievements of the Mayans and Incas came later.

Most educated people will concede these points on prehistoric and ancient history, but it is more controversial to say that Africa's technology was equal to other continents during the majority of the last two thousand years. Africans were masters of iron-making technology, which put them well ahead of the peoples of the Americas and Australia. The technological and military sophistication of Africans, combined with Africa's challenging geography, led Europeans to bypass the continent and colonize other lands. A rich trade system developed between Africa, Asia, and Europe during the Islamic era, and it was a trade among equals. Only when the Atlantic slave trade changed the dynamics of this exchange did Africa lag behind Europe. Even then, careful analysis reveals that Africa did not actually fall behind, and neither did any other continent. Instead, Europe took an unprecedented leap forward with the Industrial Revolution. The key to Europe's new levels of technology lay in the population densities in Europe, which pushed Europeans to develop more intensive and sophisticated economic methods.[11]

Understanding the development of medicine, science, and technology in Africa requires a knowledge of the unique characteristics of the continent. Unlike Europe at the time of the Industrial Revolution, Africa has rarely been the site of dense concentrations of people. Instead, the principal demographic traits in Africa have been large amounts of available land and low population densities. The reasons for this are simple: the vast majority of the continent does not have the resources to support high population levels. Much of Africa has precipitation levels that are too low or soils that are too poor to support urban civilizations. In addition to these basic constraints, the diseases, insects, and unpredictable climate cycles in many African environments present unique challenges for humans. There are, of course, some important exceptions to the rule. Certain river systems, such as the Nile Valley and the Niger Valley, have supported dense populations, and these favored regions have often been the sites of Africa's great kingdoms.[12]

---

11. Van Sertima, ed., *Blacks in Science*, 5-26.

12. Alfred W. Crosby, *Ecological Imperialism: The Biological Expansion of Europe, 900-1900* (New York: Cambridge University Press, 1986), 132-144; Iliffe, *Africans*, 1-5, 65-69; Mazrui, *The Africans*, 41-61; Newman, *The Peopling of Africa*, 119-120, 202-205; Griffiths, *An Atlas of African Affairs*, 12-15, 18-25; Schneider, *The Africans*, 45-57.

These ecological challenges have had a profound impact on the levels of tech-nological innovation in Africa. Africa's favored regions have made great techno-logical leaps, while the more challenging environments have limited human progress. The peoples of Africa have managed to settle virtually the entire conti-nent, and their adaptations represent some of the greatest achievements in human history. Even today, humans have not developed sustainable methods to live in re-gions as arid as Africa's Sahara and Kalahari Deserts, or America's Death Valley. Members of modern societies who reside in such places rely on food and supplies from outside sources, but African peoples long ago developed the ability to live in such incredibly harsh areas. The Khoisan people who remain in today's Kalahari represent the genius of Africans in adapting tool kits to find food and sustain life in almost any ecosystem.[13]

The hunter-gatherers of the Kalahari are not the type of people that are usu-ally discussed in essays on technology, but they represent a very important seg-ment of human history. Hunting and gathering supported human life for much of the existence of our species. In evaluating the broad range of human technological developments in Africa up to the colonial era, these early ecological pioneers must be recognized. They represent the great achievements of Africans in establishing human cultures that could persist against the immense challenges of their conti-nent. Africans can be seen as the greatest colonizers in the world since they ex-panded to populate all of their own continent, and then spread throughout the world. For much of the long history of people in Africa, humans have led mobile rather than settled existences. They moved across the landscape and successfully developed the tools and techniques to adapt to widely varied regions. Rarely did these Africans completely transform the environment, as they did not seek to con-quer the land. Intensive land use methods such as those used in Europe do not pay off unless population densities are high. The frequent movements of Africa's semi-nomadic peoples limited their tool kits to what they could carry, but their ecologi-cal adaptations were extensive and complex. This gradual migration of peoples to populate the corners of the continent was still going on early in the colonial era.[14]

Developing an appreciation for the typical African as well as for the great kingdoms is an important part of viewing Africa in an African context. The vast majority of African people have been hunter-gatherers, cattle-herders, and farm-ers, and all of these groups have innovated in order to expand into new regions. Thus, most Africans have engaged in pursuits closely tied to the land, and many of them have lived in decentralized societies. Western cultures often have trouble recognizing these very different societies, especially in relation to a topic like tech-nology. Westerners have an idea of the steady progress of civilization, and often like to view today's industrial societies as the culmination of the achievements of

13. Douglas H. Johnson and David M. Anderson, eds., *The Ecology of Survival: Case Studies from Northeast African History* (Boulder: Westview Press, 1988), 1-24; Iliffe, *Africans*, 1-5, 65-69; Mazrui, *The Africans*, 63-69; Joseph O. Vogel, ed., *Encyclopedia of Precolonial Africa: Archaeology, History, Languages, Cultures, and Environments* (Walnut Creek, CA: AltaMira Press, 1997), 179-198; Phillipson, *African Archaeology*, 8-10.

14. Gregory Maddox, James L. Giblin, and Isaria N. Kimambo, eds., *Custodians of the Land: Ecology & Culture in the History of Tanzania* (Athens: Ohio University Press, 1996), 1-6; Johnson and Anderson, eds., *The Ecology of Survival*, 2-23; Iliffe, *Africans*, 1-5, 120-126; Mazrui, *The Africans*, 63-79; Vogel, ed., *Encyclopedia of Precolonial Africa*, 179-198; July, *Precolonial Africa*, 93-95.

the Greeks, the Romans, and the Renaissance. There were some centralized, densely populated societies in Africa, and kingdoms like Egypt, Mali, and Zimbabwe deserve great praise even when viewed through the lens of an industrial society. However, these urban centers are not the only African groups worthy of study.

If we step back from today's Western viewpoint and expand our perspective, we can see that the African societies that adapted to seemingly uninhabitable environments developed remarkable technological sophistication. Their ability to sustain human life in these regions for century after century shows that they had achieved a level of harmony with the natural world unmatched in modern society. The tool kits of hunter-gatherers in areas like the Kalahari Desert and the Congo basin are triumphs of technological simplicity and continuity. These ways of life may well become increasingly respected in the future, as all the world's peoples cope with the ecological problems created by industrial societies. For a different approach to technological adaptation to life on this planet, we can study precolonial Africans. Their ways of life had in common a limited impact on the environment, a high level of sustainability, and the virtue of controlling technology instead of being controlled by it.[15]

The Centrality of Technology in African History

Technological change lies at the heart of the story of human history in Africa. An overview of the major periods in Africa's history will reveal that a wide array of fundamental developments in human knowledge and capabilities profoundly shaped events. I will briefly analyze the prehistoric period, the civilization of ancient Egypt, and the age of Islam and African kingdoms, and conclude with the slave trade and the colonial era. This short chronology will demonstrate the central role of technology and also establish a basic framework in which to place advances in the individual fields of medicine, science, and technology.

African Prehistory

Africa can be properly called the cradle of humanity. The first steps that our ancestors took were upon African soil, and Africa has been the site of many fundamental advances in technology since then. Bipedal locomotion allowed the hominids who lived in Africa over two million years ago to carry objects with their forelimbs, and this made the use of tools possible. The ability to create tools made our species unique, and this achievement shows that the history of technology cannot be separated from human history. The earliest human innovations were slow adaptations by foragers and gatherers to the diverse and changing African ecology. Over huge stretches of time, humans learned to form stone tools, to hunt,

---

15. Maddox, Giblin, and Kimambo, eds., *Custodians of the Land*, 1-6; Phillipson, *African Archaeology*, 8-10; Vogel, ed., *Encyclopedia of Precolonial Africa*, 179-213; July, *Precolonial Africa*, 93-95, 285-288.

to utilize fire, and to build shelters. Our earliest ancestors survived by their knowledge of Africa's environment, and they succeeded because they were able to alter that world. Their development of the first tools, weapons, and shelters represent profound changes in technology. Related advances in culture and communications grew out of the need for group cooperation, and gradually led to critical developments such as language, society, and religion.[16]

The technological sophistication of prehistoric groups evolved slowly over several million years, but more rapid changes began when our ancestors shifted to a settled existence. A settled lifestyle requires the technological ability to obtain adequate nourishment in a fixed location. For a long time, experts believed that agriculture was the necessary prerequisite to establishing a sedentary society, but there is some evidence suggesting that fish may have been the crucial food supply for the earliest settled groups. Archaeological sites show that settled human groups subsisted on fish, wild cattle, and wild grains near Lake Turkana and near the Nile River at least eleven thousand years ago, and possibly as far back as twenty thousand years ago. These groups possessed the technology to harpoon fish, and also had grinding stones for grains.[17]

The mix of foods used in these early fishing societies suggest that these Africans were quite close to two of the most revolutionary technological changes in history: the development of agriculture and the domestication of livestock. Until quite recently, the consensus among experts has been that these key advances occurred first in the Middle East, and then spread to Africa and elsewhere. This is not certain, however, and there are ongoing debates on the exact beginnings of agriculture and domesticated livestock. These advances were made over ten thousand years ago, but experts cannot agree on whether there was one original site of innovation, or if these practices evolved in separate locations at similar times. It is obvious that ancient peoples in the Americas reached these advances on their own, so there is no reason to rule out an independent discovery in Africa.[18]

Diverse evidence from Ethiopia, West Africa, the Sahara, and the Nile Valley leads some experts to argue that Africans may have developed agriculture and domestic animals largely without outside help. Some archeologists go beyond claiming an independent but parallel innovation and assert that the oldest sites of these discoveries anywhere were in Africa rather than Asia. It is possible that the cultivation of crops and the raising of livestock began in the then much wetter southern Sahara region well over ten thousand years ago, and it seems likely that pastoralism preceded farming on the continent. Africa did possess indigenous wild cattle, but African peoples would eventually herd both African and Asian cattle, as well as goats, sheep, and camels imported from the Middle East. Far fewer crops were brought in from outside the continent, as the barley and wheat grown by Asians did not prosper in Africa much beyond Egypt. Instead, African farmers success-

16. Newman, *The Peopling of Africa*, 11-21, 202-205; Spear, *Kenya's Past*, 2-6; Oliver and Fage, *A Short History of Africa*, 1-9; Vogel, ed., *Encyclopedia of Precolonial Africa*, 281-288.

17. Newman, *The Peopling of Africa*, 22-39, 202-203; Shillington, *History of Africa*, 12-13; Vogel, ed., *Encyclopedia of Precolonial Africa*, 289-304.

18. Van Sertima, ed., *Blacks in Science*, 58-66; Newman, *The Peopling of Africa*, 22-39, 202-203; Phillipson, *African Archaeology*, 8-10; Vogel, ed., *Encyclopedia of Precolonial Africa*, 215-234.

fully domesticated a variety of indigenous crops, including sorghum and millet near the Sahara, teff and ensete in Ethiopia, and yams, plantains, and African rice in West Africa. This list of domesticated crops proves that Africans had great agricultural skill even if they did first learn farming from Asia. Africans of varied regions engaged in food production very early in human history, but debates on the dates and the first sites of these innovations remain unresolved at this time.[19]

Egypt's Ancient Civilization

There are debates on the origins of food production in the Nile Valley, but nobody disputes the fact that the people of ancient Egypt made stunning technological advances. Egypt was the greatest of the ancient societies that flourished once farming was used extensively by Africans. Farming was widespread in the northern half of Africa seven thousand years ago, and this fundamental technological advance allowed for the development of more complex societies. The surplus created by human control of food production supported dense populations along the Nile River, and this led to new levels of specialization and a need to organize this large and diverse society. Many of the great Egyptian achievements stemmed from their efforts to exert control and achieve order in this complex world. The people of the ancient Nile Valley were organized under centralized governments, and ruled by pharaohs who combined political and religious power. The Egyptians developed mathematical systems to quantify and account for tax payments and crop yields, and invented a writing system known as hieroglyphics to record this information. These were remarkable developments, but the most obvious symbols of the technological genius of ancient Egypt are the glorious pyramids and temples. These huge structures still stand five thousand years later, and they are timeless monuments to the power, organization, and technological skills of the ancient dynasties of Egypt.[20]

The Nile River was the central reason why Egypt developed into a great civilization, and it shaped everything in this society. Perhaps the greatest of all the Egyptian achievements was their effective domestication of the river without harming this great natural gift. The Nile Valley was a uniquely favored place for human life, and its position in an arid region increased the concentrations of people. The Nile supplied water, excellent fishing and hunting sites, and floods which regularly replenished the fertility of the valley with silt. The Egyptian systems of irrigation allowed them to distribute the Nile's waters and fertile silt to extensive areas of farmland. Ancient Egyptian achievements, even in seemingly separate scientific fields like astronomy, connect back to the Nile River. The flood cycles were so central to this way of life that Egyptians studied the skies to predict the arrival of the rejuvenating floodwaters, and out of these efforts they developed the world's first twelve-month, 365-day calendar.[21]

---

19. Van Sertima, ed., *Blacks in Science*, 58-66; Phillipson, *African Archaeology*, 113-116; Newman, *The Peopling of Africa*, 40-59; Shillington, *History of Africa*, 14-18; Iliffe, *Africans*, 6-36; Oliver and Fage, *A Short History of Africa*, 21-30; Vogel, ed., *Encyclopedia of Precolonial Africa*, 215-234.

20. Shillington, *History of Africa*, 14-18, 23-27; Van Sertima, ed., *Blacks in Science*, 58-82; July, *Precolonial Africa*, 262-266.

21. Shillington, *History of Africa*, 23-27; Van Sertima, ed., *Blacks in Science*, 67-82;

There are serious problems with the Western view that history has seen a steady progression of ever more sophisticated civilizations, each building upon the previous model. In some ways, Egypt's glory was unequaled in ancient history, and it is unlikely that any empire will ever again last as long as the Egyptian dynasties that spanned several thousand years. Civilization and technology do not advance in a straight line, and with the decline of Egypt, much information was lost forever. However, ancient Egypt still exerted a great influence upon later human societies, and its legacy can be seen in Africa, Europe, and Western Asia. Europeans have often claimed Egypt's great achievements as part of their Mediterranean world, and denied that Egypt was African. It is ridiculous to argue that Egypt was not part of Africa, as the extensive links between Egypt and the Nubian kingdoms further up the Nile River demonstrate that Egypt was part of both the African and the Mediterranean worlds. Great kingdoms like Egypt and Nubia were linked to each other and to smaller African groups, and these ties were always two-way streets, with ideas and technologies traveling in both directions.[22]

Islam and Africa's Great Kingdoms

The Egyptian and Nubian dynasties are remarkable because they began about five thousand years ago, and continued for nearly three thousand years. In the long period of history since then, a variety of other kingdoms grew by developing the technology to build dense population centers in Africa's ecologically favored regions. West African agricultural lands fed by the Niger and other rivers supported the empires of Ghana, Mali, and Songhai, while the Congo River basin was home to the Kongo people. In Eastern Africa, Ethiopia developed a long-lasting empire, the highland lakes supported varied kingdoms, and a complex society arose in Zimbabwe. This narrative of intertwined advances in African culture and technology took place across much of the continent, but northern Africa remained the focal point of technological developments, especially with the important role of Islam.

The spread of Islam was one of the defining events in the history of Africa in the past two thousand years, and the major movements of people and ideas during the Islamic era had important impacts on medicine, science, and technology. However, the impact of Islam must not be taken too far, as some people have mistakenly argued that Africa was civilized by Muslims from the Middle East. The reality is that Africans were equal partners with Asians and Europeans in an expanded world of trade and exchange. Africans developed closer ties to the Middle Eastern and Mediterranean worlds as Islam spread, and there was also more contact between African societies. This growth in trade, travel, and cultural exchange enriched numerous African kingdoms, and facilitated the spread of knowledge and technology inside and outside Africa. Africa experienced a Golden Age of sorts from the twelfth to the sixteenth centuries, but these high points are often overlooked because of the lows that followed. One symbol of this era of African advancement was Timbuktu, the leading city of the Songhai Empire. West African societies earned tremendous wealth from the camel caravans that crossed the Sa-

July, *Precolonial Africa*, 262-266.

22. Iliffe, *Africans*, 6-36; Van Sertima, ed., *Blacks in Science*, 67-82; Shillington, *History of Africa*, 39-45.

hara laden with gold and salt, and Timbuktu was known throughout the Islamic world as a great center of learning. On the other side of the continent, trading communities on the East African coast from Zimbabwe to the Swahili islands prospered in the Indian Ocean market. Technological developments supported both these large trade systems, as gold and salt mining produced the key products in the Saharan exchange, and unique sailing ships called dhows made the Indian Ocean trade possible.[23]

The centralized societies in favored regions of Africa thrived during this long period, but there is another story to tell about events across the broad expanse of Central and southern Africa. Increases in the movement of peoples and ideas also occurred outside the great kingdoms and the Islamic world, and these developments were just as noteworthy in Africa's history. Our overview of technological developments in ancient Africa focused on the northern half of the continent because farming and dense societies expanded south very slowly. It is important to note that sweeping changes were taking place beyond this region. Beginning during the age of ancient Egypt, and continuing into the colonial era, Bantu-speaking peoples from western Africa pushed east, and then turned south in their steady movement across the continent. The population of the southern half of Africa gradually changed with this migratory drift of people and ideas.

The long, steady Bantu expansion is the leading example of the constant pattern of Africans moving into and adapting to new ecological regions. The Bantu migration fed off the gradual movement of everyday African farmers and herders on to new lands in a world of low populations and abundant territory. These movements required the African pioneers to learn their new environments, and to adapt their tools to new food sources and their medical systems to new diseases. The success of this lengthy colonizing movement was powered by several technological advantages, particularly in the later stages. The migrants often possessed superior iron-making skills, and they were also talented fishermen, cattle-herders, and farmers, while the earlier peoples of southern Africa were hunter-gatherers. Bantu migrants did not forcibly displace existing societies, but the newcomers originating in West Africa effectively colonized the southern half of the continent with the aid of their advanced technologies and their high fertility.[24]

The Slave Trade and Colonialism

There is a terrible irony in the fact that one of the greatest achievements of precolonial Africans was their ability to adapt to new ecological regions, and the Atlantic slave trade turned this strength against them. Africans had not yet completed their expansion across their own continent when Europeans began buying African slaves and moving them to the Americas against their will. This forced migration to a new land brought Africans into contact with new geographic regions and new diseases, and it required them to perform grueling agricultural labor on plantations. The remarkable ability of Africans to survive these hardships made them a more desirable labor supply than Native Americans, who were not used to intensive farming in tropical regions and were not resistant to the dis-

---

23. Iliffe, *Africans*, 42-61.
24. Maddox, Giblin, and Kimambo, eds., *Custodians of the Land*, 1-6; Newman, *The Peopling of Africa*, 140-149, 158-174, 180-193; Iliffe, *Africans*, 33-36, 66-69, 97-115.

eases of the Europeans. Over ten million Africans were transported to the Americas during this four-hundred-year period, and this massive loss of young, productive people had a powerful negative impact on Africa. The slave trade and the colonial era mark a low point in Africa's long history of technological adaptations and achievements.[25]

During much of the last five centuries, efforts to build strong societies and make technological innovations in Africa have faced huge obstacles because Africans were being forced to help enrich Europe and Europe's colonies. When African societies traded slaves to Europeans for guns and manufactured goods, they were involved in a profoundly unequal exchange. Africa gave up the productive value of young Africans who would provide their labor and the labor of their descendants to Europeans; in return the continent received weapons of destruction. Firearms were a technological advance that Africans did not possess, and the constant violence of the slave trade led African societies to engage in slave raiding in order to obtain the guns that would protect them from slave raiders. This vicious cycle caught regions of Africa affected by the slave trade in a web of mutual destruction. European traders became a predatory force, as the Atlantic slave trade reduced Africa's already low population, dramatically escalated regional warfare, and strongly discouraged technological development. Africans had no incentive to manufacture goods when the only items they received in exchange for the slaves they supplied to Europeans were guns and cheap manufactured goods.[26]

A substantial technological gap emerged along with these dramatic changes in the economic exchanges between Africa and Europe. This gap was primarily defined by Europe and certain colonies jumping ahead of the rest of the world during the Industrial Revolution, although Africa did fall backward in some areas. One way to grasp this leap in technology is to see that Europeans increasingly developed the ability to exploit forms of energy other than their own labor. Europeans utilized the muscle of animals and Africans slaves to perform their work, they effectively harnessed wind and water power, and they eventually powered machinery with steam produced by burning fuels such as coal. While Europeans used Africa as a springboard for their Industrial Revolution, the primary energy source in Africa continued to be human labor. African diseases often prohibited the use of draft animals, and low population densities discouraged the growth of intensive mechanical systems. Meanwhile, the labor of African slaves and the wealth that Europeans gained in the immensely profitable slave trade fueled Europe's rapid rise.

By the time the four century-long Atlantic slave trade ended in the late nineteenth century, Africa was no longer on an equal technological level with Europe. Africans were still in control of the vast majority of their continent, and they were in far stronger positions than the indigenous peoples of the Americas and Australia. However, European nations had developed significant wealth and technology with the help of the labor of millions of enslaved Africans, and they had developed efficient systems to extract wealth from colonies. In the late nineteenth and early twentieth centuries, the European empires turned to Africa. The European scramble for colonies in Africa came directly on the heels of the slave trade, and it was a second period of great adversity for Africans.

---

25. Crosby, *Ecological Imperialism*, 140-141.
26. Mazrui, *The Africans*, 99-113, 159-177; Iliffe, *Africans*, 127-158.

The continent's population growth was adversely affected by both the slave trade and the colonial period, and some populations may have gone down in actual numbers. Africans were no longer being moved to the Americas, but brutal forced labor conditions in colonial enterprises, such as rubber production in the Belgian Congo, killed many. Africa was being stripped of raw materials, and very little technological development took place under these conditions. The changes brought on by colonization also led to deadly epidemics in many areas. Some historians believe that railroads and trade spread illness by expanding the contacts between previously isolated African regions, but other experts have theorized that Africans' previously effective measures against endemic disease were destroyed when colonial rulers reordered entire societies. Both may be true, and the continuing legacy of colonialism means that similar upheavals still affect Africa today. The AIDS crisis is an example of the ongoing challenges that Africans face in adapting their medical, technological, and scientific systems to a rapidly changing world. Many of the most important changes in precolonial Africa centered around technological adaptations to the continent's challenging environment, and similar problems continue to face its people.[27]

Conceptual Categories

Having established the central role of technological change in each major period of African history, I will now examine the fields of medicine, science, and technology individually and in greater detail. The primary goal is to determine how these three areas of knowledge were approached and what they meant in an African context. The chronological overview centered on technology rather than on medicine or science for several reasons. First, today's society places great importance on technology, as we often name periods of human history the "stone age," the "iron age," and the "nuclear age." It is worth remembering that few precolonial African societies would define themselves based on technology; they might instead see religion as a defining characteristic. Second, technological changes in ancient times are visible because material goods like tools and great achievements like the pyramids of Egypt still survive. Science and medicine, in general, are less tangible. Both science and medicine are bodies of knowledge or ways of knowing that may not take on a physical form. A society's gains in scientific understanding might not leave obvious traces behind, and medicine can be even more mysterious. It is a difficult task, but we must now explore what each of these fields meant to the peoples of precolonial Africa.[28]

One of the great challenges to understanding a culture distant in time and place comes from the need to grasp how that society defined its world. All societies develop abstract ideas to organize and explain their world, and modern societies use science and technology to do this more than any previous civilization. Indeed, discussing precolonial Africa using categories like medicine, science, and technology reflects the organizing principles of the current era. The boundary between science and technology may be somewhat vague, and some might see medicine as contained within science, but these three categories are reasonably clear

---

27. Griffiths, *An Atlas of African Affairs*, 22-25; Iliffe, *Africans*, 66-69.
28. John S. Mbiti, *African Religions & Philosophy* (New York: Praeger, 1969), 1-5.

to us today. Medicine, science, and technology did not have these clearly under-stood meanings in precolonial Africa. In applying these abstract terms to Africa, we must discuss the sharp differences in the ways these bodies of knowledge have been defined and understood. Precolonial Africans did not see medicine, science, and technology as clearly distinct fields, and in defining these terms, they would include ideas from religion, philosophy, and magic that are far outside the mod-ern view. Therefore, the first goal must be to define what each of the conceptual categories meant in its precolonial African context and then to analyze the major advances made by Africans.[29]

Medicine

Medicine in an African Context

Medicine is a fascinating topic, because its meanings can be so different in di-verse cultures. In precolonial African societies, medicine and religion were indis-tinguishable concepts. This is in sharp contrast to today's Western societies, where there is a wide gap between science and religion, and people place medicine on the science side of the divide. It is worth remembering that the vast majority of our current medical knowledge is only the product of the last century. Our focus is on Africa up to the late nineteenth century, when the scramble for Africa began and doctors in Europe and America had very little of the expertise they have today. We may believe that we can easily define modern medicine and explain how it works, but many parts of the medical world remain a mystery. Modern doctors frequently cannot explain why some patients are cured and others are not. One common feature in medicine across time and space is the fact that all humans eventually die, no matter how effective their medical treatments are. Medicine's close connections to birth and death create much of this complexity.[30]

In today's technological society, we make efforts to distance medicine from these mysteries of life and death. Medicine is often narrowly defined as the treat-ment of specific symptoms or illnesses in a patient. Medicine had a far different meaning in precolonial Africa, as it played a much broader role in society. It was seen as more than just one patient's disease. Instead it involved the whole commu-nity and mingled with religion to become the way that people understood life and death. Modern medicine has made amazing advances, but it has also moved away from this broad community role in mediating health and illness. A workable defi-nition for medicine in precolonial Africa is to call it the culture's cumulative knowledge and experience with healing and health.[31]

---

29. Terence O. Ranger and Paul Slack, eds., *Epidemics and Ideas: Essays on the Histori-cal Perceptions of Pestilence* (New York: Cambridge University Press, 1992), 241-269; Mbiti, *African Religions & Philosophy*, 1-5.

30. Steven Feierman, "Struggles for Control: The Social Roots of Health and Healing in Modern Africa," *African Studies Review*, vol. 28 (September 1985); Makinde, *African Phi-losophy, Culture, and Traditional Medicine*, 101-107.

31. Mbiti, *African Religions & Philosophy*, 166-193; Feierman, "Struggles for Con-trol," *African Studies Review*; Makinde, *African Philosophy, Culture, and Traditional Medi-cine*, 91-92, 101-107.

Medicine played a truly central role in African societies. It was synonymous with religion, and was intertwined with all aspects of African culture. The practitioners of medicine were labeled witch-doctors or medicine-men by critics in the colonial era. In the Swahili language these medical experts were called *waganga*, and they had various names in other societies, but there is no term in our society that captures their cultural role.[32] We might call them priest-healers, but the simple word healer sums up their major function. These skilled men and women played a combination of roles, but they were all important figures in their communities. African cultures varied widely, but many healers served as religious leaders, as political leaders, and as philosophers, in addition to ensuring people's health. African medical practitioners did not just treat illnesses, but provided for the health of the entire community. They might be asked to heal the crops or to bring rain as well as to cure a disease. They explained why rains had failed, or why a disease had entered the group, and they sought to correct these community problems.[33]

Medicine's pivotal role in precolonial Africa stems from a number of linked ideas and values. African religious beliefs are often described as animist systems, which means that precolonial Africans commonly saw religion as intertwined throughout the natural world. Thus, the animals and plants that people depended upon for food could be said to have their own spirits. In such a world, the health and prosperity of each community was interlocked with and dependent on the ability of the healers to perform their medical and religious duties. These healers were powerful because they mediated the links between people and the natural world, and sought to ensure that the society would continue and prosper. Precolonial Africa was relatively underpopulated, and fertility was a critical concern in most societies. Medical experts or healers assisted in prenatal care, delivered babies, and treated infertility, so they were at the focal point of the community's efforts to reproduce and multiply. In seeking to ensure fertility, healers played key roles in building families and entire communities.[34]

Matters of health and healing also played a central role in African societies because of the ecological setting. The continent of Africa was and is an incredibly challenging environment for human life. Broad expanses of Africa can barely support human societies because of low or irregular rainfall. Africans in these arid and semi-arid regions can never be confident about the land. Humans also share much of the continent with dangerous diseases. Tropical Africa is host to many dangerous micro-organisms and parasites that threaten humans and make it very difficult to raise livestock. There are specific reasons for the unusually challenging disease problems in Africa that go beyond the tropical climate. Humans have inhabited the continent for millions of years, while humans first reached the Americas perhaps as late as fifteen thousand years ago. The long period in which hu-

---

32. Mbiti, *African Religions & Philosophy*, 166-193.

33. Steven Feierman, *Peasant Intellectuals: Anthropology and History in Tanzania* (Madison: University of Wisconsin Press, 1990), 69-93; Ranger and Slack, eds., *Epidemics and Ideas*, 241-269; Mbiti, *African Religions & Philosophy*, 166-193; Makinde, *African Philosophy, Culture, and Traditional Medicine*, 87-107.

34. Feierman, "Struggles for Control," *African Studies Review*; Feierman, *Peasant Intellectuals*, 69-93; Iliffe, *Africans*, 1-5, 66-69; Ranger and Slack, eds., *Epidemics and Ideas*, 241-269; Mbiti, *African Religions & Philosophy*, 166-193.

mans have shared the African ecosystem with animals, insects, and micro-organisms has given other organisms plenty of time to evolve in ways that make use of the human body in their life cycles. Important examples of these ecological links are the ways in which strains of malaria and sleeping sickness use humans as hosts and reach them through mosquito or tsetse fly vectors. The existence of chronic, debilitating diseases like malaria in Africa increases the societal importance of medicine in two ways. Important steps must be made to forestall these diseases, and the many people who continually suffer from these illnesses need ongoing treatment.[35]

African Approaches to Healing

Precolonial African ways of understanding medicine differ from the limited definition of medicine in Western society. The specific approaches to healing within Africa include practices that are quite similar to today's modern medical approaches, but are also mixed with ideas that fall well outside the realm of modern medicine. African healers followed pragmatic steps in which they would examine patients, reach a diagnosis, and prescribe a treatment based on their experience with curing the patient's problem. Specific writings about African medical practices, ranging from ancient Egypt to West Africa during the slave trade, describe physical examinations that revealed a solid understanding of both human anatomy and the symptoms of diverse diseases. Healers prescribed a wide range of treatments including herbal medicines and surgery. There was a variety of medical specialists, including bone setters, dentists, midwives, and surgeons.[36]

Healers actively worked to prevent illness before it occurred, and this was often done at the community level. There is evidence that precolonial African societies threatened by river blindness, sleeping sickness, and malaria took careful measures to remove people from areas infested with the organisms that carried these diseases. This often entailed the establishment of clear codes about the medical and spiritual safety of village areas versus the dangers of the "bush." Most African societies placed a strong religious emphasis on hygiene, which helped fight disease. Healers are also believed to have sporadically exposed people to the smallpox virus by pricking people with thorns. This practice of a form of inoculation suggests a sophisticated grasp of disease, and some understanding of the idea of immunity.[37]

Such examinations, treatments, and preventive measures can be called the pragmatic side of African medicine, but there was also a symbolic aspect. The

---

35. John Ford, *The Role of the Trypanosomiases in African Ecology: A Study of the Tsetse Fly Problem* (Oxford: Clarendon Press, 1971), 1-11, 86-90, 493-496; Feierman, "Struggles for Control," *African Studies Review*; Crosby, *Ecological Imperialism*, 132-144; Griffiths, *An Atlas of African Affairs*, 16-25; Newman, *The Peopling of Africa*, 119-120, 202-205; Iliffe, *Africans*, 65-69; Mazrui, *The Africans*, 41-61.

36. Van Sertima, ed., *Blacks in Science*, 140-155; Mbiti, *African Religions & Philosophy*, 166-171; Makinde, *African Philosophy, Culture, and Traditional Medicine*, 87-92.

37. Maddox, Giblin, and Kimambo, eds., *Custodians of the Land*, 127-148, 213-236; Ford, *The Role of the Trypanosomiases in African Ecology*, 1-11, 86-90, 493-496; Feierman, "Struggles for Control," *African Studies Review*; Ranger and Slack, eds., *Epidemics and Ideas*, 241-269; Makinde, *African Philosophy, Culture, and Traditional Medicine*, 97.

ideas in African healing that are foreign to Western views of medicine can be described as symbolic, and these approaches are more difficult to discuss. It is not enough to say that healers mixed medicine and religion, because to Africans, these practices could not be separated. People avoided the "bush" for unified medical and religious reasons, and healing was an all-embracing system. Observers in the colonial era described healers performing chants, incantations, or exorcisms, and they saw these treatments as ridiculous attempts at magic or divining. Many healers did attribute illness to societal imbalances rather than to a biological cause, and they often sought to restructure social relations in order to cure the patient and the group. This treatment might not directly cause a physical change in the body, but such actions can improve a person's health and solve larger problems. To dismiss these symbolic actions as meaningless ritual is foolish, as we are only beginning to understand the psychological and emotional aspects of illness. African healers' chants relied on the power of words to heal, and so does modern psychotherapy. Studies using placebos reveal the importance of the patient's belief in a cure, and African healers could call upon the unified force of the patient's religious faith and the community's cultural beliefs in their treatments.[38]

Precolonial Africans made impressive achievements in medicine in both the limited, modern definition of the field and in their broader sense of healing the community. It is impossible to go through Africa by region or by period, both because there is so much richness among African cultures and because so much more research is needed. However, two examples will be used to discuss medical advances at the beginning and the end of the precolonial period. The ancient Egyptians developed astounding healing skills that certainly influenced the Western medical tradition. Hippocrates and the Greeks are credited with laying out the field of medicine, but they were deeply indebted to the expertise developed in the Nile Valley. The Egyptians had a huge range of medical specialists including gynecologists and eye doctors, and they successfully performed surgeries as advanced as piercing the skull to ease pressure on the brain. Much African medical knowledge is lost because written documents were so rare before the Islamic era, but Egypt was different. Hieroglyphics carved in stone record the details of some medical techniques and herbal cures, and archeologists have discovered what amount to medical textbooks written on papyrus.[39]

Another specific example of remarkable medical expertise comes at the other end of the long precolonial period. In 1879 a British missionary doctor was amazed to observe a successful Caesarean section performed by a Banyoro surgeon in Uganda. In the same decade that antiseptic surgery was first being developed in England, this skillful operation was truly remarkable. Europeans had performed Caesareans only to save the infant, but this operation saved both the infant and the mother. This surgery also revealed an advanced knowledge of surgical techniques, including cauterization, antisepsis, and anesthesia. It is impossible to say what further advances would have been made in African medicine, had

---

38. Maddox, Giblin, and Kimambo, eds., *Custodians of the Land*, 127-148; Feierman, "Struggles for Control," *African Studies Review*; Ranger and Slack, eds., *Epidemics and Ideas*, 241-269; Makinde, *African Philosophy, Culture, and Traditional Medicine*, 97; Mbiti, *African Religions & Philosophy*, 166-203; July, *Precolonial Africa*, 270-272.

39. Van Sertima, ed., *Blacks in Science*, 127-137, 140-155; Makinde, *African Philosophy, Culture, and Traditional Medicine*, 100-101.

not colonial officials actively worked to suppress the practices of traditional African healers in Uganda and all their other colonies.[40]

The broader medical achievements of precolonial Africa are equally impressive, but they can only be described in sweeping brushstrokes here. Between Egypt's great ancient achievements and the African surgeon who surpassed English medical skills in 1879 there were countless successful African healers. Unfortunately, very few of their achievements were ever documented, in part because these healers kept their specialized knowledge secret. They worked in widely varied regions, and one of their great achievements was their extensive use of local herbs and other natural substances to treat illness. African herbal remedies were as diverse as the continent's ecosystems and individual healers often understood the curative properties of hundreds of plants. A wide variety of symptoms and diseases were treated effectively, and there were remarkable advances in drugs. Current medicines such as salicylic acid, the active ingredient in aspirin, were also traditional herbal medicines, and modern cancer researchers are currently studying some African herbal cures.[41] However, the most important medical achievements made in precolonial Africa may be in the broad African sense of building an all-embracing system of healing to help the entire community. This holistic approach to healing satisfied a greater range of needs of the community than our narrow, illness-centered focus. Much of the success of Africans in adapting to new regions and in surviving great adversity can be related to this strong system of medicine. Healing was integrated with cultural goals such as health, fertility, and group harmony, and this made medicine a central pillar of precolonial African society.[42]

Science

Science in an African Context

Like medicine, science is a difficult term to translate from its current meaning to the world of precolonial Africa. As we understand the word, science is a systematized approach to understanding the natural world based on experiments. Precolonial Africans also sought to understand and explain the physical world, but they did not require everything that they held to be true to be demonstrated and proven. Their view of science, like their approach to medicine, accepted that there were mysteries in the natural world that were unknowable or should be confined to the realm of religion. The divide between faith and reason that exists in modern society was far less visible in precolonial Africa, just as it was less prominent earlier in Europe and Asia. This meant that African science was often linked to other ways of seeing the world, in relationships that seem foreign today. The peoples of precolonial Africa sought to explain the workings of the natural world, and in this effort they developed systems that we identify as mathematics,

---

40. Van Sertima, ed., *Blacks in Science*, 23-24, 151-154; Makinde, *African Philosophy, Culture, and Traditional Medicine*, 100-101.

41. Van Sertima, ed., *Blacks in Science*, 22-24, 154.

42. Maddox, Giblin, and Kimambo, eds., *Custodians of the Land*, 127-148, 213-236; Mbiti, *African Religions & Philosophy*, 166-203; Makinde, *African Philosophy, Culture, and Traditional Medicine*, 87-107; Feierman, "Struggles for Control," *African Studies Review*.

physics, and astronomy. At the same time, these ways of ordering the world over-lapped with ideas that Westerners categorize as religion, magic, or philosophy. Modern society sees a clear break between astronomy and astrology and between mathematics and numerology, but precolonial Africans had scientific systems that were more broadly defined. Their approach to the natural world was also system-atized, but in ways appropriate to African cultures.[43]

One of the difficulties in understanding science in an African context is the problem of categorizing human scientific knowledge. In addition to defining the scientific and the non-scientific, we group different scientific pursuits into separate fields. We divide the broad world of science into the fields of physics, mathemat-ics, chemistry, and biology, and see this as the logical way to organize our analysis of the natural world. In fact, these groupings do not represent the only way to di-vide the study of the world. These fields, like the larger field of science, are cul-tural constructs that do not easily translate to precolonial Africa. However, using these modern categories does provide an approach to an overview of precolonial African science, because it creates a commonly understood framework.[44]

It is also useful to revisit the differences between science and technology. There is an area of overlap between these two fields, but for the purposes of this study, science can be understood as a system of thinking about the natural world, while technology represents more tangible tools and adaptations. By defining sci-ence as theory, and technology as the practical application of these ideas, we can break a complex topic into more manageable segments. Due to the general lack of written documents from precolonial Africa, it is a great challenge to recover the scientific theories that these societies developed. It is obvious that early African societies such as Zimbabwe or Buganda had an understanding of mathematics, physics, and engineering from the complex structures they built, but we have not recovered these ways of thinking. Thus, many practical applications have sur-vived to prove that precolonial Africans mastered key scientific principles, but much of the underlying theory is lost.[45]

The scientific theories of many African societies are unknown, but there are two important exceptions to this general lack of information. Some of ancient Egypt's scientific knowledge survived in hieroglyphic form, and the Islamic era created a second body of written documents related to science. Both of these eras played important roles in the development of the Western world's current organi-zation of the sciences. Egypt's legacy profoundly shaped Greek and Roman thought, as has already been discussed, but Islamic culture has received far too lit-tle credit for its scientific achievements. The Islamic world of Northern Africa, the Middle East, and the Mediterranean had sophisticated systems to organize all human knowledge. Islamic scholars had a profound influence on European scien-tific advances due to their innovations, their classification systems, and their ef-forts to collect and preserve the scientific advances of earlier peoples. Much of Re-naissance Europe's knowledge of ancient Greek and Egyptian science was carried to Europe by Muslims. Islamic society's advances in mathematics were particu-larly significant, and Westerners often ignore this even though they use Arabic nu-

43. Constance B. Hilliard, ed., *Intellectual Traditions of Pre-Colonial Africa* (Boston: McGraw-Hill, 1998), 222-226; Mbiti, *African Religions & Philosophy*, 1-5, 48-57.

44. Hilliard, ed., *Intellectual Traditions of Pre-Colonial Africa*, 222-226.

45. Van Sertima, ed., *Blacks in Science*, 5-10, 14-17, 84-91.

merals and study algebra. Islamic society also helped spread medicine, astronomy, and botany to the West. In order to evaluate precolonial African science beyond the achievements of the Egyptian and Islamic eras, I will explore different categories of science, including physics, mathematics, chemistry, and biology.

Scientific Categories and Achievements

Physics is a basic category of the human pursuit of science that examines matter and energy, and African innovations involved physics from the earliest periods of human history on the continent. Prehistoric Africans initiated the human quest to understand physics with their tool-making efforts. Their achievements in hunting with projectiles and in using fire depended on their knowledge of physical properties and mechanics. Astronomy is a specific field beneath the umbrella of physics, based on the human desire to explain the celestial bodies. Diverse African groups developed scientific expertise, as the nomadic Somali people carefully studied astronomy in order to guide their travels across desert regions. Astronomy had varied practical uses, such as celestial navigation and the calendars Egyptians created, but humans interested in the mysteries of life and death also found answers in the stars. The Dogon people of Mali had incredibly sophisticated knowledge of the orbits of the Sirius stars, and their astronomer priests held ceremonies to celebrate the return of these stars every sixty years.[46]

The ability of these early societies to track and predict the cycles of celestial bodies reveals a knowledge of mathematics as well as physics. Mathematics, or the science of numbers, has connotations of certainty, but we forget its mysterious side. Mathematics, like medicine and astronomy, was mixed with ideas of divination and prophecy through systems of numerology. However, there were practical applications that went beyond those of astronomy, as all centralized governments needed to be able to make calculations in order to organize their societies. Governments used arithmetic to calculate taxes and to plan large irrigation, construction, or military projects. Complex trade interactions relied upon weights and measures and on currency systems. Different African societies developed their own counting systems, with some cultures using the numbers five or twenty as their base, rather than the number ten. The numerical calculations used in political and economic applications included the use of geometry, algebra, and trigonometry. The construction of the pyramids and other large projects was based on difficult and precise calculations of angles and area equations. Ancient Egyptians had a definition of *pi*, the ratio of a circle's circumference to its diameter, that was far more exact than many later approximations. Western society usually links the principle of *pi*, like so much of our understanding of mathematics, to the ancient Greeks. Just as we ignore the Islamic role in modern science, we rarely acknowledge that much of Greek mathematics was a revival of Egyptian principles.[47]

Chemistry is the third of the four basic scientific fields. This science examines the structures of substances and the transformations they undergo, and it has an

46. Van Sertima, ed., *Blacks in Science*, 11-14, 27-44, 177-194; Shillington, *A History of Africa*, 23-27.

47. Van Sertima, ed., *Blacks in Science*, 14-15, 100-126; July, *Precolonial Africa*, 262-266; Shillington, *A History of Africa*, 21-25.

African past almost as ancient as physics. Prehistoric hunter-gatherers had complex understandings of the poisons of the natural world, avoiding deadly plants and using poison as a weapon. Africans learned how to manipulate chemical properties in nature, as they processed certain foods to remove their toxins. Cassava, a relatively recent African crop, requires a complex process of detoxification before it can be consumed. Practical applications of chemical principles also underlay precolonial African production of medicines, alcoholic beverages, oils, soaps, textile dyes, and ceramics.[48]

However, the most important chemical transformation achieved in precolonial Africa was iron working. African experiences with chemistry, like other areas of science, were not sharply separate from areas that are considered unscientific today. Africans experimented with alchemy, and they saw the working of iron as a miraculous or magic transformation. In widely varied cultures, iron smiths occupied special places in society. In some places, these smiths were set apart as dangerous, and in others they held high status. Linking this powerful transformative process to religion and to human fertility was common. Iron furnaces were often decorated to resemble women, while only men were allowed to take part in or observe the iron smelting process. Iron production represented a high point of precolonial African science and technology, and iron tools helped Africans adapt to many different environments. Iron production and use spread rapidly across Africa, showing the weakness of claims that African groups were isolated or unwilling to accept innovations. Iron fit well into most African contexts, and it played key roles in both small, decentralized societies and large kingdoms. Some experts believe iron smelting originated independently in Africa, and others have claimed that African metallurgy techniques were so advanced that temperatures were hot enough to produce steel before Europeans made this leap. There is a need for more research into the origin and diffusion of these techniques.[49]

The science of biology is the last field to examine for African achievements and approaches. Africans faced a challenging ecological world, and they were highly skilled in understanding their continent's diverse plant and animal life. Early people in all regions of the world possessed a deeper understanding of their local ecosystems than we do today, and Africans were no exception. They were exceptional botanists, as they were well-acquainted with hundreds of wild plants and herbs, and used them for food, medicine, clothing, shelter, and tools. In the modern world, we live in a less diverse ecosystem, using just a handful of crops for our foods, and eliminating many other plants. Precolonial Africans rarely eliminated species within their environment, and Africa is one of the few places on earth where varied megafauna such as elephants and lions and huge migrating herds of herbivores still exist. Africans hunted almost all of these animals, but

48. Gloria Thomas-Emeagwali, ed., *Science and Technology in African History With Case Studies from Nigeria, Sierra Leone, Zimbabwe, and Zambia* (Lewiston, NY: Edwin Mellen Press, 1992).

49. Peter R. Schmidt, *Iron Technology in East Africa: Symbolism, Science, and Archaeology* (Bloomington: Indiana University Press, 1997); Eugenia W. Herbert, *Iron, Gender, and Power: Rituals of Transformation in African Societies* (Bloomington: Indiana University Press, 1993); Van Sertima, ed., *Blacks in Science*, 9-10, 157-162; Schneider, *The Africans*, 10, 18, 32-33.

they did not put so much pressure on them as to push them to extinction like the megafauna of Europe and the Americas.[50]

As the birthplace of humanity, Africa was the site of many of the greatest biological achievements in history. Some of these crucial innovations were discussed in the introductory chronology of African developments, including the domestication of crops and of animals. The agricultural achievements of African farmers were of immense importance, no matter the outcome of the debates on the true geographical origin of farming. Africans domesticated a wide variety of plants indigenous to the continent, including sorghum, millet, African rice, and yams. These crops were carefully adapted to a wide variety of climates, and many have been made drought resistant. Africans found that few European crops could grow on the continent, but they did succeed in adapting American crops such as corn, sweet potatoes, and peanuts to African ecosystems during the era of the slave trade. Despite intense research efforts in recent years, modern science has not added any major new crops to the collection of plants that ancient civilizations domesticated. The domestication of animals reveals a similar talent for biology, and animal husbandry was crucial across Africa. African adaptations to diseases and their medical systems also centered around biological knowledge. All these achievements were necessary to sustain life amidst the challenges of the African continent. The successes of so many African peoples in building stable and continually reproducing societies reveal that Africans developed a complete and functioning scientific system.[51]

Technology

Technology in an African Context

Technology is the final area of African knowledge to be examined individually, and in many ways it is easier to discuss than medicine or science. Unlike the two previous fields, technology is more tangible than abstract, and scholars do not suffer from the same lack of information on the past. Objects recovered by archeologists and surviving structures can provide a great deal of information about the tools and abilities of early African peoples. Written documents are still valuable, but they are not as crucial since we are not searching to understand another culture's way of systematizing knowledge. There are fewer large gaps in our understanding of technology in Africa, but this field still needs more research. The raw data on African technology and material culture are more widely available than information on early science or medicine, but much interpretation remains to be done.

One aspect of technology that stirs debates among experts is the difficulty in identifying the original source of a tool or technique. This issue stems from the fact that it is quite possible and even common for one group to borrow specific

---

50. Hilliard, ed., *Intellectual Traditions of Pre-Colonial Africa*, 420-423, 458-460; Makinde, *African Philosophy, Culture, and Traditional Medicine*, 99-107; Van Sertima, ed., *Blacks in Science*, 22-24, 154; Schneider, *The Africans*, 42-57.

51. Maddox, Giblin, and Kimambo, eds., *Custodians of the Land*, 1-6; Schneider, *The Africans*, 29-37, 42-57; Phillipson, *African Archaeology*, 8-10.

technologies from another group, or from another continent. Precolonial African medicine and science were deeply interconnected with local belief systems, but technology can be much more flexible and transferable. Some basic technologies were developed independently in different places and times, but others have a single point of invention. An example is the idea of the alphabet, which may have been invented only once, and then diffused through the world over time. During the slave trade, firearms were the piece of European technology that African leaders most desired. Originally developed by Asians, then adopted in turn by Europeans, Africans, and Americans, guns were easily added into an existing culture, although they did help cause major changes.

Technology may not involve as many abstract concepts as medicine or science, and it may be transferable between diverse cultures, but it does still have a cultural context specific to Africa. Firearms were adopted from outside the continent, but once in Africa, they were utilized within African traditions of warfare. In a few cases, such as firearms, Africans used a technology they did not have the means to produce. However, it is worth noting that in today's modern society, most individuals use tools, such as computers and automobiles, that they could not possibly build for themselves. The majority of precolonial Africans used tools that they built, which is an entirely different technological context.

Technology can be understood as the practical application of a culture's knowledge to the environment through tools and adaptations. The tools that Africans invented or adopted had to fit both their ecological situation and their cultural goals. In this chapter's introduction, the plow and the wheel were discussed as two technological systems that were fundamental in much of Europe and Asia. The plow and the wheel were not adopted in Africa because they would not work in Africa's harsh environment. Other technologies were not adopted because of cultural barriers, either between Africans and non-Africans, or between specific societies within the diverse continent. Two of the major cultural differences between Africans and Europeans in the eras of the slave trade and colonialism concern their comfort with risk and their interest in material accumulation. In comparing the value systems of these two groups, some scholars have argued that Africans were often quite conservative, while Europeans would take more risks in their accumulative efforts. These are sweeping generalizations, but there is some logic to these arguments, and some relevance to the different rates of technological change in Africa and Europe.[52]

Africans inhabited a challenging land, and most made a living directly off the land as farmers, herders, or gatherers. A greater number of people in densely populated Europe lived in urban communities, and they were less vulnerable to ecological risks. Africans faced a hostile environment, and often had no surplus of food. The poor quality of their lands often required them to adopt a more mobile lifestyle than Europeans. Thus, most Africans were not in a position to freely experiment with new technologies, and they did not have safety nets to support failed attempts at innovation. This explains the relatively slow rate of technological change in many areas, but there is a key distinction to make. Africans living in complex centralized societies such as the leading kingdoms of West Africa would have values more like

52. Schneider, *The Africans*, 8-10, 32-33, 43-44; Phillipson, *African Archaeology*, 8-10; July, *Precolonial Africa*, 285-288; Iliffe, *Africans*, 81-83.

those of Europeans than those of a cattle-herder in a decentralized group. The African societies in favored river valley regions usually possessed a food surplus and were able to take part in long-distance trade. These were the African groups more open to adopting new technologies, and the societies most likely to make important innovations. Africans struggling to eke out a living in the harsher regions of the continent, such as the Khoisan hunter-gatherers of the Kalahari, had simple but time-tested technological systems that enabled them to survive in a challenging world.[53]

Technological Adaptations and Achievements

In discussing African science, I utilized Western categories such as physics and biology as an organizational structure, but there is no equivalent framework for technology. This discussion of specific tools and techniques will target areas of technological expertise that played central roles in precolonial Africa. The emphasis will be on Africa's situation approximately five hundred years ago, since the chronological overview traced the major technological developments in Africa across the entire span of precolonial history. I will skip over the tool-making achievements of prehistoric Africa, and begin with the technological adaptations in the fundamental areas of farming and livestock. These tools and methodologies were known and used by the great majority of precolonial Africans who made their living directly off the land. Next I will survey important manufactures and crafts. Specific skills such as metal-working, pottery, and textile production were known to smaller numbers. The review of technologies will conclude with significant artistic and architectural achievements, which were the focus of even more specialized groups in certain centralized societies.

Precolonial farming techniques reflect the skillful adaptations that Africans made to the challenges of their continent. Africans did not usually practice intensive agriculture, since the soil did not allow land to be continually farmed. Instead, African farmers took advantage of the general availability of land and they practiced a more mobile form of cultivation. They regularly cleared new lands when the fertility of their fields declined. These rapid clearing techniques are often called "slash and burn" agriculture, but this term has a negative connotation today as it is linked to the destruction of rain forests. "Slash and burn" techniques are seen as "primitive" and ecologically destructive by some, but in Africa the lands were not permanently cleared. There was a cycle in which land was cultivated and then allowed to restore itself over time. This system was often better for the environment than intensive farming, and the nutrients from burned vegetation provided an efficient fertilizer. Clearing was done quickly, and stumps were left in place, another reason why plows were ill-suited to African agriculture. Africans used iron hoes and axes as their primary farming tools, and the wide use of human-powered technology meant that the majority of Africans were involved in agriculture.[54]

Precolonial Africans were careful to spread out their risks in farming and livestock herding through strategies learned over time. In many areas, these two main

---

53. Johnson and Anderson, eds., *The Ecology of Survival*, 2-23; Maddox, Giblin, and Kimambo, eds., *Custodians of the Land*, 1-6.

54. Newman, *The Peopling of Africa*, 1-8, 202-205; Schneider, *The Africans*, 42-57; Iliffe, *Africans*, 81-83; Maddox, Giblin, and Kimambo, eds., *Custodians of the Land*, 1-6.

ways of life in Africa were combined, so livestock could supply food when crops failed and vice versa. Even when the environment did not allow such a mixed economy, Africans diversified their risks. Farmers often raised a complex mixture of crops to avoid over-reliance on one food source. They sequenced their crops over time, which helped the soils recover. Planting varied crops also spread out the demands on labor, which was in shorter supply than land. Africans developed a variety of engineering applications to improve their farming efforts. Technological systems of water-raising and irrigation were fundamental to agricultural communities across Africa. The ability to regulate water was the key to farming in many regions of the continent.[55]

Livestock herders also shared and diversified risks in a number of ways. Some raised a mixture of animals; different Maasai groups raised cattle, goats, and camels, and varied the ratios of these animals according to ecological conditions. It was common for pastoralists to form alliances, often through kinship ties, to split herds up and send them to different areas to increase the odds of finding water and vegetation. Loose economic alliances were also common among different types of societies. Despite the perception that Maasai herders subsisted only on animal products, there is strong evidence from East Africa that economic and cultural networks linked pastoralists like the Maasai, hunter-gatherers such as the Dorobo, and diverse farming societies. These peoples would exchange livestock, wild game and honey, and crops, and intermarriage was common. Particularly in times of ecological crisis, people could move from one ethnic group to another, ethnicity being a very fluid concept in precolonial Africa.[56]

In addition to their widespread expertise in agriculture and pastoralism, most African communities had varied and complex manufacturing technologies. Precolonial Africans had metal-working skills that equaled those of Europe and Asia and far surpassed anything in the Americas. Metals were adapted to a variety of uses, and they made Africans more efficient farmers, hunters, and warriors. The process of smelting iron in furnaces has been discussed, but Africans were also involved in varied mining efforts and sophisticated metal-working techniques. Iron ore was mined all over Africa, and certain areas of West and South Africa also had major gold-mining operations in precolonial times. Gold from West Africa flowed to North Africa and Europe for centuries, and gold mines in Zimbabwe had shafts over one hundred feet deep. The people of Zimbabwe halted their gold production when the Portuguese arrived in the Indian Ocean in the sixteenth century, perhaps realizing that the European thirst for gold would lead to colonization. Europeans would eventually exploit southern Africa's rich gold reserves using African laborers, but not until a hundred years ago. Before the interruptions created by the slave trade and the colonial era, skilled African metal-workers used iron, copper, and gold to create efficient tools and beautiful objects.[57]

---

55. Maddox, Giblin, and Kimambo, eds., *Custodians of the Land*, 1-6; Johnson and Anderson, eds., *The Ecology of Survival*, 2-23; Schneider, *The Africans*, 29-37, 45-53; Spear, *Kenya's Past*, 10-20; Shillington, *A History of Africa*, 21-25.

56. Johnson and Anderson, eds., *The Ecology of Survival*, 2-23, 94-95; Spear, *Kenya's Past*, 10-20.

57. Schmidt, *Iron Technology in East Africa*; Thomas-Emeagwali, ed., *Science and Technology in African History*, 90; Iliffe, *Africans*, 18-36; Vogel, ed., *Encyclopedia of Precolonial Africa*, 125-148.

Other manufacturing industries that were prominent in precolonial Africa include textile production, pottery, and wood carving. These crafts were at high technical levels at the time the Atlantic slave trade began, but many of them were adversely affected by this huge cultural disruption and the influx of cheap European goods. Textiles were a central part of cultural expression in precolonial times, and this was particularly true in West Africa. Cotton and other fibers were dyed with rich colors and woven on looms into fabrics of great beauty. The complex patterns on textiles and in jewelry were both an aspect of daily life and an art form. Pottery and wood carving also played dual roles, as they were technologies vital to the community economy and also forms of artistic expression. In many areas, crafts other than metal working were dominated by women, who also played central roles in precolonial market and trade systems. Surviving examples of precolonial African textiles, jewelry, pottery, and wood carving demonstrate the exceptional technical proficiency and the creativity of these women and men. The sculptural forms of wood-carvings and metal-castings from early kingdoms can be seen in art museums around the world.[58]

The line between everyday technology and art is impossible to identify, but there is a break between the tools used by typical Africans and the technologies used only by elite craft workers in centralized societies. Some of the finest works of bronze and gold were made by specialists working for West African kings. In the same way, architecture was an arena in which it is worth distinguishing between African farmers and African elites. The shelters used by the vast majority of Africans were clever adaptations to local environments and building materials, but they did not use complex technologies. The architectural achievements of some large African kingdoms stand in sharp contrast to the homes that most Africans built of earth and plant materials. Many kingdoms, however, had sophisticated structures designed for military purposes, such as the huge earthwork defense systems of Buganda, and other societies had the wealth and power to build monuments to their glory. Egypt's pyramids, Great Zimbabwe's towers, and Ethiopia's rock-cut churches are stunning feats of engineering and organization. These structures are still standing today, and thus they are the most obvious examples of Africa's technological achievements. These massive projects symbolize the power of these ancient civilizations and express their cultural and religious values.[59]

Conclusion

Many observers can recognize that Egypt and other African kingdoms had great technological expertise, but they do not see the way that these societies relate to the rest of Africa. These technological heights were not aberrations in the history of precolonial Africa; there were many other peaks. African peoples made profound medical, scientific, and technological advances throughout their long his-

58. Thomas-Emeagwali, ed., *Science and Technology in African History*; Vogel, ed., *Encyclopedia of Precolonial Africa*, 115-124; July, *Precolonial Africa*, 260-262, 280-285.

59. Van Sertima, ed., *Blacks in Science*, 15-17, 67-91; Shillington, *A History of Africa*, 21-27.

tory. The great monuments of precolonial Africa are some of the most easily recognizable signs of this history of innovation, but the technological adaptations of African hunter-gatherers, cattle-herders, and farmers are just as significant. We must recognize the breadth of precolonial Africa's achievements in building diverse human societies that were adapted to life in a challenging natural environment.

Review Questions

1. What led Europeans to assert that Africa had no medicine, science, or technology, and how can these claims be rebutted?
2. How did changes in the trade relations between Africa and other continents affect Africa's technological development?
3. What is the significance of the fact that precolonial Africans defined medicine much more broadly than we do today?
4. What roles did Islamic culture play in the history of medicine, science, and technology in Africa, and to what extent are these roles recognized today?
5. How can you explain the different rates and levels of technological innovation in centralized and decentralized African societies?

Additional Readings

Iliffe, John. *Africans: The History of a Continent.* New York: Cambridge University Press, 1995.

Mazrui, Ali. *The Africans: A Triple Heritage.* Boston: Little, Brown, and Company, 1986.

Thomas-Emeagwali, Gloria, ed. *Science and Technology in African History With Case Studies from Nigeria, Sierra Leone, Zimbabwe, and Zambia.* Lewiston, NY: Edwin Mellen Press, 1992.

Van Sertima, Ivan, ed. *Blacks in Science: Ancient and Modern.* London: Transaction Books, 1983.

Vogel, Joseph O., ed. *Encyclopedia of Precolonial Africa: Archaeology, History, Languages, Cultures, and Environments.* Walnut Creek, CA: AltaMira Press, 1997.

Chapter 13

Cities and Architecture

Jacqueline Woodfork

At first glimpse, traditional African architecture may appear to be unrefined, the layout of villages, towns, and cities random. Closer inspection reveals that Africans have carefully crafted dwellings and living patterns that correspond with their varying needs and circumstances. Traditional architecture reflected climactic conditions, available building materials, and the lifestyles, cultures, and systems of beliefs of the people who created and used them. Although the majority of Africans were rurally based in pre-colonial times, great cities flourished across the continent. There were as many types of houses as there were cultural groups. Since it would be virtually impossible to examine all of them, this chapter will discuss a variety of housing and spatial arrangements from different parts of Africa. Evidence for the pre-colonial period draws heavily upon the field of archaeology as many of the groups of people in this study did not put their architectural concepts into written form. The accounts of early European travelers also provide evidence, but equally important are the continuities that many of these styles of housing maintain to this day.

The Great Pyramid of Khafre

Although Egypt lies on the northeastern corner of Africa, it is often regarded as separate from the African continent. Even today there are people who claim that the achievements of Ancient Egypt could not have been created by people of African origin. This is untrue. Not only did Ancient Egyptians build awe-inspiring monuments, they developed remarkable systems of irrigation, great urban centers, a vast bureaucracy, a complex language and civilization, and a wide body of knowledge. Some of the best-recognized landmarks of Ancient Egypt are the pyramids at Al-Jizah (Giza). These were neither the first nor the last pyramids built in Ancient Egypt, but their location and durability make them the most famous. Other well-known structures from Ancient Egypt include the royal tombs at Memphis, the temples of Karnak and Edfu, Abu Simbel, and the Valley of the Kings, Queens and Nobles in Luxor, the burial site of King Tutankhanem. We will examine the architecture of the pyramid of Khafre (Chephren) to give us an insight into the complexity of the pyramids' construction and the civilization that they represent. Although treasure seekers have pillaged the pyramids and the elements have taken their toll, these monuments are a breathtaking testament to Ancient Egypt and its architectural achievements.

Figure 13-1. Great Pyramids, Al-Jizah, Egypt

Ancient Egypt was not monolithic. There was a distinction between Lower (Northern) and Upper (Southern) Egypt, which gained greater prominence around the Fourth and Fifth Dynasties. Egypt's position as an empire necessitated the incorporation of new peoples, their knowledge and customs into the realm. Egypt was a nation of subsistence-level agriculturalists governed by a king-god, or pharaoh. It was a two-tiered society in which the ruler and the ruler's courtiers and families exerted their power over the peasant populace. The word "pharaoh" originally meant "great house" and later became synonymous with the word "king." These kings were originally believed to be gods. Later, as Egyptian thinking about religion evolved, these rulers were no longer perceived to be divinities.

These kings built great houses in which they were to be buried. These tombs give us clues about their societies and their inhabitants. Al-Jizah, the site of the Great Pyramids, is on the outskirts of Cairo, to the west of the great city and the Nile River Valley, at the edge of the vast Sahara desert. Its rocky plateau is approximately 50 meters above the level of the Nile. Recent work has done a great deal to challenge the myth that the pyramids were built by slaves who were abused to glorify the Egyptian pharaohs. Some speculate that these structures were erected by unbound workers who labored in groups that were supervised by an overseer. The recent discovery of a bakery at the pyramids had led contemporary observers to believe that the workers received ample rations. Skeletons of workers have been discovered that lead researchers to believe that emergency care for the injured was offered at the site.[1] Although the work force may not have

---

1. NOVA Online/Pyramids/Who Built the Pyramids. http://www.pbs.org.wgbh/nova/ pyramid/explore/builders.html

been coerced, a great amount of the state's resources were allocated for the erection of these monuments instead of being spent on the welfare of the populace.

Most of the work was done during the late summer and early autumn when the annual flooding of the Nile precluded agricultural work, thus the builders were not being used for pyramid construction during times that their labor was required for required for farming. These workers ensured the afterlife of their divine king and themselves, as well as the prosperity of their kingdom as a whole by building these structures. There is a great debate about the number of laborers required to build the pyramids. The Greek historian, Herodotus, of the fifth century B.C., stated that the building of the pyramids required over 100,000 laborers. More contemporary estimates range from a 4,000 to 40,000 workers.

The stones used to construct the pyramids came mostly from the Al-Jizah area, although the more rare stones traveled the Nile from Upper Egypt by barge. The massive stones were probably pulled up a stone embankment made of earth, sand and brick with papyrus ropes. The stones were cut with iron tools. The construction required support from non-builders such as bakers and health care providers as well as a variety of people who were directly involved with construction. Laborers varied from the unskilled ones who helped to move the massive stones, to artisans who carved statues, to the architects who drew the plans for the pyramids.

The construction of the pyramids was an amazing feat. It was not until the twentieth century that taller buildings were erected. There was barely a millimeter of space between the stones, not even enough space to insert a playing card. Modern tour guides relate that an unwrapped loaf of bread left in a burial chamber would still be quite edible after twelve months. This was accomplished over two millennia before the birth of Christ by an African society.

There are three pyramids at Al-Jizah, and it is only the Great Pyramid of Khufu (Cheops) that is on the list of the Seven Wonders. The monument was built by the pharaoh Khufu of the Fourth Dynasty circa 2560 B.C., the first of the three pyramids constructed at Al-Jizah. Khufu is the largest of the three pyramids at Al-Jizah, and of all the pyramids of Ancient Egypt, but that of his son, Khafre, was built on higher ground and it looks equally large. Of the three pyramids at Al-Jizah, it is that of Chephren that is the most intact. The last pyramid, built by Menkaure, was smaller than that of Khafre. The pyramids at Al-Jizah were the largest built in Ancient Egypt. By the Fifth Dynasty, there was a change in the planning and design of the pyramids. This change in structure reflects changes in the way that Egyptians conceptualized the role of the pharaoh in their society.

The death of the king became a mythical fate, and mysteries became central to the burial rites and cult practices as the burials became more Upper Egyptian in character. In the Fourth Dynasty, the undisputed power of the pharaoh, who was called the "Great God," extended over the religious life of all his subjects. At the time of the death of Khafre, the god Osiris became more prominent. Osiris was a king who ruled in prehistoric times who was murdered by his brother who was jealous of his power. Osiris was resurrected and judged to be "true of speech" in a court of the gods and was awarded rulership of the underworld. Osiris was also a god of fertility. His power granted life to all things that developed from the underworld, thus the agricultural production and the annual flooding of the Nile, both essential to Egypt and its people, was his responsibility. The funerary rites of "becoming Osiris" and "opening of the mouth" were performed in the valley temple.

The *ka* was the immortal spiritual sustenance of people which was set free from the physical body at death, the *ba* was the soul that could enter the body or become one with the body at will. The "opening of the mouth" ceremony was performed so that the statue of the deceased would accept the *ka*. Thus, the pharaoh, upon his death, became again attached to the prosperity of Egypt through his transformation into the god Osiris. Later, when Egyptian conceptualizations of religion evolved and the pharaoh's claim to divinity became less secure and he was no longer believed to be a god incarnate, it was thought that all men became Osiris upon their deaths. The pyramids are elite structures that were created for the specific purpose of carrying out the death rites for their owners and for their glorification. Burial customs in Lower and Upper Egypt varied. In Lower Egypt, the moister climate and water table demanded that burials protect the deceased from the elements.

The complex of the pyramid of Khafre was built approximately 2558-2532 B.C. It was originally 157 meters tall (three meters lower than Khufu) with a base that measured 235 meters. The average weight of the stones is 2.5 tons, and some of the outer blocks weigh as much as seven tons. The angle of the incline is 53 degrees. The masonry has a limestone core with granite siding. The pillars, architraves and roof beams are granite as well. The temple walls are red granite from Aswan, deep in Upper Egypt. The floors are paved with white alabaster. The loss of height is due to the erosion of the covering of the pyramid which served aesthetic purposes and concealed the entrance to the pyramid. The only remaining covering of the three is found on the pyramid Khafre. There are two separate structures: a valley temple and a funerary temple. The valley temple was the locus of the preparations for burial with an embalming room. There are green diorite statues in the interior whose walls are plain, unrelieved surfaces. The family cemeteries were less elaborate than those of his predecessor, Khufu. The valley temple is connected the to the funerary temple by a covered causeway. The entrance to the funerary temple is laid out in much the same manner as the valley temple. The court is reached directly from the causeway corridor through a system of entrance halls, a system simplified by the following pharaoh. The large temple room at the foot of the pyramid was created by a row of statues.

The pharaoh's burial chamber was at the center of the mass and it was covered with granite. It measured 11.5 meters by 5.5 meters and reached a height of 6.3 meters. The chamber contained 23 statues of Khafre enthroned. The pharaoh's sarcophagus was made from red granite, in contrast to the magnificence and grandeur of the structure in which it was placed, there was neither ornamentation nor inscription on it. The body of Khafre was carried west from the Nile Valley, through the temples to its final resting place in a very elaborate ritual to prepare the pharaoh for his next life. The deceased was supplied with the provisions that he would need in the afterworld: adornments, alimentation, and armaments. The completion of the service did not signal the end of the pharaoh's recognition by his subjects as offerings to Khafre were made by funerary priests outside the pyramid. These offerings fed the pharaoh's *ka*, which protected and comforted the deceased.

The temple also boasts another highly recognizable artifact from Ancient Egypt: the Sphinx. Lying next to the subterranean causeway on the sand's surface, the Sphinx is 57 meters in length with a face six meters wide. The Sphinx was created for the spirit of Khafre to keep watch over his funerary complex. It has the body of a lion and the head of Khafre in royal headdress. The Sphinx was carved

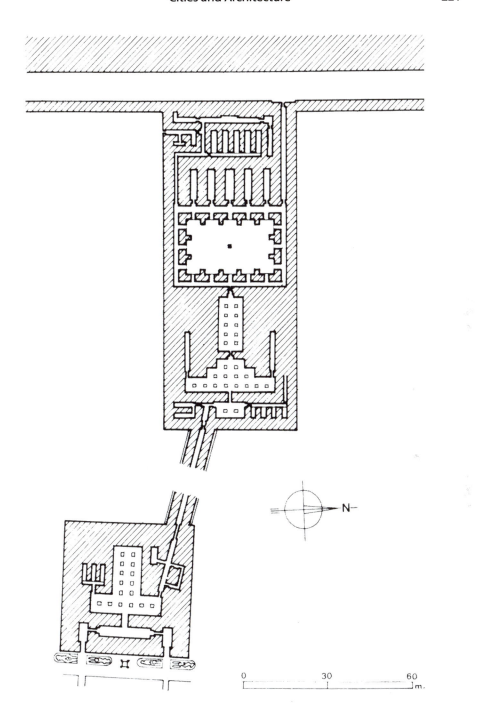

Figure 13-2. Plan of the Pyramid Complex of Khafre, Al-Jizah, Egypt

from the soft natural limestone of Al-Jizah and pieces of the monument have fallen off with the passing of time.

Figure 13-3. The Sphinx, Al-Jizah, Egypt

The pyramid was a great house for a king. As a monument to his death, it demonstrated the importance of the pharaoh to his people and displayed the items essential to the afterlife. An architectural feat, the pyramid is a testament to the knowledge of the Egyptians who built it, and their commitment to the pharaoh it enshrined.

Fez

In the northwest corner of the continent, in what is now Morocco, is the city of Fez. The city was founded as early as 789 A.D. by Idris b. Abdallah, a descendant of the Prophet's son-in-law, Ali, a Shi'a Muslim who was at odds with the Sunni administration in Baghdad. One of the most sacred cities in Morocco, Fez is the site of the Al-Qarawiyyin Mosque (the Mosque of the Dead), built under

Figure 13-4. Al-Qarawiyyin Mosque, interior

the direction of two sisters from Qairawan. It was remains one of the greatest structures and holiest sites in Morocco.

The city is located in the north-central portion of the country, about 195 kilometers southeast of Tangiers, on the Oued Fez River in the northern foothills of the Middle Atlas Mountains. The "old city" was built around the river and descended into the river valley in a series of winding streets. The city experienced natural, not planned growth. There were a number of natural springs within the city, and easy access to water was but one of the elements that attracted settlers. Fez drew many different people within its walls, and influxes of refugees from Spain (because of the Christian reconquest of that country that ended in 1492) and Tunisia increased the city's diversity. Neighborhoods in the old city were built along ethnic lines.

Fez prospered because its main market was located close to the great routes of the trans-Saharan trade system that linked the desert and the gold mines to the south with the Mediterranean Sea. The market was situated between the two largest sanctuaries of the city, the Adrisis II and Al-Qarawiyyin mosques, and the market had its own gates that were closed at night. It was not considered at all inappropriate to have the commercial center in such close proximity to religious shrines.

The houses were built in compact groups, leaning against each other and resembling honeycombs. Inhabitants were able to remain separated from their neighbors since each house opened onto an inner courtyard. The courtyards were an extremely important part of the household, often surrounded by a cloister of arcades and occasionally enlarged to create a garden with flowers and trees. At

Figure 13-5. Al-Qarawiyyin Mosque, exterior

the center there was almost always a fountain or a pool of water. The courtyard created a sanctuary of sorts from the busy city life outside; it also collected cool air to help the inhabitants in their efforts to endure the sweltering summer temperatures. The flat rooftops were used for summer sleeping and storage.

The inhabitants of Fez lived on small winding streets that bustled with activity and people. Each house was a refuge from the constant activity that took place outside its walls. With the exception of women in wealthy households, the people of the city were in frequent contact with each other when they performed regular activities such as using bathhouses, saying the five daily prayers, and marketing. Privacy from the outside world for the family was an important consideration in architectural design in Islamic society; thus, the residential quarters were situated in such a way that they were separated from the public byways while the backs of the houses faced the street. Heavy doors guarded the occupants of the houses, especially the women of wealthy families. They remained within the confines of the house, leaving only when suitably escorted by a male family member. Likewise, windows afforded protection from the outside world. These doors and windows were not just functional, they were richly decorated. The degree of ornamentation of the houses in Fez and much of the Islamic world was remarkable for its intricacy. Tiling was a favorite medium, and many examples of North African tile have been preserved and are still in use.

Tuareg Tents

The Tuareg, one of the many nomadic groups in Africa, were once heavily involved in the trans-Saharan trade. They acted as agents who carried gold from the interior of West Africa to the merchants of Mediterranean North Africa who then sent the precious metal to Europe. The Tuareg trace their origins matrilineally to the Sanhaja Berbers of northwest Africa, but they moved further and further away from their ancestors and into the Sahara. This dispersion resulted in eight distinct groups among the Tuareg who all spoke mutually intelligible languages derived from the Berber language of *tamachek*.

The degree of transhumance practiced depended upon the area in which the Tuareg lived. The range for those in the Sahara was up to a thousand kilometers; for those in the moister *sahel* to the south, the distance was approximately two hundred kilometers. Most important among the livestock were camels; goats, sheep, and cattle (in the *sahel*) might also be included. As nomadic pastoralists, the Tuareg needed to be able to move quickly in response to the needs of both humans and their livestock; this necessitated a minimal amount of possessions for each family to ensure a greater ease of transportation. The tents of the Tuareg displayed the importance of mobility to the society.

Figures 13-6. Tuareg Tent Encampment near Timbuktu, Mali

The Tuareg believed that their ancestors learned to build the first tent by studying the stars. The tents, which were low and circular, represented the image of the Tuareg cosmos. Depending on the sub-group, there were distinct varieties of tents that were used, but all had common traits. The tents were erected by women upon arrival at a new site, often pitched with openings that faced towards the east to allow the warming rays of the morning sun to enter and to keep out the intense afternoon heat. Depending upon the season, the flexible poles that composed the frame were covered with mats that were made from either woven animal-hair or animal skins. The elements of the Sahara were often extreme and it was essential that the tents protect the inhabitants to the greatest degree possible. The mats were raised and lowered to permit ventilation. Additionally, they provided a shield from an average of ten hours of penetrating sunlight per day, extreme daytime heat, and overnight cold temperatures, as well as severe sandstorms.

Unlike living quarters in many other Islamic societies, the tents of the Tuareg were sexually integrated. Women enjoyed a relatively high status in Tuareg society and were not secluded; today most of the men are not literate, but most of the women are. Although there were clearly demarcated male and female sides of the tents, there were no internal symbolic or physical partitions between men and women.[2]

The Dogon

The Dogon have been called one of the African societies the least touched by the Western world because their geographic location has kept them in relative isolation until recent times. The Dogon originally came from the Mande area of present-day southwestern Mali and northeastern Guinea and arrived at their present location in the fifteenth century. Legend holds that they were guided by a crane. Their arrival displaced the Tellem people, whose name means "we found them there." When the Dogon arrived in their new home, they diverged into three separate, but very much related, groups. "Dogon Country" is made up of two hundred kilometers of cliffs (the *falaise*) that reach as high as five hundred meters; these cliffs have, until recently, protected them from outside influences.

The very complex Dogon cosmology was manifested in everyday life, from the spatial living arrangements to the doors on the granaries. It would not have been difficult for the visitor to become lost at night in the tight and winding passageways of a Dogon village that were the spatial and architectural manifestation of the Dogon myth of creation and conceptualization of the working order of the universe. Even the farms were laid out in a pattern that demonstrated the spiral upon which the Dogon conception of the universe was, and still is, based.

The Dogon village was anthropomorphic and designed to represent the cosmos. It was laid out in the form of a square or oval with an opening at one end representing the original egg (from the creation myth) bursting forth from its shell. The orientation of the village was always on a north-south axis. Nommo was the original Dogon, reputed to have the reproductive capabilities of both

_____

2. Daphne Spain, *Gendered Spaces* (Chapel Hill, The University of North Carolina Press, 1992), 57.

sexes. The village was in the shape of Nommo lying on his side, and as in many other African cultures, smiths, cobblers, wood and leather workers, *griots*, and menstruating women were relegated to the outskirts of the village, as they were either involved in transformative processes or were in a "polluted" state. At the northern end the blacksmith could be found, his location corresponding to the head of Nommo. The houses used by menstruating women were located to the east and west, their position representing Nommo's hands. The family homesteads formed the chest and the shrines made up the feet.

Twins were very important to the cosmology of the Dogon, representing the original ancestors as well as the proliferation of life. The importance of human reproduction was represented in the foundation shrine, which was in the form of a cone and a hollowed stone, representing male and female genitalia. The cone and stone were used to produce oil from *lannea acida* seeds. "Twin-ness" was also demonstrated by villages being built in pairs; two villages were intertwined, just as the two genders were woven together in Nommo and in the Dogon people themselves.

Figure 13-7. Dogon Village Granary Door

**Figure 13-8. Houses and Granaries in
a Dogon Village near Sanga, Mali**

The granaries that flanked the houses are among the structural features of a Dogon village most recognizable to Westerners. The granaries stored millet and other foodstuffs and were vital to the survival of the Dogon. They were constructed of adobe and had distinctive, conically shaped thatched roofs. The granaries' entrances were often protected by carved wooden doors, usually carved by the village blacksmith who also made the window shutters.

Compounds were built on a circular plan. The roof was freestanding and flat, made from poles and straw; the walls were made of adobe. The houses were arranged in tight clusters, usually built into the surrounding walls. The walls were painted and it was common to find decorations incised on them. The house of the paramount chief, like that of the village, is based on anthropomorphic symbolism. The house took the form of a man, as the interconnecting rooms formed a body complete with head, torso, and limbs. The house of the spiritual leader had a central room (*ginna*), which corresponded to Nommo's breast. The *ginna* had a raised living area that was accessible by ladder and a windowless facade that depicted the original eight ancestors and their descendants. Around the *ginna* were found ordinary homes that were smaller and were rectangular in design with flat tops. In these dwellings there were also granaries, stables, towers, and storage space, as well as a kitchen, work area, shrine, and goat house, all of which were connected by passageways and opened into an inner courtyard. Additionally, the Dogon procreative and nurturing abilities were represented as the two water jars at the entrance to the main room which represented breasts, and the narrow passageway to the workroom where grinding stones and jars of water were kept replicated the male sex organ.

Figure 13-9.   A View of Rooftops from the Bottom of the *Falaise*

Found in each lineage homestead was the *togu na*, literally "the big shelter," the meeting house where men sat to discuss village matters and make important decisions. It was a shelter covered with branches and leaves, its roof almost always square or rectangular. The *togu na* was sometimes covered with clay in which symbolic figures were carved. The Dogon belonged to three different groups; the differences in their cultures manifested themselves in their architecture, but certain aspects were common to all. Traditionally, the corners of the *togu na* were aligned with the four cardinal points of the compass. Supporting the roof were eight pillars, which were situated in three rows, running from north to south; these pillars represented the eight mythical ancestors who described such a structure to Nommo. The ground plan of the series of pillars also resembled a serpent coiled along a broken line. Although there were exceptions, usually all pillars in *togu na* were of the same style, all were usually carved by the same carver, who more than likely came from that village; thus, the art of the *togu na* represented the community in which it was situated.

Gedi: A Swahili City-State

The word "Swahili" is derived from an Arabic word meaning "coast." The Swahili people, their language and culture grew from the meeting of Bantu Africans on the coast of East Africa and Arab traders who arrived in the area around 500 A.D. Between 800 and 1500 A.D. A number of city-states developed on the coast and the offshore islands in response to the increased trading demands for such goods as ivory and slaves. This meeting of cultures (Bantu, Arab, and Portuguese) produced, among other things, its own distinct style of architecture. The fortunes of cities such as Mombasa, Malindi, and Kilwa and the islands of Pemba and Zanzibar waxed and waned through the years. The cities were disunited and subject to the fluctuations of the international market and European attempts at domination. Yet the Swahili city-states maintained their importance in the Indian Ocean trade for many years.

An interesting example of Swahili architecture and spatial layout can be found in Gedi. The city of Gedi was probably not occupied until the late thirteenth century. Its importance peaked approximately in the mid-fifteenth century, and it was abandoned at the beginning of the seventeenth century. Although the history of Gedi was somewhat short-lived, its abandonment and relative isolation have left ruins that allow the student of architecture to see a relatively clear picture of a small trading city of the Islamic East African trading coast.

There were great similarities between the architectural styles of Southern Arabia and the Swahili city-states. In the earlier stages of the development of these city-states, housing construction was simpler than in the later forms. A typical house consisted of a narrow courtyard with a main room that ran along the long side of the house with private quarters behind it. These quarters held a long room with a small bedroom, a kitchen and a storeroom. Later, the private middle room was divided into two separate rooms, one long chamber and two private suites (presumably to be used by the owner's wives[3]) and included the addition of a domestic court that facilitated food preparation. The houses had many windows and flat roofs—the influence of the Portuguese traders who visited the coast.

Initially single-storied, multi-level houses began to be built in the fifteenth and sixteenth centuries. Originally, the city's planning was based upon a grid, with well-laid out streets, and at the center were the great mosque and palace, around which the greatest concentration of houses could be found. Gedi's size peaked at approximately forty-five acres. The city experienced natural growth; the result was a compact city with close-knit houses that exhibited a great deal of variety in structure. A nine-foot high wall with three gates surrounded the city.

There was extensive use of stone. The stone was primarily coral ragstone, which was commonly found on the coast. Coral was an excellent building material: lightweight and easy to transport. The stone is soft when initially cut, but hardens with exposure to water and sun. The blocks of stone were cemented and plastered with white lime that was produced by burning of the coral. The roofs of the houses were waterproofed with a thick layer of lime. This lime coating also created an insulating effect against heat. The ceilings were often carved and were

---

3. Paul Oliver, *Shelter in Africa* (New York and Washington, Praeger Publishers, 1971), 84.

Figures 13-10. Ruins of Gedi, Kenya

crafted from hard woods brought in from the interior of the continent. There is no evidence that the flat roofs were used for storage or any other activity. Floors were also made of coral stone and lime concrete. Stone and mortar were the materials used to construct the houses of the elite. Those with less wealth lived in houses made of timber and adobe, roofed with palm or grass thatch.

As in Fez, the courtyard was an important feature of the domestic dwellings, offering refuge from summer heat. The need to conduct business in surroundings that would be hospitable and amenable to visiting traders in a hot, moist climate combined with the increase of European influences resulted in the unique architectural structures of the Swahili city-states. Enlarged front courtyards were used in the commercial activities that dominated the economy of Gedi. The forms of the doorways were generally designed with a wide, painted arch set into a recessed rectangular range. Niches were often carved into the doorways and lamps would be inserted into them.

As cities grew, graveyards came to be built between houses in the effort to use all available space. This resulted in the outlying sections having less formal structure than the older sections of the cities and created some interesting variations and innovations. For example, the pillar tombs that developed in the fourteenth and fifteenth centuries seem to be a feature unique to the Swahili city-states.

The Kingdom of Buganda

The Kingdom of Buganda was located on the northern shores of Lake Victoria in Uganda and was considered to be one of the greatest of the pre-colonial in-

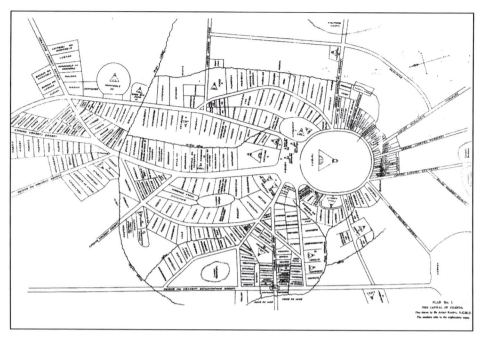

Figure 13-11. Plan of the Capital City of Buganda

tralacustrine states. The size, culture, and highly centralized government of the kingdom impressed the first Europeans who visited the area. Buganda had productive soil and reliable rainfall, which provided the Baganda (or Ganda, the people of Buganda) with a reliable harvest of bananas—the staple food of their diet—as well as many other essential items.

Buganda had enough arable land to provide for the needs of all its citizens. The nature of the land-tenure system had most Ganda working on the farms of a landlord and receiving usufructory rights in return. Because of the size of the land holdings, most Ganda lived outside of the view of their closest neighbors. They lived in family households with a banana garden just outside the compound walls. A village was a group of households, a group not necessarily related by kinship. Extended family homesteads were extremely rare, as there was little kinship continuity in villages, and village composition was mixed and fluid.

By the end of the nineteenth century, it was rare for more than thirty percent of a village to be composed of one clan, and a son rarely lived in the village in which he had been raised. Landlords were more concerned about retaining their farmers than the peasants were about holding up their end of the bargain. Landlords had to be fair and popular to keep peasants from moving; it was not uncommon for the peasants to work more on their own gardens than on those of their landlords. The high level of productivity of the banana made it possible for the peasant to be able to produce an adequate amount of tribute for the landlord and the king while leaving time to for other, more leisurely, pursuits.

The houses of the peasants were built in the same way as those in the capital city, but on a smaller scale. They were round, and attached to the ceiling of the house were three rings of varying sizes made from the fronds of palm leaves. These rings supported the roof. From the center ring, the roofing material was attached. The roofs were made from elephant grass, a type of grass that is plentiful in Buganda that is not suitable for grazing livestock. The roof was normally about seven feet high and descended at a gentle angle from the center to a height of approximately five feet at its lowest edge.

The floor was a hard, smooth surface made from earth beaten with plantain stems and covered with a mixture of clay and cow dung, which hardened into the desired surface. Making floors was a specialized task—the work was done in such a way that the floor's integrity was not compromised by rain. The floor was constructed at an angle that allowed water to run off, avoiding the house. The walls were constructed from reeds. There was only one entrance to the house. There were neither chimneys nor holes to let the smoke of fires escape from the interior of the house. Smoke would eventually find its way out of the only door.

When Europeans first ventured into Buganda in the nineteenth century, they were amazed by the capital city; it was judged to be spacious and very clean, and the visitors were greatly impressed by the system of roads that led into the city and the broad avenues within the city walls. The capital city (*kibuga*) was mobile; when a new *kabaka* (king) took control of the government, it was traditional to move it to a new location.

Although the capital city was relocated at the installation of a new king, regularity in form was maintained. The enclosure was in the shape of an ellipse and held a great number of buildings and people; it was estimated that three thousand people lived within the *kibuga* in 1858.[4] The capital was divided into districts that corresponded to the districts of the kingdom. The leading chiefs resided in the capital when their presence was required, and houses were built for them in the *kibuga*. Lands that lay outside were available for peasants to build temporary homes when the peasants needed to be in the capital city for required labor. Within the walls of the capital, there were cultivated lands with banana trees that were used to supplement the food brought into the capital as tribute from the countryside. There was also a road with a private exit that led to Lake Victoria—in case the king needed to make a quick escape.

The king had his own enclosure in the capital city containing over four hundred buildings. The queen's residence was built about a mile from the king's. Near the entrance to the city there was a sacred flame that was never allowed to go out. The outer enclosure was surrounded by bark cloth trees, and inside it were twelve foot-high fences woven from elephant grass. The fences were supported by posts carved from fig trees. Since the fences were woven, they required a great deal of maintenance. The houses were also made of perishable materials and constantly needed to be rebuilt, demanding a work force of "no fewer than a thousand men."[5]

The Tswana

The Tswana live in the present-day Republic of Botswana, a country where the eastern fringe holds the greatest percentage of inhabitants because the rest of

4. Peter C.W. Gutkind, *The Royal Capital of Buganda. A Study of Internal Conflict and External Ambiguity* (The Hague: Mouton & Co., 1963), 15.

5. John Roscoe, *The Baganda* (London: Macmillan, 1911), 366.

the land is part of the Kalahari Desert. The Tswana were mixed agriculturalists, raising crops and keeping livestock both in urban areas and in rural settings. Archaeological evidence suggests that the typical Tswana house has not undergone any significant changes either in pre-colonial or post-colonial times,[6] although some recent modifications have been made in order to respond to the changing environment.

Towns were common amongst the Tswana, and tensions in southern African region prompted many Tswana to live in communities for increased of protection. The Tswana houses were called "rondavels" by the Europeans who encountered them; the name came from their conical shape. A family's compound had a number of houses arranged in a semi-circular pattern. The Tswana desire for order is evident in the structure of the settlements: towns were divided into wards and sections. Where one lived indicated one's place in society.

A high degree of mobility was an accepted fact of life in the search for productive agricultural lands, water, and grazing land. Just as the people moved, so did the chief and his capital. Each of the different locally based political units had its own chief. The largest unit of the village or town was the ward. In the ward, there were sections, then household clusters, then individual households. When townspeople moved to a new location, households were set up to permit one to have the same neighbors and orientation to the chief's house. The new town had to be consecrated for protection at the time that it was established. Traditionally, the king and his wife were the first to sleep in the new town.[7] Although town planning was quite precise, no provisions were made for growth.

The houses were round and varied in interior design. The construction of walls and thatching were done by women. A common design would have the interior divided into an inner and an outer room that opened on to a verandah where the children often slept. For security reasons, there was only one opening to the house. The rest of the family would sleep in the central area of the house. Smaller units were created for those who needed to be separated (such as servants and girls of marriageable age) and for storage units. Raised granaries were found behind the main house.

Roofs were thatched with grass that hung down over the sides of the houses. Houses were placed in the middle of enclosures creating both a front- and a backyard. The yard (*lolwapa*) was often finished with clay and sloped to allow the water to run off. The front yard was the scene of cooking and grain threshing. The *lolwapa* was also where the family ancestors were located and where visitors were entertained. The *lolwapa* was considered to be a controlled area; the area outside the fence was thought of as an untamed area, and it was not often used. Widows and widowers lived on the outskirts of town; their distance from the rest of the village was to ensure that the rains would not be hampered.

The chief's *kgotla* was in the center of the town. The *kgotla* was a large, open space encircled by a fence of poles that contained shade trees if possible. The *kgotla* was the seat of local administration, where issues concerning the settlement were discussed, and where justice was administered. The great cattle *kraal* (corral) that led up to the *kgotla* also had ritual and political importance. This

---

6. Graeme John Hardie, *Tswana Design of House and Settlement — Continuity and Change in Expressive Space* (Ph.D. diss., Boston University, 1980), 32.

7. Ibid., 172.

was where chiefs would have secret meetings with their advisors and where initiation ceremonies would take place.

The Kuba

The Kuba were agricultural Bantu who inhabited the savanna of the Democratic Republic of Congo. Jan Vansina described their architectural style as one that was characterized by an "overall sense of proportion to which details were often subordinated."[8] Horizontal lines dominated. Kuba houses have been de-

Figure 13-12. Royal Bedchamber of the Kuba Palace with King Nyim Mbop Mabinc maKyen (r. 1939-1969) and His Two Sons

---

8. Jan Vansina, *The Children of Woot. A History of the Kuba People* (Madison: University of Wisconsin Press, 1978), 233.

Figure 13-13. Houses of the Royal Wives of the Kuba King

scribed as basketry upon poles because the walls were constructed of highly decorated woven mats.

Houses were rectangle-shaped with saddle roofs and courtyards. The roof and walls were constructed from woven palm fronds. There were two doors, one on a long side, another on a short side. Sliding doors were added at the end of the nineteenth century. Each house was divided into two rooms by a partition. The Kuba created attics by laying screens between the top of walls and the roof. Because of the lightweight of the building materials, all houses, even those of the king, were easy to transport.

The capital city was mobile and *corvée* labor was required for its construction and maintenance. The lightweight houses were moved from one location to another as the king changed residences. The royal houses were rarely higher than fourteen feet and were pyramidal in shape with steeple-crown roofs. With the exception of the harem, the responsibility of building and maintenance of each structure in the area of the palace as well as the buildings of the public domain and enclosures were relegated to a specific village. The capital's main avenues separated public buildings of various heights and widths. The builders' principal architectural feature was the use of open, walled spaces designed in such a way that the perspective would not be evaluated from a stationary position, but rather by walking along the street.

The Mbuti

As this study moves farther into the interior of the Democratic Republic of Congo, into the heart of the continent, we encounter a group greatly mythologized and misunderstood in the West. The Mbuti (sometimes referred to as "pygmies") inhabit the central and southern parts of the Ituri forest, just north of the equator in eastern Congo—one of the most inaccessible places on the African continent. Mbuti is a blanket term that is used to describe a number of different ethnic groups: the Efé, the Asua, the Kango and the Çwa. They have lived in the Ituri forest for at least 2,000 years.

The "band" was the social organization of the Mbuti. The "band" was a unit of hunters and their dependents who preferred to use hunting territories instead of kinship relations in the construction of social boundaries. The Mbuti were a nomadic hunting and gathering society who only occasionally made forays into the farms of neighboring agriculturalists. Virtually all their needs were provided for by the dense rain forest in which they lived, including the materials from which their houses were built.

**Figure 13-14. Mbuti Forest Camp, Ituri Forest,
Democractic Republic of the Congo**

Men, women, and children worked together to prepare the camp area by cutting saplings and leaves. The dwellings were constructed of leaves that were pushed through frames to form walls that could be erected in two hours' time. The time factor was important as the sun set very rapidly on the equator and the area was subject to frequent rain. The houses were set up communally by women as the Mbuti moved to new camps. The houses were low—usually about four and a half feet high—and beehive shaped, consisting of one room with a leaf door. The ubiquitous leaves of the Ituri provided protection from the rain, and leaves were constantly being added and changed to prevent leaks.

The Mbuti moved from camp to camp according to their needs, primarily to ensure the availability of food. The houses were abandoned as the band moved on. Bands never camped twice in the same place and did not use the same camp for more than a month. If there were two groups inhabiting the same camp, the houses would be arranged in such a way that the two entities overlapped. The houses were usually arranged in a circular shape, depending upon the location of the trees in the area. Family units lived together in a house and changes were made to allow for change in family size or status. For example, an addition would be built for a girl who was about to reach puberty or because of the addition of an in-law.

Because of the intense level of contact among the Mbuti, due to their communal hunting and gathering activities and camp size, the location of the houses in the camp was based more on the lines of friendship than upon lineage. When tensions among the group flared, the women would change the orientation of the houses so that the parties concerned would not have to face each other upon entering or leaving their homes. The Mbuti cherished sounds and a lively atmosphere characterized the camps, with the sounds of work, singing and children playing; it was said that a silence was the mark of a group that was living in extreme tension. All efforts were made to bring any disharmonious people in the camps back into mutual accord as swiftly as possible. Because of the extreme proximity in which the Mbuti lived, any lack of mutual goodwill between two individuals was bound to affect the band as a whole.

Conclusion

In this discussion of indigenous African architecture we can see that the styles of dwellings, use of space, village layout, and construction of houses varied greatly. The elements used to erect houses corresponded directly with the needs of those who dwelled within their walls. One of the most important considerations was that people's houses should meet the needs of their occupations. The Mbuti were the only group studied here who made their houses entirely from leaves and these hunter gatherers moved no less than once a month. The Ganda and Kuba had centralized political organizations with mobile capital cities—stone would have been an impractical building material. The commerce-oriented city dwellers of Fez and Gedi were firmly entrenched in their urban areas and their buildings were made of stone. African people worked with the materials that were locally available to produce dwellings that were suited to their lifestyles and modes of production. The continuity of many of these styles is a testament to their practicality and aesthetic values. Through the study of African architecture one gains further insights into the lives and beliefs of the people who created and lived in these structures.

Review Questions

1. How did the cosmology of certain ethnic groups reflect the ways in which they created their spatial living arrangements?
2. What environmental considerations were taken into account in the creation of dwellings?
3. How did dwellings correspond to the modes of production/life styles of the inhabitants?
4. Many of the houses discussed mention outdoor sections used for village discussions, family gatherings, business dealings, and chores. What does this demonstrate?

Additional Reading

Denyer, Susan. *African Traditional Architecture*. New York: Africana Publishing Company, 1978.

Duffy, Kevin. *Children of the Forest*. New York: Dodd, Mead & Company, 1984.

Felix, Marc L. *Ituri: The Distribution of Polychrome Masks in Northeast Zaire*. Munich: Lerlag F. Jahn, 1992.

Garlake, Peter S. *The Early Islamic Architecture of the East African Coast*. Nairobi & London: Oxford University Press, 1966.

Griaule, Marcel and Dieterlen, Germaine. "The Dogon," in *African Worlds. Studies in the Cosmological Ideas and Values of African Peoples*. London: Oxford University Press, 1954.

Gutkind, Peter C.W. *The Royal Capital of Buganda. A Study of Internal Conflict and External Ambiguity*. The Hague: Mouton & Co., 1963.

Hardie, Graeme John. *Tswana Design of House and Settlement — Continuity and Change in Expressive Space*. (Ph.D. diss., Boston University, 1980).

Huet, Jean-Christophe, "The Togu Na of Tenyu Ireli," in *African Arts*, 21, 4 (August 1988).

Hull, Richard W. *African Cities and Towns Before the European Conquest*. New York: W.W. Norton & Company, Inc., 1976.

Hutt, Antony. *Islamic Architecture, North Africa*. London: Scorpion Publications, 1977.

Mair, Lucy. *African Societies*. London: Cambridge University Press, 1974.

Oliver, Paul. *Shelter in Africa*. New York: Praeger Publishers, 1971.

Prussin, Labelle. *Hatumere: Islamic Design in West Africa*. Berkeley: University of California Press, 1986.

Prussin, Labelle. *African Nomadic Architecture. Space, Place and Gender*. Washington, D.C.: Smithsonian Institution Press, 1995.

Roscoe, John. *The Baganda: An Account of the Native Customs and Beliefs*. London: Macmillan, 1911.

Spain, Daphne. *Gendered Spaces*. Chapel Hill & London: The University of North Carolina Press, 1992.

Turnbull, Colin M. *Wayward Servants. The Two Worlds of the African Pygmies*. London: Eyre & Spottswoode, 1966.

Vansina, Jan. *Les Tribus Ba-Kuba et les Peuples Apparenées*. London: International African Institute, 1954.

———. *The Children of Woot. A History of the Kuba People*. Madison: University of Wisconsin Press, 1978.

Chapter 14

Art

dele jegede

We begin by posing a set of related questions: What is African art? In what ways is it different from other art forms like the ones that we are familiar with in our museums and galleries—sculpture, paintings, prints, assemblage, photographs, installation, even video arts, for example? And what do we stand to gain by studying it? While we may affirm that, stylistically and conceptually, African art differs from, say, Western art, we must also quickly point out that being different is not a disadvantage; it does not imply that one is superior to the other. This observation is central to our study of the arts of Africa. Of course, studying the arts generates its own aesthetic pleasure. But beyond this, we gain considerable insights into the social structure and value systems of other cultures, for the arts are a record of a people's history and achievements. Art offers us immense opportunities for appreciating epochs and cultures. In particular, African art provides us with a platform from which to take an insightful journey into history and learn about cultures, many of which have long ceased to exist. The tremendous diversity that exists in Africa creates an added dimension, one which teaches us to value diversity and be wary of generalizations and stereotypes.

As we become exposed to a plethora of multicultural precepts and practices which are reflected by the arts of this continent, we may experience culture shock: we may be provoked or irritated; challenged, astonished, or humbled. The perception that we gain through our exposure to the arts of other lands and cultures may leave us bewildered, sometimes nauseated, even alarmed. Hopefully, it will also lead us to an appreciation of our own individual limitations, prejudices, or even arrogance, all or some of which we manifest, sometimes unintentionally. Studying the arts of Africa also exposes us to issues of diversity. At the same time that it helps us to appreciate historical antecedents, it also helps in developing a sense of our own place in history. It will be important for us to learn this important point: that in matters pertaining to art, there is not a single correct approach or answer. Some have said that the word "art" does not exist in some African cultures. True as this may be, it does not mean that such African cultures do not have art; it simply means that they perceive, create, and relate to it in ways that are sometimes radically different from those we are used to. Thus, it is best for us to develop an open and critical mind in studying the arts of other cultures—to adopt the approach that is known in anthropological circles as cultural relativism, which demands that we should strive to relate to other cultures on their own terms, without attempting to impose our own values on them.

Over the years, the notion that African art is synonymous with wood sculpture has gained currency, especially in the West. But such a perception could be misleading, for African art finds expression in a wide variety of media. The perception that African art is executed predominantly in wood dates back to the turn of the century, around 1905, when a group of artists based in Paris—André Derain, Amedeo Modigliani, and Pablo Picasso among others—brought international attention to African art through an innovative adaptation and use of African sculptural forms in their own works. Coming shortly after the 1897 British expedition to Benin during which thousands of precious art works were looted and shipped to Europe, this development stimulated interest in the study of African art, and there emerged a group of scholars—anthropologists, archaeologists, linguists, and art historians among them—who began to concentrate on this. In turn, museums, galleries, collectors, and dealers became involved, although not necessarily in that order. In the process, sculpture in wood became not only the most accessible, but also the most readily collectable genre. As exhibitions were held and as books and exhibition catalogues on African art became widespread, sculpture became the favored idiom.

Another important issue concerns the tendency to separate Egypt from the rest of Africa. As a result of the way scholars have partitioned the study of the arts of Africa (most studies have concentrated on sub-Saharan Africa), and partly in accordance with an attitude, now mostly discredited, which saw African art as primitive and barbaric, it has become customary to treat Egyptian art as something extraneous to the continent. This notion not only reflects Western prejudices, but it is supported neither by history nor geography, nor by Egyptian religious and cultural practices, most of which find abundant echoes in other parts of Africa.

In this chapter, African art does not exclude the arts of Egypt. Although our main concern is with art, an important secondary consideration will be the people and cultures without which no art would be created. Who were the artists and how did their concept of art differ from ours? What were the dominant themes and precepts that gave rise to the creation of specific art forms at a particular time and in a particular culture? How did African peoples use art as a handmaiden of social, political, and religious organization? Why did people produce art and how has art changed over time and space? What materials did they use and when were certain art works produced?

In attempting to find answers to these questions, we must study the arts and learn about their purposes. And in studying the arts, we must learn about the worldview that sustained their creation as well as the period in which they were created. Africa, the world's second largest continent (after Asia) and home to fifty three countries and over six hundred million people, presents us a challenge in the diversity of its peoples, the plurality of its art forms, and the vibrant adaptability which characterizes its traditions. Thus, it is neither desirable nor feasible for us to cover the arts of the continent in one fell swoop. The arts and ideas that are presented here are therefore representative and not exhaustive. An added dimension is the difficult issue of chronology. Since we do not have adequate information about the history of most of the art works under consideration, we have learned to reconstruct their history by having recourse to archaeology at times; at other times, it is oral history that has come to the rescue. This chapter will thus look at the diverse art forms that were produced in selected areas of Africa prior to the last quarter of the nineteenth century. While we shall grapple with the issue of chronology, it should be borne in mind that considerable lacunae do exist which caution us about the dangers of thinking about African art history on a linear scale.

Diversity of the Arts: Use and Media

The range of materials employed is as diverse as the age, use, and location of the art works themselves. Although personal embellishment or institutional aggrandizement featured prominently, African art has also found use within the context of religious, judicial, agricultural, and regulatory performances. In other words, some African art was used in contexts that reflected a worldview that we may here refer to as "art for life's sake." A detailed study could be rewarding in that the world of a people—their religious beliefs, their technological and economic systems, their socio-political organization—is often interred and encapsulated in their arts. Admittedly, the period under consideration provides us with no incontrovertible information concerning art forms other than those that have survived. But studying the arts reveals the presence of a hierarchy in which the arts were interrelated. Frequently, sculpture, costuming, jewelry, dance, poetry, music, and oratory are involved in a variety of educational, ritual, political, juridical, religious, and socio-political ceremonies.

Many of the art works that were produced in Africa during the period under consideration have been lost for a variety of reasons. Many were lost as a result of such ecological and man-made disasters as flood, fire, and wars; at other times, it was humidity and frequent use that accelerated decay. Because many pieces were made of perishable materials and also because not much premium was attached to their preservation (after all, the process was much more important than the objects, which were often casually placed in the sacred environments of personal or community shrines from which they would then be summoned for periodic ceremonial use), they provided ready materials upon which the ubiquitous termites pounced. It is true that through the planned and certified system of preservation that prevailed in Egypt, a significant body of work exists in relatively good state. But the same cannot be said of many other cultures in other parts of Africa. From the exquisite examples of works that have come to us from Djenne in Mali, Asante in Ghana, Igbo-Ukwu, Ife, and Benin, all in Nigeria, not to mention the various other cultures from Zimbabwe to Zaire, and from Burkina Faso to Botswana, we do know that African craftspeople and artists produced works in a variety of media which included terracotta, cast gold and copper alloys, iron, beads, stone and ivory. These are media that are capable of surviving in conditions where wood, animal hides and skins, yarns, raffia, gourds, and calabashes among others —materials in which a significant number of objects were produced—will perish. What of the use of the human body as a canvas? If there is any lesson that the arts communicate through their physical appearance, it is that the practice of ornamentating and scarifying the human body is an age-old one. From the tomb walls in ancient Egypt to the terracotta figures from Ile Ife, there is abundant evidence revealing the compulsive fascination that Africans have for surface decoration. Of course, we know that while the human body may be one of the most mobile art works, it is one of the most perishable. But there is yet another genre that has borne surface decoration for thousands of years; this is an extremely pervasive genre that is as fascinating as it is enigmatic: rock art.

Rock Art

The oldest and also the most widely distributed genre in Africa is rock art. Thousands of rock paintings and engravings have been found across the continent, especially in the northern, eastern, and southern parts. The first batch of rock paintings and engravings was discovered in Mozambique in 1721, more than one and a half centuries before the now famous Altamira cave paintings were discovered in Spain.[1] Since then, significant quantities of rock art have been discovered across the continent—in Zambia, Tanzania, Uganda, and Kenya; in the Kalahari Desert to the south; and, to the north, in the Sahara Desert. In the southern part of Africa, rock paintings have been discovered in the mountain ranges of the western Kalahari districts of Botswana. Many more have been found in the extensive rock shelters and overhangs that abound in such countries as Namibia, South Africa, Zimbabwe, Lesotho, and Swaziland. While many of these paintings and engravings are believed to have been made by Bantu-speaking peoples, many others are believed to have been made by the San peoples before they were forced into the Kalahari Desert. The sites where rock art has been found are too many to itemize. It is probably not an overstatement that in Southern Africa, wherever there are caves, overhangs, and rock shelters, there is a strong possibility that there are rock paintings.

In the Sahara Desert area, an equally astounding number of prehistoric rock engravings and paintings abound. The first discovery in this area was made in 1847 in the ancient city of Oran in northwestern Algeria by a contingent of French army officers[2]. A spate of discoveries has since followed. In 1850, Heinrich Barth, the legendary German geographer and explorer, embarked upon a journey across the Sahara. Setting out from Tripoli, he headed south for Timbuktu. In Fezzan, southwestern Libya, he came upon thousands of rock engravings. But it is in Tassili-n-Ajjer in southern Algeria that we have the largest concentration of rock art and paintings: fifty percent of the thirty thousand examples that have been discovered in this area are in the high cliffs and mountains of the Tassili plateau.

In considering rock art, certain questions arise which pertain to chronology, manufacture and purpose. While it has been established that Africans were the producers of these rock paintings and engravings, their chronology and purpose remain problematic. First, we must admit that the age of rock art is not easy to ascertain. Quite unlike the relatively recent practice whereby artists append their names on their works, sometimes even dating them, prehistoric artists did not provide us with such luxuries. Added to this is the particular difficulty presented by the ground, that is, the surface, on which the artists rendered their work. In order for us to have an idea of the age of rock art paintings and engravings in Africa, we must therefore look to archeologists who, employing a battery of analytical and scientific methods, including radiocarbon dating, have come up with

---

1. Frank Willett, *African Art* (New York: Thames and Hudson, 1993), 43.
2. Willett, op. cit.

suggested dates for certain sites. In attempting to establish dates, archaeologists may aim at achieving relative or absolute dating. Relative dating is much more easily established because, rather than depending solely on the artwork to generate evidence from which a conclusive date may be extracted, archaeologists cast their net wide and look for associative evidence that may be obtained from a variety of sources like such as human occupation of the site, the artwork itself, the subject-matter favored by the artists, and even stylistic development over a period or periods of time.

Thus, a number of dates have been suggested for the prehistoric rock art of Africa. Each of these dates must be treated individually, and on its own merit. While, for example, the Tassili paintings have been dated to around 4000 B.C., the age of the seven small slabs of prehistoric paintings which were discovered in the Apollo II Cave in the Huns Mountains of Namibia has been put at between 25,000 and 27,500 years. At the other extreme are those rock paintings in southern Africa which, because they depict such items as European dress and the use of horses, could not have been painted earlier than the eighteenth century. On the assumption that most of the rock paintings, especially those in southern Africa, were done during the Late Stone Age, some experts have come to the conclusion that rock art started about ten thousand years ago. In general, however, it is believed that the rock art of Africa spans a period of about thirty thousand years.[3] Although we may not know the absolute dates for thousands of these sites, this much we know, and can say without any equivocation: art is as old as humankind. And, on the basis of our knowledge of Africa as humankind's first home, it would not be farfetched for us to state that art originated in Africa.

As to what the paintings and engravings were used for, several possibilities offer themselves, depending upon the way the subject-matter is scrutinized. Based upon the presence of an overwhelming profusion of animals, are we to assume that the art was connected with some form of hunting magic? Was it a reflection of some trance experience? Or was this art merely for home decoration and pleasure? In other words, was this art for art's sake? Regardless of how we interpret the themes, contents, and subject-matter, we are left with one enticing thought: in these rock paintings and engravings are contained a record of the activities of prehistoric Africans. Perhaps in much the same way that we keep our journals today or document our family history, these art works can be studied as a reflection of their worldview, their religious beliefs, their law and customs.

Animals are by far the largest objects depicted in these paintings and engravings. Certain stages of development in the portrayal of these animals are discernible. First, they were depicted in simple monochromatic hues. Evolving from this was the technique of unshaded polychromes, from which they moved to the sophisticated, fully shaded, bi-chromatic and polychromatic methods, during which the artists also displayed knowledge of foreshortening.[4] A variety of animals has been identified. The rock engravings of the Sahara depict such animals as

---

3. See D.N. Lee and H.C. Woodhouse, *Art on the Rocks of Southern Africa* (New York: Charles Scribner's Sons, 1970), 15. For a detailed view of rock art in Africa, see also Willett, *African Art*.

4. Monochromatic hues are light and dark shades of a single color. When black is added to a color, it is called a shade; white added to the same color produces a tint. Bi-chromatic colors are obtained by using tints or shades of two colors. An artwork that is done in several

the elephant, rhinoceros, hippopotamus, and buffalo, all of which have since ceased to exist in the area. There are also depictions of the camel, the horse, the giraffe, large antelopes, ostriches, oryx, gazelles, humped cattle, goats, and moufflon which still exist in the Sahara. Four distinct phases have been identified in the rock engravings, on the basis of subject-matter and style. These are, in order of ascendancy, the Bubalus Period; the Bubalus Antiquus Period; the Horse Period; and the Camel Period.

Egyptian Art

We have seen that rock art, in spite of its antiquity and extensive distribution in Africa, is filled with riddles, many of which may remain unsolved for a long time. But Egyptian art belongs in a different category. From the extensive work that has been done by a succession of scholars, we are privileged to behold the splendor of Egyptian art, to learn some things about this ancient civilization, to marvel at its architecture, contemplate its religious doctrine, and understand some factors that actuated change over a period of time. You may have learnedsomething about Egypt; probably through the pictorial images of the great pyramids at Giza, considered to be some of the most impressive edifices of the world. Perhaps you have watched *The Ten Commandments*, a film based upon the biblical narrative which pitted Moses against an Egyptian pharaoh in an epic battle for freedom for the people of Israel. What about the Nile, the world's longest river and Egypt's life-source? The Nile was the principal source of irrigation for Egypt and its annual floods provided the necessary soil fertility without which survival would have been a Herculean task. Rising from the Kagera River in Burundi, the Nile courses through the Lake Plateau of East Africa, flowing on its more than four-thousand-mile journey northwards, finally emptying into the Mediterranean Sea. Prior to its unification by Menes, ancient Egypt comprised Upper Egypt (which was actually the southern part) and Lower Egypt, to the north.

From whatever perspective you look at Egypt, what comes across is a magnificent civilization which clearly reveals a rationalized worldview. Egyptian art and architecture are a reflection of the majesty, grandeur, and opulence of the pharaohs. The following summation may be offered in connection with ancient Egypt:

(i) Dating back more than five thousand years, Egyptian art and architecture reveal Africa's most enduring legacy to world civilization;

(ii) Egyptian art is a record of the country's history: its philosophical, artistic, intellectual, religious, and political pursuits;

(iii) Often on a grandiose scale, Egyptian art and architecture are a manifestation of the doctrine of divine kingship, and the belief in life hereafter.

One of the best examples of Egyptian art comes in the form of a large, twenty-five-inch stone slate which was used by Menes for applying cosmetics to his face. Although this may seem strange to us today, it was quite a routine prac-

---

colors is referred to as polychromatic. In foreshortening, the artist shortens the dimensions of an object or a figure in order to depict it in a believeable and spatially correct position.

tice in ancient Egypt for men as well as women to wear cosmetics. And palettes such as this one were regular items on the cosmetic table; one of the two sides usually had a circular depression that was used for blending the cosmetics that were then applied to eyelids. Known as the *Palette of Narmer* (the other name by which King Menes was known), this double-sided slate is rich in iconographic symbols, the analysis of which reveals much about the role of King Menes in the history of ancient Egypt.

We begin around the year 3150 B.C., when King Menes succeeded in unifying Upper and Lower Egypt, thus establishing the first in a long succession of dynasties which lasted for about two thousand years. It was during this two-thousand-year period that Egyptian civilization developed a well articulated system in which fresco painting, sculpture (both three-dimensional and relief) and architecture attained their impressive majesty and monumentality. This was also the period when the papyrus was developed and the hieroglyphic form of writing was invented. The period has been divided into three main sections, each with its own set of dynasties, or ruling families. Altogether, there were twenty dynasties, beginning from the unification of Egypt in 3150 B.C. These were the Old Kingdom—ca. 2700-2190 B.C. (Dynasties 3-6); the Middle Kingdom—ca. 2040-1674 B.C. (Dynasties 11-14); and New Kingdom—ca. 1552-1069 B.C. (Dynasties 18-20).

Made between 3150 and 3125 B.C., the *Palette of Narmer* was found at Hierakonpolis. Its trapezoidal shape is divided, on both sides, into registers which bear low relief carvings. On the obverse side, the figure of the king clutching the hair of a kneeling victim with one hand and wielding a mace with the other, looms large. Undoubtedly, this gesture signifies the power of the king, the divine presence who subjugates his enemies. The powerlessness of his victims can be seen in how pathetic the kneeling figure appears. The two figures in the lowest register are paralyzed by fear, a situation that is amplified by the way they are hemmed in, suggesting that their fate is sealed, literally, by the towering presence of Narmer under whose feet they crouch. The king is depicted larger than others in this pictorial composition, in consonance with his status as a divine ruler. This social hierarchy —arranging pictorial subjects according to their social standing—is encountered in other African cultures like Benin and Yorubaland in Nigeria which also have kingship institutions. Narmer is seen wearing the conical crown of Upper Egypt (which is white; red is the color of the crown of Lower Egypt). Facing him and perching on six papyrus plants which sprout from the back of a figure is Horus, the falcon god of the sky and of kingship. Horus, the falcon with a human hand, is seen holding a rope tied around a man's neck. The papyrus upon which Horus stands is a plant that grows in considerable quantity in the lower Nile area. The meaning of this plaque is clear: Narmer is the triumphant ruler, the all-conquering hero under whom Egypt's destiny as a united entity is sealed. Behind Narmer is a diminutive figure, a court official who is the king's sandal-bearer. That Narmer is portrayed barefooted is indicative of the holiness of the ground on which he stands.

The reverse side of the palette is divided into four registers. Reading from the top, the second compartment employs the social hierarchy method in revealing King Narmer. There he is resplendent in his majesty, towering above all else. He is preceded by a column of devoted soldiers with standards held aloft. Behind him we see his court official once again, still bearing the king's sandals. In this same

**Figure 14-1 a-b. Palette of Narmer from Hierakonpolis,
1st Dynasty, c. 3000 B.C., (recto, left; verso, right)**

compartment, look to the far right and you will see a graphic manifestation of divine rulership: arranged in two rows are ten bodies whose decapitated heads are tucked between their legs. Another look at the pharaoh reveals him wearing the crown of Lower Egypt. In the third register, the interlocking necks of the two central animals create a circular spot which may have been used by the pharaoh for blending his cosmetics. The symbolism in the gesture of the animals apparently underlines the unification of Upper and Lower Egypt, with the two handlers emphasizing, perhaps, the necessity for co-operation. On the first register on both sides of the palette is Hathor, the cow goddess, who is represented framing (and thus protecting) the king, whose name appears in the rectangular pictographs situated in the middle. Pictography, or picture writing, is common in Egyptian art.

A careful consideration of this palette reveals significant imprints of an Egyptian stylistic canon. It is a canon that would endure for several hundred years, defying a spirited even if short-lived attempt to remove it by Akhenaten during the New Kingdom, in the mid-fourteenth century B.C. This canon is guided by the principle of clarity. The attempt was not for the artist to be held slave to a faithful representation of the human figure in biologically correct postures. Rather, the artist was interested in finding the most characteristic angle from which the human body could be represented. And once this was found, it became the benchmark from which no deviation was tolerated. Thus, the artist devised a stylized schema which reduced the possible angles from which the human figure could be represented to two—the full face and the profile—both of which were frequently combined into one in a single pictorial representation. Take a look at any ancient Egyptian painting or plaque; the chances are that the human figures are depicted using this creative canon. The head is shown in profile as are the waist and legs, while the shoulders are depicted frontally. Although the head is shown from the side, the eye is believed to be most communicative when viewed not in profile but frontally. Accordingly, a head shown in profile usually has an eye that is depicted as if seen from the front. Because the waist must be shown, the Egyptian artist came up with the tradition of placing the two feet of a figure perfectly on the same line, in profile, one foot behind the other. Of course, this convention was applied mainly to royalty and other dignitaries; representations of persons of lower ranks did not always follow this tradition. Egyptian artists were quite capable of representing the human figure in naturalistic rather than stylized forms as can be seen in their three-dimensional sculptures.

The logic of the interrelationship between ancient Egyptian art and architecture is to be found in a religious belief that placed a considerable premium on life after death. Indeed, the art of ancient Egypt epitomizes a concept that is widely upheld in many other parts of Africa: art for life's sake. As a handmaiden of religion, Egyptians believed that everyone had a *ka*, (a spirit or life force) which continued to live even after the body had died. The concern for catering to this *ka* in an afterlife, to honor it and make life as comfortable for it as it was during its life, was central to the evolution of certain practices, including mummification and the making of lifelike statues. Large-scale tomb sculptures in the round emerged as a complement to mummified bodies. Supposing something unexpected happened to the mummy? What if it decomposed or otherwise became unsuitable as a repository for the *ka*? It was for this reason that three-dimensional sculptures emerged, to serve as sanctuaries for the *ka*. Art and architecture were a vital component in the observance of all activities and events relating to the dead.

One of the most vital and well-veiled functions of the pyramids, for example, was as a burial chamber for Egyptian kings, members of the royal court, and eminent personages. The earliest construction of Egyptian tomb structure was the *mastaba*, a one-story, flat-topped trapezoidal building which originated during the Early Dynastic Period (ca. 3150-2700 B.C.; Dynasties 1-2). In Dynasty 3, during the reign of Djoser, we witness the construction of the earliest monumental architecture in ancient Egypt: a funerary complex of six *mastabas* placed upon one another, forming a seriated pyramid. This was the brainchild of Imhotep, the first architect in world history whose name was recorded. Built above an underground burial chamber, the *mastaba* provided the template for later Egyptian pyramids which have a square base and four slanted triangular sides. The pyramids are a testimony to the ingenuity of ancient Egyptian architects and builders. They are a monument to the awesomeness of the pharaohs, including Menkaure, Khafre, and Khufu—three Old Kingdom kings for whom the three pyramids at Giza were erected in the fourth Dynasty between 2601 and 2515 B.C. Constructed of limestone blocks, the largest of these three pyramids, that of Khufu, is 480 ft. high, with the base of each of the sides measuring 755 ft. So impressed were the Greeks that they listed the three pyramids at Giza as one of the Seven Wonders of the World. The stone sculptures from this period were no less impressive. Every ruler was interested in perpetuating his or her own memory, as well as in providing lifelike sculptures as an abode for his or her *ka*. One of the remarkable stone sculptures from Dynasty 4 is a double portrait of King Menkaure and his radiant Queen, Khamerernebty. About five feet, six inches in height, this sculpture typifies the standard Egyptian pose: the king stands, as does his queen, one foot in front of the other. With clenched fists and taut arms by his side, the king presents an athletic posture, as intended. But his tensed figure is softened by the gentle, curvilinear forms of the queen, whose embrace conveys both affection and deference.

As I have hinted above, there was an attempt during the New Kingdom to change the direction of Egyptian art. Of course, there had been changes, some subtle, others more obvious, in the period intervening between the Old and New Kingdoms. The Middle Kingdom (2040-1674 B.C.) witnessed socio-political upheavals which resulted in the whittling away of the authority of the pharaohs as local and regional chieftains gained ascendancy. Indeed, for about 150 years, the northernmost parts of Egypt were dominated by the Hyksos, a western Asian race, until they were expelled in 1552 B.C. The New Kingdom was thus a period of prosperity, a time when Egypt once again asserted itself, extending its frontiers to other domains. The most unusual change during this period was brought about by Amenhotep IV, the most radical personage of Dynasty 18. Having ascended

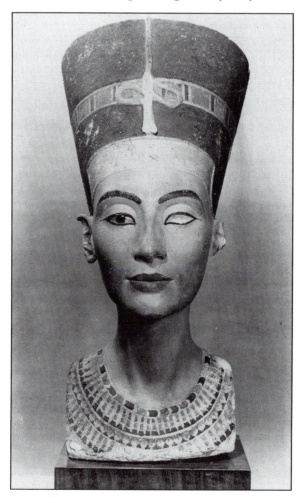

Figure 14-2. Bust of Queen Nefertiti

the throne in 1352 B.C., he began by initiating fundamental changes in the cultural, political, and spiritual life of Egypt. First, he proclaimed a new religion, devoted to the worship of one supreme god, the sun disk Aten. This was indeed remarkable, particularly when we realize that until then, Egypt had always practiced polytheism, that is, belief in several gods. The pharaoh followed this up by changing his own name from Amenhotep IV to Akhenaten. Third, in order to assert his power and weaken the firm grip which the priests of Amun had exerted on Thebes, he built a new capital in a new location much farther north, close to the place that is now called Tell el'Amarna. That is why this event has been dubbed "The Amarna Revolution." Akhenaten's revolutionary measures affected the arts, as artists strove to break with the established canon and introduce new artistic principles.

One masterpiece from this period is the bust of Queen Nefertiti, Akhenaten's dynamic Queen, confidant and collaborator. Measuring 20 inches in height, this elegant limestone figure at once reveals and conceals the character of a powerful personage. It exudes an inner strength and dignity which is matched by a gracious outward serenity. Busts were a rare form of art in the Old Kingdom, a fact which underlines the innovations that Akhenaten encouraged during his time. In less than two decades, the whole experiment was over. Akhenaten's rule lasted for only seventeen years, from 1352 to 1335 B.C. Soon after his death, the Amun priests regained their power, signifying an end to Akhenaten's monotheistic religion. Tutankhamun, the young pharaoh who succeeded Akhenaten, moved the capital to Memphis and ordered a return to the status quo. If ever there was any iota of doubt about the lavish attention paid to the residence in which pharaohs and other dignitaries would spend their life after departing this one, Tutankhamun's arrangements disproved it. His sarcophagus or ornamented coffin revealed a ruler that was buried in opulence. Buried with him were precious items which included jewelry, gold-plated furniture, textiles, and four gold chariots. The innermost of the three coffins in which he was buried was made of solid gold, and weighed several hundred pounds.

Nigeria

Nok

After Egypt, the next major culture whose art reveals an appreciable degree of technological knowledge and sophisticated artistry is located in north-central Nigeria. However, Nok, the name that has been given collectively to the terracotta corpus that has been discovered in this area, does not denote any particular group. In reality, Nok is a small village. It lent its name to the body of work that has been discovered over a geographical expanse of about three hundred by one hundred miles, because it is an archaeological practice to name a culture after the site that produced the first artifact. The first "discovery" was a fortuitous occurrence. The first Nok head that was found was used by a tin miner as a scarecrow in his farm. In 1943, Bernard Fagg, a British archaeologist and administrator in Nigeria, drew the attention of the mining community to the historical significance of the terracotta pieces, an example of which had been brought to his attention by the manager of a tin mine in the Jos Plateau area. The pieces were found deep in alluvial deposits. Since the first was found, more than 150 terracotta figures have been discovered.[5] Radiocarbon and thermoluminescence dating have placed these works from the middle of the first millennium B.C. to the first two centuries A.D. Thus, Nok provides us with the oldest category of terracotta works yet discovered in Africa, outside of Egyptian civilization.

A cursory look at these works reveals a stylistic homogeneity. A more detailed analysis, however, reveals the presence of subtle stylistic differentiation. As in relation to ancient Egypt, Nok art shows that its creators worked within a culturally sanctioned stylistic tradition. All the works so far discovered in this area are made of terracotta, that is, fired clay or pottery. It is of course possible that they also produced items in other media like wood, none of which survived. Certain standard features characterize Nok art. First, the eyes are schematized: they are rendered in the form of a triangle, or a soft V, or a segmented circle. The pupil is dilated, while the presence of the eyebrow, often arched, completes the studious gaze of the face. Second, the ears, lips, and nostrils are often pierced. Some have surmised that this was an ingenuous technical ploy that allowed for the circulation of oxygen during the firing process, thus minimizing cracks. The third stylistic characteristic of Nok art is that most of the human heads (which are basically geometric: cylindrical, conical, or spherical) come with sensitively modeled hair styles, some parted into buns while others are sorted into knobs or plaited. Nok art reveals the artists' general tendency for profuse ornamentation, as has been shown by the few relatively complete figures, which are bedecked with beaded collars, strings of beads worn across the body (dangling from the chest or worn around the waist), and rows of bracelets and anklets. But Nok art was not all based on the human body; animals, too, are represented. There are examples, all fragmented, of snakes, an elephant, and monkeys; no complete animal or human figures have as yet been found.

The presence of common stylistic traits, as well as the fact that the pieces were found over a wide geographical area have suggested to some scholars that the people who produced Nok art must have lived in a well-structured society, with a clearly defined religious or political philosophy. In the absence of any extant records—oral or inscribed—these art works become the most reliable tools from which an understanding of the past may be meaningfully contemplated. Based on the evidence of the works themselves, it is clear that the people who made them had a mastery of the technology to fire them successfully. For example, one fragmented head is more than fourteeen inches in height, prompting the suggestion that the full figure could not have been less than four feet in height. If this assumption is correct, it follows that the antecedents of Nok art must have dated to much earlier times, for all of the items that exist to date are proof of a sophisticated culture with an understanding of the strengths of the materials it worked with. At any rate, the discovery of slag from furnaces and clay nozzles at some of the sites proves conclusively that the people who made these pieces had iron technology. In addition to being iron smelters, they were also agriculturists, as has been demonstrated by the discovery in Nok deposits of a number of stones

---

5. Ekpo Eyo and Frank Willett provide helpful insights into the arts of Nok, Igbo-Ukwu, Ife, and Benin in their book, *Treasures of Ancient Nigeria* (New York: Alfred A. Knopf, 1980).

Figure 14-3. Nok Culture Head, Jemaa, Nigeria

for grinding grains. Nok is one strong example of how art could be our only window—often a reliable one—into the past.

Igbo-Ukwu

In 1938, a few years before the first terracotta piece was discovered in the village of Nok, a man had chanced upon an unusual find in Igbo-Ukwu, a village located east of the Niger River, also in Nigeria. In the process of digging at the back
of his house, Isaiah Anozie struck a set of artifacts—the first of a collection of ancient objects. Although he did not realize it at that time, he had just disturbed a
deposit containing a group of precious ritual objects that were kept in what experts believed was either a shrine or a storehouse for ceremonial items. Twenty-
one years after this discovery, in 1959, Thurstan Shaw, an archaeologist, began
formal excavation of the Isaiah Anozie site[6]. Two more sites, belonging to Isaiah's

---

6. Detailed analysis of the excavations at Igbo-Ukwu are contained in Thurstan Shaw's

brothers, Richard and Jonah, were also excavated. These three sites have thrown up priceless objects of considerable age, all of which attest to a culture that once thrived and produced superbly crafted objects using precious media including bronze and beads.

At the Igbo Richard site was found what is believed to be the burial chamber of an important personage. Recall Egypt and the Egyptian belief in life after death. Recall, also, the elaborate extent to which ancient Egyptians went, in order to ensure that their revered rulers had access to maximum comfort in their journey to the other world. The burial chamber in Igbo Richard Anozie resurrects our memory of ancient Egypt. But did the man in this burial chamber occupy a social status comparable to that of the pharaohs in Egypt? Although experts are not agreed as to the political or religious role of the person buried in this pit, they are of the opinion that whosoever was buried there was a high dignitary whose burial commanded tremendous pomp and pageantry. No less than five people had been sacrificially buried with this personage, perhaps to ensure that he had access to their services in the world beyond. Their remains were located in the burial chamber, above the level where the dignitary was buried. The central character in this burial chamber was seated on a stool, displayed as he probably was in real life in a show of affluence, with all the paraphernalia of office: a beaded crown on his head, breast collar around his neck, bracelets and anklets adorning his limbs with his foot resting on one of three precious elephant tusks on the burial chamber floor. His arms were propped up by two metal brackets which are sunk into the floor, in the same way as his decorated staff. Among other items from this burial site were thousands of beads: more than sixty thousand were also found at the Igbo Isaiah site.

Radiocarbon dating has confirmed that the Igbo-Ukwu objects were cast from leaded bronze (an alloy of copper, tin, and lead) between ninth and tenth centuries A.D. The items recovered from the Igbo-Ukwu sites vary a great deal, ranging from finely crafted ornamented staffs to a variety of bowls and vessels, some of which are decorated with concentric motifs. One piece that exemplifies the superb artistry of the artists is the *Roped Pot on a Stand*. Excavated from Igbo Isaiah, this is an exemplary two-piece combination: a globular waterpot with a decorated, spherical rim sits atop a stand which is decorated with a system of perforated swirling motifs. The stand and the pot are united by a network of knotted ropes. This piece is a testimonial to the proficiency of the artists in the use of the lost-wax casting method. The makers of the Igbo-Ukwu objects knew the distinct characteristics of their materials; they used leaded bronze—copper and lead with some tin—for their castings while they forged, hammered, or incise their copper. Going by the date of these pieces and judging by the excellent command of technique that they manifest, Igbo-Ukwu is a solid example of the efflorescence of an indigenous art industry about five centuries before the advent of European adventurers.

Ile Ife

Located in southwestern Nigeria, the ancient city of Ile Ife, regarded as the cradle of Yoruba civilization, had existed as early as the ninth century A.D. According

Igbo-Ukwu: An Account of Archaeological Discoveries in Eastern Nigeria (Evanston, IL: Northwestern University Press, 1970), and *Unearthing Igbo-Ukwu: Archaeological Discoveries in Eastern Nigeria* (Ibadan, Nigeria; New York: Oxford University Press, 1977).

Figure 14-4. Roped Pot on a Stand, Igbo-Ukwu

to one Yoruba myth of creation, the high God, Olodumare, once sent one of his sons on a mission to create the world. He armed Obatala with a five-toed chicken and a mound of earth in a snail shell. Unfortunately, Obatala chanced upon a party on his way from his heavenly abode and, having taken a sip too many, fell asleep, drunk. His younger brother, Oduduwa, thus seized the items and descended from heaven on a chain, accompanied by a chameleon. What was known of earth at this time was a vastness populated by water. Oduduwa it was who accomplished the mission of creating the world—the Yoruba world—by setting the chicken upon the piece of earth that he had set down, and by placing the chameleon on it to confirm its habitability. Oduduwa became the first oni (this is the generic title assumed by all Yoruba kings, or obas) to rule in Ife. It was from Ife that the sons of Oduduwa spread out to establish their own domains, all in a homogeneous cultural area that is now known as Yorubaland[7]. Although there is no reason to doubt

7. For publications dealing with the Yoruba myth of creation, see William Bascom, *The Yoruba of Southwestern Nigeria* (New York: Holt, Rinehart and Winston, 1969); and Daryll

that the Yoruba of today are direct descendants of the Yoruba of ancient times, it is important to note that the art which we are here concerned with flourished between twelfth and sixteenth centuries A.D. In other words, there is a chasm between this art and the art that is currently being produced by the Yoruba although, admittedly, there are very strong stylistic parallels between the two.

Ife was a well endowed city by the standards of its times. Its key location in the network of trade contacts that linked several West African cultures to the trans-Saharan trade route ensured that it had access to, and benefited from, the products and services engendered by the transactions. From all accounts, Ife was a substantial urban settlement: it had a glass-making industry, foundries, and ateliers where the art works were produced. Its courtyards and shrines, as well as other important public sites were paved with potsherds. At the royal palace, the oni presided, resplendent in his majesty; a divine entity who symbolized all the power and beauty of the Yoruba people. We catch the dignified presence of the oni in one figure, dated somewhere between the early fourteenth and early fifteenth centuries. Cast in zinc brass, this figure portrays the oni dressed in royal regalia. He wears a crown with a finial while his neck is heavily laced with rows of varying forms of beads. There is a delicately pleated breast collar, on top of which sits a thick necklace that ends in a double bow (his badge of kingship) which rests on the breast collar. This necklace is in turn encircled by a smaller row of beads. All of this is accented by a heavy rope of beads that ends in a loop around the oba's knees. In both hands, he holds instruments of power; in his left hand, he holds *ase*, a potent medicinal preparation that is sealed in a ram's horn. *Ase* is the power to energize the unseen powers that inhabit the universe, the force to set in motion a cosmic energy which will not stop (and cannot be stopped) until it has accomplished its charge. Because of its potency, it is used by the oba only sparingly. The right hand holds yet another symbol of office, a scepter made of beads and cloth. The proportion of this figure is typically African: in the ratio of 1:3, that is, one figure equals three heads.

It was a German ethnologist, Leo Frobenius, who first drew world attention to Ife art[8]. In 1910, he traveled to Nigeria where he succeeded in unearthing a number of artifacts, in bronze as well as terracotta. Frobenius was already aware of the practice whereby the people of Ife would bury sculptures under certain trees, to be exhumed and used again for rituals as occasion demanded. This practice has been confirmed by the discovery of both recent and ancient items buried in the same site. The works discovered in Ife are unique in the history of African art for their superb realism and sensitive modeling. Indeed, it is only in Ife that we find portraits—in bronze as well as terracotta—that, in naturalism and quality, recall Greco-Roman classical traditions. Indeed, Frobenius was so astonished at the beauty and quality of Ife art that he attributed the works to the lost city of Atlantis, a view that has

Forde, *The Yoruba-speaking Peoples of South-western Nigeria* (London: International African Institute, 1969). On Yoruba art, see Frank Willett, *Ife in the History of West African Sculpture* (New York: McGraw-Hill, 1967); and Henry John Drewal et al., *Yoruba: Nine Centuries of African Art and Thought* (New York: Center for African Art in association with H. N. Abrams, 1989).

8. See Leo Frobenius, *The Voice of Africa: Being An Account of the Travels of the German Inner African Exploration Expedition in the Years 1910-1912* (New York: B. Blom, 1968).

Figure 14-5. Standing Figure of an Oni, Ife

since been thoroughly discredited. Bear in mind that Frobenius belonged to a period when it was customary in certain parts of the world to regard the arts of Africa as primitive or barbaric. Although vestiges of such notions still exist, they are no longer taken seriously because they have no credible basis. As we have now seen, the arts provide strong evidence that helps to counter such pernicious notions.

With the departure of Leo Frobenius, the excavation of art in Ife came to a halt until 1938, when a chance discovery led to a renewal of interest in these ancient works. In circumstances that bear a striking resemblance to Nok and Igbo-Ukwu, eighteen precious bronzes were revealed just two feet under the ground at Wunmonije compound, as a man started digging the foundation for his house. This site was close to the palace of the oni, who, not unexpectedly, was interested in preserving what he considered as the treasures of his ancestors. Scientific excavation of several sites in Ife by archaeologists, including Frank Willett, Ekpo Eyo, and Peter Garlake, yielded several items in shrines and burial sites: terracotta animals and pots with animal lids, a bronze vessel and a variety of figural objects, mostly portraits, male and female, in bronze or terracotta. About thirty Ife sculptures are cast in metal, including some copper but mainly made of zinc brass. (Adding alloys of tin, zinc, or lead to copper decreases oxidization, thus making the job of the caster easier). All of these are generally referred to as "bronze." While Ife art is noted for its naturalism, there are a number of objects which are executed in a stylized fashion. The striations on the faces of some of the pieces are a remarkable stylistic characteristic of Ife portraits.

Benin

In 1897, the glory and splendor of Benin City was terminated by British soldiers who invaded the city and set it ablaze, sent its oba into exile, and executed some of his chiefs. The immediate cause for this was the death of seven out of the nine-man team led by British Vice-Consul J. R. Philips. They died during a fight that broke out when some Benin chiefs, led by Ologbosere, tried to prevent the Philips team from imposing themselves on the oba during the annual Igue festival (when the oba could neither see nor be seen by any outsider). It was during this time that thousands of precious artworks were looted from the oba's palace and shipped abroad. Benin art was royal art. It revolved around the ruler, around whose palace there were guilds of craftsmen who worked almost exclusively for him, casting in bronze, carving in ivory, and producing other items that added to the pomp and pageantry of the ruler. The oba was the sole patron of the artists and had the right to half of the elephant tusks harvested by any hunter. In addition, anybody desiring to commission an artist to make a bronze casting must first receive his blessing. In spite of the fact that Benin art was looted without any regard to proper documentation of what was removed from where, or even who had made what, we do have records—oral, written, and visual—through which our appreciation of Benin art is enhanced.

The connection between Ife and Benin dates back to the thirteenth century A.D., when Eweka, the son of Oranmiyan, a prince from Ife, founded the dynasty that succeeded that of the Ogisos. That dynasty has continued to rule in Benin, until today. According to Jacob Egharevba,[9] following their inability to resolve a dispute which had arisen during an interregnum, the people of Benin sent an emissary to Oduduwa, the Oni of Ife, to send one of his sons to rule over them. By way of testing their resolve and ability to take care of his son, Oduduwa sent seven lice to Benin, to be returned to him after three years. The status of the lice would determine whether or not the prayers of the people of Benin would be answered. Once Oduduwa was satisfied that these conditions were met, he dispatched Oranmiyan to Benin as the new ruler. After a while, Oranmiyan decided to return home to Ife. By that time however, he had married a Bini woman, Erinmwide, who bore him a son, Eweka, the one who founded the dynasty that has continued to rule Benin since then. If we accept Egharevba's version of the history of Benin, Ife was not only responsible for the introduction of the tradition of obaship to Benin; it also introduced the art of bronze casting. This is said to have taken place late in the thirteenth century, during the reign of Oguola, the fourth oba of Benin. In order to produce works of art similar to the ones sent to him

9. Jacob Egharevba. *A Short History of Benin* (Ibadan: Ibadan University Press, 1968).

Figure 14-6. Uhumwelao, Bronze Head

from Ife, oba Oguola implored the Oni to send him a brass-smith. Iguegha was then sent to Benin, and thus began the Benin brass-casting tradition. Today, Iguegha is a deified ancestor among the Bini.

Benin art is a reflection of the history of contacts that Benin kingdom made not only with Ife but also with Europeans. By the last quarter of the fifteenth century, the Portuguese had established such a strong presence in Benin that they were immortalized in several of the art works—in bronze as well as ivory—the Benin craftsmen produced. Several of the plaques which once decorated the royal walls and columns in the oba's palace in Benin contain visual references to the Portuguese, who are easily distinguished by their costumes. The plaques are generally rectangular in shape, with the visual composition modeled in high relief. The introduction of the rectangular plaque is believed to have occurred some time early in the sixteenth century when Benin artisans decided to commemorate their success in a war in which the Portuguese had assisted. As we have seen in regard to ancient Egypt and the *Palette of Narmer*, Benin artists employed social hierarchy in the portrayal of royalty. All figures occupy positions in terms relative to their social status, with the oba or, as the case may be, the queen mother, being the most dominant.

When the British invaders descended upon Benin, they found shrines and ancestral altars which were filled with brass bells, figures, and memorial heads bearing ivory tusks with relief carvings of Benin royalty and court attendants, as well as Portuguese soldiers. The corpus of Benin art has been divided into three periods: the Early Period (1400-1550 A.D.); the Middle Period (1550-1700 A.D.); and the Late Period (1700-1898 A.D.). Works attributed to the Early Period are the most naturalistic and least cumbersome, supposedly because of remnants of Ife influence. The more stylized memorial heads belong to the Middle Period. It has been suggested that works cast in heavy metals, with profuse ornamentation and attention to detail, are those produced during the Late Period. Following this classification, the memorial heads from the Early Period are those with the fewest coral bead necklaces while, by the Late Period, the number of beaded necklaces had grown remarkably, from the neck to the lower lip, completely covering the chin. One remarkable piece belonging to the Early Period is the Queen Mother Head, an elegant piece with a cone-like projection. This form is believed to have been invented by Benin artists in the sixteenth century when oba Esigie decided to confer the title of queen mother on his mother, Idia. During this time, brass was available in sufficient quantity as a result of contact with Portuguese traders.

Djenne

One significant feature of ancient civilization in several African states was urbanism. From the evidence provided by the art works, it is clear that indigenous African cultures—Egypt, Nok, Igbo-Ukwu, Ife and Benin, among others—had technologies that were considered advanced in relation to their period. Contrary to the suggestion of some scholars, there was considerable cross-fertilization of ideas amongst African peoples. Through the numerous trade routes that cross the continent—the trans-Saharan route, routes through the sudan, and the southeastern networks—goods ranging from gold to salt, ivory, spices, and skins were exchanged, a process that also facilitated the communication of ideas and visual concepts. The legendary cities of Mopti, Timbuktu, and Djenne were major centers where commercial transactions between West African traders and merchants from the Mediterranean took place. Impressive architectural designs complemented trade and learning. Accounts of early European visitors to Africa speak eloquently of the beauty of urban centers such as Benin and Luanda.

The city of Timbuktu which was founded in the twelfth century A.D. enjoyed considerable importance as a trading post on the trans-Saharan caravan route and a center for Islamic studies. Situated to the south of Timbuktu but founded much earlier was the ancient city of Djenne which, like Timbuktu, was also both a flourishing trading outpost and a center of Muslim scholarship. Today, in art circles, the name Djenne has acquired a somewhat dubious reputation due to the activities of looters who have done incalculable damage to history by destroying precious and irreplaceable material at unauthorized sites. A French archaeologist, Theodore Monod, first drew attention to the expressive terracotta figures from the Djenne area when, in 1943, he discovered a terracotta figure of a kneeling woman. Unfortunately, Djenne has since become an all-comers' market as commercial exploitation of these items has taken precedence over their historical import. The importance of archaeology in the reconstruction of prehistory is dependent upon controlled study of sites, something that has been completely neglected by these looters. Our appreciation of art is contingent upon an understanding of its conditions of existence: by our knowledge of who produced it, when, and why. In other words, the context of art is important to its appreciation. Artifacts like the ones from Djenne constitute our main link with antiquity, especially where the culture that produced them has become extinct. "The preservation of archaeological evidence," to quote Paul Bator, "thus requires not only that objects as such be protected from destruction or mutilation, but, further, an opportunity to study and record exactly where and how each object was buried and how it related to other objects."[10]

Because of the reckless plundering that is associated with the Middle Niger objects, we must take some of the dates ascribed to some of them with an open, questioning mind. Roderick McIntosh, an archaeologist who has done considerable work on Djenne, estimates that before 1977 (when he and his wife conducted their first excavation), hundreds of terracotta figurines from the area had been looted. Many of these items have been dated to the fifteenth through eighteenth centuries, although McIntosh has challenged the basis of these dates. His own work reveals that these artifacts may indeed have been made much earlier: charcoal associated with some of the terracottas has been radiocarbon-dated to between the eleventh and late thirteenth centuries. The objects themselves vary in form and content, ranging in media from clay and iron to bronze and gold. Among the numerous items that have been retrieved from archaeological sites are pendants, bracelets, earrings, animal figurines in copper, horse trappings, and bells. The booty from illegal diggings is even more extensive: a large number of ornamental items like chains, necklaces, finger-rings, horse ornaments, equestrian figures, pectoral ornaments, amulets and pendants. Figural representations abound: these are figures engaged in a variety of activities—kneeling, hugging, horse-riding, and others.

In terms of style, there is a pronounced expressiveness and dignity. Faces are characterized by a stylized elongation which becomes most visible at the chin. Oblong protrusions represent eyeballs, while beards are depicted in sharp flanges. Bodily ornamentation and cicatrization appear on many of the figures. What were these objects used for? What was the social structure that sustained their production? What about the artists: Did they produce these items for religious reasons? Unfortunately, answers to these and similar questions are at best conjectural; at worst, we will never know. But Roderick McIntosh has determined that the Middle Niger area of the Djenne as a locus of long-distance trade and an urban metropolis began a thousand years earlier than had been previously claimed, and that the existence of functioning craft and production groups dates to even earlier times, perhaps as much as a millennium earlier. But several issues remain as yet unresolved regarding, for example, the impact of the introduction of Islam on production.

---

10. Paul Bator, *The International Trade in Art* (Chicago: University of Chicago Press, 1983), 25. Quoted in Roderick J. McIntosh, "Just Say Shame: Excising the Root of Cultural Genocide," in Peter R. Schmidt and Roderick J. Macintosh, eds., *Plundering Africa's Past* (Bloomington: Indiana University Press, 1996).

Figure 8. Mother and Child, Djenne People, Mali

Zimbabwe

While comparing the arts of West and southern Africa, it is customary, in some circles, to conclude that very little art was produced in places like Zimbabwe in ancient times. Such a claim has no basis in history. For although a great deal remains undeciphered about this culture, soapstone sculptures of birds and the magnificent stone architecture, now in ruins, provide incontestable evidence that Great Zimbabwe was, as early as the fourth century A.D., a thriving center for skillful masons (see Figures 10-4 and 10-5). Today, Zimbabwe is preserved in the impressive remains of an architectural complex that provides evidence of a great civilization. Indeed, the word "zimbabwe" is derived from the Shona term for "houses of stone."

Three groups of buildings have been identified in this area. The first is the "Great Enclosure," or "Imba Huru," an elliptical structure which is considered to have been a temple. It has a huge outer wall that is thirty-two feet high, seventeen feet thick at the base, and eight hundred feet long. Built of dry stone without mortar, and sloping inward toward the top, it serves as enclosure for a complex comprising two small towers (one of which is conical in shape, about eighteen feet in diameter and thirty feet tall) and a smaller, incomplete wall. This complex was the royal palace where the monomotapa reigned as a divine king. About a quarter of a mile to the north of this site is the "acropolis," a structure of stone walls built between the boulders of a granite hill, serving as a protective shelter from enemy attacks. Based upon the evidence provided by archaeology, Frank Willett has identified three phases of the occupation of Zimbabwe. The first phase included the second and third centuries A.D., while the second phase (which utilized clay as part of the construction of their round huts) arrived in the fourth century A.D. It was during the third phase, between the tenth and sixteenth centuries, that the stone buildings were erected. A series of carved soapstone sculptures, each of which depicts a bird perched atop tall monoliths, has been discovered. Other finds include Portuguese medallions, Persian pottery, and Chinese porcelain—items which testify to the importance of Great Zimbabwe as the nucleus of an important fourteenth-century city of over ten thousand people who controlled the profitable southeast coastal trade. By the mid-fifteenth century, the power of Great Zimbabwe had declined, and the city was eventually abandoned.

Conclusion

From the foregoing examples we have seen that although certain trends and practices attest to underlying homogeneous traits, the geographic, linguistic, religious, and political diversity of Africa alerts us to the dangers of applying broad generalizations that are only capable of supporting unhealthy stereotypes. While it is true that the continent is one geographic entity, it is also true that it is made up of a profusion of languages and cultures, many of which evolved independent of each other, and each of which has its distinctive cultural features. Thus, within what may initially appear to be a homogeneous capsule are heterogeneous characteristics that warrant particular attention. Using the arts as our point of departure, we have embarked upon a journey into the African past—a journey that has offered tremendous insights into the social, religious, political, and creative activities of ancient cultures. In this chapter, we have realized that the visual arts are in themselves history: they constitute the physical dimensions of history through which temporal and spatial interactions can be accessed, analyzed, preserved, and disseminated for our own benefit.

Review Questions

1. List and discuss three advantages that we derive from studying the arts of other cultures.
2. What are the factors that contributed to the popularity of African art in the West?
3. Discuss the range of art that was produced in ancient Africa, as well as some of the media in which it was produced. In what ways are the arts of Africa different from the arts in your own society?

4. What does "art-for-art's-sake" imply?
5. What are the distinctive features—themes, subject-matter and media—of rock art? In which parts of Africa is such art to be found?
6. List some of the significant achievements of Egypt after its unification by King Menes.
7. Discuss three of the major contributions made by Egypt to world civilization.
8. Describe the evolution and functions of Egyptian pyramids.
9. Evaluate the significance of the Amarna Revolution in Egyptian art and religion; who was the prime mover of this revolution, and what did it entail?
10. What are the distinctive stylistic features common to all Nok art? In what circumstances was this art discovered?
11. Explore the connection between class and social structure in the arts of Igbo-Ukwu.
12. Compare and contrast the arts of Ife and those of Nok, Igbo-Ukwu, and Benin. What are the cultural, stylistic and socio-religious differences and/or similarities? Compare the media in which these arts were produced, and construct a chronology for them.
13. Examine the connection between Ife and Benin with particular reference to the production of art. Analyze the role of Imperial Britain in the subjugation and eventual dissemination of Benin art.
14. Discuss the claim that Benin art is royal art.
15. Artworks often enhance our understanding of ancient cultures and civilizations. In what ways does Djenne confirm or contradict this statement?
16. Describe the typical Djenne sculpture in terms of style, form, and media.
17. What is the significance of Zimbabwe to African art and architecture?

Additional Reading

Eyo, Ekpo and Frank Willett. *Treasures of Ancient Nigeria*. New York: Alfred A. Knopf, 1980.

jegede, dele. *Art by Metamorphosis: African Art from the Spelman College Collection*. Atlanta: Spelman College, 1988.

Phillips, Tom. *Africa: The Art of a Continent*. New York: Prestel, 1996.

Ritchie, Carson A.I. *Rock Art of Africa*. New York: A.S. Barnes and Co., 1979.

Roy, Christopher D. *Art and Life in Africa: Selections from the Stanley Collection*. Iowa: The University of Iowa Museum of Art, 1992.

Schmidt, Peter R. and Roderick J. McIntosh. *Plundering Africa's Past*. Bloomington: Indiana University Press, 1996.

Sieber, Roy, and Roslyn Adele Walker. *African Art in the Cycle of Life*. Washington, DC: Smithsonian Institution Press, 1987.

Thomas, Nancy, ed. *The American Discovery of Ancient Egypt: Essays*. Los Angeles: Los Angeles County Museum of Art, 1996.

Willett, Frank. *African Art*. New York: Thames and Hudson, 1993.

Chapter 15

Music

Steven J. Salm

This chapter provides an introduction to the "traditional" music of Africa. In this context traditional music is defined not solely by its precolonial existence (because it still exists to a large degree in many African societies today), but by its performance setting, instruments, and functions within African societies. Traditional music should not be seen as unchanging or stagnant. Its ability to adapt from one generation to the next is emphasized by the many variations that remain extant within all levels of African societies. Even the popular African music styles heard frequently on the radio today, incorporate many characteristics from traditional music forms.

African traditional music was a vital part of society and for this reason has much to offer to the study of African history and culture. It is important to study traditional African music in its social context, in order to gain some insights into the musical experiences that are so prominent in the personal and social life of Africans. Throughout the chapter, examples from the musical culture of individual groups are interspersed with larger regional variations to present a well-rounded and balanced understanding of the past and present. The cultural past contains features that reveal important things about a people and their way of life. Music, like oral literature and archaeology, provides a piece of the precolonial history puzzle where written records are scarce at best. The chapter is organized as follows: Section I presents a broad survey of the musical traditions of Africa in the context of their social, cultural, and historical backgrounds; section II describes the characteristics of the performances, including the location, the audience, and the performers themselves; section III reviews the instruments prominently used in the performance of traditional music; and section IV looks at the functions of the music as they relate to social, religious, economic and political factors.

Classifications of Music

This section addresses the problems inherent in the classification of African traditional music and investigates the factors that influenced the unique musical development of certain societies and regions. Although far from exhaustive, this section will develop the essential characteristics and historical background necessary to reach a greater understanding of traditional African music as a whole.

It is difficult to generalize about African music because Africa is not a culturally homogenous region. Cultural and musical development varied greatly according to the differences in historical background, environment, and lifestyle, that placed emphases on certain aspects of the past and present while omitting others. Differences in musical styles can be explained by a combination of internal and external factors. Interactions through trade and diplomacy brought cultural exchanges that influenced the transformation of musical traditions. Although there were great variances in musical styles throughout the continent, it is nonetheless helpful to divide Africa into two distinct musical regions. The first region includes North Africa, the Sahara desert, some societies in northern Sudan, as well as the East African coast. The second region consists of societies on the southern fringes of the desert and the rest of sub-Saharan Africa. Although this is a far from perfect division, it is helpful in understanding the overall picture.

The development of traditional music was affected by external influences, such as Islam, and internal exchanges, like local and regional trade, that resulted in the transference of cultural traits from one society to another. Although its impact was felt over much of the continent, the depth of the imprint made by Islam varied. Its influence was felt in differing degrees in North and West Africa and the coastal areas of East Africa. For example, in North Africa and some regions of northern Sudan, there was a high level of interaction between the indigenous people and those from the Arab states. The cultures of these societies were more closely related to those of the Arab world than other cultures were. This was reflected in the music which was Arab in origin, style, and tradition. With the establishment of Islam in the seventh century, the Arab world became relatively unified, and Egypt soon became part of its realm. In the early part of the second millennium A.D., much of North Africa was pulled into the Islamic world, and Arab musical style became firmly established in the region.

In other areas, the effects of Islam were not as profound. A society did not always experience a wholesale conversion to Islam, but selectively borrowed cultural items from Islamized neighbors, or from other contact agents such as Muslim traders. In these cases, Islamic influence was present, but it was integrated with local traditions. Adjustments and modifications in resources or refinements in style were made, while the basic structure and social functions of the music remained intact. In some societies, drums, lutes, reed pipes, and trumpets were added to the musical inventory, but they did not usually replace the instruments that were already used. It was easier to adapt these instruments to the local environment than to adapt many Western instruments because the former could be made with local materials. Islamic styles were readily integrated into the local culture because some aspects of the Islamic musical tradition served to reinforce African musical structures. Members of the Yoruba Islamic community, for example, used orthodox Arabic music during worship, but performed traditional Yoruba music for social activities as well as during some Muslim festivals. Muslim musicians performed not only for their own religious community, but for other social groups and non-Muslim festivals and ceremonies as well.

The influence of Islam helped to link societies together musically, but there were other important agents that performed a similar function. For example, musical connections were created in areas that formed around centers of economic or non-Islamic religious activities. In Ethiopia, the musical styles of the Coptic Church, which has been separated from both Western and Orthodox Christianity for more than fifteen hundred years, and the Jewish influence of the Fellasha, affected the development of cultural forms. This music was characterized by the presence of unique instruments including a variety of long trumpets, zithers, lyres, harps, and kettle drums that connected a number of different communities into a single musical family. There were many shared features between this music family and others in Africa, but religious, historical, and environmental factors combined to produce a unique musical culture.

In the sub-Saharan region, there were also many differences between one society and another; but with few exceptions, they formed a relatively close-knit musical family within the African continent that was distinct from the musical traditions of northern Africa. There were similarities in the types of instruments used and in the methods of integrating music with social institutions and practices. Internal influences from extensive trading systems and long traditions of intermarriage spread musical forms and structures from one society to another. One result of these cultural exchanges was the existence of musical types having the same names in different areas. For example, the *asafo* music of warrior organizations could be found in Akan, Ga, Adangme, and Ewe areas of Ghana, while among the Dagomba, a music and dance type called *kanbonwaa* combined the Akan and local styles. *Jongo*, another type of music from northern Ghana, existed in many different societies within the region.[1] The prevalence of some instruments, such as the xylophone which was found from the east to the west coasts, also reflects the historical importance of regional and local trading systems in spreading cultural forms.

Other factors that helped determine the development of musical forms within a society were the combined elements of environment and lifestyle. The particular lifestyle that a society engaged in had an impact on the focus and functions of its music. For example, communities that had an everyday relationship with water as a central means of livelihood, had songs that reflected this. One society had songs that pertained to the different contexts of using a canoe. One song was used when placing a recently constructed canoe in the water for the first time, another when paddling against a strong current, and yet another when paddling with the current or to make the work of the paddlers more efficient.[2] Among the Tutsi, for whom cattle were very important, there were a number of songs that proclaimed this. These included boasting songs called *ibiririmbo*, in which two men sang in competition against each other. They exchanged musical phrases in which each one extolled the merits of his own cattle over those of the other. They also sang *inyambo*, or praise songs for the royal cattle, songs for taking the cattle home in the evening, songs for when the herders were drawing water for the cattle, and songs for when they were relaxing with other herders in the evening.[3] Societies that gave a great deal to prestige to hunting also had songs that reflected this. Among the hunter's associations of the Yoruba, for example, there was a specialized chant known as *ijala* which was performed on the way to a hunt. During the Ogun festival which gave recognition to the god of iron, hunters and warriors performed chants during the vigil before and also after the hunting expedition attached to the festival. The hunters took turns performing the chants which recounted past hunting glories and sang the praise of Ogun.

---

1. J.H. Kwabena Nketia, *The Music of Africa* (New York: W.W. Norton, 1974), 7.
2. Alan P. Merriam, *African Music in Perspective* (New York and London: Garland Publishing, 1982), 68.
3. Merriam, *African Music in Perspective*, 69.

The names of traditional music forms were sometimes derived from the functions they performed. For example, among the Akan of Ghana, a category of songs performed by women during wartime when the men were away, was called *asrayere* ("visiting the wives") because it united the women and reflected their support for the fighting men. At times, the social occasion on which a particular musical form was performed gave its name to it. The songs of the puberty rite *(bragoro)*, for instance, were called *bradwom* (*dwom* is "song" in Akan). In other cases, the main instruments that were used in the performance of certain forms lent their name to those forms. In Ethiopia, the music of trumpets was called *ntahera,* the same name used for the trumpets themselves.[4]

The type of music used at specific events was determined by the norms of societies. Some musical instruments and styles were reserved for specific ceremonial rites or festivals and banned from others. Some instruments, like certain royal drums, were used only for the worship of divinities, while others were played only before kings. Among the Sukuma of Tanzania, specific types of drums performed specific functions. The announcement of the funeral of a chief was sent through the drums of that chief. These drums, known as *lugaya* or *milango*, were turned upside down soon after the chief's death. As the corpse was being carried to the grave, another drum, the *itemelo*, was played, and all those who heard it understood that the "drum has burst—that is, the chief is dead." In addition, societal beliefs sometimes limited the times of the day when music could be performed. Among the Lele of Kasai, drumming was considered to be an activity appropriate for the evening hours and was not to be done during daylight except on days of rest. Drums were not to be played at all in one particular Lele village during periods of mourning that sometimes lasted up to three months.[5] It was common for societies to ban musical activities such as drumming for a fixed period of time before the annual harvest festival began.

Although many types of music were associated with specific occasions, the most common types were usually recreational forms unconnected with any particular ritual or ceremony. Music often served as a background for a wrestling match, a general sing-along, a solo song of praise or insult, or an instrumental improvisation. In each of these instances, the atmosphere of the situation dictated the type of music and its instrumentation. The Hutu in Rwanda identified at least twenty-four social song types that were distinguishable from those of a religious nature. They included songs for beer-drinking, war, hunting, and harvesting.[6] Many other African societies shared a similar range of musical types.

In general, community life placed more emphasis on group musical activities than on solo performances. Groups included choruses of singers, troops of drummers, and ensembles of musicians playing instruments such as the xylophone, flute, and trumpet. On the other hand, it was not uncommon to find individuals playing music for their own enjoyment or for the enjoyment of small groups of close friends or family. At times, music had a religious meaning in an individual setting and a different meaning at a group level. The Konkumba lute players, for example, performed for themselves when they wanted to keep in close communion with their god, but, in a group setting, they sometimes sang or played dirges

---

4. Nketia, *Music of Africa*, 25.
5. Nketia, *Music of Africa*, 27-29.
6. Merriam, *African Music in Perspective*, 68.

or praise songs that carried symbolic messages and they were prominent on social occasions.

Music provides an important window into cultural life. By assessing the musical repertoire of a given society, one can gain additional evidence of that society's social and cultural norms. Although it is impossible to detail the many different characteristics and styles of African music here, it should now be possible to incorporate further information into the larger categories of analysis provided above.

Characteristics of Performance

The difficulties in classifying the multitudinous characteristics of traditional African music are also reflected in the performance context. The interactions between the audience and the musicians, the location of the performance, and the nature and training of performers differ from one society to another. There are, however, a number of common features that help to elucidate the context of specific musical occasions and enhance the understanding of the dynamic roles played by both the audience and the performers.

Location and Audience

Music was performed in many different settings depending on the context of the performance. It was sometimes performed in a public place where the community gathered for a celebration, or, at other times, in a private area where participation was limited to those connected with a particular rite or ceremony. It could be held in the courtyard of a house, in the fields where people cultivated their crops, or a market place or dance plaza. Among the Sonjo of Tanzania, for example, plazas were specifically constructed for religious festivals and dances. The religious plaza was located at or near the center of every Sonjo village and consisted of an area large enough to hold several hundred dancers. At one end of the plaza was an enclosure where the village council met and, behind that, another building which was used as a sanctuary. There was one sacred dance plaza which was the largest and most central of all, but every section of the town had a smaller plaza built on similar lines for recreational singing and dancing.[7]

In performances of African music, the members of the audience rarely practiced restrained contemplative behavior. They were most often outwardly involved with the performance and dramatically expressed their feelings. The audience often shouted in appreciation, or indicated their satisfaction in other ways. Their conduct revealed their satisfaction level; disapproval was shown when the performance did not meet their expectations or desires. There were accepted norms of behavior relating to the roles of the performers and the audience. In some societies, it was considered taboo for the dancers to glance at the audience while they were performing, because it was believed that they should be so deeply engrossed in what they were doing, and doing it so well, that the audience would notice them without the dancers having to make themselves seen.

---

7. Nketia, *Music of Africa*, 31.

Audience participation occurred at many different levels. The audience some-times joined the chorus or entered into the dancing ring either to dance or to give moral support to the dancers. Support and recognition was given by placing money on the foreheads of the performers, or by spreading cloths on the ground for the dancers to step on. The presence and response of the audience influenced the effec-tiveness of performance. It affected the selection of music and the range of textual and musical improvisation, and provided an energetic stimulus to further activity. In a public performance, there was not usually much physical separation between members of the audience and the performers. Instead, the audience often sur-rounded the performers, leaving only a small opening for them to pass in and out. The atmosphere was generally informal and the spectators were free to move about as they wished. Performances were generally in the open air, except in limited cases such as those given by specialized musicians for royalty. In most settings the focus was on music performance as a communal activity, one that emphasized artistic merits, but displayed social, political, or religious values as well. Music was per-formed for entertainment purposes, as an opportunity to enhance social interac-tion, to express the sentiments of the community, as a tribute to an individual, or an offering to a deity. Music performance was closely linked to the working of society and ensured popular participation and identification with the life of a community.

The Performers

In traditional music cultures, the performers included spontaneous groups, popular musicians, and specialized musicians with certain restrictions on their po-sition in society. The first two groups were autonomous and not attached to tradi-tional powers or royal courts as the last mentioned group was. They included any members of society that congregated to make music on an informal basis, as well as organized groups of musicians who were skilled in specific genres and were sometimes invited to play at social events that incorporated those genres into the festivities. Popular groups were hired to perform on social occasions such as funer-als, weddings, and dancing contests. In every Nyasa village in Tanzania, for exam-ple, music contests were organized to determine the best of these quasi-profes-sional groups. The contestants that were chosen for the competitions practiced their playing often to improve their skills. In many African societies, associations existed that helped to enhance musical skills and enrich creativity in musical pro-duction. It is important to remember that, although certain types of music were close to immutable, the range of musical styles constantly changed. Performers were not limited to the styles that were passed on to them by previous generations. New ones were added to the repertoire, but those who learned the previous styles and performed them on social occasions were the ones who sustained the tradition.

Specialist musicians included the royal musicians, and those attached to tradi-tional courts and ruling establishments. Music specialists among the Hausa of Nigeria were often tied to occupational groups whose members were their pa-trons. Musicians were attached to blacksmiths, butchers, hunters, and farmers, each group having a different set of musical instruments.[8] Music was very impor-

---

8. David Ames, "A Socio-cultural View of Hausa Musical Activity" (unpublished manu-script, n.d.); and Nketia, *Music of Africa*, 43.

tant in the courts of kings, and both the music and the instruments were integrated into the beliefs of society. Among the Lovedu of South Africa, for example, there were four sacred drums, the smallest which was believed to be mystically linked to the queen and the welfare of the state.[9] Harvest festivals and other important state functions nearly always included music. Ceremonies and rituals, such as the installation of kings, queens, and other political officials usually included music provided by the royal court musicians. The music was in the form of praise songs to the ruler, or historical chants that recalled important events. These performers, such as the *griots*, were skilled singers who combined the roles of performer and historian.

In West African Mande societies, *griots* were part of a caste system. They were trained from childhood in the art of performance and narration. The *griots* were adept narrators as well as skilled musicians renowned for their skill on the *kora*. Their lineages were attached to the courts of kings and royal families as well as the families of great hunters. Part of their purpose was to enhance the prestige of their employers by remembering the great deeds and accomplishments of their family's past and presenting songs of praise for the present rulers and other members of the nobility. The *griots* began a long training process at an early age. They were highly esteemed in society and admired for their knowledge, as well as for their creativity and command of performance.

Other musicians were attached to the courts as servants who came to perform when it was requested of them. Their membership was sometimes organized on the basis of caste or kinship. Among the Dagomba of Ghana, for example, the son of every drum leader was expected to become a drummer like his father—a daughter was expected to send her first son in replacement. There were also qualities that were expected of the performer. Within Dagomba society, bands of musicians were attached to a chief and, as that ruler rose in power, so did the prestige of the band. The lead drummer, who also served as the voice of the archives, had to be well-versed in Dagomba oral literature and the history of the society. This included the chronicles of the chiefs and the praise names that were associated with each of them.[10]

Whether the performers were spontaneous participants or skilled practitioners, there was a training process that they had to undergo. For some, training was done on an informal basis through social interactions and exposure to musical situations. Watching and participating in performances was a means to learn the techniques of the musical culture. This often began when children were still very small and the mother sang them to sleep. When children were old enough to sing, they often sang along with their mothers and learned to imitate the rhythm of the drums. Participation in children's games and stories that incorporated songs encouraged further learning and nurtured appreciation for musical talents.

In other cases, formal training was employed to educate musicians in the skills necessary to achieve success. Schools of music were established in ancient Egypt, training people in the arts of vocal and instrumental expression. These schools developed and taught a theory of musical notation and were among the

9. F.J. and J.D. Krige, "The Lovedu of the Transvaal," in Daryll Forde, *African Worlds* (London: Oxford University Press, 1954), 66-67.

10. See Christine Oppong, "A Preliminary Account of the Role and Recruitment of Drummers in Dagbon," *Research Review*, 6, 1 (1969); and Nketia, *Music of Africa*, 53.

Figure 15-1. Wodaabe Men During a Dance

first to promote music as a profession. In some societies, the importance of certain musical forms, even for non-professional musicians, could not be left to informal training alone. Among the Akan of Ghana, it was a social duty of women to mourn their kinsmen with special chants, and, therefore, mothers had to teach their daughters directly, to ensure that they would know these dirges when the appropriate time came. In other societies, such as the Chopi and the Baganda, the training of their musicians began at a very young age. The Chopi of eastern Africa trained their youth in the art of playing the xylophone from the age of seven or eight until the necessary skills were mastered. Among the Baganda, people wanting to become flutists in the royal ensemble had to spend their time at the palace beginning at the age of ten to twelve years. There they lived with the older musicians who were often their fathers or relatives. They spent many hours watching the royal ensemble perform and, when they were deemed capable of playing up to the standards of the ensemble, they were introduced to the king and sworn in as royal musicians.[11]

Instruments

The history of instruments, more than any other aspect of the musical culture, can be traced back to ancient times because of available evidence. In Egypt, for example, more instruments have been preserved in the sandy, arid climate than in

---

11. See Hugh Tracey, *Chopi Musicians: Their Music, Poetry and Instruments* (London: Oxford University Press, 1948); Lois Anderson, "The Miko Modal System in Baganda Xylophone Music" (Ph.D. diss., University of California at Los Angeles, 1968).

other parts of Africa, and the close association of life and music resulted in the creation of a number of paintings and carvings that depicted musical performances. The legacy of music in ancient Egypt can be seen even today in the shapes, tuning patterns, and playing styles of such instruments as the *argul* double clarinets in Egypt, the many end-blown flutes of the Near East, the *halam* of the Wolof, and the sistrums of the Ethiopian Coptic groups.[12]

Drums are probably the most commonly recognized African instrument today. Whenever there is an African dance troupe on an international tour, it inevitably includes a large number and variety of drums. Although the drums were certainly pervasive in many African societies, their prominence is sometimes overstated. Historically, early explorers, travelers, and missionaries overemphasized the role of drums, which was significant when compared to their own societies. The rhythm of the drums was "mysterious" to them and the images provided by the drums were used to reinforce the stereotype of the "savage African." But there are many other types of African instruments as well, many of them even more prominent than the drum.

There are many instruments that were unique to individual African societies. The use of specific instruments among certain groups was related to environmental factors, to the kind of occupation in which a society engaged, or to the type of historical contacts. There were some nomadic societies, for example, that did not use drums because they were much too cumbersome to transport on a continual basis. Instead, these societies used sticks and other portable items to create musical rhythms. Rhythms emerged through hand-clapping, complex body movements, foot stomping, and even vocals. Variances in musical instruments were also found between people who lived in the savannah areas and those who lived in the forest regions. Differences in the availability of resources affected the range of drums that could be produced and the types of skins that were used for covering them. Environmental differences did not always mean an instrument was exclusive to one society, for these differences were sometimes eclipsed by trade and other activities that enhanced interaction between members of one musical culture and another. With these differences and similarities in mind, it is useful to classify the instruments used to create traditional African music into four main categories: idiophones, membranophones, aerophones, and chordophones.

Idiophones

These included the most commonly found African instruments. Idiophones used vibrating bodies to produce sound. They included not only those instruments played independently by a performer, but those that were attached to their costumes or their instruments as well. Rattles worn around their legs, waists, or wrists, or attached to the top of the drums, accentuated the rhythm of the music and the body movements of the performers. Another form of idiophones was groups of stone chimes. The variance of size and pitch allowed the performer to play melodies. Drums that were not covered by a skin were also considered idiophones. Among the Ijo and Igbo of Nigeria, for example, clay pot drums were

---

12. William P. Malm, *Music Cultures of the Pacific, the Near East, and Asia* (Englewood Cliffs, NJ: Prentice-Hall, 1967), 59.

Figure 15-2. Drum, Lobala People, Congo

common. Changes in pitch were created by filling each drum to an appropriate level; they were struck with a palm frond. The slit drum, known as the *kele* by the Limba of Sierra Leone, was also very popular in many African societies. It was made of a single log of wood with slits cut into it at different lengths to form keys with different pitches. The slit drum's ability to carry over long-distances and to produce contrasting tones made it a viable medium for the transmission of messages in African tonal languages, as was done by the Lokele of Central Africa.

Another prominent idiophone was the gourd rattle, the largest form known as a *sekere* among the Yoruba of Nigeria. This was a net rattle made by covering a gourd with a woven net of hard objects, such as seeds, nutshells, beads, or animal teeth. Loosely placed around the gourd, these objects produced sounds when the gourd was shaken. The instrument was played by tossing it from one hand to another, bouncing it up and down between a hand and a thigh, shaking it with both hands, or tapping it with the fingers. There was also another type of rattle known as a vessel rattle. It was made of a hollowed gourd which had hard objects placed inside, but it was usually not as large or as loud as the *sekere*.[13]

More intricate forms of idiophones found in traditional African music were the *mbira* and the xylophone. The *mbira* was found throughout Africa and known by many different names, but was especially popular among the Shona of Zimbabwe (from whom the name *mbira* comes) and other societies in Zambia and Mozambique. It consisted of metal tongues, often made of iron or brass, which were fastened to a wooden chamber by a metal bar. The tongues of metal were plucked with the thumbs and the different lengths, weights, and

---

13. Nketia, *Music of Africa*, 70.

flexibility of these tongues determined the pitches that it could produce.[14] Xylophones were found in many societies from the east to the west coasts. They were usually made from wooden bars of different lengths laid out parallel to one another on a wooden frame. Some of them had gourds placed under the wooden bars to help resonate and amplify the sounds. The number of keys varied from four to twenty-two. Xylophones were usually played in small groups, but did occur in ensembles of up to thirty performers among the Chopi of Mozambique.

Membranophones

A second category of African instruments is the membranophones; this category includes all of the drums that were covered by membranes, usually made from animal skins. Drums came in all different shapes and sizes: some were carved from a tree and stood ten to fifteen feet tall, making it necessary for the performers to stand on a platform while they played; some were made of coconut shells that were small enough to hold in one hand; some of them had two membranes while others had only one; and some were played with the hands while others were beaten with a stick. The tone and pitch of drums was determined by the shape and size, as well as the type of skin and the material used to strike it. Children often began playing makeshift drums, made from a hard fruit or other suitable material, at a very young age. Drums were widespread in Africa, but different ethnic groups often specialized in specific types.

The *atumpan* was a single-headed drum that was the master drum of the Asante. It was associated with high office and, because of this, intricate ceremonies had to be performed during its construction. The proper tree had to be selected and, before cutting it down, libations had to be made to appease the spirits that lived in the tree. When the body of the drum was being prepared, the woodcarver carved an eye on the drum, designed to prevent misuse. Other drums included small hand drums found in different regions of Africa. The Ethiopian *atamo* was held in one hand and played with the fingers or the palm of the other. Seeds or beads were sometimes put inside to provide additional sound qualities. Groups in Uganda had a drum of a similar design that was fastened to leather straps thrown over the shoulder and played with both hands. Double-headed drums were also very common throughout Africa. The hourglass or pressure drum had two heads of roughly equal size, but only one of them was played. The name was derived from the shape of the body and the two heads were connected with rope that ran the length of the drum. Changes in pitch were obtained when the drum head was tightened or loosened by squeezing the rope when the drum was placed under the arm of the performer.

A drum was sometimes played solo or, more commonly, in an ensemble that included a combination of high, medium, and low pitched drums. It was not uncommon to find large drum troupes with more than forty or fifty drums being played together. The fifteen *entenga* drums of the Buganda king, for example, were so finely tuned to different pitches that the music produced by them could

14. For a more detailed discussion of the *mbira*, see Paul F. Berliner, *The Soul of Mbira* (Los Angeles: University of California Press, 1978).

duplicate the form and structure of xylophone songs; this music has even been called a "drum chime."[15] Drum ensembles were sometimes combined with vocalists, or played with other instruments such as the *sekere*, xylophone, or other idiophones. Drums were often found connected to royal courts or political offices and had many religious functions. These aspects will be discussed in more detail in section IV below.

Aerophones

Aerophones make up the third class of African instruments. This group consists of instruments that produce sound from the vibrations within a pipe created when air is forced through them. It includes flutes and whistles, single- and double-reed pipes, as well as horns and trumpets. The most widely distributed flutes were made of bamboo and were usually found where bamboo grew. They were played singly, in duets, or as a part of a larger ensemble. One type found in Ethiopia, the *embilta*, had no finger holes and played at only one pitch, and thus several performers with flutes of different pitches were required to play a melody.

Flutes existed for thousands of years in parts of Africa. In evidence culled from rock paintings dated c. 2700 B.C., a piper was shown with a double-pipe instrument; one pipe was used to play a melody and the other acted as an accompaniment. It is still a common aerophone today throughout the Islamic world. Further evidence from a painting in Gizeh, dating to around 2,000 B.C., shows a band of seven players playing flutes of different lengths. In ancient Egypt, the flute was associated with love, pastoral music, and wind. It was a symbol of fertility, life, and rebirth, and was sometimes buried with the dead. It was used at weddings and circumcision ceremonies, as well as healing, initiation, and sacrificial rites.[16]

Other common types of aerophones included the single- and double-reed pipes. A popular double-reed instrument in North African music was the *zorna*. It had seven holes on the top and an octave hole on the back. With a large number of possible notes, one could play a wide range of intricate melodies on it. Double reed aerophones also appeared in many societies of sub-Saharan Africa where the Islamic tradition flourished. In Chad, they were prominent in ensemble performances, and were also found in areas of what is now Sudan, Somalia, Kenya, Tanzania, Cameroon, and Nigeria.

Trumpets and horns were also prominent in certain African societies. They were made from bamboo, gourds, elephant tusks, animal horns, wood, or metal. The majority of them had no finger holes, and variations in pitch were created by changing the amount of air forced through them or altering the tension of the lips. They were played by blowing either from the end or from the side. The Berta of eastern Sudan, for example, had an elaborate end-blown trumpet called the *waza*. It was made of gourd tubes fastened together with beeswax, strings, and thin

---

15. See K.P. Wachsmann, "Some Speculations Concerning a Drum Chime in Baganda," *Man*, 65, 1 (1965): 1-8.

16. See H. Macaulay Fitzgibbon, *The Story of the Flute* (London: William Reeves, 1929). See also Ashenafi Kebede, *Roots of Black Music: The Vocal, Instrumental, and Dance Heritage of Africa and Black America* (Englewood Cliffs, NJ: Prentice Hall, 1982), 69-70, 98.

slices of bamboo. The *waza* varied in width and length with the biggest being up to seven feet in length. Each had its own distinctive sound, and sometimes ten performed together to form a melodious orchestra. Similar styles were found in Nigeria among the Hausa, and in areas of Ethiopia, Uganda, Tanzania, and Chad.

Chordophones

A fourth category of African instruments is the chordophones. They were generally more common in northern Africa than elsewhere and included stringed instruments such as lutes, lyres, zithers, and harps. Lutes were characterized by the strings that ran parallel to the neck of the instrument. The simplest of them was often considered to be a children's instrument, consisting of a single string attached to a bowed stick. Some, such as the one-stringed Ethiopian *masinko*, resembled a fiddle with a resonator made of wood and covered with animal skin; it was played with a bow. The *masinko* was played exclusively by the Azmari poet-

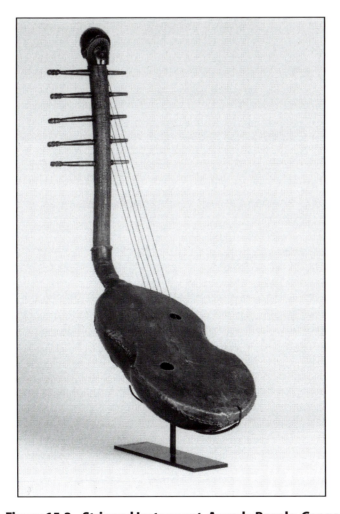

Figure 15-3. Stringed Instrument, Azande People, Congo

musicians and was often paired with a vocalist in a performance.[17] More elaborate forms were common, some zithers having more than one hundred strings. Lutes and zithers have been played for thousands of years. Early Egyptian paintings showed women playing lutes which resemble the modern banjo or guitar. Today, the short-necked 'ud (from which the word "lute" derives) is the dominant musical instrument used in Islamic music, but may be found in non-Islamic regions as well.

Lyres were different from other chordophones in that they had two wooden sideposts that emerged from the sides of a sound resonator. The sideposts were connected at the top by a crossbar or yoke, and the strings stretched from the crossbar down to the bottom of the resonator. Some lyres had a circular or bowl-shaped resonator, while the resonator in others was square or box-shaped. They were popular in many northeast African, Near Eastern and Mediterranean cultures. Early Egyptian and Sudanese paintings portray ritual dances with musicians playing the lyre as far back as 2000 B.C. Lyres were common in Ethiopia and parts of East and Central Africa, but were rarely found in West African societies. One variety, the Ethiopian *begana*, was very large and had eight to twelve strings. It was used primarily during religious festivals of the Ethiopian Church. Another very large lyre was the *obukano* of Kenya. Its length of more than three feet and its resonator of eighteen inches gave it a low sound that leads it to be referred to as "the double bass of East Africa."[18]

A zither was an instrument with horizontal strings that ran the length of its wooden base. One zither has been found with up to 105 strings. In North Africa it was played with picks worn on the index fingers. In Madagascar there were two types of zithers. The *valiha* was a tube zither whose strings ran across the shell of a hollow tube, such as a bamboo stem. It had up to twenty wire strings. Another type was the *jejo vaotano*, a stick zither with four to twelve strings. It is believed that they were brought to the island by a Malayan people, the Hovas, during the fifteenth century, but the performance style and musical content was adapted into a distinctively African style.[19]

Harps differed from other chordophones in that the strings did not run parallel to the soundboard. Harps were used in Mesopotamian cultures as long ago as 3000 B.C., and are found in India and in European societies as well. Some African harps had a gourd resonator; this was the case with the *kora*, which was actually a combination of lute and harp. The *kora*, found mainly among the *griots* of West Africa, was a beautiful instrument that produced a complex and melodious sound. It usually had twenty-one strings that stretched in two rows across the bridge. The tuning was done by moving rings around the neck that tightened and loosened the strings. It was played with the bridge of the instrument facing the musician who plucked the strings with the thumb and forefinger of each hand, while the other fingers were used to support the bridge. It was a complex instrument to make and play, and was, thus, usually found only in the hands of professionals.

The instruments of traditional African music were varied indeed. There were many that were unique to individual societies and regions because of varying cul-

---

17. Kebede, *Roots of Black Music*, 78-79.
18. Nketia, *Music of Africa*, 107.
19. Malm, *Music Cultures of the Pacific, the Near East, and Asia*, 36-37.

tural emphases and differences in the availability of environmental resources. The above discussion certainly does not reflect an inclusive list or even begin to touch on the thousands of different types. Yet it does provide a starting point and a system of classification that can be used to categorize other instruments that one may meet in the study of traditional African music.

Functions

Performances of African traditional music were involved in virtually every aspect of culture, and were inseparable from the context in which they were performed. They involved the community to a much greater degree than performances found in the Western setting today. African music has been defined as "fundamentally a collective art…a communal property whose spiritual qualities are shared and experienced by all." Another definition refers to music as "that aspect of traditional African life which provides the repositories of traditional beliefs, ideas, wisdom and feelings."[20] Traditional music was a vital part of African communities. It performed many different functions that helped organize and give meaning to the development of a particular society.

Musical performances were sometimes organized as social events. They occurred on occasions when members of a community came together for entertainment, for recreational purposes such as sport, or for the performance of a social or religious observance. Music helped bring different members of a community together and provided an important means of encouraging participation in society. It was also used to give order to social events and to impart lessons about social relations and the individual's place within community life. Music, therefore, operated at two levels in relation to the community: it provided an opportunity for sharing and participating in specific experiences, and it was used as a medium for the inculcation of societal beliefs and values. Unlike a typical music performance of today, with the band on a stage located in front of the audience, in traditional African music performances there was little separation between the artist and the audience. Music was participatory and was integrated into the daily routines of people.

Music was important in virtually every aspect of existence. It included domestic songs such as grinding songs, pounding songs, and songs sung while building a new house. These helped to reduce the tedium of these tasks. Music was found at all stages of life such as birth, rites of passage, marriage, and death. It was prominent as a form of social control because the song text allowed the expression of thoughts that might otherwise have remained unsaid. Hugh Tracey wrote about the Chopi:

> Sly digs at the pompous, outspoken condemnation of those who neglect their duties, protests against the cruel and overbearing, outcries directed against social injustices as well as philosophy in the face of difficulties,

---

20. W. Komla Amoaku, "Toward a Definition of Traditional African Music: A Look at the Ewe of Ghana," in Irene V. Jackson, ed., *More Than Drumming* (Westport, CT: Greenwood, 1985), 32, 34.

are all to be found in their songs and shared through their music and dancing...One can well imagine the forcefulness of the reprimand conveyed to a wrongdoer when he finds his misdeeds sung about by thirty or forty strapping young men before all the people of the village, or the blow to the pride of an overweening petty official who has to grin and bear it while the young men jeer to music at his pretentiousness.[21]

According to Tracey, the ability to say in public that which could not otherwise be said helped to maintain a spiritually healthy community.

Some of the functions of music were determined by the presence and needs of women, who played an important role in performance. In Akan society, for example, the songs and the drum music played during the girl's puberty rite were performed by adult women. These songs were not only intended to celebrate the rite of passage, but also to teach the initiates their duties as adult women. In other societies, the rites for healing the sick were performed by women who sang special songs, accompanying themselves with rattles and drums. Women also played a special role at funerals, performing choral laments and dirges.[22]

Children used music to learn and impart lessons in certain contexts. Among the Asante of Ghana, for example, a group of children sang a song to an habitual bed-wetter as a special corrective ceremony.[23] Songs were frequently incorporated into stories or embodied in games, particularly counting or number games, language games, and games involving dancing or other forms of movement. Sometimes children were taught a song to commemorate a special event. Among the Fon of Dahomey, children sang a traditional song to celebrate the moment they lost their first tooth. Children learned songs from their parents, other adults, and their peers. The Venda of South Africa had a large repertoire of play songs which formed an integral part of children's games. Venda children would sing a song to mock a boy who was considered effete or to tease women who were working hard. Songs played an important role in what children learned about their families, important people and events, and the norms of right and wrong. In the following example from Ghana, a cradle song reflects important images and values of society:

If you are hungry, cook yourself a meal.
    Why do you cry?
You are the child of a yam farmer.
    Why do you cry?
You are the child of a cocoyam farmer.
    Why do you cry?[24]

Although no one expected small children to cook themselves a meal when they were hungry, the song was a way of imparting lessons that would allow the children to take better care of themselves once they were grown. This song also shows a level of pride in the agricultural profession of the parents that was meant to be transmitted to the infant.

---

21. Hugh Tracey quoted in Merriam, *African Music in Perspective*, 70, 129.
22. J.H. Kwabena Nketia, *Funeral Dirges of the Akan People* (New York: Negro Universities Press, 1969).
23. Nketia, *Music of Africa*, 36.
24. Ibid. 191.

Music also performed important functions in the funeral rites and remembrances of particular societies. Funeral songs were evidenced by writings on the walls of tombs and monuments in ancient Egypt. A translation of one of these reveals the importance of music in that society:

> Let music and song be before you. Leave behind all evil and think only of joy until the day comes when we journey to that land that loves silence.[25]

Other areas of Africa showed an equally important integration of music and funeral rituals. In the *fika ya ngoma* ceremony of the Shambaa of Tanzania, the entire community joined in to remember the death of a male relative. Participants outside approached the house singing, "Evil enters the house of the master." The people inside sang the reply, "They come in, they go out," meaning that evil spirits may enter the house, but the ceremonies would soon drive them away. The master of ceremonies tied bells around both legs and sang: "May I tie the string of ornaments of the master of ceremonies? Let us work to please him." As he started to dance, he took small steps along the walls of the hut and other people joined him in singing and dancing. This usually lasted for about four hours, and then the main ceremony of invocation and appeasement of the major ancestral spirits began. Throughout the *fika ya ngoma* ceremony, singing and dancing played a central role in the ritual.[26]

Music was also used as a communication device to attract people to a central area for a specific purpose. Among the Chopi and the Igbo, for instance, the women of the village occasionally assembled to judge a woman accused of a crime against another member of the group. A song was used to announce to the women that they should begin to make their way to the area where the judging was to take place. In some areas of Ethiopia, Nigeria, and Cameroon, stone chimes were used as a call to prayer, or as a way of summoning the community in the case of meetings, festivals, and emergencies. Music was also used to denote seasonal changes, as in northern Togo, where the sound of stone chimes marked the end of the rainy season and announced the feast of the millet harvest.[27]

Traditional music also served an important function in political organization. This was apparent in praise songs performed for chiefs and elders during state-sponsored events. Constructive criticisms aimed at the politicians or household elders that could not be raised through regular channels could be raised through music:

> He sits under the short palm tree drinking palmwine.
> Some day you will see our king.
> Some day you will see our king and be envious.

Criticisms such as these were phrased in ways that were not disrespectful, and yet the subject clearly received and understood the message. Like those songs that taught the beliefs and values of society, there were songs that served as tools with which to learn the laws, customs, and political institutions. Political functions

---

25. Malm, *Music Cultures of the Pacific, the Near East, and Asia*, 59.
26. See Nketia, *Music of Africa*, 39-41.
27. See Merriam, *African Music in Perspective*, 129; and Kebede, *Roots of Black Music*, 96.

were also reflected in the use of some musical instruments. Among the Tutsi, for example, drums were a symbol of political power and only the king and the wife of the king could have them. In Ghana, the association of the *atumpan* with high office was evidenced in the requirement that two recently built drums be present whenever a new paramount chief was being installed. Drums such as the *naqquara* of the Saharan Tuaregs and the *negarit* of Ethiopia symbolized political power, just as the Hausa *taushi* reflected aristocratic status and was played by court musicians.[28]

In economic life, songs functioned as an aid to co-operative labor. Members of a Dahomean co-operative work group were led to the field where they would work by a flutist whose loud shrill notes could be heard for great distances. There were also drums, gongs, and rattles that were used to emphasize a work rhythm. For example, among the Frafra of northern Ghana, a player of a one-string fiddle and a rattle player accompanied teams of men who cut grass. As they played, the workers moved their cutlasses to the rhythms of the music. This increased speed as well as efficiency. Music was also performed by people selling their wares to attract customers, or by teams of fishermen as they rowed their boats or hauled in their nets.[29]

Another function of traditional music was as a mnemonic device that recalled past events, such as famous battles or the reigns of great rulers. One scholar wrote about music in Dahomey:

> Songs were and are the prime carriers of history...This function of song came out with great clarity. The informant at one point could not recall the sequence of important names in the series he was giving. Under his breath, to the accompaniment of clicking finger-nails, he began to sing, continuing his song for some moments. When he stopped he had the names clearly in mind once more, and in explanation of his song stated that this was the Dahomean method of remembering historic facts. The role of the singer as the "keeper of records" has been remarked by those who visited the kingdom in the days of its autonomy.[30]

Historical songs, as a form of oral literature, existed for many generations and often commemorated a particular event. For example, songs referring to battles which took place in the eighteenth century can still be heard in parts of Nigeria today. The lead drummers in the Dagomba bands mentioned earlier were responsible for preserving the chronicles of the kings and for pointing out genealogical references that linked contemporary society to the ancestors. In that context, music served as an historical medium that transmitted stories of the past from one generation to the next, while acting as the contemporary archival source for society.

Of course, music also had an important function in, and was closely associated with, religious life. In Egypt, for example, particular gods were distinguished by their role as inventors or "lords" of music and dancing. Performers were sometimes associated with supernatural powers. Professional musicians such as

---

28. See Merriam, *African Music in Perspective*, 69; and Kebede, *Roots of Black Music*, 64.

29. See Merriam, *African Music in Perspective*, 70; and Nketia, *Music of Africa*, 28-29.

30. Melville J. Herskovits, *Dahomey: An Ancient West African Kingdom*, vol. 2 (New York: J.J. Augustin, 1938), 321.

the *essawa*, *gnawa*, and the *griots* often performed healing ceremonials that used music as the medicine. Instruments also had symbolic or mythological associations with religious imagery or rituals. Instruments were initially used by *shamans*, healers, and religious leaders, not for their aesthetic purposes, but to attain magical and religious powers. Some African drums were considered sacred and used for no other purpose but religious ceremonies and the worship of gods. In some cases, different gods had different instruments reserved for their honor only. One writer commented on the relationship between religion and music in African cultures: "Music helps us to pass into other realms of consciousness. The heightened feeling enhanced by musical experience is aligned with spirituality and the other world...the world in which things are no longer subject to time and space."[31]

African traditional music was found in virtually every aspect of society. Its functions were diverse, but they differed from one society to the next and also over the course of time. Its dynamic and adaptive character can be useful for historical reconstruction. A particular song must have existed for a reason, and the existence of specific musical types can give insights into a previous lifestyle or the environment of a community that no longer survives. In addition, song texts can reveal hidden political processes and structures of social organization. Even in traditional music used for recreation, there are often messages that illustrate the values and beliefs of a society.

Conclusion

This chapter has given a broad overview of the styles, instruments, and functions of African traditional music. The abundance of music styles and instruments makes a more detailed portrait impossible in this small space. Nonetheless, the numerous examples from individual societies provide a base from which one can easily incorporate further knowledge into the larger musical context. Many styles of traditional African music were associated with specific social situations and, in this way, music was an essential part of society and played an integral role in its evolution. The most pervasive music types were those that provided entertainment and relaxation and were usually separate genres from the religious ones.

Participants in a performance of African music made a contribution to the success of the occasion, and they behaved with the understanding that what they did was an act of artistic participation as well. The study of traditional African music provides a looking-glass into African culture. Music was sometimes the central focus of an event, as in a spontaneous performance by non-professional musicians, a music competition, or a praise song for the nobility. At other times, it existed as part of an event, as an instructional tool within a children's game or a choral refrain in a storytelling performance. Regardless of the context where it was found, music added to (and continues to enhance) the quality of life and the overall happiness and functioning of society.

---

31. Kebede, *Roots of Black Music*, 94. He is, in part, quoting, John Blacking, *How Musical is Man?* (Seattle: University of Washington, 1973), 51.

Review Questions

1. Describe some of the factors that led to the evolution and development of different music cultures in specific regions. How did these music styles reflect the historical and environmental influences present in that region?
2. Which sectors of society were performers drawn from, and what types of training did they undergo?
3. Briefly describe the four categories of instruments used in the production of African music. What evidence exists to reveal the importance of music in ancient Egyptian societies?
4. How was music used to organize society in terms of economic and religious functions? What function did it have in the education of children?
5. Discuss how music was used as an archival source to recreate the history of societies. What role did the *griots* play in recording history?

Additional Reading

Akpabot, Samuel Ekpe. *Ibibio Music in Nigerian Culture*. East Lansing: Michigan State University Press, 1975.

Blacking, John. *Music, Culture and Experience: Selected Papers of John Blacking*. Chicago: University of Chicago Press, 1995.

Chernoff, John Miller. *African Rhythm and African Sensibility: Aesthetics and Social Action in African Musical Idioms*. Chicago: University of Chicago Press, 1979.

Kebede, Ashenafi. *Roots of Black Music: The Vocal, Instrumental, and Dance Heritage of Africa and Black America*. Englewood Cliffs, NJ: Prentice Hall, 1982.

Merriam, Alan P. *African Music in Perspective*. New York: Garland Publishing, 1982.

Nketia, J. H. Kwabena. *The Music of Africa*. New York: W.W. Norton & Co., 1974.

Suggested Recordings

Music of the Former Bandia Courts (Central Africa). Chant du Monde Records, no. 2741009.

Raakotozafy, *Valiha Malaza* (zither music from Madagascar). Globestyle, no. ORBD028.

Music of the Cushitic Peoples of South-West Ethiopia, no. BM30L2305, and *Music of the Ethiopian Coptic Church*, no. BM30L2304, UNESCO Collection, Ethiopia I.

Sounds of Africa (General). Verve, no. FTS3021.

Kora Manding: Mandinka Music of the Gambia (Kora music). Ethnodisc, no. ER12102.

Chapter 16

Written and Oral Literature

Steven J. Salm

This chapter will focus on the precolonial literature of Africa, including both oral and written literature. Within these two types there are a number of sub-genres that help define and characterize the role of literature in society. Much attention is given in this chapter to oral literature, as its influence and importance in precolonial African society—and still today—are extensive.[1] In the first section, the concept of "oral literature" and its relevance to research in African history is addressed. The second section looks at the classifications and functions of oral literature and the characteristics of the specialist practitioner. Examples of oral literature from different regions of Africa follow in the third section. The fourth section discusses some examples of the independent development of unique writing systems on the continent. The final section considers the influence of outside religious systems and their impact on written literature.

Oral Literature: An Overview

It seems fitting to begin this chapter on African literature with a discussion of oral literature because it has, undoubtedly, provided some of the most significant revelations and sparked a re-evaluation by scholars of previous interpretations of the precolonial history of Africa. This is not to say that Africa as a whole was without any written literature before it was introduced by the West; there were a number of independently developed writing systems, as well as extensive use of the Arabic and Latin scripts in African literature, dating as far back as the third millennium B.C. These are discussed in detail below, but let us turn first to the characteristics of oral literature and its acceptance by scholars as a historically relevant source.

Many readers are, no doubt, somewhat familiar with contemporary written African literature. Writers such as Chinua Achebe, Ngugi wa Thiong'o, and others have written many works that are read the world over by peoples of diverse

---

1. It is impossible to adequately cover the entire field of oral literature in the space allowed here. I will focus only on the major forms as they pertain to historical reconstruction, as well as their cultural and social relevance. For more detailed discussions of the types, structures, and functions of oral literature in Africa see the additional reading list below.

backgrounds. Many African novels, short stories, and volumes of poetry are read for enjoyment and used extensively as teaching tools. But, "Oral literature?" one may ask, "Is that not a contradiction in terms?" How can something be considered "oral" and "literature" at the same time? Such a narrow definition of literature is purely Western. *The Random House Dictionary* defines literature as "writings in which expression and form, in connection with ideas of permanent and universal interest, are characteristic or essential features."[2] Other definitions similarly use the words "writing" and "printed material" in every description. But, if we take a broader view and define literature as "an artistic form that uses language as its medium," then we can accept that literature is not limited to the written or printed word alone. Using such a definition, African oral literature has all the necessary qualities to be considered "literature" in the truest sense of the word.

Furthermore, it is erroneous to view oral literature simply as part of a "preliterate" culture, a primitive precursor to written literature; for oral literature is neither less structurally complex than written literature, nor is it inferior in artistic value. One might even argue that the poetics and paralinguistics of performance make it a more complicated genre, with impromptu dynamism and interaction with the audience, demanding a considerable amount of skill on the part of the practitioner. It is interesting to note that much of contemporary African literature is influenced, in some way, by the long tradition of oral literature that preceded it.

When the colonial powers set out to assert their dominance over the African societies they encountered, they denied the historical existence of African civilization. It suited their hegemonic aims to view Africans as culturally inferior, or "without culture" and "without history." They wanted to believe that Africa's past was devoid of any significant events, and that its society must be in its infancy and thus ripe for the "civilizing mission" of colonialism. History, it was assumed, must be recorded in a written form to be valid. This notion was later dismissed, largely through the acceptance of oral literature as an historical source to reconstruct the African past. The abundance of oral literature contains a great deal of historically valuable information.

Only since the 1950s has the use of oral tradition as a valid historical source gained general acceptance in the field of African studies. Before that time, oral literature was recorded and studied for its aesthetic and textual qualities, but it was often dismissed as mythical and too prone to change and adaptation to be useful as a historical source. However, a closer examination of oral literature has helped advance our knowledge of precolonial African history. In the 1950s and 1960s, some historians set out to validate the use of oral literature to reconstruct the history of a society. One such scholar was Jan Vansina whose seminal work, *De la Tradition Orale*,[3] described the techniques necessary to use oral tradition as a source. This work opened new avenues to unravel the precolonial African past.

Intense ethnographic research is necessary to derive the historical content from the oral literature. To perform such research well, a scholar needs to be well versed in history, sociology, linguistics, and anthropology. He or she must also be

---

2. *The Random House Dictionary of the English Language* (New York: Random House, 1967).

3. Jan Vansina, *Oral Tradition: A Study in Historical Methodology*, trans. H.M. Wright (London: Routledge & Kegan Paul, 1965).

willing to devote a significant amount of time to living in the community, learning the unique cultural features that distinguish one society from another. Extended fieldwork is required to understand the customs, traditions, values, proverbs, and other images contained within the narrative. One example is found in the Mbegha myth, the story of the founding of the Shambaa kingdom in southern Kenya.[4] The myth contains popular Shambaa phrases such as: "Where once a lion sat, there is now a pig." Without understanding that in Shambaa society the lion represents strength and power and the pig represents famine, one would not realize that this phrase is saying that the kingdom thrived during the powerful Mbegha's reign and lost stature with his departure. Successful techniques of deconstruction demand this in-depth understanding of the culture.

Scholars have been documenting examples of oral literature for many years now. However, there are a number of problems when attempting to translate an artistic performance into a static text. As will be shown below, the text alone cannot reveal the entire message of the performance. The performance transcends the spoken words and transmits cultural insights in a way similar to dance, music, sculpture, and paintings. As with these art forms, there is a loss of power in the translation from the oral performance to the written page.

There are, of course, certain advantages to the written word. One of these is availability and accessibility. Once recorded, a written history or literary work can be saved and replicated and is a more static and easily accessible document of the historical period from which it comes. Oral literature, on the other hand, is subject to change and requires a greater effort to unravel the strands of fact and fiction, of myth and reality.

Classifications of Oral Literature

There are many different types of oral literature. It is impossible to make accurate generalizations about the oral literature of the continent because the prevalence and usage of different forms vary widely from one society and region to the next. Nevertheless, this section will attempt to present an overview of the different types, with more detailed descriptions provided when necessary. Not all of these genres do or did exist in every society in Africa. The many categories of oral literature include, but are not limited to: (i) oral narratives such as epics, legends and explanatory tales; (ii) poetry such as praise poetry, chants and songs; and (iii) epigrams such as proverbs, riddles, puns, and tongue twisters. The last category is the most pervasive in everyday life, but is less useful than others as a historical source; they will not be discussed here.

Oral Narratives

Oral narratives are generally defined by their use of prose, but they are not limited to prose alone. They are distinguished by their use of belief and unbelief,

---

4. See Steven Feierman, *The Shambaa Kingdom: A History* (Madison: University of Wisconsin Press, 1974). This work provides a brilliant deconstruction of the myths and history contained within the Mbegha myth, using different techniques of analysis.

by their perception of reality and unreality. Epics are defined by their rich and profound use of narrative and poetic style; they are neither solely prose nor poetry. They exist in slightly different forms in many different regions of Africa and include, for example, the Mande *Epic of Sundiata* in Mali; the *Ozidi* epic of the Ijo in southern Nigeria; and the *Mwindo* epic of the Nyanga of eastern Zaire.

Epics and legends combine the facts of history with the creation of myth, giving the stories an artistic quality while maintaining a semblance of historical fact. They may be accounts of great leaders and hunters of the long-ago past or they may approach topics nearer to the contemporary world. If their topic is that of ancient history, they are likely to contain more myth and tales of the supernatural.

Another type of oral narrative is the explanatory tale, which explains characteristics of the environment and defines expected behaviors and values. Such narratives include creation myths that interpret the origins of the natural environment, as well as tales that anthropomorphize animals and physical features of the world. In this example from the San of southern Africa, an explanation of the origins of death is presented in a story of why hares have split noses. It is common for explanatory tales to be set in a time before creation or at the beginnings of humankind.

The Origin of Death

The Moon, it is said, once sent an insect to men saying, 'Go to men and tell them, "As I die, and dying live; so you shall also die, and dying live."'

The insect started with the message, but, while on his way, was overtaken by the hare, who asked, 'On what errand are you bound?'

The insect answered, 'I am sent by the Moon to men, to tell them that as she dies and dying lives, so shall they also die and dying live.'

The hare said, 'As you are an awkward runner, let me go.' With these words he ran off, and when he reached men, he said, 'I am sent by the Moon to tell you, "As I die and dying perish, in the same manner you shall also die and come wholly to an end."'

The hare then returned to the Moon and told her what he had said to men. The Moon reproached him angrily, saying, 'Do you dare tell the people a thing which I have not said?'

With these words the Moon took up a piece of wood and struck the hare on the nose. Since that day the hare's nose has been slit, but men believe what Hare had told them.[5]

In different regions a variety of animals are used to personify human traits: The monkey personifies stupidity; the dog, greed; and, in what are known as trickster tales, the tortoise and spider personify cunning. Explanatory tales use their characters to reiterate values important to society. Tales of this type are pervasive throughout Africa and have been recorded by scholars in a number of works.[6]

---

5. "The Origin of Death" in Paul Radin, ed., *African Folktales* (New York: Schocken Books, 1983), 63.

6. For books of such tales, see Harold Scheub, *The African Storyteller: Studies from African Oral Traditions* (Dubuque, IA: Kendall/Hunt Publishing, 1990); and Paul Radin, ed., *African Folktales.*

Poetry

Poetry is more dramatic and performance-oriented than oral narratives. Poetry is often characterized by rhythmic patterns and rhyme, assonance, and alliteration. It is sometimes partly performed in song and, in other cases, it may be entirely sung. Poetry, including songs, chants, praise poetry, and funeral dirges, often uses words and phrases that have distinct shades of meanings to particular societies and, therefore, can distinguish them from one another.

Poetry was used in Africa for a variety of purposes, including entertainment. It was often considered the most effective means of exerting popular pressure and influencing opinion in matters such as politics, and was an accepted method of addressing private disputes and grievances. Among the Somali people, poets engaged in verbal duels, either in person or through the use of messengers who conveyed the text orally to the recipient. These duels were used to vent grievances and also for entertainment purposes. Praise poetry was used during celebrations to enhance the prestige of certain individuals or families within the audience. In warfare, poetry was used to strengthen the troops' morale and to commemorate previous victories, as well as to grieve for the dead.

Examples of poetic chants include: *ijala* (chanting done by hunter-poets) among the Yoruba; the *heello* of the Somali, *intsomii* of the Xhosa, and *izibongo* (praise-chant) of the Zulu. A stanza of an *izibongo* is presented in this example:

Izibongo to Shaka

The joke of the women at Nomgabhi,
Joking as they sat in a sheltered spot,
Saying that Shaka would not rule, he would not become chief,
Whereas it was the year in which Shaka was about to prosper.
The beast that lowed at Mthonjaneni,
And all the tribes heard its wailing,
It was heard by Dunjwa of the Yangweni kraal,
It was heard by Mangcengeza of Khali's kraal,
Fire of the long dry grass, son of Mjokwane;
Fire of the long grass of scorching force,
That burned the owls on the Dlebe hill,
And eventually those of Mabedlana also burned.[7]

This chant was written in praise of Shaka, the king of the Zulu. Such a chant was performed rapidly in a high-pitched voice and at high volume. The presentation straddled the realms of narration and song. A performance like this created rising emotional excitement within the audience and in the artist as well. Though differing in form, poetic songs and chants were used by many societies and in virtually every major event of the life cycle: birth, adolescence (initiation or puberty rites), marriage, and death. Themes varied according to the occasion and included love, praise, criticism, war, and death.

---

7. See T. Cope, *Izibongo: Zulu Praise Poems* (Oxford: Clarendon Press, 1968). This passage was quoted in Isidore Okpewho, *African Oral Literature* (Bloomington: Indiana University Press, 1992), 81.

Characteristics and Functions:
The Art of Performance

It is important to understand some unique characteristics of oral literature before we embark on a discussion of its functions within society. The first point is that, while written literature is an interaction between the reader and the book, oral literature is performed. There is a dynamic interaction between the artist and the audience that demands additional talents. Extra-linguistic features are invoked to create an atmosphere of emotion. The audience reacts to the performer's intonation and dress, to song, dance, body movements, and swift glances with the eyes. The artist, in turn, feeds off the energy of the listeners and adjusts the performance accordingly. The point to remember is that when an oral performance is reduced to words alone and the power of the aesthetic is diminished, it also loses much of the artistic form and the energy that shaped the story.

This leads to a second point: that oral literature is prone to change. It is inherently dynamic because it is transferred from one generation to another by memory alone. It does not often retain the original textual passages, nor the exterior details, but a change in thematic focus is not due to failed memory or an error in transferring the message between generations. Rather, it is a result of the high respect for creativity that gives merit to those who are capable of creating new twists to often-told stories. The changes in the story are used to bring the history and tradition into a contemporary context. On the other hand, the essential message of the story remains intact over time. The changing "texts" have made it difficult for scholars to fully accept the verities of such literature, yet the continuity in the essential message shows how it can be of use to historians and other scholars wanting to reconstruct the African past.

Performers are creators, and a story is seldom retold without a change from the previous telling. Part of the creativity depends on the interplay between the performer and the audience. The talent of the artist is based on his/her ability to captivate the audience by changing the story and making it interesting to the listeners. The interaction with the audience helps determine the course and the very nature of the narrator's creativity in reconstructing the events as they unfold. The message of the story is "reinvented" as a result of the relationship between the performer and the audience. The involvement of the audience begins from the first moments of the performance. There is a call and response, an exchange between the performer and the audience that is called antiphony, which opens a story. Among the Hausa of West Africa, for example, the teller calls out "ga ta nan, ga ta nan" ("here she is, here she is") and the listeners respond "ta zo mu ji" ("let her come so that we can hear"). The audience is thus involved from the very start of the performance and their presence is crucial to the development of the themes.

In this way, the past and the present, the traditional and the contemporary worlds are united. The past—the realm of history, the setting of the story and the center of tradition—is modified and contextualized into the contemporary without losing the central, or core message. This adaptability is best represented by Ruth Finnegan's work among the Limba of Sierra Leone in the late 1960s. She told the story of Adam and Eve to a respected artist in Limba society. After a few years, she returned to find the story had been completely recontextualized to fit the local setting. The names were changed, for instance: Eve became Ifu, Adam was changed to Adamu, and the serpent became a local snake called *bankiboro*.

The relations between men and women and the relationship of people to their environment were also changed to present a more local meaning.[8] With this thematic volatility of oral literature in mind, the next section will address the functions of oral literature and the ways in which it can enhance our understanding of precolonial African history.

Functions of Oral Literature

Literature in general, like music or other art forms, opens a window into cultural characteristics not always readily accessible through other sources. In Africa, the study of epics, poetry, and praise songs can reveal the political, cultural, and social structures important to a society. Oral literature provides a view of a society's history, motives, and traditions. The functions of oral literature are many and thus, only the most important functions and their relevance to society will be addressed here.[9]

Oral literature links the past with the present. Therefore, we can view the functions of oral literature in the precolonial era by investigating a continuity of characteristics as found in present societies. As Harold Scheub writes:

> The materials and methods of composition have remained constant through the centuries—images from past and present, representations of fantasy and reality, worked together and artfully crafted into rich metaphorical parallels in performances that enlist the emotions of the members of audiences... That past, the paradigm of the culture, continues to exert its influence on the shaping of the present, giving it a mythical heart, a traditional context, and a nascent form.[10]

Scheub describes oral narrative tradition as "a repository of emotions" that are "regularized and controlled during the performance."[11] The images invoked during the narrations are incorporated from the contemporary world of the storyteller and the audience, as well as from "ancient artistic tradition." This "borrowing" from two worlds links the past and the present and calls forth emotional stimuli that have a profound effect on the audience.

The functions of oral literature can be related to its use to scholars in unveiling the political, social, and cultural history of African societies. The first function is to record the history of a society and transmit that history from generation to

---

8. See Ruth Finnegan, *Limba Stories and Story-telling*, trans. Ruth Finnegan (Oxford: Clarendon Press, 1967), *Oral literature in Africa* (London: Clarendon Press, 1970), and *Literacy and Orality: Studies in the Technology of Communication* (New York: Blackwell, 1988).

9. For a more detailed account of the functions of oral literature, see Okpewho, *African Oral Literature*, 105-124.

10. Nongenile Masithathu Zenani, in Harold Scheub, ed., *The World and the Word: Tales and Observations from the Xhosa Oral Tradition* (Madison: University of Wisconsin Press, 1992), 3.

11. Harold Scheub, "Zulu Oral Tradition and Literature," in B.W. Andrzejewski et al., *Literature in African Languages: Theoretical Issues and Sample Surveys* (London: Cambridge University Press, 1985), 511.

generation. For historians, it provides descriptions of historical facts and objects that would be otherwise unavailable. Oral literature can reveal the history of heroes and heroines of the past. It gives unique insight into the political, social, and cultural institutions of previous societies by relating that history to the contemporary world. For many African societies, oral literature was the only means to archive traditional customs.

A second, and very important, function of oral literature is in educating the youth. Exposure to oral literature enhances verbal skills and inculcates knowledge about the origins, ideals, and proper conduct of society. Oral literature reveals the values and morals that motivate a society, how it represents the past, and how it forms its social context in relation to other societies. Through oral literature, the youth learn what factors are important in the maintenance of cultural continuity and why change happens.

A third function of oral literature is that it contributes to a society's worldview and its concept of collective identity. Adopting local variances in similar historical myths gives a sense of belonging to one group that is in competition with another. There are oral traditions which were disseminated throughout large areas. Different groups within these regions adjusted the stories to fit their own contexts. For scholars, a comparison of these local variances within a single story can reveal how societies set themselves apart from another; how the story has been changed through transmission; and what parts of the story one group has emphasized in contrast to another. The different types and messages of oral literatures can divulge the cultural rigidities and social structures that differ from one group to another.

A fourth function of oral literature is to express individual beliefs or group grievances. Oral performances also allow a medium for political expression or lobbying for particular actions by an individual or the entire community. An example of this was mentioned earlier in the use of poetry among the Somali. There was a high level of respect for elders, and criticism could not be made of such persons directly. One method that was accepted was the use of proverbs addressed to a general audience, yet obviously pointing to one certain individual.

The fifth, and most common, function is to provide entertainment and relaxation, focusing on the aesthetic pleasures. Traditional African societies used storytelling as a means to relax and pass the time at the end of the day before retiring. The men gathered around in the village meeting place, and the women and children met together at home. In their respective places, each engaged in lively communication ranging from riddles, proverbs, and trickster tales to longer stories of ancient glories. It helped boost people's spirits and relieve some of the pressures of daily life. An example of this can be found in Chinua Achebe's *Things Fall Apart* among the Igbo of Nigeria. These storytelling times were also important to the youth because they provided knowledge of the literature and helped them to learn the artistic skills necessary to carry on the tradition.

Case Studies

The following examples will focus on the epic form among the Mande in West Africa, the Swahili in East Africa, and the Xhosa in southern Africa.

The Mande Epic in West Africa

The Mande epic is a highly developed literary form that was only performed by specially trained bards. Epics are long historical narratives that celebrate the adventures and heroism of great rulers and hunters of the past who are described as having supernatural powers. Mande is a term used to designate a language family made up of many ethnic groups who occupy a large area of West Africa between the Sahara to the north and the rain forest to the south.

The bards, or *griots*, as they were called in Mande societies, were part of a caste system in which they were trained from childhood in the art of performance and narration. The *griots* were adept narrators as well as skilled musicians, and a performance was often a blend of poetic chants and narration accompanied by a *kora*. They were admired for their knowledge and command of performance and creativity and entertained the courts of kings and other noble families as well as the families of great hunters. D. T. Niane, in the preface to *Sundiata: An Epic of Old Mali*, describes the *griots* as "counselors of kings."[12] They worked to preserve the history and acted as the archives of the constitutions, records, traditions, and customs of their kingdoms; this was all done by memory alone. Their knowledge of the past was also invoked to train and tutor heirs to the throne. They served as a reservoir of the past and as the means of recreating that past within the present society.

The Mande epics celebrated and glorified the great rulers of the past. The most famous and most celebrated was Sundiata, the founder and first king of the Mali Empire in the thirteenth century. Though the many versions of the epic vary greatly, they all maintain a core message about Sundiata's life. He struggled through childhood, unable to walk, but he not only emerged victorious over his disability, he even exhibited superhuman strength. After a period of exile, he returned home to defeat Sumanguru and establish the empire. The tale of *Sundiata* is still told over a large area of West Africa today, in classrooms and in theaters, for the lessons in political and social history that it imparts.

Swahili

Inhabiting much of the East African coast of Tanzania and Kenya, the Swahili have a long tradition of literature, both oral and written. There are many written court chronicles in Swahili. The most celebrated of them is the *Tarekhe ya Pate* (Pate Chronicles), which covers the period from 1204 to 1895. Much of the literature reflects the syncretic culture and language that grew out of the combination of the local African and the imported Islamic and Arabic elements.[13]

When the Arabs first settled in the coastal towns, there was a dividing line between the literature of the townspeople, the Arabs, and the literature of the rural folk, the Africans. The literature of the former was the work of privileged groups such as theologians, Islamic scholars, and members of the courts. The perfor-

---

12. D.T. Niane, *Sundiata: An Epic of Old Mali*, trans. G.D. Pickett (London: Longman, 1965).

13. For a brief translated version of the *Pate Chronicles* as well as a similar set of chronicles from Kilwa, see G.S.P. Freeman-Grenville, *The East African Coast: Select Documents from the First to the Early Nineteenth Century* (Oxford: Clarendon Press, 1962).

mances included narratives with music and dance developed in the urban context. The literature of the rural areas comprised historical narratives, fables, songs, and proverbs. As the Arab presence and the economic prosperity of the coastal towns grew, some of the rural Africans began moving into the towns—sometimes willingly and sometimes as slaves—where the two cultures gradually became one.

One form of literature that developed was a religious poetry that reflected the syncretism of the culture. The most widely recognized form of Swahili poetry is the *utenzi* (pl. *tenzi)*. It was influenced by the Islamic and Arabic traditions, but the *tenzi* became a unique African art form; they were written in Swahili and the creative energies were drawn from the East African context. It is modeled, in form, on Arabic poetry in that there are four parts to each line with the first three set in a rhyming pattern. The *utenzi* narrative is interesting because it combines the written and the oral forms. It exists in manuscript form, but is also orally transmitted between generations, and is designed for public performance.[14]

The oldest and, some would say, the finest preserved work of this form is *Utenzi wa Tambuka* (The Epic of Tambuka), written in 1728 for the sultan of Pate. This represents one type of *utenzi* which can be classified as an epic. Unlike the Mande epics, the artist performs the work as it is written and adds little or no impromptu material. Another example of an *utenzi* is *Habari za Wakilindi* (The Story of the Wakilindi Lineage) written in 1895 by Abdallah bin Hemedi bin Ali Ajjemy (ca.1840-1912). It is the story of the Shambaa people and the rise to power of the Kalindi lineage. It combines historical facts with mythical images, and relies on the use of specific cultural references that assume an in-depth understanding of Shambaa traditions.

Xhosa

The oral tradition of the Xhosa people in Southern Africa also includes the epic narrative. In Xhosa society it is called *intsomi* (imaginative narrative). It is a highly developed epic form in which stories have been known to last for more than a hundred hours and can take up to one full month to complete. These stories are intricate narrations sewn together cohesively to captivate the audience and teach them about a particular historical event or figure. An *intsomi* might give cultural descriptions of Xhosa society, including insights into circumcision, purification, and marriage ceremonies. The artists who perform these stories are considered the very best in their community. These stories help disseminate and preserve the traditions and rituals of the society.[15]

There are many other forms of Xhosa oral literature including the *irhayirhayi* (riddle), *iqhalo* (proverb), *ibali* (oral history), and *izibongo* (poem). As in Mande society, royal bards were significant among the Xhosa. Many of the leaders had their own *iimbongi* (poets) to proclaim their greatness in poetic verse and to reinforce their position among their people.

---

14. For written examples of tenzi, see Haji Chum, ed., *Utenzi wa Vita vya Uhud* (The epic of the Battle of Uhud), trans. by H.E. Lambert (Nairobi: East African Literature Bureau, 1962), and Zuberi Hamadi Lesso, *Utenzi wa Zinduko la Ujamaa.* (Nairobi: East African Literature Bureau, 1972).

15. See Harold Scheub, *The Xhosa Ntsomi* (Oxford: Clarendon Press, 1975).

Development of African Scripts

The merging of written and oral works, discussed above in the context of the Swahili *tenzi*, was influenced by contacts between Africans and the imported Islamic and Christian cultures. More will be said about these interactions in section V. Before addressing this, it is important to note that Africa was not devoid of the ability to write apart from the use of Islamic and Christian scripts. For instance, it is commonly known that one of the oldest writing systems in the world is that of Egyptian hieroglyphics, dating to the beginning of the third millennium B.C. There were also a number of other African societies that developed writing systems with structures not based on Arabic or Latin scripts. These include the Mende of Sierra Leone, the Kpele of Liberia, the Bamun of Cameroon, and the people of Calabar in Nigeria. But these systems were never implemented for widespread use and were rarely available in the public domain. They were sometimes reserved for courts or restricted to recording the affairs of limited circles, and they were not employed to document the history of the larger society or to write other literature. In Calabar, for example, the writing system (*nsibidi*) was used exclusively within the Ekpe secret society, while the Vai system was used to translate the Bible and the Qur'an, and even an autobiography of the system's creator, Momolu Duwale Bukele, but never established a widespread presence.

In contrast to those mentioned above, there are a number of African languages that sustained a position of importance over many centuries and whose use was more pervasive. These languages include Ge'ez in Ethiopia and Libyo-Berber in Libya. There are numerous inscriptions written in Ge'ez, but the oldest existing evidence of this writing dates to the fifth century B.C. in an inscription on an altar to the gods Astar and Nawraw. The intricate writing system consisted of about 200 symbols, with each consonantal sign having seven different shapes depending on the vowel with which it was joined.

The origins of the Ge'ez writing system derive from a group of people who entered into what is now northern Ethiopia during the first millennium B.C. They mixed with the Ethiopian population and, in the first century A.D., set up the first Ethiopian state at Aksum. It is believed that Christianity became the state religion some time in the fourth century A.D. and Ge'ez became the official spoken and written language of the state soon after. Ge'ez writing was developed by the Ethiopian clergy and used within the ruling structures of the emperor and other nobility. Some of the early writings include a translation of the Bible made some time between the fourth and seventh centuries. From the fourth to the eleventh centuries, the Aksumite period, a number of indigenous hagiographies about Ethiopian saints were also written.[16]

The fourteenth century marked the beginning of Ethiopian historiography written in Ge'ez. *The Chronicle of the Wars of Amda Seyon I*, believed to have been written by a monk in the service of the king's court, addresses the period of the king's rule and includes eyewitness descriptions of events, speeches made by the king, and passages relating to the private life of the royal family. Another vol-

---

16. See I. Guidi, *Storia della Litteratura Etiopica* (Roma: Instituto per Oriente, 1932), and E. Cerulli, *Storia della Letteratura Etiopica* (Milan: Nuova Accademia Editrice, 1956).

ume of works titled *Kabra Nagast* (The Glory of Kings) consists of 117 chapters and includes many important topics in Ethiopian history: the birth of the future king of Ethiopia, Menelik I; the journey of Menelik I to Ethiopia and his subsequent coronation; and the important standing of Ethiopia within the tribes of Israel and its ultimate glory and heroism.[17]

The purpose of this short section has been to present a few examples of the independent development of written forms on the African continent. The examples reveal the presence of written forms in Africa apart from Arabic and Roman scripts. On the other hand, the introduction of Islam and Christianity did have a major impact on the way history and literature were recorded. This will be examined in the next section.

The Islamic Influence: Literature in Arabic

The introduction of Islam and Western Christianity had a tremendous influence on the development of African written literature. Some of the social and cultural changes that were set into motion by the arrival of these new religious systems are discussed elsewhere in this book. The Arabic language and script were introduced to North Africa, at least by the late seventh century. From there, it spread across the Sahara. On the East African coast, the changes were slower—but no less significant—because of a more gradual process that led to the development of the Swahili culture and language.

After the Prophet Mohammed's death, his teachings were compiled into a volume known as the Qur'an, and the language of this book is Arabic. Islam is based on the Qur'an just as Christianity is based on the Bible. One difference lies in the fact that, while the Bible was freely translated into many local languages, the Islamic belief is that the Qur'an should not appear in any language but Arabic because it is the language in which the Prophet received his revelations. Thus, converts wanting to gain a better knowledge of Islamic teachings needed to understand Arabic at least as it pertained to religious doctrine. Further, those who wanted to excel in an Islam-dominated society had to advance their knowledge of Arabic beyond a basic understanding of religious tenets. Hence, Arabic and the Qur'an have had a significant impact on the themes, language, and rhythms of all subsequent literature in North Africa.

The Arab conquests of North Africa began a gradual absorption of the conquered peoples into the Arabic culture and the Islamic community. This had a profound effect on the production of written literature. During the early days of Islam, an independent group of historians arose in Egypt, and much later the same occurred in northwest Africa. In the tenth century, at Qairawan in Tunisia, a center of legal studies stimulated the production of new literary works. In the lat-

---

17. See *The Glorious Victories of 'Amda Seyon, King of Ethiopia*, trans. G.W.B. Huntingford (Oxford: Clarendon Press, 1965), and *Kebra Nagast*, trans. Sir E.A. Wallis Budge (London: Oxford University Press, 1932).

ter part of the tenth century, Cairo became the center of Islamic learning and one of the premier cities of the Islamic faith.

The best-documented and best known epic history of Arabic oral literature is the *Sirat Bani Hilal*.[18] It describes the spread of the Banu Hilal between the tenth and twelfth centuries out of the Arabian peninsula and into Egypt, their conquest of North Africa, and their subsequent defeat. It is a rich and complex story made up of a series of intricate tales that are strung together into a larger narrative about their passage into a new homeland and their trials and battles on the way. It has been retold for nearly a thousand years. The epic has been performed in many different forms: in narrative prose, in poetic narration, and as sung verse accompanied by musical instruments. The story, like the Xhosa *intsomi*, has been known to last for more than one hundred hours. It has existed as an oral tradition for nearly one thousand years and has been told in Egypt, across North Africa, in Mali, and in Nigeria. It has also existed in a written form since the fourteenth century and can now be found throughout the Arab world.

There were a number of other works produced in the fourteenth and fifteenth centuries, relating to the geography of the region, the history of Islam, and other encyclopedic and biographical subjects. One writer was al-Maqrizi (1346-1442). His extensive volumes of reference works include: the *Khitat*, a meticulous topographical description of Egypt; historical depictions of the Fatimid, the Ayyubid, and the Mamluk dynasties; a biographical dictionary of prominent Egyptians; and other writings on historical subjects.

Cities in Northwest Africa such as Tunis and Fez also rose to prominence as centers of Islamic activity. One cannot speak of literature in this region without recalling the names of Ibn Battuta (1304-1377) and Ibn Khaldun (1332-1406). Hailing from Tangier, Ibn Battuta set out on a pilgrimage to Mecca at the age of twenty-one. His curiosity and interest in Islam and history led him to visit many countries and interview many prominent citizens. He traveled for twenty-four years and wrote accounts of his journeys along the east coast of Africa, and in Eastern Europe, India, China, and Mali. His keen interest and his ability to interact with people enabled him to portray vividly the manners, popular customs, types of government, and trading systems of the many peoples he encountered. His writings provide some of the most detailed records of this era

Of no less merit is Ibn Khaldun of Tunis, a great historian who was politically involved in the courts of Fez and Tunis. His works include the monumental *Kitab-al-'Ibar* (Universal History) and a three-volume *Muqaddimah* (Introduction to the History). The former has been called "the most detailed socio-historical study of the Maghrib ever written."[19] One volume is devoted to the empire of Mali and gives a list of rulers that provides a starting point for further research into the political structures of the kingdom. In the latter, he reveals a greater respect for oral

---

18. For a detailed account of the Sirat Banu Hilal epic, see Dwight Fletcher Reynolds, *Heroic Poets, Poetic Heroes: The Ethnography of Performance in an Arabic Oral Epic Tradition* (Ithaca: Cornell University Press, 1995).

19. Ibn Khaldun, *Kitab al-'Ibar wa-diwan al-mubtaba wa 'l-Khabar* 14th century, (republished in 1868), 7 vols. (Bulak) and (Beirut: Commission Internationale pour al Traduction des Chefs d'oeuvre, 1956-59); *The Muqaddimah*, 3 vols., trans Franz Rosenthal (London: Routledge and Kegan Paul, 1967); and see D.T. Niane, "Introduction," in D.T. Niane, ed., *Africa from the Twelfth to the Sixteenth Century*, UNESCO General History of Africa, vol. 4 (Berkely: University of California Press, 1984), 8.

poetry and includes passages of poetry from the *Sirat Bani Hilal*. His work also helped establish the foundations of sociology and emphasized the importance of seeking an objective view of history by critically analyzing the sources.

The influence of Islam was not limited to areas north of the Sahara. In West Africa, there were contacts dating at least to the eighth century, but beginning in the eleventh century Islam made inroads into the government and civil structures of the Empire of Ghana. The traders and government leaders in Ghana and, to an even greater extent, in its successor, the Empire of Mali, adopted Islam and established new towns of economic and religious significance. Some of these were important centers of the trans-Saharan trade.

Islam gradually spread eastwards from Ghana. Throughout the regions, contact was established with the states of North Africa and the rest of the Islamic world through the trans-Saharan trade. The importance of trade to these regions furthered the spread of the Arabic language and, thus, it became an important lingua franca for trans-Saharan and intra-regional exchange.

Islamic societies promoted the use of Arabic in scientific and educational writings. As more Africans began converting to Islam, local Muslim scholars emerged and helped to encourage an increasing number of Islamic institutions of higher learning. Many great works relating to religion, history, and science came out of these educational centers. These include two of the greatest political and ethnographical accounts of the Western Sudan and the Songhai kingdom in particular. Written in the middle of the seventeenth century, the *Ta'rikh al-Sudan* (History of the Sudan) and the *Ta'rikh al-fattash* (Chronicle of the Researcher), written by al-Sadi and Mahmud Ka'ti respectively, remain the fundamental historical sources for the region for the period from the thirteenth to the seventeenth centuries.[20] Valuable as they are, the *Ta'rikhs* also have some weaknesses. They are dominated by images of the cities and give few glimpses, or distorted pictures, of the majority of the people who continued to live outside the major urban centers and were less influenced by Islam and formal education. Nonetheless, these volumes provide evidence of the existence of a large number of written historical documents pertaining to North Africa and the Sudan regions long before the advent of colonialism.

The early nineteenth century jihad of Usman dan Fodio (1754-1817) helped the spread of Islam to other parts of West Africa, and, likewise, the spread of writing in the Arabic language.[21] The effects of the jihad are seen in the abundance of Fula literature over a wide area of West Africa. Many poems were composed by Dan Fodio himself and members of his family. They were recorded in a modified Arabic script called *Ajami*. These poems were written with the intent of teaching people the tenets of Islam, and many are still in wide use today.

The carriers of Islam helped spread the Islamic faith throughout a wide area of North, West, and East Africa. But its impact went beyond the religious conver-

---

20. See *Ta'rikh al-Sudan*, ed. and trans. O. Houdas (Paris, 1901) and *Ta'rikh al-fattash*, ed. and trans. O Houdas and M. Delafosse (Paris, 1913).

21. See Usuman dan Fodio, *Ihya' al-sunnah wa-ikhmad al-bud'ah* (Cairo: Matbu'at al-Idarah al-'Ammah lil-Thaqafah al-Islamiyah, 1962). For writings about dan Fodio, see Ibraheem Sulaiman, *A Revolution in History: The Jihad of Usman dan Fodio*, (London; New York: Mansell, 1986) and M. Hiskett, *The Sword of Truth: The Life and Times of the Shehu Usuman dan Fodio* (New York: Oxford University Press, 1973).

sion of millions of people. Islam carried with it the Arabic writing system and contributed to the development and forms of literature in these regions.

The Influence of Christianity

Christianity also had a conspicuous influence—albeit, at a much later date— on the written literature of precolonial Africa. For many African societies, written literature in the Roman script developed in the early to mid-nineteenth century with the introduction of Christian missionaries and missionary schools. Perhaps the most significant impact made by Christian missionaries was the development and standardization of the orthographies of African languages.

During the nineteenth century, Christian missionaries began recording many African languages using the Roman script. Even for the Swahili language, with its long history of writing in Arabic, the Roman script was made the official alphabet, replacing Arabic in the late nineteenth century. The prevalence of the missionary influence ensured that the first written works were translations of the Bible. Most of the literature written in African languages during this time was focused almost exclusively on the spread of Christianity.

There are a number of collections of stories from oral tradition that were recorded in Western languages, but the emphasis in writings in African languages continued to be of a religious, not a cultural or historical nature. Gradually, however, literacy began to be employed for other purposes. For instance, the first recorded texts written by the Zulu of southern Africa were the *Iinncwadi ya-muhla uumbishops wase Natal ehambela kwaZulu*. This was an account by three Zulu missionaries who traveled with the Bishop of Natal throughout Zululand in 1859 and recorded their experiences. In southern Africa, some of the written literature of the Zulu was characterized by a blending of oral tradition and the written form. It consisted largely of the transcription of stories from oral tradition and the composition of new literature that sometimes bore a close resemblance to its oral counterpart. Many of the stereotyped characters of the written literature were pulled out of the oral tradition and put into a contemporary context—usually in relation to conflict with the West.

The written literature of another southern African group, the Xhosa, dates to the early years of the nineteenth century. The Xhosa language was used extensively in journals, newspapers, and elsewhere from a much earlier date than in other societies. The first piece of literature in Xhosa is generally believed to be a hymn of praise written by a Christian convert, Jonas Ntsiko, in 1824, and published by Lovedale press. Lovedale press was named for the Rev. John Love who, with others, in 1775 formed the organization that would later be called the London Missionary Society. The London Missionary Society and the Glasgow Missionary Society arrived in South Africa in 1799 and 1821 respectively. They established a number of Christian mission schools that educated Xhosa-speaking people in a Western manner. The Glasgow organization, in particular, was instrumental in developing the use of the printed word in education. They set up the first printing press in 1823 and printed copies of the alphabet for classroom use.

Still, the majority of works produced were oriented towards religion. A number of Xhosa-language newspapers and journals were produced. Although they occasionally provided a voice of black resistance, they were still under the control of the missionary-owned presses. This restricted the potential of the newspapers and journals and no significant resistance literature was generated until the last decades of the nineteenth century.

In general, African literature written in Western languages during the nineteenth century was Western in focus. Most of the people capable of reading and writing in these languages had been schooled in the tradition of the West and had become acculturated to some degree. Most were converts to Christianity, some became preachers, and some worked as civil servants in colonial governments. Not until the twentieth century was there an abundance of literature written *by* Africans that was based *in* an African tradition.

Conclusion

This chapter has presented an overview of the literature of Africa. It is important, first, to recognize the existence of African precolonial literature in both oral and written forms. Its historical existence precedes the advent of colonialism and provides a refutation of the "civilizing" mission of colonialists. Oral tradition, which has been flourishing in Africa from time immemorial, captures the spirit of life and is an artistic and creative art form that helps us form a clearer picture of the political, social, and cultural history of societies throughout the continent.

A second point to remember is that African oral tradition must not be seen solely as a form of entertainment, filled with mythical events and figures. There are veritable facts embedded within the narrative and cultural insights that can be derived from the poetics of performance. Oral tradition is and must continue to be taught as a significant part of African culture, because it ties the present to the past.

It is also important to recognize the existence of written literature in the precolonial era. This includes Egyptian hieroglyphics, early Ge'ez writing in Ethiopia, and an abundance of Arabic literature. Its importance to historical reconstruction is inestimable. The evidence it contributes to the history of ancient African cultures goes a long way towards helping scholars to unravel the African past.

Review Questions

1. What are the benefits and difficulties of using oral literature as a source with which to reconstruct the African past? How can it help historians re-evaluate the colonial hypothesis of an African past devoid of history?
2. Discuss the functions of oral literature. How did it contribute to the cohesiveness of society? How does it act to link the past and the present worlds? Provide examples.
3. Describe the development of scripts invented by Africans and the types of literature that are recorded in them.
4. How did the introduction of Islam change the method of recording history in the affected societies? Provide examples of these effects.
5. How did the effects of Christianity on the production of literature differ from those of Islam? What types of materials were recorded in the Roman script?

Additional Reading

Andrzejewski, B.W., S. Pilaszewicz and W. Tyloch, eds. *Literatures in African Languages*. London: Cambridge University Press, 1985.

Gibb, H.A.R. *Arabic Literature: An Introduction*. Oxford: Clarendon Press, 1963.

Okpewho, Isidore. *African Oral Literature*. Bloomington: Indiana University Press, 1992.

Radin, Paul, ed. *African Folk Tales*. New York: Schocken Books, 1983.

Scheub, Harold. *The African Storyteller: Studies from African Oral Traditions*. Dubuque, IA: Kendall/Hunt Publishing, 1990.

Vansina, Jan. *Oral Tradition as History*. Madison: University of Wisconsin Press, 1985.

Chapter 17

The Europeans in Africa: Prelude to Colonialism

Apollos O. Nwauwa

Perhaps the nineteenth century—the period just before direct European invasion and conquest—remains the most complex and yet interesting epoch in African history. While some scholars refer to this period as the "transitional age," others call it the "revolutionary years."[1] In this century, internal events were much affected or even provoked by European activity on the coast, even more after 1850 when the Europeans began to penetrate the African interior. Similarly, European actions on the coastal enclaves were largely dictated by the nature of African events in the hinterland. Some of the transformations within Africa included the Islamic jihads and reformation in West Africa, developments in trade and politics in the Omani Sultanate, the rise of Mohammed Ali Pasha and the Egyptian revolution, and of Shaka and the *Mfecane* in southern Africa. This chapter will focus on the increasing European political and commercial influence, together with African reactions to the dramatic changes of the period before 1885.

In broad terms, the nineteenth century in Africa is marked by three major periods of European activity: (i) the suppression of the slave trade; (ii) the gradual shift to "legitimate" commerce, and the increasing European interference through exploration; and (iii) missionary, trading, and consular activities, all of which acted as precursors to invasion and conquest. For more than half a century following the official British abolition of the slave trade in 1807, Europeans had "nibbled" on Africa. However, the traditional assumption has been that European colonization of Africa occurred after 1885 and not before. It is argued that before 1885, other than a few French forts in Senegal and Algeria, British settlements in the Gambia, Lagos, and the Gold Coast, and the Portuguese coastal locations in Angola and Mozambique, centuries of European contact and commercial activities had not been geared to any real political colonization of Africa. This is erroneous.

---

1. See to J.F. Ade Ajayi, "West African States at the Beginning of the Nineteenth Century," in J.F. Ade Ajayi and Ian Espie, eds., *A Thousand Years of West African History* (Ibadan: Ibadan University Press, 1965), 253-266; and J.B. Webster and Adu Boahen, *The Growth of African Civilization: The Revolutionary Years, West Africa since 1800* (London: Longman, 1967).

European Exploration of Africa

It seems absurd to continue to credit European explorers with the "discovery" of African peoples, rivers, lakes, waterfalls, mountains, and creeks when Africans themselves knew about the existence of these things. Although in the fifteenth century the Portuguese explorers, Bartholomew Diaz and Vasco Da Gama, had circumnavigated Africa, they did not make any effort to venture into the interior. Systematic efforts to explore the African hinterland did not begin until the last decade of the eighteenth century when the Scot, James Bruce, followed the Blue Nile into the highlands of Ethiopia in 1766. In 1795, another Scot, Mungo Park, made his first expedition to the River Niger. For the explorers, curiosity and a spirit of scientific inquiry, plus the desire to seek economic and commercial opportunities, were vital to their enterprise.[2] What is often overlooked is that Africans served as indispensable guides to these explorers as in the case of Chuma who accompanied David Livingstone in his explorations.

Hitherto, the map of Africa as sketched by Europeans, suggested that the River Niger rose from Lake Chad and flowed westwards to the Atlantic through the Gambia. Park was determined to find the course of this river. He was able to report that the great Niger River flowed eastward and not westward as Europeans previously believed. But Park died at Bussa in 1806 during his second expedition in search of the mouth of the Niger. It was not until 1830 that Richard and John Lander demonstrated that the Niger flows into the Atlantic Ocean through the Gulf of Guinea. Earlier, however, Hugh Clapperton and his group had crossed the Sahara via Tripoli to Kano and Sokoto, in search of the best overland gateway to West Africa. Later, the German emissary of the Royal Geographical Society, Heinrich Barth, and the French explorer, René Caillé, reached Timbuctu (a medieval intellectual and commercial center in West Africa) and finally confirmed its legend. The reports of these visitors certainly pricked the curiosity and interests of European traders, governments, and scientific and missionary bodies. Consequently, steps were taken toward a large-scale exploration of the whole of Africa.

Soon the search for the source of the River Nile began with Richard Burton, John Speke, James Grant, and Samuel Baker.[3] Speke ultimately solved that mystery when he reached Lake Victoria and identified it as the source of the great Nile River. An ambitious exploration project was begun in 1841 by David Livingstone, who was sponsored by the Church Missionary Society (CMS). Livingstone was the first European to cross Africa, from Lake Ngami (on the east coast) to Luanda (on the west coast); then he retraced his footsteps to the Zambezi River where he encountered the great waterfall, which he named "Victoria Falls." Stanley Livingstone was one of the greatest explorers of Africa.[4] In 1872 he circumnavigated Lakes Victoria and Tanganyika, and crossed to the west coast of Africa through

---

2. See A.E. Afigbo et al., *The Making of Modern Africa*, vol. 1 (London: Longman, new edition, 1986), 62-63; and J.D. Fage, *A History of Africa* (New York: Alfred A. Knopf, 1978), 329.

3. Burton was credited with the discovery of Lake Tanganyika while Baker was the first to reach Lake Albert. Speke and Grant concentrated on finding the source of the River Nile.

4. See Ieuan Ll. Griffiths, *An Atlas of African Affairs* (London: Routledge, revised edition, 1985), 39.

the River Congo. The mystery of the three great African rivers—the Niger, Nile, and Congo—was solved.

To Africans, however, the activities of the explorers meant little or nothing, except that some African rulers had begun to be wary of these itinerant white men wandering "aimlessly" within their domains. In East Africa, these explorers came to be called *wazungu*, the wanderers. Although African rulers often received Europeans visitors with some show of hospitality, there were usually some underlying apprehensions. Europeans coveted African land and resources but Africans misunderstood this, and often regarded them "with wonder and pity" because these explorers "seemed so wise, and yet so ignorant; so strong, and yet so helpless."[5] Soon, they criss-crossed Africa and by the time Africans realized the real motives of the European "wanderers," it was already too late. Exploration provided the essential groundwork for the subsequent increase in European interference in African affairs.

The Abolition of the Slave Trade

The suppression of the trade in 1807 will be highlighted here to show the dynamics of European influence in Africa in the period before 1885. The abolition of the slave trade helped to provoke the subsequent European colonization of Africa. It led to an aggressive effort by Europeans to penetrate the African hinterland to stop the slave trade at source, establish model farms, and by-pass African middlemen.

Denmark abolished the trade in slaves in 1802, and Britain and the United States followed suit in 1807 and 1808 respectively. Similarly, Latin American countries joined the crusade for the suppression of the slave trade. But the British initiative remains the most remarkable, because not only had Britain hitherto dominated the trade but it also took active diplomatic and military steps toward ensuring that other nations complied with abolition. The first major success recorded by the anti-slavery movement came in 1772 when Chief Justice Mansfield ruled in favor of James Somersett—a runaway slave from the West Indies—that English law could not uphold slavery. Henceforth, the legality of the whole slave business came under serious attack ultimately resulting in the passing of the 1807 Act in British Parliament which made slave trading illegal for British subjects.

The reasons for the abolition of a trade that once constituted the mainstay of the British, French, and American economies have been controversial. Two broad approaches dominate the debate: the humanitarian and the economic analyses. Reginald Coupland put forward the humanitarian thesis, revolving around a movement led by Thomas Clarkson, Fowell Buxton, William Wilberforce, and Granville Sharp.[6] The contention is that it was the ideas of the Enlightenment coupled with the relentless efforts of the humanitarians and evangelicals that

---

5. See W.E.F. Ward and L.W. White, *East Africa: A Century of Change, 1870-1970* (New York: Africana Publishing, 1971), 1-2.

6. Reginald Coupland, *The British Anti-Slavery Movement* (London: Frank Cass, reprint, 1964).

compelled the British government to outlaw the trade in slaves. In other words, abolition was seen as a victory for "men of goodwill" who were shocked by the immorality and inhumanity of the slave system.

Insisting that "philanthropy was never disinterested," Eric Williams challenged the humanitarian analysis.[7] Dismissing its proponents as "men who have sacrificed scholarship to sentimentality and, like the scholarstics [sic] of old, placed faith before reason and evidence," Williams argued that it was economic circumstances in Britain which forced the British to lead the crusade to outlaw the trade in slaves.[8] The Industrial Revolution had led to a great increase in manufactures. But the British Caribbean islands had declined as a market for British manufactured goods. Furthermore, the high cost of slaves and the economic crisis of the last quarter of the eighteenth century had demoralized leading slave dealers. Under these conditions, the importance of slaves waned as British industrialists and traders competed for alternative, profitable ventures.

It would appear as if the two analyses—humanitarian and economic—are opposites; in actuality, however, they are inter-related and reciprocal. It was the coalescence of the economic situation and emerging humanitarianism that ultimately shaped the British decision to outlaw the slave trade. Research has shown that the humanitarian and evangelical movements were both products of industrialization, beginning as a means of placating new restive urban dwellers (now industrial workers) displaced from their lands by aristocrats and gentry.[9]

It was in the interest of British industrialists that industrial workers and plantation slaves should imbibe industrial ethics including cleanliness and moral virtues as the best security against disloyalty and insurrection, and this was the crux of the evangelical message.[10] However, the evangelical and philosophical ideas of liberty, equality, and fraternity of all men before God, was implicitly inciting to the slaves. The attendant contradictions in these liberal ideas of the time coupled with the uncooperative attitudes of slaveowners and planters resulted in the transference of the evangelicals and humanitarians from "local good work" to an anti-slavery campaign.

When the British Parliament decided to outlaw the slave trade in 1807, it was mostly responding to economic conviction rather than sheer moral sentiment. The interests of the industrialists and the humanitarians often coincided. A.G. Hopkins captured the mood of that time when he concluded that the abolitionists "were a less romantic and more complex band than they have often been depicted."[11] Paradoxically, however, rather than diminish it, the abolition of the slave trade boosted European influence in Africa by inaugurating an alternative trade known as the legitimate trade, with its own attendant problems.

---

7. Eric Williams, *Capitalism and Slavery* (New York: Capricorn Books, reprint, 1966).

8. Williams, *Capitalism and Slavery*, 178.

9. See Mary Turner, *Slaves and Missionaries: The Disintegration of Jamaican Slave Society, 1787-1834* (Urbana: University of Illinois Press, 1982), 4; and J.E. Flint, "Economic Change in West Africa in the Nineteenth Century," in J.F. Ade Ajayi and Michael Crowder, eds., *History of West Africa*, vol. 2 (London: Longman, 1974), 391.

10. Turner, *Slaves and Missionaries*, 4

11. A.G. Hopkins, *An Economic History of West Africa* (New York: Columbia University Press, 1973), 116.

New Economic Pattern: "Legitimate" Trade

The "legitimate" trade was a nineteenth century Western concept which refers to the various commercial transactions that replaced the slave trade. The term "legitimate" was used to denote the trade in goods as opposed to the outlawed trade in human merchandise; it hardly considered changes in African production processes. While it can be argued that the Industrial Revolution led to the suppression of the slave trade, it also inaugurated legitimate commerce. In other words, both the abolition of the slave trade and legitimate commerce were products of the same economic changes engendered by the Industrial Revolution.

Legitimate trade was considered a vital instrument in the effective destruction of the slave trade. It is true that in the first quarter of the 19th century, both the slave trade and legitimate commerce coexisted. By 1830, however, Thomas Buxton, a humanitarian, had articulated the idea that the most effective way to destroy the slave trade and bring civilization to Africa would be the encouragement of legitimate commerce along with colonization and Christianity.[12] Humanitarians could also be imperialists. Thus the combination of abolition, legitimate commerce, and Christianity served to foster the consequent colonization of Africa.

Industrialization resulted in an immense increase in the volume of manufactured goods, particularly textiles, which demanded newer and wider markets. Many of these untapped markets lay in Africa. To take advantage of African cravings for cotton cloth and other manufactures, British industrialists and financiers considered that Africans should remain at home and be consumers, especially if they could produce cash crops in exchange, rather than be traded as human merchandise. Furthermore, European factories needed African raw materials such as peanuts, cotton, dyes, gum, and palm oil more than other commodities, including slaves.

In England, in particular, palm oil was in great demand for soap-making and lubrication of industrial machines. Soap had been a hand-made article which only the rich could afford, but with the Industrial Revolution and its grime and grease, a mass demand for soap arose and palm oil proved to produce the best lather. The factories were demanding lubricating oil for their machines. Palm oil again provided the answer. Later, in the Senegambia region, another equally important source of vegetable oil—peanuts—was also developed, and France dominated this trade. By the 1880s the Senegambia was exporting an average of 29,000 tons of groundnuts a year.

The switch from the slave trade to legitimate commerce, though not smooth or easy, inaugurated a new economic pattern. Not all African traders and societies hitherto involved in the slave trade could readily make the transition to legitimate trade. In many ways, the dynamics of the slave trading system were easier to understand and manage. Participation in legitimate trade depended upon the availability of suitable local export crops such as palm oil, peanuts, rubber, cocoa, etc. and proximity to navigable rivers such as the Niger, Congo, Senegal, Zambezi, and Nile.

---

12. See Thomas Fowell Buxton, *The African Slave Trade and Its Remedy* (London: Dawsons, reprint of 2nd edition, 1968).

Palm oil was abundant on the west coast of Africa. But it was very difficult to process and the profits to the traders were not as "good" as those from the slave trade. In addition, the real profits usually went to wealthy merchants who bought in bulk and controlled transport. Nevertheless, the expansion of the palm oil trade with England between 1810 and 1855 "represented a triumph of African organizing power and ingenuity in the face of a major technical challenge."[13]

Within Africa, the new pattern of trade provoked conflicts between African middlemen and European merchants. While Europeans wanted to go inland to increase their profit margin African middlemen struggled to preserve their positions and control. Conflicts also arose between African traditional elites, many of whose incomes had been drastically reduced as a result of the suppression of the slave trade, and the new "merchant princes." The major cause of these conflicts involved taxes levied by the traditional rulers, which the merchants saw as exploitative. This was the case in the Senegambia over the peanut trade and in the Niger Delta over palm oil. The dislocation resulting from the introduction of legitimate trade was employed as an excuse for the subsequent European invasion and conquest.

Missionaries as Agents of Imperialism

Scholars of European imperialism now recognize the complex connection between missionary activity and the colonization of Africa. Missionaries "were an essential ingredient of increasingly assertive European presence which was a forerunner of imperial control."[14] Sometimes, the interests of European politicians and traders coincided with those of missionaries and explorers. Citing David Livingstone, who insisted that Christianity and commerce were inseparable, George Brooks has argued that "missionaries shared merchants' interests in commercial prospects and potential areas of mineral wealth."[15]

The last decades of the eighteenth century witnessed a great religious revival in Europe, particularly in Germany and Britain, resulting in a rapid growth of missionary activity. This movement spread to United States. Mission stations were set up in many parts of Africa. Since missionaries desired to penetrate the African hinterland to convert the "heathen," their goals sometimes coincided with those of explorers in the mapping of rivers, lakes, and mountains. Sometimes, too, missionaries collaborated with traders and consuls to accomplish "the civilizing mission."

Roman Catholics began evangelization in Senegal, Gabon, and southern Nigeria. Protestant missions took root in Sierra Leone, Liberia, the Gold Coast,

---

13. Elizabeth Isichei, *History of West Africa Since 1800* (London: Macmillan, 1977), 152. In 1810, one thousand tonnes of oil were exported to England and by 1855 the figure rose to forty thousand tonnes.

14. Kevin Shillington, *History of Africa* (New York: St. Martin's Press, 1989, revised edition 1995), 292.

15. George E. Brooks, "African 'Landlords' and European 'Strangers': African-European Relations to 1870," in Phyllis M. Martin and Patrick O'Meara, eds; *Africa* (Bloomington: Indiana University Press, second edition 1986), 115-116.

Figure 17-1. Rev. David Livingstone

and also southern Nigeria. However, the nineteenth century missionaries were intolerant of African traditional institutions such as polygyny, domestic slavery,
aristocracy, and kingship. Inspired by a sense of moral and technological advantage, missionaries flaunted European values and traditions as the ideals with
which Africans must be imbued.

For a long time, however, missionary activity was restricted to the African
coasts for a number of reasons. European missionaries who ventured inland died
in great numbers from malaria and those who survived the disease had to contend
with the hostility of African rulers. Consequently European missionaries con-
trived the use of African "recaptives" as agents for proselytization.[16] Protestant
missions, in particular, employed African pastors and laymen and sent them to
their homelands for missionary duties. Samuel Ajayi Crowther was one of the
most outstanding of these people, becoming Bishop of the Niger in 1864. Al-

---

16. The term "recaptives" refers to those African slaves and their descendants who were
recaptured at the sea by the British anti-slavery squadron, freed, and resettled in Sierra
Leone. They were quite different from the freed slaves from Nova Scotia and the West Indies
who were also resettled in Sierra Leone.

though nineteenth-century missionary activity was far more successful than earlier efforts, it would be an exaggeration to assume that a general conversion of Africans occurred. Real conversion was a more gradual process, taking many years to accomplish. But with the use of quinine as a prophylactic against malaria from 1850s, sustained European penetration of Africa hinterland began. The great age of missionary expansion was ushered in.

Yet early African converts in the nineteenth century were mainly drawn from the ranks of the needy, the poor, and the rejected or outcasts. Chinua Achebe has suggested that among the Igbo, it was the *osu* (outcasts), the *efulefu* (worthless), and the weak who flocked to the missionaries and became converted.[17] This group of converts had nothing to lose by becoming Christians. If anything, they had much to gain. To these classes, the traditional African social and political order was highly oppressive and thus they saw European missionaries as saviors, since they preached, even though it might be hypocritically, about social justice and the equality of all men before God. Nonetheless, freemen, aristocrats, and rulers continued to view Christianity, missionaries, and conversion with suspicion.

From Informal Influence to Direct Intrusion

European colonization of Africa was hardly as sudden and dramatic as has often been depicted. Thus J.D. Fage views it as "the culminating stage in a process of interaction between Europeans and Africans which had been growing in momentum and intensity over a much longer period."[18] From the successful circumnavigation of Africa by the Portuguese in the fifteenth century, through the early nineteenth century, Europeans had built many trading forts, castles, and lodges along African coasts, from Morocco through the Bight of Biafra to East Africa. However, they had no territorial jurisdiction since they rented the land from the local African rulers. They recognized the indigenous authority and operated through alliances with African rulers. In the nineteenth century the situation changed dramatically.

With the abolition of the slave trade and the establishment of legitimate commerce, European merchants increasingly sought to gain control over the trading systems of the African hinterland. European governments began to secure for their subjects some of the fruits of empire while at the same time limiting their own military and financial responsibilities. Nevertheless, although the first seventy years of the nineteenth century witnessed a very limited extension of colonial control and "informal empire," European nibbling on Africa proceeded. The principal European powers—Britain and France—gradually began to jostle for more influence by increasing their stake in Africa. At first, colonial expansion was a matter of seizing coastal enclaves with the aim of controlling areas of viable

---

17. See Chinua Achebe, *Things Fall Apart* (New York: Fawcett Crest, 1991), 133-143. Also Elizabeth Isichei, *A History of the Igbo People* (London: Macmillan, 1976), 162.

18. Fage, *History of Africa*, 325-326.

commerce under the guise of suppressing the slave trade. Anxiously, European agents waited for the slightest opportunity to begin to lay hold on the trade and politics of the interior.

In addition to Sierra Leone, established in 1787 by private evangelical initiatives as a settlement for freed slaves, Britain established itself on the mouth of the Gambia, and on other parts of the coast of West Africa. By 1849, a British consul was appointed (to assist British merchants) in the Bights of Benin and Biafra. This unprecedented event signaled that the era of informal empire was gradually drawing to a close and the beginning of a new imperial policy backed by politicians was emerging. Soon the naval bombardment of African states and kingdoms alleged to have obstructed foreign commerce, missionary activity, and European civilization followed. Britain meddled in Lagos politics in 1851, deposed King Kosoko and installed Akitoye, and bombarded Lagos island under the pretext of suppressing the slave trade. In reality, British activity in Lagos had economic and political underpinnings—to tap and dominate the commerce of Dahomey and Yorubaland. In 1861, Lagos was annexed to the Crown, signaling the beginning of formal colonial encroachment.

In the Niger Delta, the British crafted "treaties" which allowed them increasing intervention in the commercial and political affairs of the region. Obviously, they were positioning themselves for the control of the palm oil trade and other commodities of the Delta and the interior. They clashed with African middlemen and merchant princes over the control of the hinterland trade. In spite of the resistance put up by Delta middlemen and rulers such as Jaja of Opobo, British steamships and gunboats ascended the Niger River to trade directly with African producers.[19] The first breakthrough occurred in 1854 when Dr. Balfour Baikie's expedition along the Rivers Niger and Benue demonstrated that quinine was a good antidote for malaria fever, which had taken the lives of many Europeans who had earlier ventured into the interior.[20] This medical innovation paved the way for subsequent and more effective European penetration.

In East Africa, British commercial, diplomatic, and political maneuvers forced the sultan of Zanzibar to rely on them. Flaunting the suppression of the slave trade as an excuse, the British in 1866 appointed John Kirk as consul to the Zanzibari sultanate, thereby eroding the authority of the sultan. By 1872 British steamers had a firm base at Zanzibar. The activity of British missionaries and traders, coupled with the subsequent appointment of a consul, indicated that political and economic interference, transcending the mere abolition of the slave trade, had been set in motion.

French activity in Africa after the end of the Napoleonic Wars resulted in the occupation of Algeria in 1830. From then on, France nursed the ambition of creating an empire encompassing all of northwestern Africa and Senegal. Control over St. Louis and Goree and other posts along the River Senegal, was re-established. From the 1840s, France moved to fortify its positions in the Ivory Coast, Dahomey, and Gabon to protect French trade, check the increasing influence of the British, and provide stations for the French navy. Between 1850 and 1860

---

19. See K.O. Dike, *Trade and Politics in the Niger Delta, 1830-1885* (Oxford: Clarendon Press, 1956); G.I. Jones, *The Trading States of the Oil Rivers* (London: Oxford University Press, 1963); and Obaro Ikime, *The Niger Delta Rivalry* (Ibadan: Longman, 1969).

20. The 1841 Niger expedition was an unmitigated disaster. Forty-eight Europeans who ascended the Niger died of malaria on the river.

under the leadership of General Louis Faidherbe, the French began an aggressive policy of empire-building in the Senegambia region after subduing the jihad of Al-Hajj 'Umar. Soon afterwards French political and commercial missions, backed by military power, were sent eastward through Futa Djallon in the interior. This also signaled the dawn of a new era of direct interference in Africa. The British were alarmed. Nevertheless, despite all these aggressive incursions, large portions of the hinterland remained under indigenous African rule until the late 1870s, when the scramble began in earnest.

The Beginnings and Motives of the "New Imperialism"

From the 1870s, European nibbling on Africa began to give way to direct political control. Opinions are mixed regarding the motives and/or justifications for these incursions. Analyses fall into four broad categories, namely: economic, psychological, diplomatic, and African factors. A brief analysis of each of these is given here.

The economic motives for imperialism had been advanced by J.A. Hobson and V.I. Lenin in their works published in 1902 and 1916 respectively.[21] While Hobson believed that imperialism resulted from overproduction, surplus capital, and underconsumption in industrial nations which forced them to expand overseas through political means, Lenin argued that it was the transition of capitalism from free competition to monopoly and finance capital which caused capitalist nations to intensify their struggle to partition the world. During the Industrial Revolution, Europe's emergent factories needed raw materials, and the products of these industries also needed newer and wider markets. It was the efforts to monopolize these raw materials and markets that resulted in direct imperial control. Thus, Lord Lugard asserted that British colonial expansion resulted from the need "to foster the growth of trade and to find an outlet for our manufactures and our surplus energy" while the French Prime Minister, Jules Ferry, declared that "colonial policy is the child of the industrial revolution."[22] Furthermore, the severe depression of 1873 deepened the need for markets, with most nations erecting protective tariff barriers to keep out each other's manufactured goods. The colonization of Africa, therefore, served dual advantages which European nations desired to exploit and monopolize.

The psychological motives include ideas of Social Darwinism, the "White Man's Burden," and evangelical Christianity. Applying Charles Darwin's concept of "the survival of the fittest" to imperialism, social Darwinists assumed that the subjugation of the weak by the strong was in accordance with the laws of nature.

---

21. J.A. Hobson, *Imperialism: A Study* (Ann Arbor: Michigan University Press, 1965); and V.I. Lenin, *Imperialism: The Highest Stage of Capitalism* (Peking: Foreign Language Press, 1975).

22. F.D. Lugard, *The Rise of Our East African Empire*, vol. 1 (London: William Blackwood and Sons, 1893), 379-382; and Harvey Goldberg, ed., *French Colonialism* (New York: Rinehart & Co., 1959), 3-4. Lugard was a British army officer who actually took part in the invasion and conquest of Africa in the 1890s. He served as British governor of both Uganda and Nigeria.

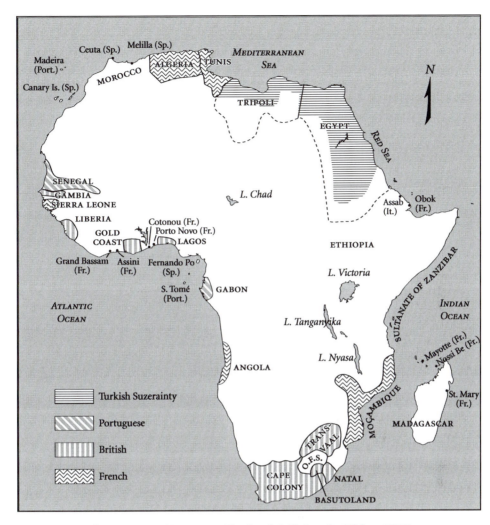

Figure 17-2. European Territorial Claims in Africa, 1879

Both "the White Man's Burden" and evangelical Christianity assumed that it was the moral duty of the Western world not so much to crush the "unfit" but to "tame," "civilize" and "Christianize" them. One major feature of these assumptions is that they carried racial imagery of a generous, superior European race and a passive, inferior African race.

The diplomatic motives revolve around national prestige, the balance of power, and strategic concerns. The second half of the nineteenth century witnessed intense competition and nationalism, and the acquisition of territories became a matter of national pride for European powers. Humbled by Prussia in the war of 1871, France's aggressive expansionist activity in Africa was desperately designed to save face. Germany's entry into the scramble in 1884 was also mainly driven by national pride. Thus, regardless of the possible economic benefits of imperialism, egocentric nationalism was a potent driving force for acquisition of territories.

Finally, the African factor has been integrated into the analysis. Not only did the commercial and diplomatic rivalry between European powers dictate the nature of the scramble, but also African resistance to increasing European influence inflamed European desire for invasion and conquest. The change-over from the slave trade to legitimate commerce and the downward turn in both the export and import trades in the last quarter of the century caused serious strains and stresses in African societies. Blaming the crisis on African middlemen, European traders, aided by the "gunboat diplomacy" of their various governments, became desperate to check, displace, or punish the middlemen. It was in the midst of these crises that European countries prepared themselves for an invasion of Africa, to assume direct control of the trade and politics of the continent.

Three major events heralded the scramble. The first was the activity of King Leopold II of Belgium who, in 1879 with the assistance of H.M. Stanley, created colonies along the River Congo in the heart of Africa as part of his personal empire. Leopold amalgamated these colonies in 1885 and renamed it the Congo Free State, which granted concessionaires control of the lucrative rubber trade of the region. The second was the flurry of expeditions sent by Portugal between 1876 and 1880 which resulted in the annexation of Mozambique to the Portuguese crown. Hence as far as the Portuguese and King Leopold were concerned, the scramble for Africa had begun by 1876. The third and by far the most important factor which precipitated the scramble was the aggressive, expansionist mood of the French between 1876 and 1880 resulting in joint control of Egypt with Britain in 1879; a foothold on the north bank of the River Congo; the revival of colonial initiatives in both Tunisia and Madagascar; and the construction of a railway from Dakar to link the French colony of Senegal with the upper Niger valley. While local political forces in France may have dictated her assertive imperial policy, it has been argued that French inroads into the savanna were "prompted in part by fears of some great British enveloping strategy" on the Lower Niger.[23]

Consequently, Britain and Germany quickly abandoned their preference for "free trade" and informal influence for a formal policy of protectionism and annexation. In 1882, Britain unilaterally occupied Egypt, began to monopolize the Suez route to India, and increased its territorial claims in West Africa. France responded that year with the declaration of protectorates over Porto Novo and the northern bank of the River Congo, and the formal annexation of Tunisia in 1883. Germany made a swift move in 1884 when Chancellor Bismarck proclaimed protectorates over Togo, Cameoon, Tanganyika, and South West Africa. At the suggestion of Portugal, Bismarck persuaded the French Premier, Jules Ferry, to join him in summoning a European conference in Berlin to discuss the African question.

The Berlin Conference and
Its Implications, 1884–1885

The conference met in Berlin from November 1884 until February 1885 and involved the major European powers. While the United States had no territorial

---

23. J.D. Hargreaves, "The European Partition of West Africa," in Ajayi and Crowder, eds., *History of West Africa*, vol. 2, 409-410.

claims in Africa, except for its influence in Liberia,[24] it participated as an observer. No African representatives were invited. The conference was intended to bring some order to the "mad rush" for territories in Africa and to avoid open armed confrontations between European powers. In any case, the map of Africa was placed before European contenders so that they could stake out their claims. These claims resulted in arbitrary boundaries being demarcated on paper.

The Berlin Conference is often seen as epochal, as if it was at the conference that Africa was actually partitioned. In reality, the partition was already underway. Even before the conference, few African coastal enclaves remained unappropriated by the various European powers. All the future colonies already existed in embryo. Whoever occupied the coastlines could, when desirable, move into the hinterland with ease. What was agreed on at the conference was the principle of "effective occupation". This principle stipulated that a European claim to any part of Africa would only be recognized by other European governments if the territory in question was "effectively occupied".[25] It would appear that this clause was a deliberate tactic by Bismarck to undermine British claims to vague, informal "spheres of influence" all over Africa.

The conference did affect the scramble and the ultimate invasion and colonization of Africa. It was no longer morally wrong or diplomatically unacceptable to appropriate territories in Africa. Thus European powers arrogated to themselves the rights to subjugate Africans and appropriate their land. As soon as the conference ended, an all-out scramble was unleashed to grab the remainder of Africa. Germany swiftly made another move in East Africa by declaring a protectorate over Tanganyika in 1885. Other European powers dispatched troops and modern weapons to invade Africa and seize territories by force. Clearly, the Berlin Conference has to be included in any serious analysis of European scramble and partition of Africa.

After the conference, the most effective method of effecting the paper partition of Africa was through treaties between Africans and Europeans and bilateral agreements between European partitioners themselves. Africans entered into these treaties for a variety of motives: they hoped that the prestige of such a treaty would give them some political advantages in dealing with their neighbors; they hoped to use a treaty as of means of renouncing their allegiance to another African sub-imperialist state; and to use such treaties as a means of preserving their independence when threatened by other European powers.[26] The treaty between Kabaka Mwanga II of Buganda and the British represents an instance where an African king sought European protection in a dispute with his subjects.

Some of the treaties were fraudulently procured by Europeans, as the case of King Lobengula of Ndebele and the British demonstrates. In the Ndebele scenario, a British missionary, Reverend Helm, was reported to have deliberately misinterpreted to King Lobengula the contents of a treaty between the British and

---

24. Liberia was founded in 1847 by the American Colonization Society as a settlement for American freed slaves.

25. For an African territory to be deemed as "effectively" occupied, the colonizing power must have some tangible evidence of its occupation through military, consular, or administrative presence. This was intended to reduce conflicts as well as discourage vague claims.

26. G.N. Uzoigwe, "European Partition and Conquest of Africa: An Overview," in A. Adu Boahen, ed., *UNESCO General History of Africa*, vol. 7 (Berkeley: University of California Press, 1985), 31-32.

Ndebele. In another event, Robert Moffat, a reverend and friend of Lobengula also advised the king to accept the Rudd Concession, which granted Cecil Rhodes exclusive prospecting rights in the area north of the Limpopo River."[27] In both of these instances, King Lobengula learned the lesson that in matters relating to colonization of Africa, not even European missionaries could not be trusted. These deceptions resulted in the subsequent British declaration of a protectorate over the Ndebele Kingdom. Furthermore, when the Fante of the Gold Coast made a treaty of protection with the British, they were interested in renouncing the overlordship of the Asante rather than surrendering their sovereignty (as the British later interpreted the treaty). In this case, it was the fear of the enemy within rather than devotion to the British that drove the Fante into the British camp.

European invasion and conquest of Africa was hardly as dramatic as has often been portrayed. Rather, it resulted from almost one hundred years of European meddling in the African continent under various pretexts. Precursors to subsequent colonization included events such as the exploration of the interior; the abolition of the slave trade; the introduction of "legitimate" commerce; missionary activity; the establishment of commercial posts; the seizure and occupation of strategic areas; treaty-making with African rulers; and the establishment of permanent settlements. The level of competition amongst the contending powers and the type of relations between Europeans and Africans dictated the momentum of European maneuvers in relation to treaty-making and gunboat diplomacy.

Indirect conquest of Africa had been underway long before Europeans actually took up arms against its people. This was accomplished through explorers who in effect claimed informal spheres of influence for those countries or societies that sponsored them. Missionary efforts were also surreptitiously targeted to "tame" and "pacify" the so-called savages, and invoke the benefits of the trinity —Christianity, civilization, and commerce—in readiness for the ultimate takeover. While traders cried out to their home governments for protection against the commercial aggression of other powers, consuls and politicians moved in to stake out areas that explorers, missionaries, and traders had mapped out for them. In light of this, the ultimate invasion and conquest of Africa in the last quarter of the nineteenth century was almost a *fait accompli*.

Review Questions

1. How did European explorers serve as precursors to the European colonization of Africa?
2. Discuss the humanitarian and economic reasons for the British abolition of the slave trade. How did abolition affect the subsequent European colonization of Africa?
3. "Missionaries were agents of European imperialism". Do you agree?
4. Discuss the motives suggested for the European colonization of Africa. To which of the arguments would you give the most weight? Why?

---

27. See Vincent B. Khapoya, *The African Experience* (Englewood Cliffs, New Jersey: Prentice Hall, 1994), 157-158.

5. Why was the Berlin Conference convened? How did it affect the European partition and colonization of Africa?

Additional Reading

Afigbo, A.E. et al. *The Making of Modern Africa*. Vol. 1, new edition. London: Longman, 1986.

Ajayi, J.F. Ade, ed. *UNESCO General History of Africa*. Vol. 6. Berkeley: University of California Press, 1989.

Isichei, Elizabeth. *History of West Africa Since 1800*. London: Macmillan, 1977.

Shillington, Kevin. *History of Africa*. Revised edition. New York: St. Martins Press, 1995.

Index